For more than a hundred centuries the Emperor has sat immobile on the Golden Throne of Earth. He is the master of Mankind by the will of the gods and master of a million worlds by the might of his inexhaustible armies. He is a rotting carcass writhing invisibly with power from the Dark Age of Technology. He is the Carrion Lord of the Imperium for whom a thousand souls die every day, for whom blood is drunk and flesh eaten. Human blood and human flesh – the stuff of which the Imperium is made.

To be a man in such times is to be one amongst untold billions. It is to live in the cruellest and most bloody regime imaginable. This is the tale of those times. It is a universe you can live in today – if you dare – for this is a dark and terrible era where you will find little comfort or hope. If you want to take part in the adventure then prepare yourself now. Forget the power of technology, science and common humanity. Forget the promise of progress and understanding, for there is no peace amongst the stars, only an eternity of carnage and slaughter and the laughter of thirsting gods.

But the universe is a big place and, whatever happens, you will not be missed...

CONTENTS

PRODUCED BY GAMES WORKSHOP

British Cataloguing-in-Publication Data. A catalogue record for this book is available from the British Library.

Printed in China.

UK	US	AUSTRALIA	CANADA	JAPAN
Games Workshop,	Games Workshop,	Games Workshop,	Games Workshop,	Games Workshop,
Willow Road,	6721 Baymeadow Drive,	23 Liverpool Street,	2679 Bristol Circle,	Willow Road,
Lenton,	Glen Burnie,	Ingleburn,	Unit 3,	Lenton,
Nottingham,	Maryland,	New South Wales	Oakville, Ontario,	Nottingham,
NG7 2WS	21060-6401	2565	L6H 6Z8	NG7 2WS

Product Code: 60 04 01 99 011

www.games-workshop.co.uk

ISBN: 1-84154-468-X

WARHAMMER® 40,000

In the Grim Darkness of the Far Future there is only War

THE ETERNITY GATE

Ten thousand years of battle, and still the war goes on. Like the glorious annals of the Imperium itself, the revered banners and relics of the Emperor's most loyal servants adorn the long march to the Eternity Gate.

Let those who would gaze at the splendour of the Imperial Palace take a moment to marvel at the achievements of His greatest warriors.

As the Emperor's sacrifice is immortal, so shall we immortalise those who sacrificed all for Him.

THE IMPERIAL PALACE

In the Sanctum Imperialis, upon the most sacred ground of all the Emperor's realm, only the feet of the Custodes may tread.

The Loyal Guard, the Unflinching Gaze, the Steadfast Hand, the Truest Blade. Protectors Eternal, they stand guard over the most holy gift the Emperor has to give: the Imperious Corporalis, the Emperor-in-Flesh.

In their domain there is no greater power before the Emperor himself. Neither pious Cardinal nor devout Inquisitor nor loyal High Lord may stand before His greatness, for that alone is the province of his Dread Guardians.

To the common masses our struggle is a fight, a war. A battle fought with sinew and muscle, with bolt, blade and bomb, with tank and warship. To those of us in high station this is nought but a conflict of will! A struggle of metaphysic dimension. The Soul of Mankind is our battleground. The very existence of the human race is the prize for victory. Our sanity is the sacrifice we make to win that laurel.

The High Lords of Terra.

They are the Will and the Word of the Emperor.
They are the Inquisitorial Representative, whose eyes see all, whose ears hear all, whose mind knows all.

They are the Power and the Glory of the Emperor.

They are the Lord Commander Militant, whose Imperial Guard wage war in the Emperor's name on a hundred thousand worlds.

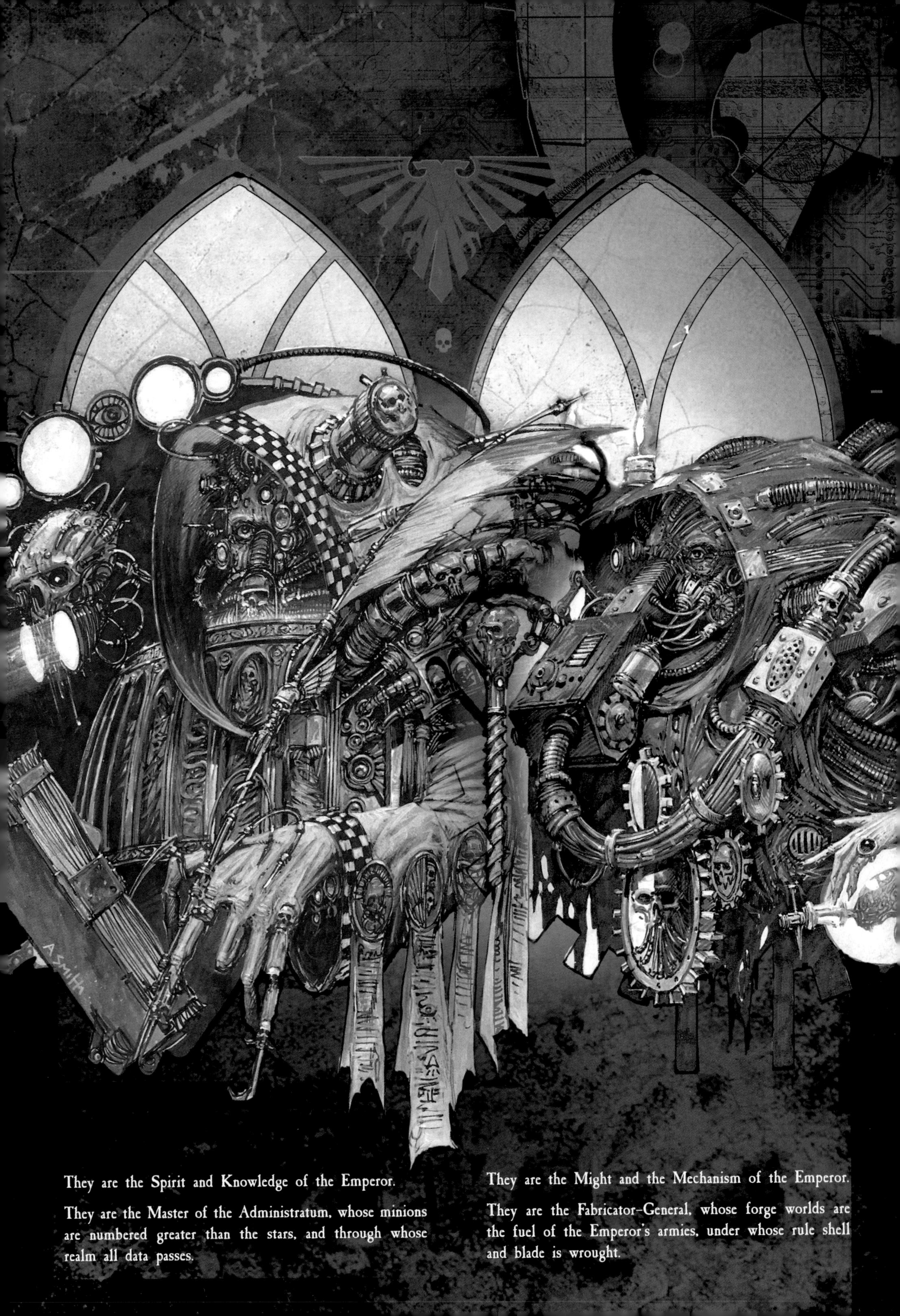

They are the Spirit and Knowledge of the Emperor.

They are the Master of the Administratum, whose minions are numbered greater than the stars, and through whose realm all data passes.

They are the Might and the Mechanism of the Emperor.

They are the Fabricator-General, whose forge worlds are the fuel of the Emperor's armies, under whose rule shell and blade is wrought.

Who is to judge what is right and what is wrong? Great and powerful foes surround us; unknown miscreants gnaw at us from within. We are threatened with total annihilation. In days such as these we can afford no luxury of morality.

Behind the bright lights hide a multitude of horrors as would disgust and repel the most stout-hearted of men. So it is with determination and unflinching duty that we must face those vile and terrible things – for if not us, then who?

The creatures of the Warp have but one trait with which you need concern yourself – their undying contempt for the Emperor. It is your task to quell the rebellion they preach, and the only sure way is to destroy them utterly.

Cast out the mutant, the traitor, the heretic! For every enemy without there are a hundred within. Beware their secret clans and hidden ways. The only cult we do not abhor is that of the Emperor!

Toll the Great Bell Once!
Pull the Lever forward to engage the
Piston and Pump...

Toll the Great Bell Twice!
With push of Button fire the Engine
and spark Turbine into life...

Toll the Great Bell Thrice!
Sing praise to the
God of All Machines!

Catechism of the Autoculus of Mars

The call to arms rings out across the dark void that is the galaxy. Its toll is answered by the iron willed devotees who are themselves but humble servants of a greater power. Who among the teeming billions of Mankind has the strength to answer the call and march to war? Come forth you mighty warriors, gather under the bloodstained banners and grisly trophies of conquest! Join now the massed throng whose aim is to rid Humanity of its blighted fate. To win famous victory on hellish otherworlds.

The Armies of the Imperium

No duty should be beyond us as we defend the holy truth of the Emperor's canon. Every device will be employed and all human skills exploited to the utmost. There is no shirking from our duty. In these darkest of times we must employ the darkest of methods. We must be vigilant, strong and unyielding lest we weaken our resolve and fracture the faith that bonds us together. We, the brothers and sisters of the great Ecclesiarchy, will fight to the bitter end. We shall not let one heretic or traitor stay us from our holy duty. Not one witch or changeling will shock us into meek surrender. Be vigilant, be strong, the Emperor is with us all!

The Great Ecclesiarchy

They shall be my finest warriors, these men who give of themselves to me. Like clay I shall mould them and in the furnace of war forge them. They wi[ll] be of iron will and steely muscle. In great armour shall I clad them and with the mightiest guns will they be armed. They will be untouched by plague o[r] disease, no sickness will blight them. They will have tactics, strategies and machines such that no foe can best them in battle. They are my bulwark agains[t] the Terror. They are the Defenders of Humanity. They are my Space Marines and they shall know no fear.

The Adeptus Astartes

FIGHTING WARHAMMER 40,000

What you hold in your hands tells you all about how to fight battles based in the Warhammer 40,000 universe, providing the core rules needed to play the game. It gives some of the background information about the Warhammer 40,000 universe, its history, environment and flavour. It can guide players towards deciding what sort of army they might choose to play, how to go about collecting the models, painting armies, putting together a tabletop battlefield and even finding an opponent to play against.

This book may seem a bit daunting to the beginner, any bound collection of almost three hundred pages of information can be intimidating, but you don't need to read it all at once. The three distinct sections – Rules, Background and Gaming Material – offer very different things. The Rules section explains the game mechanics, and once you've grasped the early parts of this, which cover Movement, Shooting, Assaults and Morale, you are pretty much on your way.

GETTING STARTED

First and foremost, you can't fight a battle without troops, which in our case are represented by models. Model armies, just like real life armies, contain different kinds of troops and vehicles under the command of an officer. Some of the armies you can collect and control in Warhammer 40,000 are human, such as the massively diverse Imperial Guard or the zealous Space Marines of the Adeptus Astartes. Other armies consist of alien races, such as the ancient and mysterious Eldar, the barbaric green-skinned Orks, or the monstrous entities of the Tyranid hive fleets.

Playing a game of Warhammer 40,000 requires models. When players first start playing games they should play with whatever models they like the look of, rather than concern themselves overly with precisely what they are and how they function. Maybe they know someone who already plays the game, and can use some of their models, or maybe they could even play a couple of introductory games in a store or at a gaming club. Familiarising yourself with how to play does not mean you need to collect a large army beforehand.

When starting to collect an army, you'll probably want to use it all at once, so the best way to begin is by collecting a few squads of troops and some vehicles that can fight equally effectively against many different kinds of enemy. Later, as your collection grows, you can add in more of the special troop types that are particularly good at fighting certain types of opponent, but may be weaker against others. The bigger the collection, the wider the choice and the bigger the battles that can be fought.

"In war victory is one part planning and nine parts faith."
Tactica Imperium

CHOOSING AN ARMY

Before you start collecting an army you'll have to decide which one you want it to be. Different races have different skills, troop types, special abilities and technological assets. For example, the Imperial Guard, the human troops of the Imperium, fight in very great numbers of men supported by a variety of tanks and artillery, while Chaos Space Marine armies usually consist of markedly fewer, more elite units of men, often supported by mutated creatures and warp-spawned daemons. Both armies can play in the same battle but will be used in very different ways.

The details that make up any army are provided in the Warhammer 40,000 Codex books, which are a collection of rules and explanations that cover the types of troops, weapons, vehicles and special rules that different armies can call upon. The army lists are a useful element of the game, as they outline the choices you will face when putting your force together, imposing certain restrictions on how you combine your troops. This is to preserve the character of the different armies and to ensure a balanced selection of troops.

Within the selections permitted by an army list, the options provided are very flexible. It is very unlikely that two players would ever pick precisely the same force and same combination of troops from any list.

CODEX BOOKS

Once you have chosen the army you want to collect, you'll need to know more about it: how it fights, what special models it can include and what its army list contains. You'll find all this, plus background information, racial histories, special characters and other details, inside the Warhammer 40,000 Codex book for that army. For example, if you decide to collect an army of mighty Space Marines, then all the information you will need to make the most of your collection will be contained within the pages of Codex: Space Marines. As well as telling you more about the race, this book also covers uniforms and painting schemes, a detailed description of the different weaponry they can use, the different troops types and the restrictions you face when selecting the models that can take part in a battle.

A TYPICAL SPACE MARINE ARMY

(A) Terminator Squad – Elite Space Marines equipped with the virtually impregnable Terminator armour and carrying the deadly storm bolter. They can teleport directly into the midst of the enemy's battle lines.

(B) Land Raider – Land Raiders are the mainstay of the Space Marines' armoured might. Their sponson-mounted lascannons give them superior firepower, and they can also be used to swiftly transport squads into battle. These tanks are heavily armoured and can withstand most firepower that the enemy can throw at them.

(C) Land Speeder Tornado – A fast attack vehicle that can fly and is extremely manoeuvrable. The Land Speeder Tornado mounts a heavy bolter for gunning down infantry and an assault cannon to take on heavier targets. It can inflict a lot of damage but is only lightly armoured.

(D) Two Tactical Squads (one with Rhino Transporter) – Tactical squads are highly flexible troops that make up the majority of squads in most Space Marine armies. Their standard equipment of rapid-firing bolters can deal with most opponents, while heavy weapons can be issued to deal with any enemy vehicles or monstrous creatures. Tactical squads can be mounted in a Rhino to transport them rapidly across the battlefield.

(E) Dreadnought – Dreadnoughts are huge, heavily-armoured fighting machines. They can be armed with a number of heavy weapons that can destroy tanks, mow down infantry or crush enemies in assaults.

(F) Assault Squad – Equipped with close quarter weapons, such as pistols and chainswords. Their jump packs enable them to quickly engage the enemy.

(G) Command Squad – This army is led by a commander who represents the player in person on the battlefield! They can be accompanied by a bodyguard which includes experienced veterans and specialists, such as Apothecaries.

(H) Bike Squadron – Fast attack Bike squadrons make excellent assault troops and are very manoeuvrable. They can engage the enemy quickly to support the Assault squad.

RULES INTRODUCTION

This section of the Warhammer 40,000 book details the rules of the game, the nuts and bolts of how things move and fight on the battlefield. It is not necessary to master all the rules to begin playing – in fact trying to learn everything at once may be confusing. If you've never played a game like Warhammer 40,000 before, we recommend starting with the basic Infantry rules and then progressing to the rules for different unit types.

Few games of Warhammer 40,000, especially if you are just starting out, will involve all of the rules given over the following sections. Our advice is to have a quick look through the rules once. You don't have to read every word, just get an idea of what's going on and where different rules can be found. After that, the best idea is to get stuck in and play a few games! As you come across situations you're not sure how to deal with, look up the relevant section and read the rules as you are playing. In particular, the sections on Characteristics, The Turn, The Movement Phase, The Shooting Phase, The Assault Phase and Morale contain all the basic rules you need to play. It's also worth looking back over the rules from time to time to make sure things really do work the way you think they do.

By starting this way you'll find that you pick up the core rules in a few sessions and will be able to play most games with just the information on the reference sheet at the back of the book. As you introduce other elements into your games, such as heroic characters, lumbering tanks and heavily-armed Dreadnoughts, read through the appropriate rules and refer to them while playing.

WHAT YOU NEED

As well as the Warhammer 40,000 book, there are a few other items you will need. For a start, you'll need two or more players with a selection of miniatures to represent their forces and a battlefield for them to fight over. Any firm, level surface will do, such as a tabletop or an area of floor – most kitchen tables will do fine. It's a good idea to protect the table from scratches and chips with a blanket or cloth. Most players use a 6' x 4' gaming board made from chipboard on top of the table to extend their playing area.

To complete your battlefield you should try to obtain some terrain, such as hills, walls, ruined buildings, wreckage, jungle or woods. Terrain, whether you made it yourself or bought it, adds realism to your battles and gives armies something to fight over or use as much needed cover from enemy fire. You can find out more about armies and battlefields in the Organising a Battle section of this book.

The Codex books give the specialised rules and army lists for the different opposing forces of the 41st millennium and are designed to work in conjunction with the Warhammer 40,000 rules.

As well as players, armies, a battlefield and terrain there are a few other things you'll need when playing. For troop movement, etc, you will need at least one measuring device marked in inches (such as a ruler or retractable tape measure). All distances in Warhammer 40,000 are in imperial measurements. You will need some ordinary six-sided dice, and a Scatter dice will also be useful. Finally, a pen and some paper can be handy for noting down damage to vehicles, casualties on units and other details that may crop up during a game.

DICE ROLLS

There are lots of occasions in Warhammer 40,000 when you have to roll dice to see how the actions of your infantry turn out – how effective their shooting is, what damage they've done to a vehicle, how far they fall back from enemy fire, and so on. All of the dice rolls in Warhammer 40,000 use a standard six-sided dice (usually shortened to 'D6'). Sometimes, you may have to modify the result of the dice roll. This is noted as D6 plus or minus a number, such as D6+1 or D6-2. Roll the dice and add or subtract the number to or from the score to get the final result. For example, D6+2 means roll a dice and add 2 to the score, giving a total of between 3 and 8.

You may also be told to roll a number of dice in one go, which is written as 2D6, 3D6, and so on. Roll the indicated number of dice and add the scores together, so a 2D6 roll is two dice rolled and added together for a score of between 2-12, 3D6 adds together the scores of three dice for a total of 3-18 and so on. Another method sometimes used is to multiply the score of a dice by a certain amount. Therefore, D6x5 means roll a D6 and multiply it by 5, giving a total between 5 and 30.

Sometimes a combination of these methods may be used, such as 2D6+5 giving a score of between 7 and 17, or 3D6-3 which will total 0-15.

In rare circumstances you may be told to roll a D3. Since there's no such thing as a three-sided dice, use the following method for determining a score between 1 and 3. Roll a D6 and halve the score, rounding up. Thus 1 or 2=1, 3 or 4=2 and 5 or 6=3.

SCATTER DICE

A few weapons are fairly random in their accuracy and require you to roll a Games Workshop Scatter dice to determine where they land. The Scatter dice is marked on four sides with an arrow, and on two sides with a special 'HIT' symbol. Simply roll the Scatter dice near the target point – if an arrow is rolled this shows which direction the shot has deviated in. If a HIT symbol is rolled this generally means the shot is bang on target. Some weapons may scatter automatically, with no chance of a direct hit, in which case you will find a small arrow on the HIT side to determine the direction.

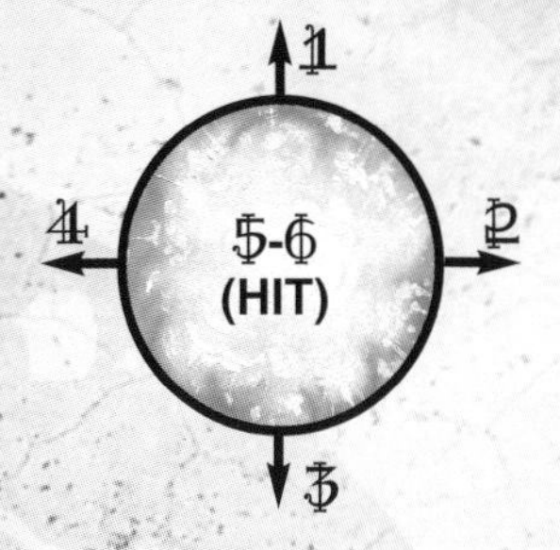

Although a Scatter dice is the best way to determine random direction, you can achieve a similar result by using a D6. Put this book flat on the table with the arrow marked 1 on the diagram facing in the direction you want the weapon to fire. Roll a D6 and on a score of 5 or 6 the hit lands on target. If you roll 1, 2, 3 or 4 then the shot scatters, as shown. This method isn't as random as a Scatter dice but suffices in most circumstances.

RE-ROLLS

In some situations the rules allow you a 're-roll' of the dice. This is exactly as it sounds – pick up the dice you wish to re-roll and roll them again. The second score counts, even if it means a worse result than the first, and no single dice can be re-rolled more than once regardless of the source of the re-roll.

THE MOST IMPORTANT RULE

The most important rule about playing games of Warhammer 40,000 is to have fun! Now while having fun may often be gained by mercilessly crushing your opponent's forces, never ever forget that you are **both** there to have fun. Whenever you play a game, you and your opponent are basically agreeing to duel according to a set of fairly abstract rules, with a theoretical ground scale, using representative forces and a thousand other subtle agreements that go together to make it work.

The battle itself is a shared experience and great entertainment for both sides if they are both willing to make it so. No one particularly enjoys playing a game with someone who is overwrought, irascible and generally mean, or who only plays to win at all costs. That kind of player soon has difficulty finding opponents because they simply aren't much fun to game against. So the most important rule is to play nice and treat your opponent with the respect you would wish to get back from them so that you both have a enjoyable and exciting game. If you can do that *and* mercilessly crush their forces at the same time, then you really are a winner.

The foolish man puts his trust in luck,
the wise man puts his trust in the Emperor.

MODELS

The Citadel miniatures used to play Warhammer 40,000 are simply referred to as **models** in the rules that follow. Each model is an individual playing piece with its own capabilities. It is convenient to define different types of models for ease of description throughout the rules.

There are two very general types of models. These are:

NON-VEHICLE MODELS

This category includes an enormous variety of troops ranging from Gretchin, the small, weak slaves of the Orks, to Wraithlords, mighty Eldar constructs containing the souls of the dead. Non-vehicle models are the most common in the game and all use a standard profile described in the Characteristics section (see page 12).

VEHICLE MODELS

Needless to say, this includes all vehicles. In practice it includes all vehicles that enclose the crew. Small vehicles, such as bikes, are not included, instead they are dealt with as an extension of their rider. All vehicles will have a profile described in the Vehicles section (see page 58).

When you see the term 'model' used in the rules, it will apply to both non-vehicle and vehicle models. If the term 'non-vehicle model' or 'vehicle model' is used it will apply to models using characteristics or vehicle characteristics respectively. To ensure that you can recognise the difference it is probably a good idea to take a quick look at these sections now.

Models will sometimes fight individually. This is commonly the case with powerful tanks or experienced army commanders. Normally, though, a number of models are combined in a group termed a **unit**. The different types of unit are detailed in the Units section.

BASE AND HEIGHT GUIDELINES

There are countless different models in Warhammer 40,000 – everything from towering daemons and immense war engines to tiny, crawling vermin. To ensure no one gets confused by the huge variety of models in the game, a couple of conventions apply to *all* models on the tabletop battlefield.

BASES

Firstly, a model is considered to occupy the area of its base, so when measuring distances use the closest edge of the base as your reference point. For models without a base (usually vehicles) use the model's hull/main body instead. Games Workshop miniatures are usually supplied with a base and this should be viewed as the minimum size base they can be mounted on – you can mount them on something bigger if you wish, but not something smaller.

All the models pictured here are classed as non-vehicle models. (A) Tyranid Hive Tyrant, (B) Tyranid Hormagaunts, (C) Tyranid Ripper Swarm, (D) Space Marine Tactical Squad, (E) Space Marine Chaplain, (F) Space Marine Bikes, (G) Space Marine Attack Bike.

In this example, the Hormagaunts, Ripper Swarm, Space Marine Tactical Squad and Bikes each form separate groups known as units.

MODEL HEIGHT

The rules will often have to take account of the height of models and terrain features. This is necessary to determine whether troops can see over obstructions. This does not mean literally their actual height, as the simple expedient of crouching, kneeling or crawling will render such direct comparisons irrelevant. Instead there are three broad height bands into which all models fall. These categories are also used to define the height of some terrain features. The following three categories are the only ones that are important in the Shooting phase when determining line of sight and target priority:

Size 1: Small Targets (see page 75).

Size 2: Standard Targets. Basically every model not included in either of the other categories.

Size 3: Large Targets. Includes Monstrous Creatures and Vehicles (see Units, page 9 and 10).

Initially, virtually every model you use will fall into the middle category. Be aware though that when you want to see over some terrain features or an ongoing close combat, these heights will become relevant. All you need to remember is that if an observer OR the observed is of a greater height category than anything in the way, then it has a clear line of sight.

All the models pictured here are classed as vehicle models. From left to right: Predator tank, Rhino APC, Land Speeder, Dreadnought.

UNITS

Warhammer 40,000 allows you to fight battles with armies of creatures and supporting units of tanks and guns. It is up to you as general of your forces to find the best way to use your vehicles and infantry to achieve victory. Of course, soldiers tend to band together to fight in squads, teams, sections, etc – individual warriors do not normally go wandering off on their own for obvious reasons! In Warhammer 40,000, we represent the way that real infantry fight by grouping them together into units.

Units of warriors fight in loose groups with gaps between each model. This gives the troopers the freedom to move over difficult terrain quickly, and enables them to take advantage of such things as minor folds in the ground, scrub, and other small features, to shelter from enemy fire. Similarly, artillery batteries consist of the guns and the crew that fire them, vehicle squadrons are made up of a number of vehicles and so on. The different elements of the unit have to stay together to remain an effective fighting force. This is detailed more fully in the Movement section.

A unit will usually consist of several infantry models or small vehicles that fight as a group, but it can also be a single, very large and/or powerful model, such as a battle tank, a monstrous alien creature or a lone hero. In the rules that follow, all of these things are referred to as units. In order to make it easier to learn the core rules the sections covering Movement, Shooting, Assault and Morale are written with respect to Infantry units, because these are by far the most common unit type in the game. The other unit types are explained in later sections, covering specific rules for Jetbikes, Monstrous Creatures and so forth. The main unit types for non-vehicle models are as follows.

INFANTRY
Infantry units include all types of foot soldiers, whether human or alien. A typical unit of infantry is between five and ten models strong but are often much larger. In rare cases, a unit may comprise of only a single model. Infantry are fairly slow moving but can cross almost any terrain (given enough time) and make the best use of cover to avoid enemy fire. Infantry are the most common and dependable units in Warhammer 40,000 and the bulk of the core rules are concerned with them.

JUMP INFANTRY
Jump infantry are equipped with jump packs, jet packs, sometimes wings, teleport devices or other means of moving quickly over short distances. They commonly take advantage of these by dropping onto the battlefield in the midst of the enemy – heroically or foolishly depending on your perspective. Jump infantry can move like normal creatures on foot or kick in their jump device to make a high speed move, combining some of the best elements of both mounted and ordinary infantry. Jump infantry usually come in units of five to ten models and tend to be a rare and valuable commodity in most armies.

BEASTS & CAVALRY

Consisting of particularly vicious hunting animals or a rider with a living mount, beasts and cavalry are able to swiftly carry the battle to the enemy. Beasts and cavalry have a profile like other infantry but are able to make use of a special faster move when they charge an enemy unit.

These units tend to be powerful in open terrain where they have room to manoeuvre, and move like infantry in denser areas, such as woods or buildings. Beast and cavalry units are typically quite small, with one to six models in a single unit. Note that riders may not dismount during the game and that cavalry models have a combined characteristic profile that factors in both the beast and rider.

BIKES AND JETBIKES

These units are riders mounted on a variety of conventional bikes or jetbikes. They are capable of moving really quickly, and will often have weapon systems mounted on their bikes. Their only major weakness is the risk of crashing when moving through difficult terrain. Both types of bike manoeuvre much faster than infantry and jetbikes are able to glide over obstructions, such as scrub, without being slowed. Bike and jetbike units normally number from three to five models.

MONSTROUS CREATURES

Some creatures are just too big to fit into the ordinary infantry unit category; towering giants that are capable of crushing a tank – like the Tyranid Carnifex, a creature bioengineered and evolved especially for killing – or a living engine of destruction, like the Eldar Wraithlord. While Monstrous Creatures use many of the Infantry rules, their size and destructive capability make them closer to vehicles in other respects. A Monstrous Creature unit will usually consist of only a single model.

ARTILLERY

These units represent large weapons and their crews, the gun models themselves being large enough to be removed separately in addition to crew casualties. Artillery units count as infantry in all respects, but when they are fired at, hits can be scored on the guns or the crew. The guns themselves have vehicle-like characteristics. Note that these units should not be confused with the heavy weapon teams found in some infantry units (such as Imperial Guard or Eldar, for example).

VEHICLES

Vehicle units include all kinds of war machines. Space Marine Land Raider tanks, Rhino personnel carriers, Dreadnoughts and Ork Wartraks all fall into this category. Some vehicles can move more rapidly than infantry but need to stick to open ground to avoid getting bogged down. Vehicle units are represented by single models, in the case of tanks and other large vehicles, or as a group of one to three smaller vehicles. Vehicle crew members – the drivers, commanders and gunners – are assumed to be an integral part of their machine, and if their vehicle is destroyed they are considered to be lost along with it.

THE ULTRAMARINES AT THE BREACH OF CORINTH

CHARACTERISTICS

In Warhammer 40,000, there are many different types of warriors, ranging from the mighty Space Marines to the brutal Orks, the agile Eldar to the massive and dreaded Tyranid Warriors. To represent the abilities of these creatures in the game, there are nine categories that describe the various aspects of their physical and mental make-up. These are called Characteristics.

All characteristics are measured on a scale of 0 to 10. The higher the value of a characteristic, the better it is, except for Saves. The characteristics are: Weapon Skill (WS), Ballistic Skill (BS), Strength (S), Toughness (T), Wounds (W), Initiative (I), Attacks (A), Leadership (Ld) and Save (Sv).

WEAPON SKILL (WS)
Defines how skilled a creature is with his weapons in close combat, or simply how determined and vicious a creature is. The higher the score, the more likely the warrior will land blows on a close combat opponent. A normal human has WS3. A battle-hardened Space Marine will have WS4 or even WS5.

BALLISTIC SKILL (BS)
Shows how accurate a creature is with ranged attacks, such as guns, rockets or energy weapons. It also includes a measure of the warrior's technical competence with his weapons and ammo supply. The higher this score is, the easier a creature finds it to hit when it shoots at something. Some monsters have natural weapons that can be used at range (they may be able to spit venom, for example) and their BS is used to determine whether they hit or not.

STRENGTH (S)
Shows how physically strong a creature is. An exceptionally puny creature may have a Strength of 1, a deadly Tyranid Lictor has S6 and most humans have S3. Strength tells us how hard a creature can hit in close combat or how easily it can hurt an enemy.

TOUGHNESS (T)
This measures a creature's ability to resist physical damage and pain, and includes such factors as the toughness of its flesh, hide or skin. The tougher a creature, the better it can survive enemy blows or shots. A human is T3, a genetically-enhanced Space Marine is T4. Things with a Toughness of 6 or more are usually monstrous creatures with special rules to reflect their great size.

WOUNDS (W)
Shows how much damage a creature can take before it either dies or is so badly hurt it can't fight any more. Most humans/human-sized creatures have only a single Wound. Heroes and large monsters are often able to withstand several wounds that would slay a lesser creature, and so have a Wounds value of 2, 3, 4 or even more.

INITIATIVE (I)
Indicates how alert a creature is and how quickly it reacts. Creatures with a low Initiative score are slow and cumbersome, creatures with a high Initiative score are much quicker and more agile. In close combat, faster creatures gain a big advantage over slower ones in that they strike first.

ATTACKS (A)
Indicates the number of Attacks a creature makes during close combat. Most creatures only attack once, although some warriors of exceptional skill or monsters can strike several times. The number of Attacks a creature makes may be increased if it has the added impetus of charging into its foe or is fighting using two weapons.

LEADERSHIP (Ld)
A creature with a high Leadership value is courageous, steadfast, and self-controlled. A creature with a low value is the opposite. Creatures with high Leadership can lead others, inspiring them on to greater feats of valour.

SAVE (Sv)
A creature's Saving throw gives it a chance of avoiding harm when it is struck or shot. Most creatures have a Saving throw based on what kind of armour they are wearing, so their Saving throw may be improved if they are equipped with better armour. Other creatures may receive a natural Saving throw from having a thick hide or chitinous shell.

ZERO LEVEL CHARACTERISTICS

Some creatures have been given a '0' for certain characteristics, which means that they have no ability whatsoever in that field. This usually applies to creatures unable to use missile weapons, and so they have a BS of 0, but it might equally apply to other characteristics too (eg, a defenceless model will have no Attacks whatsoever).

LEADERSHIP TESTS

Sometimes, a unit may be called upon to make a Leadership test, most commonly to direct its fire or hold its ground. To take a Leadership test, roll 2D6 and compare the combined score to the unit's Leadership value. If the dice score equal to or under the Leadership value, the test is passed. If the dice score over the characteristic, the test is failed. Modifiers may apply to the Leadership characteristic in particularly trying circumstances, eg, -1 if the unit is below half its starting strength. Characteristic tests are used for other things, as detailed in the army's Codex book.

CHARACTERISTIC PROFILES

Each creature in Warhammer 40,000 has a profile that lists the value of its characteristics. In the Codex books, you will find profiles for many races and creatures.

Below are the profiles for a Tyranid Termagant and an Imperial Space Marine.

	WS	BS	S	T	W	I	A	Ld	Sv
Termagant	3	3	3	3	1	4	1	5	6+
Space Marine	4	4	4	4	1	4	1	8	3+

As you can see, both are similar in some respects. They have the same Initiative value which means they are equally quick in close combat. Both creatures have 1 Wound and 1 Attack which is the norm for man-sized creatures. When it comes to BS and WS, S and T, however, the Space Marine is superior to the Termagant.

The Space Marine's Ballistic Skill of 4 and Weapon Skill of 4 mean the Space Marine will hit more often in shooting and close combat. The greater Strength value gives the Space Marine a better chance of injuring or killing the Termagant in hand-to-hand combat. Space Marines are extremely robust, with their high Toughness meaning they are better than ordinary humans in surviving damage inflicted on them. The Space Marine has a Leadership of 8, which is slightly higher than the average Leadership for most warriors. Termagants are animalistic, bioengineered predators which can be easily confused without the telepathic control of the larger hive organisms, and so have a low Leadership of 5. The Space Marine's thicker armour gives him another marked advantage over the Termagant, as any shot or blow that hits the Space Marine is deflected on a D6 roll of 3 or more. The Termagant needs a roll of 6 to be saved by its chitinous armour plates.

Obviously, Termagants are no match for Space Marines when fighting one to one but, as Termagants are usually found in large broods this can make them challenging opponents, even for Space Marines.

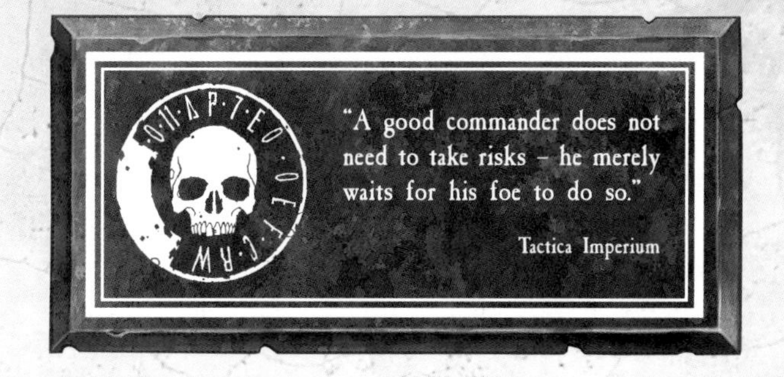

POINTS VALUES

Generally, you'll find characteristic profiles come with one other piece of information – the points value per model. This represents the relative battlefield value of the creature in question. Points values are an abstract calculation which take into account a huge number of different factors including characteristics, different races' overall strengths and weaknesses, basic weapons, unit size, rarity and so forth.

For comparison, Space Marines are worth 15 points, and Termagants 7. This means Space Marines can be outnumbered by Termagants by at least two to one and still have an even chance of winning.

VEHICLE CHARACTERISTICS

Set in the far future, the Warhammer 40,000 universe is home to all sorts of tanks, war machines and other combat vehicles, both human built and alien. To reflect the many differences between creatures of flesh and blood and constructs of steel and iron, vehicles have many different rules and their own set of characteristics. Vehicle characteristics are described in more detail in the Vehicles section (see page 58).

THE TURN

Warhammer 40,000 battle is unlike other games, such as chess or draughts, where you only move a single piece at a time. A tremendous amount of action takes place in a battle: squads are constantly manoeuvring and shooting, tanks rumble into action and artillery fire roars overhead in a torrential downpour of destruction.

A Warhammer 40,000 game represents the whole ebb and flow of battle but, in order to determine its outcome, players alternate taking turns moving and fighting with their units. So, in a battle, player A will move and fight with his forces first, then player B will move and fight, and then player A will move and fight again and so on until the end of the game.

During his turn, the player can move and fight with all of his units if he wishes. For convenience, the actions of moving, shooting and fighting are dealt with one after the other. This means you move any infantry and vehicles you want to first, and then you shoot with anyone who can and so on. This process helps everyone to keep track of what is going on and makes it easier to know when one player's actions are over and their opponent can start taking his turn.

TURN SUMMARY

1 THE MOVEMENT PHASE
The player can move any of his units that are capable of doing so. See the Movement rules for more details of how to move your forces.

2 THE SHOOTING PHASE
The player can shoot with any of his units that are within range of the enemy. See the Shooting rules for more details about how to resolve shooting.

3 THE ASSAULT PHASE
The player can move any of his units to assault the enemy if they are close enough. Assaults are bloody, desperate affairs where units are fighting in close combat and firing at very close range.

This means that both forces can fight in an Assault phase, but only the player whose turn it is can move into an assault. The Assault rules will tell you more about assaults.

THE GAME TURN

In a complete game turn, each player gets a turn and performs their actions in the appropriate phases – the Movement, Shooting and Assault phases to be precise. Exactly what happens in each phase is described in the Turn sequence. Hence one game turn will comprise two player turns, or sometimes more depending on the number of players and the mission being played.

WHO GETS THE FIRST TURN?

Which player gets the first turn of the game can be determined in a number of different ways. Normally, both players roll a D6 and the player with the highest score can decide to take the first or second turn (first being a popular choice unless you have a really cunning plan). Sometimes, the kind of game you are fighting will decide it for you. For example, some missions, like ambushes or sneak attacks, may specify that the attacking side will get the first turn.

Fighting all sorts of different battles is covered in more detail in the Organising a Battle section of the rules.

ENDING THE BATTLE

A battle can end in a number of ways. One of the most common is playing a pre-set number of game turns. Most games are set to a limit of six game turns, ensuring an equal number for each player. However, in some kinds of battle, players might be able to win a 'sudden death' victory that ends the game immediately – for example, if they destroy the power generator they win straight away. Alternatively, the number of game turns being fought might be random, possibly determined by a dice throw. You could also decide to end a battle at a pre-set time if you only have a limited amount of time to play in. Some different kinds of battles and ways of ending them are shown in more detail in the Organising a Battle section.

EXCEPTIONS

There are times when a player performs actions when it is not their turn, such as fighting in a close assault, for example. It may also be convenient to interrupt a player's turn because of some event occurring, like a booby trap being triggered. The thing to remember is that after the interruption, the turn sequence always continues as normal.

MOVEMENT PHASE

The Movement phase is your chance to move your units around the battlefield. For example, you can send them into the attack, move them into cover, retreat from a superior foe or sweep around an enemy's vulnerable side or rear. Although the Movement phase is the easiest to perform, it's probably the most tactically important. For the time being we'll just explain how warriors on foot move, as they are by far the most common units in the game. Vehicles, jump/mounted infantry and certain other units move in different ways to represent their greater mobility, and these will be discussed in detail later.

In his turn, a player may move all or some of his units up to their maximum movement distance. Once a unit has completed all of its movement, the player selects another unit and moves that one, and so on, until the player has moved all of the units he wishes to move.

MOVEMENT PHASE SUMMARY

1. Choose a unit to move.
2. Move any or all of the models in the unit up to their maximum move distance.
3. Repeat the above until movement is complete.

Note that a player doesn't have to move all (or indeed any) of his units. A unit that doesn't move is often more effective at shooting, as we will explain later in the rules. Once you have started moving a unit you may not go back and change the move already made by a previous unit.

MOVEMENT DISTANCE

Infantry on foot move up to six inches (6") in the Movement phase. This represents most creatures moving at a run but stopping several times to observe the surrounding landscape for enemies, snap off a few quick shots with their weapons, etc. Even warriors who are moving in a part of the battlefield where no enemies may be apparent move 6". This is because your units lack your own god-like knowledge that there is no enemy around.

A model may not move into/through the space occupied by a friendly model or through a gap between friendly models smaller than its own base size. A model cannot be placed so that it touches an enemy model during the Movement phase – this is only possible in the Assault phase. To keep this distinction clear, a model may not move within 1" of an enemy model (ignore wrecked vehicles) during the Movement phase.

DIFFERENT MOVEMENT DISTANCES IN A UNIT

All models in a unit move at the speed of the slowest model.

MAINTAINING UNIT COHERENCY

As mentioned before, units are normally groups of models operating together on the tabletop. They fight in a loose formation with gaps between each model. This gives the individual troopers freedom to move quickly over difficult terrain, and enables them to disperse somewhat to take advantage of cover.

When you are moving a unit, the individual models in it can move up to their maximum movement distance – remember that units have to stick together, otherwise individual models become scattered as the unit loses its cohesion as a fighting force. So, once a unit has finished moving, the models in it must form an imaginary chain where the distance between one model and the next is no more than 2". We call this *unit coherency*.

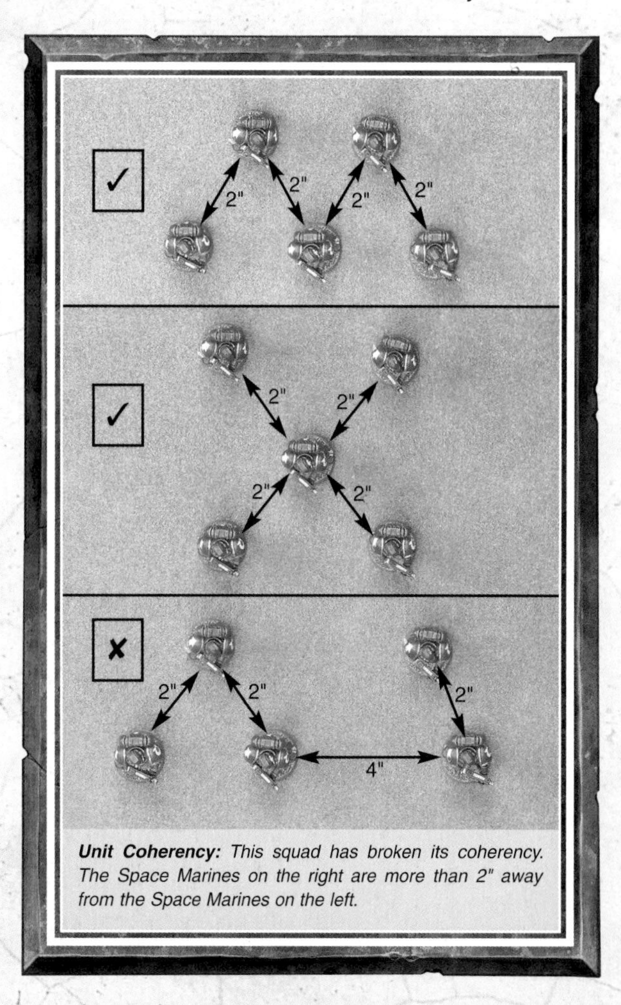

Unit Coherency: *This squad has broken its coherency. The Space Marines on the right are more than 2" away from the Space Marines on the left.*

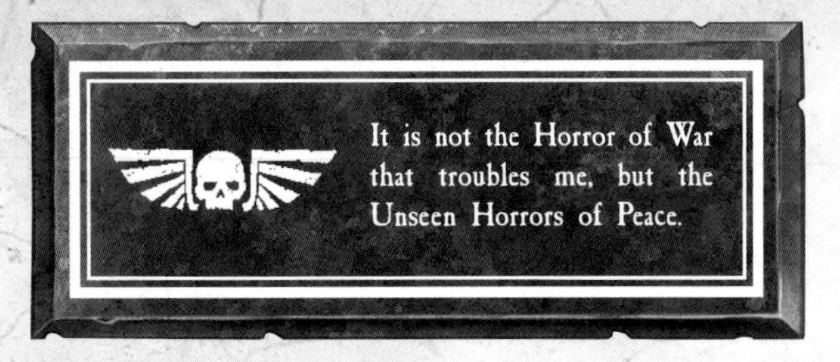

It is not the Horror of War that troubles me, but the Unseen Horrors of Peace.

During the course of a game, it's possible a unit will get broken up and lose unit coherency, usually because it takes casualties. When this happens the following rule applies:

If a unit is broken up for any reason, the models in it must be moved to restore unit coherency in the next Movement phase. If they cannot do so, the unit may not shoot or launch an assault until it is in a coherent formation again. If the unit cannot move for some reason in its next turn (because they are pinned down by a barrage or sniper fire, for example), then they must move to restore unit coherency as soon as they have the opportunity.

TURNING & FACING

As you move models in a unit they can turn by any amount, without any penalty, to the distance they are able to cover. Infantry models can be turned to face their targets in the Shooting phase, so don't worry about which way they are pointing at the end of their Movement phase (although dramatically facing off against their foes is traditional).

RANDOM & COMPULSORY MOVEMENT

Sometimes, a unit will be specified as being subject to random movement and/or be forced to move in a certain way. Most commonly this will be D6" or 2D6" of additional movement and/or moving directly towards the closest enemy. Unless covered otherwise in the special rules for the unit, such movement is subject to all the normal penalties for moving through difficult and dangerous terrain. A unit using random movement slowed by difficult terrain halves the distance rolled (rounding up), unless specified otherwise.

TERRAIN

The galaxy is a vast place with millions of different worlds: ice worlds, desert worlds, hive worlds, feral worlds and many other exotic types of battlefield – if you can imagine it, then it probably exists somewhere. The terrain covering these worlds can vary from broad, empty plains to sky-scraping towers of plexiglass and plasteel, from verdant jungles to icy peaks or baking hot deserts. One factor is common to all of them – they have areas seemingly designed to make it difficult to wage war.

Of course, areas that provide cover from which warriors can fight or which present an obstacle to the enemy are vital in war, and these are destined to become the bloodiest battlefields. How to represent terrain on the battlefield is discussed later. For now, we're going to discuss terrain only in relation to how infantry moves through it.

TERRAIN TYPES

Terrain provides useful cover from enemy fire, but can also impede the movement of your units. Troops can be disorientated or physically slowed by the need to push through or climb over entanglements and obstructions. There are three general classes of terrain: clear, difficult and impassable.

• Clear terrain can be moved across without any penalty, and generally covers most of the battlefield.

• Difficult terrain slows down models wishing to move through it. Difficult terrain can sometimes be dangerous to models passing through it.

• Impassable terrain prevents all movement through it.

GUIDELINES ON CATEGORISING TERRAIN

It is a relatively simple matter to classify terrain within these three categories, and it is important that you and your opponent agree what class of terrain each feature falls into before starting your game.

• Clear terrain represents terrain that can be traversed easily. This includes open areas, such as fields, moorland, grass, deserts, ash wastes and gentle hills. This could be embellished with the odd tree, shrub or cactus (or alien equivalents) for visual appeal.

• Difficult terrain includes areas of jungle, woods, forest, ruins, brush and scrub, rocky outcrops, boggy ground, marshes, low walls, hedges, steep hills and shallow water, such as streams. It also includes terrain features that combine several of these types, such as a ruin surrounded by woods. If the terrain feature includes hazards, such as carnivorous plants, toxic vents, erupting geysers and the like, then it may be additionally categorised as dangerous.

• Impassable terrain includes deep water, lava flows, fully enclosed building models and towering cliffs.

It is quite possible that a very large building could be classed differently in different locations, most of it counting as ruins and therefore difficult, whilst an intact tower at its corner counts as impassable terrain.

You will notice that buildings appear in more than one category. A building model with roof and walls attached can be difficult to position models on. In these circumstances it is best to categorise them as impassable. If the roof lifts off, or models can be safely balanced on top, then they should be categorised as difficult.

AREA TERRAIN

For most terrain features, what you see is what you get. Thus a hill or an enclosed building is as high as the model used to depict it. Sometimes, however, it is necessary to take liberties and make assumptions about terrain. This is where Area Terrain comes in. Area Terrain, like models, comes in size classes, ranging from Size 1, representing low-lying terrain, to Size 3, representing very high terrain such as woodland that can obscure tanks.

The types of terrain where this approach works best are marshes, woods, ruins and all types of rough going area. Realistically a wood might be a tangled, overgrown mass of foliage. If it is represented like this then it will be very difficult to position models on it with any degree of precision (or safety). What is important is where the boundary of the terrain feature is. You can show the boundary by using a flat baseboard, an outline of lichen or by painting a slightly different colour on your gaming board. Within this boundary loosely place trees or sections of ruins as appropriate for the type of terrain it represents. The exact placement and size of the terrain items used are not important and you can freely move them to allow models to be accurately positioned. Each area feature should be given a height, and it is this that will decide who can see over it. This is explained in more detail under Line of Sight and Area Terrain (page 21).

In all cases, you should discuss any unusual terrain features with your opponent before the game and agree exactly what everything counts as and where boundaries of terrain features lie. When the game is underway, it will be harder to discuss it quite so dispassionately…

IMPASSABLE TERRAIN

Models may not be placed in impassable terrain unless the models concerned have a special rule in their profile granting them an exception, or are able to fly above the terrain like a skimmer, or both players agree to it.

MOVING IN DIFFICULT TERRAIN

If an infantry unit moves into, through or out of difficult terrain, it will generally be slowed down. Units that are slowed must take a Difficult Terrain test, rolling two D6 and selecting the highest.

Moving in Difficult Terrain : *A unit moving through difficult terrain rolls two D6 and selects the highest. In this case, the unit moves 5".*

Moving Up & Down: *This model has rolled a 6 on its Difficult Terrain test. It can travel up or down the same distance it moves along.*

This is the distance in inches they may move. Some units may be able to roll more than two dice and select the best, or even re-roll their dice. Where this is the case, it is explained in their profile or in their relevant section later in this book.

If a unit that starts its move outside difficult terrain does not roll high enough to enter the terrain, it is still only moved the distance rolled. This represents them approaching the terrain in a cautious fashion.

If you take the Difficult Terrain test, you are never compelled to move the models, considering you may not have rolled enough movement to make it worth moving at all. However, if you roll the dice, the unit is still considered as having moved for the purposes of firing, as detailed in the Shooting rules.

MOVING UP & DOWN

When a unit is moved, it can travel up and/or down the same distance as it moves along, subject to the Difficult Terrain rules. For example, if a unit moves 6" into a building, then it could be placed 6" above ground level inside that building as well.

DANGEROUS TERRAIN TESTS

As mentioned previously, some terrain features will be dangerous to move through. This is represented by the unit taking a Dangerous Terrain check. Roll a D6 for every model in the unit. Each roll of a 1 indicates a model suffers a wound with no Save possible (Saves are explained in the shooting rules, all you need know for now is that in this case you don't get any of them!).

SHOOTING PHASE

In the Shooting phase, you have the opportunity to fire at the enemy with your forces. As the two sides engage each other at a distance, the guns thunder ceaselessly and there is an almost constant exchange of fire between foes. In a Warhammer 40,000 battle, we split the firing up so that each player's force fires during their own turn. This keeps shooting simple to work out and keeps the game moving at a good pace.

During the Shooting phase, each of your units may fire. You can choose any of your units to shoot with, but you must complete all the firing by one unit before you move onto the next. Every model in a unit can shoot – infantry can fire with just one weapon each, but some units (like vehicles) may be able to fire more than one weapon per model, as detailed later. The whole unit has to fire all of its weaponry at a single opposing unit of your choice – you may not split fire between two or more target units. Note that individual models within a unit can choose not to shoot.

The shooting process can be summarised in six steps, as shown below. Once you've completed this sequence with one of your units, select another and begin at Step 1 again. Once you have completed Steps 1 to 6 for each unit in your army, you've finished shooting and can go on to the Assault phase. The rules for the Shooting phase also include details on weapons later in the section.

SHOOTING PHASE SUMMARY

1. Choose a unit to shoot with.
2. Resolve the shooting process (see below) for the chosen unit.
3. Repeat the above until shooting is complete.

THE SHOOTING PROCESS

1. **Choose a target:** Select an enemy unit for one of your units to fire at. Your unit may have to pass a Leadership test if they want to shoot at any but the closest enemy.
2. **Check line of sight and range:** See if the target is within sight and range of the weaponry of your firing unit.
3. **Roll to hit:** Roll a D6 for each shot fired by the firing unit. The model's BS determines what score they must equal or beat to hit their target.
4. **Roll to wound:** For each shot that hits, roll again to see if it wounds the target. The score needed is determined by comparing the Strength of the firing weapons with the Toughness of the target.
5. **Make Saving Throws:** Each wounding hit may be deflected by making a Saving throw. Saving throws derive from the armour worn, or any special Invulnerable Saving throws, or by being in cover. Models that fail a save become casualties.
6. **Remove casualties:** The owner of the target unit removes any casualties inflicted.

CHOOSE A TARGET

As mentioned previously, a firing unit can choose a single enemy unit as its target. There are several considerations when choosing a target; namely, can your unit see it, and will their weapons have enough range to reach it?

TARGET PRIORITY

Your units will have a natural tendency to shoot at the nearest enemy, as in the tumult of battle these will be the easiest to spot and often the most threatening. However, a well-trained and led unit will overcome this and follow your orders to the letter. To represent this, you must pass a Leadership test (see page 13) if you want a unit to target any enemy unit other than the closest. If the test is failed, resolve the unit's firing at the nearest enemy unit instead.

Exceptions: Units are always able to ignore targets which cannot be fired on (units with all models engaged in close combat, for example) and units that are falling back (see the Morale section for more on this).

The Leadership test must be taken even if the unit does not normally have to take Leadership tests, or is assumed to automatically pass them.

If there is any real contention over which unit is closest, take a Leadership test anyway and then find out what's closest. You may not measure the range to a target before choosing.

Target Priority: The Space Marines' closest target is Unit A. To fire at Unit B, the Space Marines must first pass a Leadership test on 2D6. If Unit A was falling back then it could be ignored if desired, making Unit B the closest target.

FIRING AT LARGE TARGETS

Many units carry tank-busting weapons, like missile launchers or lascannon, and are able to spot marauding vehicles, walkers or large creatures with ease. To represent this, when it comes to choosing a target you can declare that your unit wishes to target enemy vehicles, artillery and monstrous creatures (these are the only unit types you can target this way, collectively referred to as 'Large Targets'). If you choose to target Large Targets then other units can be ignored in terms of determining the closest target. A Leadership test is still required to target anything other than the closest Large Target.

Firing At Large Targets: By targeting Large Targets, the Imperial Guardsmen can ignore the Chaos Marine infantry (A) and shoot at the Predator (B) without needing to test their Leadership. Shooting at the Daemon Prince (C) or the Rhino (D) would require passing a Ld test to ignore the Predator. Note that Large Targets can also physically block line of sight and prevent a shot.

CHECK LINE OF SIGHT & RANGE

LINE OF SIGHT

You can only select an enemy unit as a target if your unit can see it, or at least part of it. Obviously, a unit can't draw a bead on their target if there is a hill, a building, or some other large and solid object in the way that stops them. In some cases, it will be difficult to tell if line of sight is blocked or not, so players might have to stoop over the table for a model's eye view. This is the best way to determine whether or not a line of sight exists. The only time you don't use this method is when you want to draw a line of sight into or past Area Terrain (see page 21, Line of Sight & Area Terrain), or an ongoing assault combat – this is dealt with later.

Models from the same side do not normally block line of sight (your unit conducts their firing at a convenient moment when their compatriots aren't in the way) and enemy models can be ignored for line of sight purposes (bearing in mind the Choosing a Target rules). However, the following models do block a unit's line of sight if they are in the way:

• All vehicles, vehicle wrecks, monstrous creatures and artillery, friend or foe block line of sight. A line of sight can still be drawn over or past such models, but not through them. Use a model's eye view to determine if you can see past them. Skimmer vehicles only block line of sight if immobilised or wrecked.

• Models engaged or locked in close combat block line of sight through them up to the height of the participating models. This is where the model's height matters (see page 7). If the model doing the spotting, or the model being spotted, is taller than the tallest model in the close combat then the line of sight is not blocked.

Above: *Targets A and B are visible to the Havocs. The Eldar Falcon (C) is also visible. Unit D is out of sight behind the building. Unit E is visible past the Falcon. Unit F is not out of sight behind the Falcon, as it is a skimmer and does not block line of sight.*

Left: *The Tau Fire Warriors can only hit three Imperial Guardsmen (models A, B and C). The rest are hidden behind the tank. Fire Warriors 1, 2, 3 & 4 do not fire at all as these models cannot see any of the Guardsmen.*

"Heresy is like a tree, its roots lie in the darkness whilst its leaves wave in the sun and to those who suspect nought it has an attractive and pleasing appearance. Truly, you can prune away its branches, or even cut the tree to the ground, but it will grow up again ever the stronger and ever more comely. Yet all awhile the root grows thick and black, gnawing at the bitter soil, drawing its nourishment from the darkness, and growing even greater and more deeply entrenched. Such is the nature of heresy, and this is why it so hard to destroy, for it must be eradicated leaf, branch, trunk and root. It must be exorcised utterly or it will return all the stronger, time and time again, until it is too great to destroy. Then we are doomed."

Galan Noirgrim Master of the Ordo Malleus, 'Prelude to The Abominatus'

Any individual models in the unit that don't have a line of sight to the target unit can't fire, and any models in the target unit that can't be seen by the attackers can't be hit or chosen as casualties (with the exception of barrage weapons – as explained later). If a model represents a weapon, such as an Eldar grav-platform, and there are separate crew figures, there must be a line of sight from both the gun model and at least one of its crew to the target. Sometimes, all that may be visible of a model is a toe or antenna or some other minor part. In these cases, the line of sight is considered blocked. Line of sight must be traced to the body of the target model. This rule is intended to ensure that players don't get penalised for having impressive banners, blades, gun barrels, spectacularly posed models, etc.

LINE OF SIGHT & AREA TERRAIN

Area Terrain does not block line of fire completely. Instead there will be a 'grey area' where the enemy fades out of sight the further in they are. Equally, a particularly large target may be visible across an area of low-lying terrain. This means that in regards to terrain defined as 'Area Terrain', the usual rules for spotting targets using the model's eye view is not used. In these cases we say it is possible to see up to 6" into Area Terrain. Models further than 6" in cannot be seen at all, nor can they see out, unless they are taller than the terrain. If both firer and target are within the same area of terrain, they can only see each other if they are within 6", unless one or both of them are taller than the terrain.

Note that although it is possible to see into Area Terrain, you cannot see through it even if it is less than 6" deep, hence if a unit is behind Area Terrain as tall as itself and the spotter, they cannot be seen. Models that are classed as taller than the Area Terrain can see and be seen over it.

A model's line of sight will be considerably improved by being on an elevated position, such as a cliff or building, so it can count the height of the terrain piece it stands on for line of sight in regards to other Area Terrain.

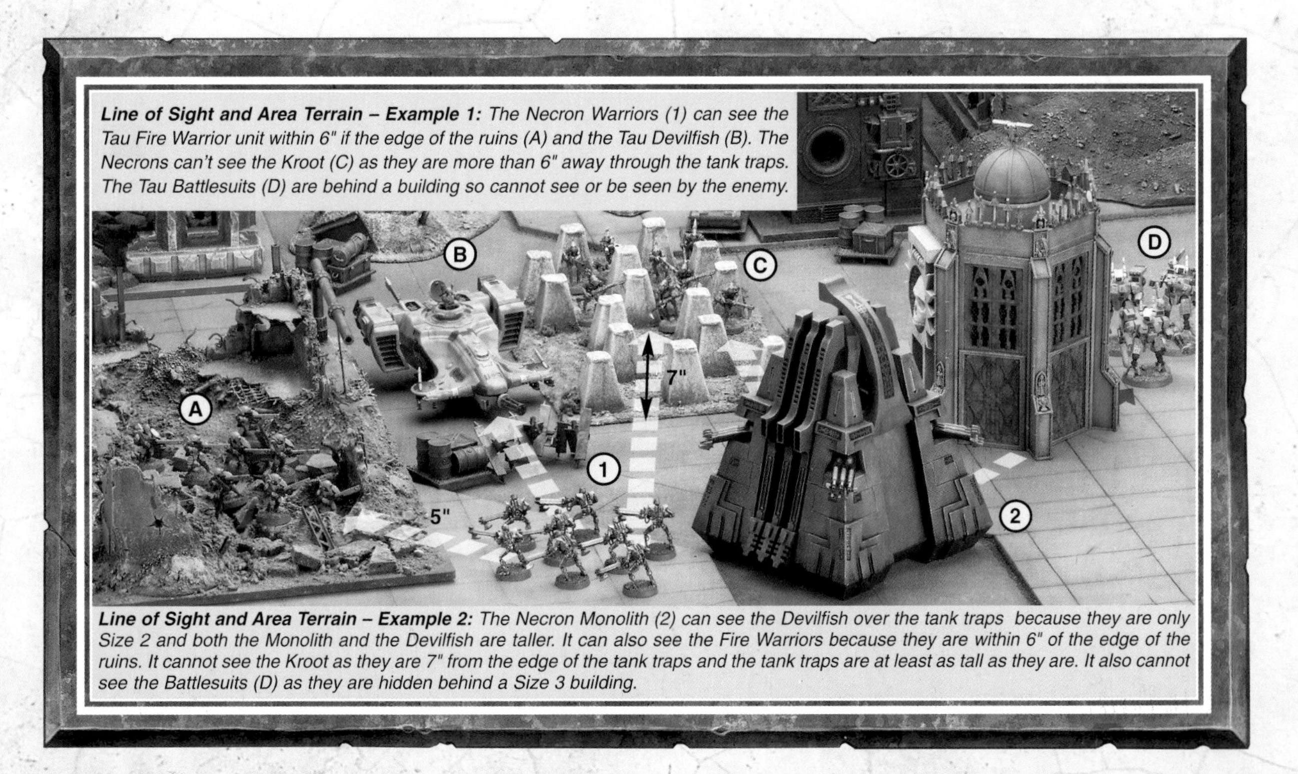

Line of Sight and Area Terrain – Example 1: *The Necron Warriors (1) can see the Tau Fire Warrior unit within 6" if the edge of the ruins (A) and the Tau Devilfish (B). The Necrons can't see the Kroot (C) as they are more than 6" away through the tank traps. The Tau Battlesuits (D) are behind a building so cannot see or be seen by the enemy.*

Line of Sight and Area Terrain – Example 2: *The Necron Monolith (2) can see the Devilfish over the tank traps because they are only Size 2 and both the Monolith and the Devilfish are taller. It can also see the Fire Warriors because they are within 6" of the edge of the ruins. It cannot see the Kroot as they are 7" from the edge of the tank traps and the tank traps are at least as tall as they are. It also cannot see the Battlesuits (D) as they are hidden behind a Size 3 building.*

CHECK RANGE

All weapons have a maximum effective range that tells you the furthest distance they can shoot. If your target is beyond this maximum range then your shot misses automatically. This is why you have to choose your target before measuring the range. Here are some examples of weapon ranges:

Weapon	Maximum Range
Laspistol	12"
Boltgun	24"
Autocannon	48"

When you're checking range, simply measure from the firer to the nearest model in the target unit. Any models in the target unit which are actually out of range can't be hit by the shooting.

MOVING & SHOOTING

Whether a unit has moved or not can make a big difference to its firing. If the warriors hold a position, take up firing stances and aim at their targets properly, they can hit targets further away than if they are firing on the move. In fact some weapons are so heavy that they can only be used if their firer halts to brace themselves. This is explained in more detail in the Weapons section later, but for the time being it's enough to know that moving can make a difference to a unit's shooting. The most important thing to understand is that the whole unit counts as moving if ANY of its models moved in the Movement phase.

Check Range: *The Seraphim's bolt pistols are range 12". Measuring shows the target unit is in range. Seraphim 1, 2 & 3 are out of range, however, and may not shoot. Only the Mutants in range (A, B & C) can become casualties.*

ROLL TO HIT

To determine if the firing unit has hit its target, roll a D6 for each shot. Normally troopers will only get to fire one shot each. However, some creatures or weapons are capable of firing more than once, as we'll explain in more detail later. The dice score needed to hit will depend on how accurate the firers are (as shown by their Ballistic Skill characteristic or BS). The chart below shows the minimum D6 roll needed to score a hit.

Firer's BS	1	2	3	4	5+
Score to hit	6	5	4	3	2

For example, if the shooters are a unit of five Space Marines with a BS of 4, you would roll five dice and each roll of a 3 or more would score a hit.

To hit rolls are easy to remember if you just subtract the BS of the shooter from 7. This will give you the number you need to hit, eg, a model with a BS 2 needs 5 or more ($7 - 2 = 5$) on a D6 to hit. As you can see, the minimum dice roll needed to hit is always at least 2. There is normally no such thing as an automatic hit and a roll of a 1 always misses.

ROLLING DICE TO HIT

When a unit fires roll all of its To Hit dice together. Sometimes there will be different weapons firing, or firers with different BS in the same unit and you might find it convenient to use different coloured dice for them so that they can be picked out. For example, you could use green dice for all shots with plasma weapons and red dice for all shots with melta weapons. Alternatively, you can simply make separate dice rolls for different weapons or shooters, but as long as it's clear which dice rolls represent which shots you can use any convention for this that you like.

ROLL TO WOUND

Hitting your target is not always enough to put it out of action. Some targets can take quite a bit of damage before they are destroyed, while some hits will not always cause damage. A hit might result in nothing more than a superficial graze or flesh wound. To decide if a hit causes damage, compare the weapon's Strength characteristic with the target's Toughness characteristic. Each weapon has its own Strength value, given in the description of the weapon. Here are some examples of different weapons and their Strength characteristics.

Weapon	Strength
Boltgun	4
Meltagun	8
Lascannon	9

Consult the chart below. Cross-reference the weapon's Strength (S) with the target's Toughness (T). The number indicated is the minimum score on a D6 needed to convert the hit into damage. As with shooting, roll the dice together and, once again, you can use different coloured dice to pick out weapons with different Strengths.

MULTIPLE TOUGHNESS

Some units will contain models which have different Toughness characteristics. To keep things simple, use the Toughness characteristic that is in the majority in the target unit. If no majority exists, use the lowest in the unit. If this roll is successful, the target has been wounded and you proceed to the Determine Casualties section.

DAMAGE CHART

Strength \ Toughness	1	2	3	4	5	6	7	8	9	10
1	4+	5+	6+	6+	N	N	N	N	N	N
2	3+	4+	5+	6+	6+	N	N	N	N	N
3	2+	3+	4+	5+	6+	6+	N	N	N	N
4	2+	2+	3+	4+	5+	6+	6+	N	N	N
5	2+	2+	2+	3+	4+	5+	6+	6+	N	N
6	2+	2+	2+	2+	3+	4+	5+	6+	6+	N
7	2+	2+	2+	2+	2+	3+	4+	5+	6+	6+
8	2+	2+	2+	2+	2+	2+	3+	4+	5+	6+
9	2+	2+	2+	2+	2+	2+	2+	3+	4+	5+
10	2+	2+	2+	2+	2+	2+	2+	2+	3+	4+

*Note that **N** on the chart means the hit has no effect. A target with the Toughness indicated cannot be harmed by a hit of such puny strength.*

***Example:** A Space Marine armed with a boltgun shoots at an Ork and hits him. A boltgun has a Strength of 4 and the Ork has a Toughness of 4. Referring to the chart, a score of 4 or more is needed to convert the hit into damage. If the dice roll is 4 or more, the Ork takes a wound – as he has only 1 Wound in the first place, he will be 'killed' and removed from play (subject to Saving throws – see later).*

"A Heretic may see the truth and seek redemption. He may be forgiven his past and will be absolved in death. A Traitor can never be forgiven. A Traitor will never find peace in this world or the next. There is nothing as wretched or as hated in all the world as a Traitor."

Cardinal Khrysdam – Instructum Absolutio

MAKE SAVING THROWS

Before he removes any models as casualties, the owning player can test to see whether his troops survive being hit because their armour stops or deflects the shot. Most troops wear some sort of protective clothing or armour, even if it's only a helmet! If a model is wearing armour it is allowed a further dice roll to see if the armour stops them being wounded. This is called an Armour Saving throw.

To see if armour successfully stops damage, roll a D6 and compare the result to the model's Save (Sv). If the player gets equal to or greater than the Sv characteristic, the wound is stopped. The following table shows how the minimum D6 score required varies between three sample types of armour:

Armour Type	Minimum D6 score required to save
Ork body armour	6
Eldar mesh armour	5
Space Marine power armour	3

For example, a Space Marine wearing power armour is hit and wounded. The Space Marine is entitled to a Saving throw of 3, so a D6 is rolled resulting in a score of 5. The damage is therefore saved, and the model is unharmed – the shot bounces harmlessly off his armour.

ARMOUR PIERCING WEAPONS

Some powerful weapons are quite capable of punching through even the thickest types of armour. This is shown by a weapon having an Armour Piercing value, usually referred to as AP. Nearly all weapons have an Armour Piercing value. Some sample AP ratings for different weapons are shown below.

Weapon	Armour Piercing
Boltgun	5
Heavy bolter	4
Lascannon	2

The lower the rating the better, because it indicates the Armour Save the weapon can ignore. A weapon shown as 'AP –' has no Armour Piercing value and always allows the target an Armour Save.

• If the weapon's Armour Piercing value is **equal to or lower** than the model's Armour Save then it is sufficiently powerful to punch straight through the armour and the target gets no save at all. The armour is ineffective against the shot.

• If the weapon's Armour Piercing value is **higher** than the armour, then the target can attempt to save as normal.

For example, a heavy bolter has an Armour Piercing rating of 4 so Saves of 4+, 5+ or 6+ are ignored. A bolter with an Armour Piercing rating of 5 can pierce armour which has a Save of 5+ or 6+. A lascannon with its Armour Piercing value of 2 ignores armour which has a Save of 2+, 3+, 4+, 5+ or 6+.

When a unit takes a number of wounds from an enemy unit shooting at it, you begin by removing all models that do not get a Saving throw and then roll all other Saving throws together. The owning player then removes one model for each failed save. If the unit has models which have different armour types, see the Universal special rules section for the Mixed Armour rules (see page 76).

For example, a mob of Orks (with an Armour Save of 6+) takes seven wounding hits from lasguns (AP -) and one wounding hit from a plasma gun (AP 2). The Ork player removes one model immediately because the plasma gun easily penetrates the Ork's armour, and then rolls seven Armour Saves for the lasgun wounding hits, removing one Ork for each failed save.

COVER SAVING THROWS

When the air is full of bullets and shrapnel, some good solid cover to lurk behind is always welcome. A position in cover shields troops against flying debris, shots, blasts and shrapnel, enabling them to get their heads down or crawl amongst rocks and (hopefully) avoid harm. Because of this, models in or behind cover get a Cover Saving throw or a Saving throw from their own armour, whichever is better. The great thing about Cover Saving throws is that they are not affected by the Armour Piercing value of the attacking weapon, so troops in cover will normally get a Saving throw regardless of what's firing at them.

WHAT COUNTS AS COVER?

Cover is basically anything you can hide in or behind.

WHEN DO MODELS COUNT AS IN COVER?

When a model is within Area Terrain or the firer's line of sight crosses over cover so that the target model(s) are partially obscured, the model receives the Cover Save shown below. Models can claim cover from Area Terrain up to one size smaller (eg, a monstrous creature (Size 3) gets cover from Standard-sized terrain (Size 2) but not from Small terrain (Size 1)). When checking for Cover Saves, ignore cover occupied by or in contact with the firers, unless the target unit also occupies that cover.

MAXIMUM COVER SAVE

Some models gain additional benefits from cover and may increase their Save by +1 or +2. However, Cover Saves may never be improved above 2+. A roll of 1 always fails.

UNITS PARTIALLY IN COVER

Sometimes, a unit will only be partially in cover (ie, some of the models are in or behind cover and some of them are in the open). If there are more models that can be hit in cover than there are outside it, then the unit may make Cover Saves for the entire unit. If this is not the case, then none of the unit may make Cover Saves.

COVER SUMMARY TABLE

Cover Type	Cover Save	Height range possible if Area Terrain feature
Bushes High Grass/Crops Fences/Railings	6+	Size 1 and 2
Crates/Barrels Pipes/Logs Partially behind hill crests Woods/Jungles	5+	Size 1, 2 and 3
Wrecks/Vehicles Wreckage/Craters Rubble/ Rocks Ruins/Walls/Buildings Trenches/Gun pits Emplacements	4+	Size 2 and 3
Bunkers Fortified buildings	3+	Size 2 and 3

Cover Saves. *A model with a heavy bolter (AP4) strafes a unit of Orks in cover behind some ruined walls. The Orks don't get their Armour Save of 6 because of the AP value of the heavy bolter, so they use their Cover Save of 4+.*

If they were Space Marines (Armour Save 3+), they would use their 3+ Armour Save instead.

INVULNERABLE SAVES

Some creatures or entities are protected by more than mere physical armour. They may be shielded by force fields, enwrapped by mystic energies or have an alien metabolism that can shrug off hits which would put holes in a battle tank. Models like these are called Invulnerable, and always get their Saving throw even if the Armour Piercing value of the weapons hitting them would normally defeat their armour. Even if a hit normally ignores all Armour Saves, an invulnerable model gets to try to make a Saving throw as normal.

MORE THAN ONE SAVE

Sometimes, a creature will have a normal Armour Save and a separate Invulnerable Armour Save – a good example is a Space Marine Chaplain who is protected by both power armour and a Rosarius generated force field. As if this wasn't enough they might be in cover as well. In these cases, the owning player can choose which save to attempt before rolling the dice, but the model still only gets to make one Saving throw.

Eg, if the Chaplain described above was standing in a fortified building and was wounded by an AP3 weapon his power armour would be of no use, as the shot's AP is equal to or lower than his Armour Save. The force field grants a 4+ Invulnerable Save. However, the fortified building grants a 3+ Cover Save. Neither of these saves is affected by the AP of the weapon so the Chaplain uses the Cover Save to give him the best chance of surviving.

Sometimes a unit will contain models with a mix of different Armour Saves and Invulnerable Saves. This complex situation is explained on page 76.

REMOVE CASUALTIES

Once the number of hits and wounds has been determined, the player that owns the target unit must remove any casualties. This means that the owning player gets to choose who is removed by the enemy's firing. Assuming that the models in the unit have one Wound each, one model is removed for each wound inflicted. Casualties are not necessarily dead, they may be merely knocked unconscious or incapacitated in some way. In any case, they are no longer fit to participate in the battle.

Remove Casualties: *Any Ork casualties must be taken from models in range and line of sight of the shooters. The Ork player doesn't have to take the Nob as a casualty unless he wishes to, but must do so if all other visible models have already been killed.*

When a unit suffers wounding hits, each will affect a different model – you cannot claim that all the hits strike a single model.

The owning player can choose to remove any models from the unit, providing they are within the line of fire and range of the attacker's weaponry. He can even remove models at the rear of the unit if he wishes – it can be imagined that these troops were slain as they advanced and that the rest of the unit continued moving forward.

Under normal circumstances, powerful weapons will be picked up by other members of the unit and it will be difficult to identify leaders (to a Tyranid, all humans look the same), so it is perfectly fair for a player to avoid taking casualties on (for example) heavy weapons or squad leaders if he doesn't wish to. Sometimes, however, a unit will be subjected to a torrent of fire so severe that a particularly significant model may die or a heavy weapon may be destroyed. When a unit suffers as many wounding hits from the firing of a single enemy unit as it has models, the shooting player can nominate one model in the target unit that could be a casualty. This model must make a save against one of the wounding hits. The owning player can choose which wounding hit he saves against and, if the model has more than one type of save, may select which he uses. Other saves are then taken as normal.

For example, a squad of five Space Marines, including one armed with a flamer, suffers wounding hits from five bolter shots, a meltagun and a krak missile. Seven

Remove Casualties: *The Space Marines rapid fire at approaching Hormagaunts. They roll ten dice, needing 3+ to hit, and score 7 hits. They roll to wound with these seven dice, needing 3+ to wound, and score 4 wounds. The Hormagaunts (with 1 Wound each) take four casualties chosen by the Tyranid player from ones in range and line of sight (represented in the above photo by the models marked with a skull). Any model within range of the shooters can be removed as casualties.*

wounding hits on a five-model unit means the firer is allowed to select an individual model to make a save. He chooses the flamer model. The owning player decides to have the flamer-armed Marine save against one of the bolter shots before making his other saves. After that he will remove two models which don't get Armour Saves (against the meltagun and krak missile) and will roll four Armour Saves against the remaining bolter wounding hits (this means that the flamer-armed Marine may die anyway).

MORALE CHECKS – CASUALTIES FROM ENEMY FIRE

Enemy fire can make even the hardiest troops waiver if their companions start to fall in great numbers. Outright flight is unlikely and unwise in the face of intense opposition, but even the most seasoned veterans may fall back to regroup, tend their injured, reload their weapons and reconsider their tactics if they suffer too many casualties.

In Warhammer 40,000, such events are represented by units taking Morale checks when they suffer casualties in the Shooting phase. Any unit of troops losing 25% or more casualties to shooting during a single Shooting phase must make a Leadership test to hold their ground. Morale checks, falling back and regrouping are covered in more detail in the Morale section of the rules (see page 47).

CREATURES WITH MORE THAN ONE WOUND

Especially tough and heroic individuals like Space Marine commanders or horrendous alien monstrosities, such as Tyranid Lictors, can sustain more damage than ordinary troopers and keep on fighting. To show this, they have more than one Wound on their characteristics profile.

When a creature like this suffers a wounding hit that it does not save against, it loses one wound. Once a creature has lost all of its wounds it is removed as a casualty, so a creature with 3 Wounds would only be killed after it had been wounded three times. Keep track of how many wounds a creature has left on a piece of scrap paper, or by placing a dice or marker next to the model.

When a unit contains several multiple-Wound models, and those models take wounds, you must remove whole multiple-Wound models from the unit as casualties where possible – wounds may not be 'spread around' to avoid removing models. Track any excess wounds with a marker as noted above.

INSTANT DEATH!

Even though a creature might have multiple Wounds, there are plenty of weapons in the 41st millennium that are powerful enough to kill instantly. If a creature is wounded by something which has a Strength value of double their Toughness value or greater and fail their save, they are killed outright and removed as a casualty. It can be imagined they are vapourised, burned to a pile of ash, blasted limb from limb or otherwise mortally slain in a suitably graphic fashion.

For example, a Space Marine Captain is Toughness 4 and has 2 Wounds. Ordinarily, he could survive being wounded once before he was removed as a casualty. However, if he were to have the misfortune to be wounded by a krak missile (Strength 8 – normally used for knocking out battle tanks), he would become a casualty immediately because the missile's Strength is double his Toughness – he just isn't that tough!

Note that some models can gain improvements to their Toughness by using wargear items, Chaos Marks and sundry other means. When it comes to Instant Death tests such bonuses do not count! (ie, riding a bike won't save you from being obliterated by a lascannon blast). This is identified by two values being shown on the Toughness characteristic of a model's stat line, one of which is in brackets. The lower value is used for Instant Death calculations.

ARMOUR SAVES & MULTIPLE WOUNDS

Creatures with multiple Wounds take their Armour Saves just like ordinary troops with only one Wound. If they make their save they suffer no damage and if they fail they suffer one wound. Against weaponry with enough Strength to cause instant death, a save can still be attempted (assuming the weapon doesn't have a good enough Armour Piercing value to just punch through their armour).

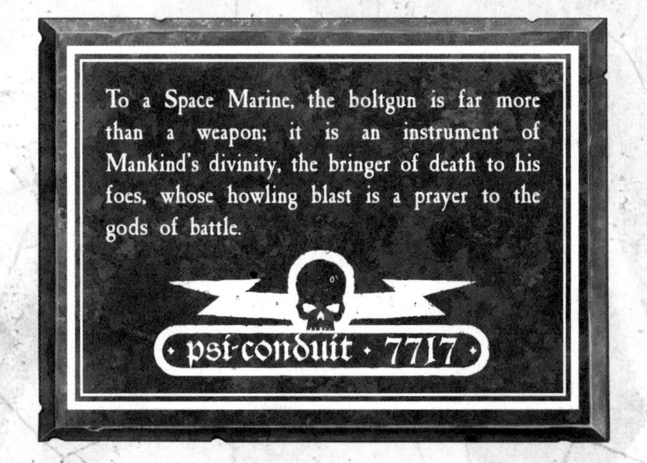
To a Space Marine, the boltgun is far more than a weapon; it is an instrument of Mankind's divinity, the bringer of death to his foes, whose howling blast is a prayer to the gods of battle.
• psi-conduit • 7717 •

WEAPONS

By the 41st millennium, warfare has spawned innumerable weapons of destruction, ranging in capability from the simple but efficient laspistol to the barely controllable energies of the plasma cannon. In this section we will be describing how characteristics and special rules reflect the differences between different weapons.

Every weapon has a profile which consists of several elements:

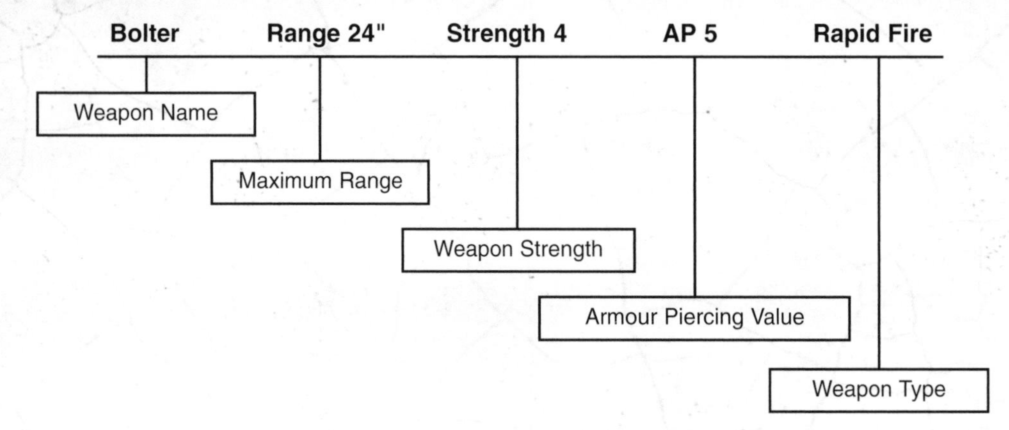

WEAPON NAME

Some weapons have several names, depending upon who is using them. The one given will be the most common.

MAXIMUM RANGE

Ranges are all given in inches. If the weapon's range is given as 'Template' then the weapon fires using the teardrop-shaped Flamer template. The exact method is explained later. If the weapon has a 'G' next to its range then the weapon can be fired over obstacles by means of the gunners guessing the range. These are called Barrage Weapons. Such a weapon may have two ranges (for example, G12"-48") – in this case the first number is the minimum range for the weapon, the second is the maximum.

WEAPON STRENGTH

As explained in the Shooting rules, when rolling to wound for shooting hits, you use the weapon's Strength rather than the firer's.

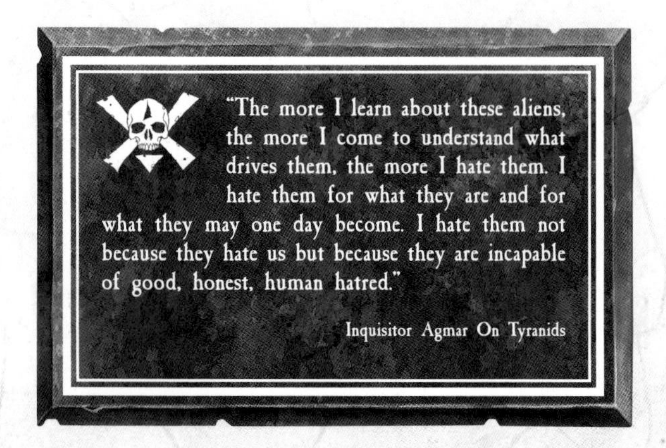

"The more I learn about these aliens, the more I come to understand what drives them, the more I hate them. I hate them for what they are and for what they may one day become. I hate them not because they hate us but because they are incapable of good, honest, human hatred."
Inquisitor Agmar On Tyranids

ARMOUR PIERCING VALUE (AP)

This shows how good the weapon is at punching through armour. The lower the number, the better the armour it can pierce without allowing an Armour Saving throw. See the Shooting rules for more on Armour Saves and AP.

WEAPON TYPE

Different weapons have unique characteristics when they fire. For example, some guns rattle off a burst of shots which means they can hit multiple targets, others may fire a single blast of energy or a shell which explodes on impact and can kill several things at once. Some weapons are so massive that they can only be mounted on vehicles and are so powerful they can destroy not only the target but anything near to it as well. These qualities are all represented by a weapon's type. All weapons will be classified as either Rapid Fire, Pistol, Assault or Heavy.

Some weapons may be able to fire in different ways, representing different power settings or different types of ammo. Where this is the case there will be a separate line in the weapon's profile for each.

Some weapons such as storm bolters and multi-lasers fire multiple shots. Where this is the case the number of shots a weapon fires is noted after its type. For example, a multi-laser fires three shots in each Shooting phase so its type is noted as Heavy 3.

In addition to the weapon type, a weapon may have some additional characteristics that define the way they work. These include things like Gets Hot or Blast. A weapon may have one or more of these characteristics.

WEAPON TYPES

RAPID FIRE WEAPONS

Weapons which are self-loading and carry a reasonably large load of ammunition are called rapid fire weapons. These are very common and usually come in the form of sub-machine guns or similar. They can lay down a withering hail of bullets, particularly at close range. Their high rate of fire means they can be fired effectively 'from the hip' when a squad is advancing, spraying shots into the enemy whenever they present themselves.

An infantry model armed with a rapid fire weapon can shoot twice at targets up to 12" away.

If an infantry model has not moved, it may instead fire once at targets over 12" away, up to its maximum range. Models carrying rapid fire weapons that wish to charge into close combat in the Assault phase may not fire in the Shooting phase – being constantly on the move limits them to short, close range bursts of fire as they charge in, the effects of which are included in the assault.

Example	Range	S	AP	Type
Boltgun	24"	4	5	Rapid Fire

PISTOL WEAPONS

Pistol weapons are similar to rapid fire weapons but are light enough to be carried and fired one-handed. As pistols often have a less powerful charge their range is limited. On the plus side, they are handy enough to allow a trooper to fight in close combat with a combination of a pistol and sword, axe or other close combat weapon.

If a model armed with pistols moves, it can shoot once at targets up to 12" away. If a model armed with pistol weapons remains stationary, it can shoot twice at targets up to 12". Models carrying pistol weapons can fire them once in the Shooting phase and still charge into close combat in the Assault phase, but cannot charge if they remained stationary to fire twice.

Example	Range	S	AP	Type
Bolt Pistol	12"	4	5	Pistol

ASSAULT WEAPONS

Assault weapons are fired by warriors as they charge forward into the attack. They either fire so rapidly or are so indiscriminate that you don't have to do much more than point and shoot. For example, a flamer is a weapon which fires a fan-shaped gout of burning fuel, so it's just as accurate whether you are moving and firing or not. These weapons shoot the number of times indicated – whether you move or not and regardless of range.

Models carrying assault weapons can fire them in the Shooting phase and still charge into close combat in the Assault phase. This means they are very good for moving and assaulting things... hence the name!

Example	Range	S	AP	Type
Big Shoota	36"	5	5	Assault 3

HEAVY WEAPONS

These are heavy, man-portable weapons, such as missile launchers or lighter weapons, that require reloading between each shot, careful set-up or bracing against their considerable recoil. If an Infantry unit moves then it cannot shoot heavy weapons – they either move or shoot, but not both (remember that even if the model armed with the heavy weapon doesn't move, it still can't fire if other members of its unit move). When shooting, heavy weapons always fire the number of times indicated regardless of range, in the same way as assault weapons. They are very good for laying down long range supporting fire or taking out tanks and such like. Infantry units that fire heavy weapons in the Shooting phase may not charge into close combat in the Assault phase, although some rare units may be an exception to this.

Note: *Vehicles, monstrous creatures, riders on bikes (including jetbikes) and certain other models are capable of moving and firing freely with heavy weapons thanks to their strength, powerful exoskeleton, internal power sources, etc.*

Example	Range	S	AP	Type
Ion Cannon	60"	7	3	Heavy 3

ORDNANCE WEAPONS

Ordnance weapons are so huge and powerful that they cannot be physically carried but must be mounted onto a vehicle or be built into the structure of a bunker or fortress. Units using ordnance weapons may not charge into close combat in the Assault phase.

Designate the target and place the large Blast marker over it with the following restrictions:

- You may not place the marker so that any of your own models or vehicles (apart from wrecks) are underneath it.
- You must place the Blast marker so that one enemy model is under the central hole; you cannot place the Blast marker over empty space.

Next, check if it landed on target. If the hole at the centre of the marker is beyond the weapon's maximum range or no line of sight exists to the target the shot is an automatic miss and has no effect. Otherwise, proceed to see where it hits.

If the target is in range and can be seen, the massive impact of an ordnance weapon means it's going to be very hard to miss completely. Nonetheless, the shot may not land exactly where it was intended to. Roll the Scatter dice and a D6 to see where the shot lands. If the Scatter dice rolls a HIT symbol the shot lands on target. If an arrow is rolled, the marker is shifted in the direction shown by the arrow the number of inches indicated on the D6. If the Ordnance weapon was fired by a moving vehicle then two D6 are rolled and the highest taken to determine the distance the Blast marker scatters. Scatter rolls can take the Blast marker beyond range or out of sight, representing the chance of ricochets, the round blasting through cover and other random chance.

Example	Range	S	AP	Type
Battle Cannon	72"	8	3	Ordnance 1; Large Blast

SPECIAL WEAPON CHARACTERISTICS

BLAST WEAPONS

Blast weapons fire shells, missiles or bolts of energy which explode on impact, potentially injuring several victims with the shock waves and shrapnel. They pose less of a threat to a well dispersed unit, but can wreak havoc among closely packed ranks of warriors.

This section covers blast weapons fired by non-ordnance weapons only (ordnance weapons fire even larger shells or missiles – these are handled using the rules for ordnance weapons).

When you fire a blast weapon roll to hit as normal; if the shot misses it has no effect. If a hit is scored take the Blast marker and place it over the target unit so that one model is under the hole to see how many models are affected.

Models whose bases are partially covered by the marker are hit on a D6 roll of 4 or more, models whose bases are completely covered are hit automatically. The defending player may remove any casualties inflicted from the unit as a whole, not just from models beneath the Blast marker.

Designer's Note: *While this is a bit odd at first glance, it prevents blast weapons being employed unrealistically as snipers to destroy leaders and heavy weapons.*

MULTIPLE BLASTS

If a unit is firing multiple blast weapons, just place one marker after another, resolving the casualties from each blast before placing the next. Remember, casualties can come from anywhere in the unit, not just under the marker.

LARGE BLASTS

There are two sizes of Blast marker: the normal one and the large one. Nearly all Blast weapons use the normal Blast marker, while ordnance weapons use the large Blast marker. Some non-ordnance weapons may use the large Blast marker and where this is the case it will be noted in their description. This doesn't convey any of the other advantages of ordnance weapons, however.

Some ordnance weapons have optional ammunition that doesn't use the large Blast marker. These benefit from all the advantages of ordnance weapons even if the large Blast marker is not used.

GETS HOT

'Gets Hot' represents the penchant of certain unstable weapons for overloading and badly singeing their user. If you roll a 1 to hit, the weapon has overheated and injured the model firing it. The model must make an Armour Save or it suffers a wound (an exception to the normal Casualty Removal rules) – the model with the overheating weapon must take the wound. Weapons on vehicles are not affected by overheating. It is possible for a model to hit with shots that also result in an overheat – the hits are still resolved as normal, even if the firer also falls victim to his own weapon.

Example	Range	S	AP	Type
Plasma gun	24"	7	2	Rapid Fire, Gets Hot!

MULTIPLE GETS HOT SHOTS

If a Gets Hot weapon is firing multiple shots, the chance of it getting hot is even riskier. The chance of suffering wounds is equal to the number of shots being fired, so firing two shots means that the weapon Gets Hot on rolls of 1 or 2, while firing three shots makes it a ludicrously dangerous 1, 2 or 3.

TWIN-LINKED WEAPONS

Weapons are sometimes linked to fire together in order to increase the chances of scoring a hit through the crude expedient of blasting more shots at the target. To represent the fusillade of fire laid down by a linked weapon you may re-roll the dice to hit if it misses; if the second roll is also a miss, you may not re-roll the dice again. Twin-linked weapons don't get more shots than normal ones, but you get a better chance of hitting with them. The big advantage of twin-linked weapons is that they only count as a single weapon being fired.

Example 1: *A Space Marine Land Raider is firing its twin-linked heavy bolters at an enemy. It gets three shots (as heavy bolters are Heavy 3) and may re-roll any To Hit dice which don't score a 3 or higher – a hit for a Space Marine's BS of 4 – because the weapons are twin-linked.*

Example 2: *A Space Marine Dreadnought with a missile launcher and a twin-linked lascannon can fire both weapons and still move, as it is allowed to shoot with two weapons and the twin-linked lascannon only counts as one weapon.*

MELTA WEAPONS

Melta weapons are devastating short-ranged 'heat rays'. Melta weapons roll an extra D6 when rolling to penetrate vehicles' Armour Value at half range or under. See the Vehicles rules later for more details on armour penetration.

Example	Range	S	AP	Type
Fusion Blaster	12"	8	1	Assault 1, Melta

TEMPLATE WEAPONS

These are particularly indiscriminate short-ranged devices, such as flame throwers, which affect a broad, cone-shaped area represented by a template. They are indicated by having the word 'Template' for their range characteristic instead of a number. Instead of rolling to hit, simply place the template so that its narrow end is touching the base of the model firing it and the rest of the template covers as many models as possible in the target unit without covering any friends. Against vehicles, the template must be placed to cover as much of the vehicle as possible without also touching a friendly model.

Any models fully or partially under the template are hit automatically. Against vehicles use the direction of the firer to determine which armour facing is attacked. Because template weapons bathe the area in burning fuel, baneful energies or something equally dangerous, Cover Saves are ignored when resolving hits. As with blast weapons, casualties inflicted by template weapons do not have to be taken from amongst the models actually covered by the template, but must come from within range of the firer.

Example	Range	S	AP	Type
Flamer	Template	4	5	Assault 1

MULTIPLE TEMPLATE WEAPONS

If a unit is firing multiple template weapons, resolve them one at a time.

TWIN-LINKED TEMPLATE WEAPONS

Twin-linked template weapons can re-roll to wound against each model hit. Against vehicles, you may re-roll the Armour Penetration dice instead.

BARRAGE WEAPONS

Certain blast weapons launch their shells high up into the air so that they plunge down upon their target, passing over any intervening obstacles en route. Weapons like these fire by the crew guessing the range to the target point and hoping the round lands close enough to inflict harm. Their greatest advantage lies in their ability to fire at targets which are out of sight. Some pieces of ordnance are used for laying down a barrage in the same way.

FIRING BARRAGES

Barrage weapons never have to test to see if they must fire at the closest enemy. Designate the target unit and place the Blast marker over it, with the following restrictions:

• You may not place the marker so that any of your own models or vehicles (apart from wrecks) are underneath it.

• You must place the Blast marker so that one enemy model is under the central hole; you cannot place the Blast marker hole over empty space.

You then see if it has landed on target. If the hole at the centre of the marker is inside the weapon's minimum range, or beyond its maximum, the shot is an automatic miss and has no effect. If its range is good, proceed to see where it hits, remembering that no line of sight is required. Roll a Scatter dice and a D6 if a line of sight exists to the target, or two D6 if not and take the highest. If you roll a HIT on the Scatter dice the shot lands on target. If an arrow is rolled, the marker is shifted in the direction indicated by the arrow a number of inches equal to the D6 roll.

Note that it is possible for a scattering shot to land beyond the weapon's range, out of sight, off the edge of the table or even on your own troops! Such are the vagaries of barrage weapons. With barrage weapons, the centre of the marker is used to determine which direction hits occur from in relation to Cover Saves. Barrage weapons are always pinning weapons as well. See the Pinning Weapons rules for details.

Example	Range	S	AP	Type
Mortar	G48"	4	6	Heavy 1, Blast

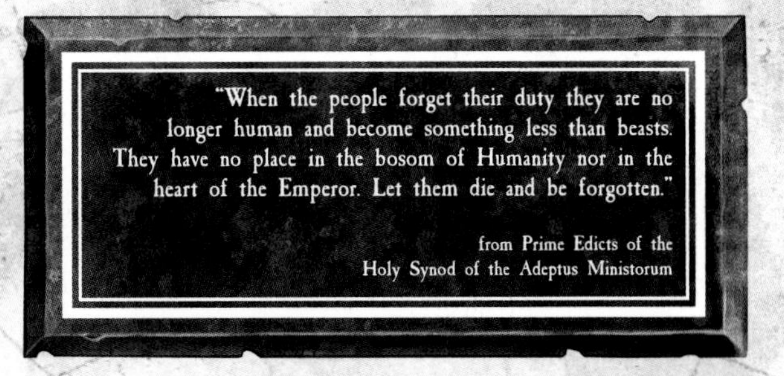

"When the people forget their duty they are no longer human and become something less than beasts. They have no place in the bosom of Humanity nor in the heart of the Emperor. Let them die and be forgotten."
from Prime Edicts of the
Holy Synod of the Adeptus Ministorum

MULTIPLE BARRAGES

If a unit has more than one barrage weapon they'll all be fired together in a salvo, with one Blast marker landing for each weapon that is within range. Place the Blast marker and roll for any potential scatter with the first shot as before, this is the 'ranging shot' for the salvo – all other shots will land nearby. Once the first marker is placed, roll a Scatter dice for each other Blast marker in the salvo.

If an arrow is rolled, place the marker in the direction indicated so that its edge is touching the edge of the marker placed for the ranging shot. If a hit is rolled, the firing player may place the marker so that its edge is touching the edge of any of the Blast markers in the salvo which have already landed.

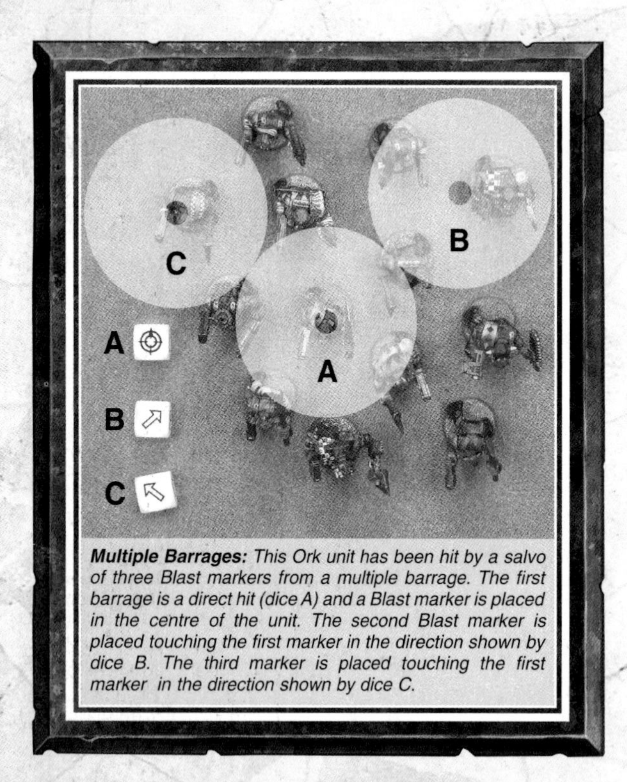

Multiple Barrages: *This Ork unit has been hit by a salvo of three Blast markers from a multiple barrage. The first barrage is a direct hit (dice A) and a Blast marker is placed in the centre of the unit. The second Blast marker is placed touching the first marker in the direction shown by dice B. The third marker is placed touching the first marker in the direction shown by dice C.*

ORDNANCE BARRAGES

Some ordnance weapons fire barrages. These use the firing procedures for barrage weapons to determine where they land but hit with all the benefits of ordnance. Just like normal barrages, ordnance barrages are pinning weapons. See the Pinning weapon rules for details. Note that ordnance barrages may not be fired from moving vehicles.

PINNING WEAPONS

Coming under attack from some weapons can be sudden and shocking, making troopers throw themselves flat and hug cover rather than risk being hit. This is usually due to momentary confusion about where they're being attacked from. Sniper fire, barrages, etc, are the most common.When the firing of a single enemy unit inflicts casualties with pinning weapons, the target must take a Leadership test to avoid being pinned down. If the unit fails the test it may not move, shoot or assault, or make any other actions in its following turn. A unit may be called upon to take multiple Pinning tests in a single turn. A pinned unit does not have to take a Morale test if it sustains 25% casualties from enemy fire, as the fact it is pinned overrides the Morale test. If assaulted by the enemy, the pinning effect is immediately cancelled and the unit will fight normally.

INCOMING!

ORDNANCE BARRAGE PINNING

Ordnance barrages are even more terrifying than normal barrages – the ground shakes and heaves under the thunderous impacts, troops caught in the open are completely annihilated and those in cover are virtually buried alive by a furious rain of incandescent death. Units suffering casualties from an ordnance barrage must pass a Leadership test with the following modifier to avoid being pinned down:

-1 Leadership for coming under fire from an ordnance barrage.

SNIPER WEAPONS

These weapons are precise and deadly and can be used to pick out a target's weak or vulnerable points. A sniper weapon hits on a 2 or more regardless of the firer's BS. Sniper hits wound on a roll of 4+ regardless of the victim's Toughness, and roll 2D6 for armour penetration against vehicles, but with no additional bonus for Strength. Against vehicles, this represents their chances of successfully hitting exposed crew, vision ports, fuel or ammo storage, etc.

Example	Range	S	AP	Type
Sniper rifle	36"	N/A	6	Heavy 1, Sniper

RENDING WEAPONS

Rending weapons fire a hail of shots so focussed they can literally chew through flesh, bone and armour alike. Any roll to hit of 6 with a rending weapon automatically causes a wound with no Armour Saving throw possible. Against a vehicle, any Penetration roll of 6 allows a further D6 to be rolled and the result added to the total score. Note that only one extra dice is ever rolled, even if this additional roll is also a 6; no further dice are added.

LANCE WEAPONS

These weapons fire a coherent, focused blast which can bore through even reinforced vehicle armour regardless of its thickness. Due to their unique nature, they count vehicle Armour Values higher than 12 as 12.

Example	Range	S	AP	Type
Bright lance	36"	8	2	Heavy 1, Lance

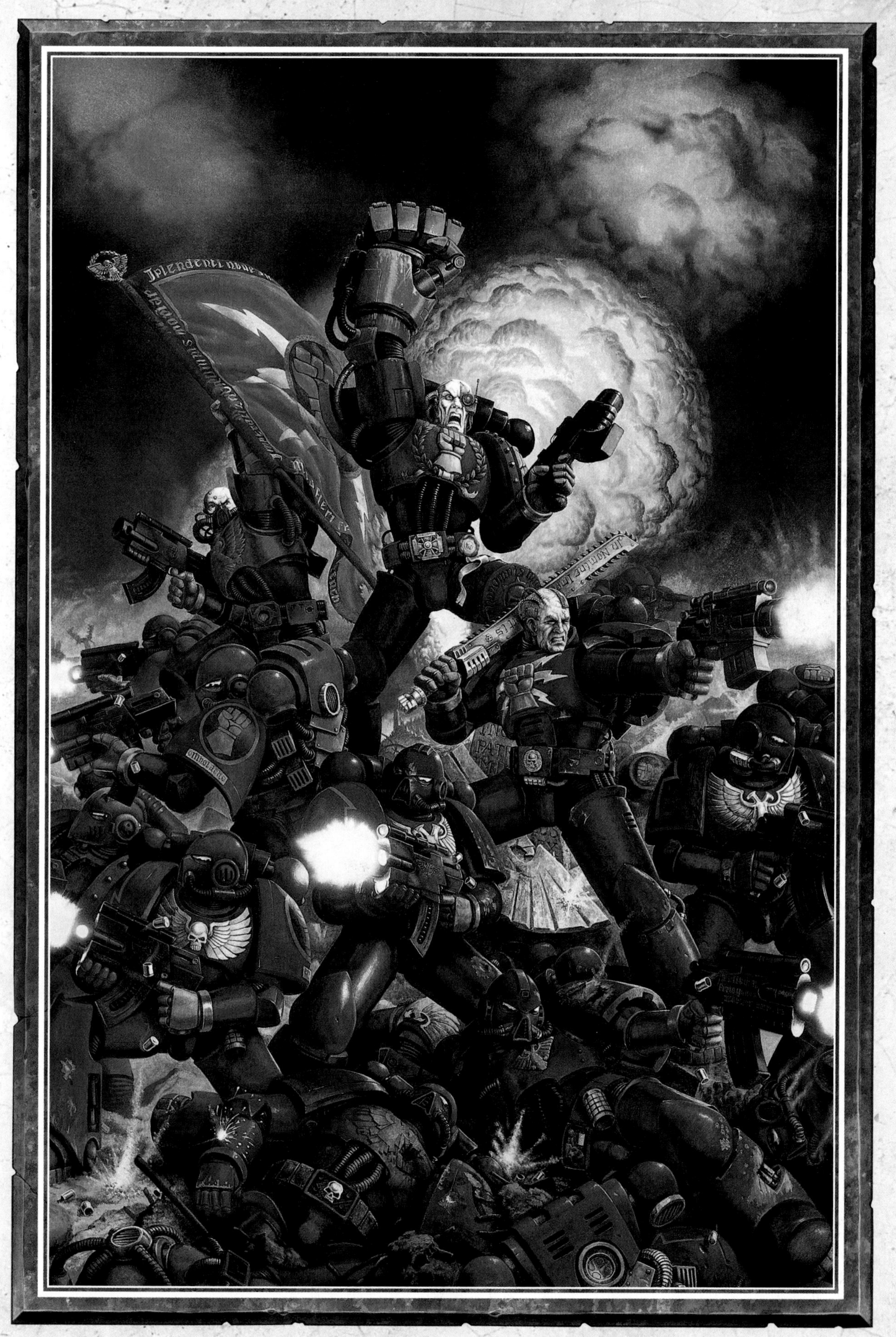

Last Stand of Commander Drakken

Boltguns

More than just a weapon, the Bolter is the holy sword of the Adeptus Astartes, the bringer of the Emperor's divine retribution. Firing a mass-reactive, explosive shell, it brings swift death and is justly feared by the unrighteous and unclean.

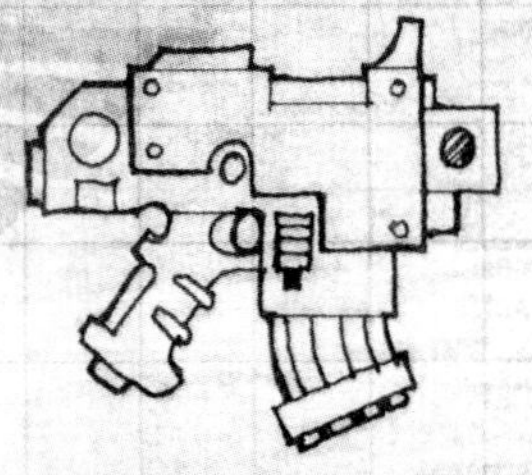

Bolt Pistol
Astartes MK III

6–10 round magazine

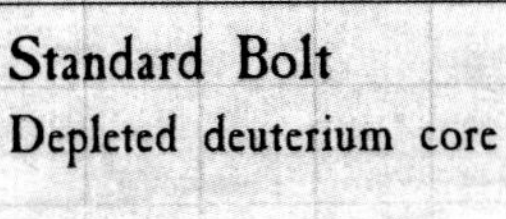

Standard Bolt
Depleted deuterium core

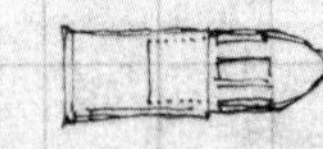

Variants include Inferno bolt, Hellfire round, Metal Storm frag shell, Stalker Silenced shell and Kraken Pattern Penetrator round

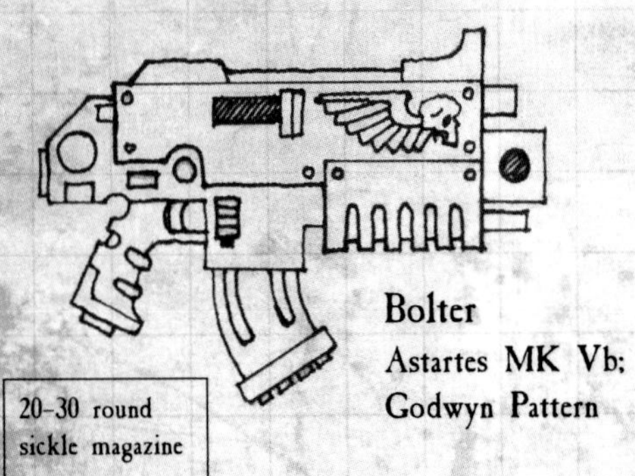

Bolter
Astartes MK Vb;
Godwyn Pattern

20–30 round sickle magazine

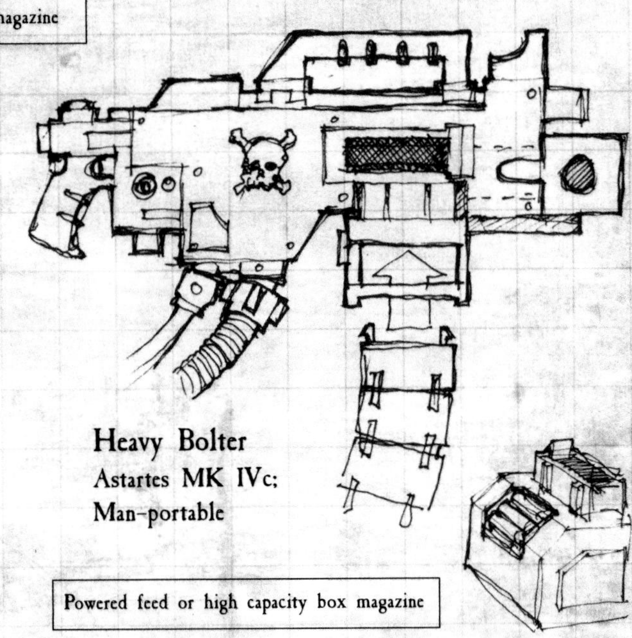

Heavy Bolter
Astartes MK IVc;
Man-portable

Powered feed or high capacity box magazine

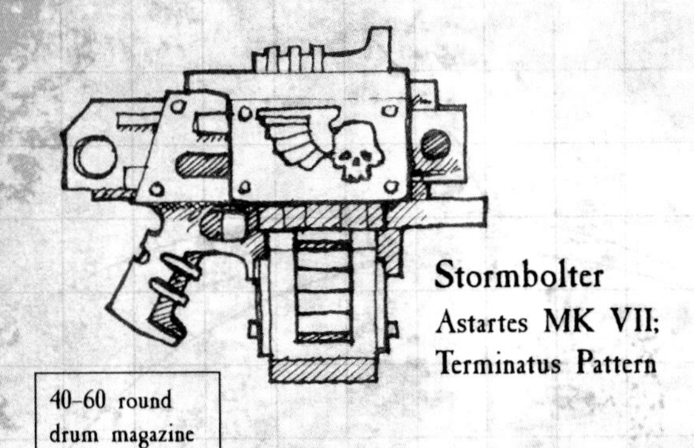

Stormbolter
Astartes MK VII;
Terminatus Pattern

40–60 round drum magazine

Close combat weapons

The Powerfist smites the unworthy from the Emperor's sight, crushing the life from their bodies with its lethal energies.

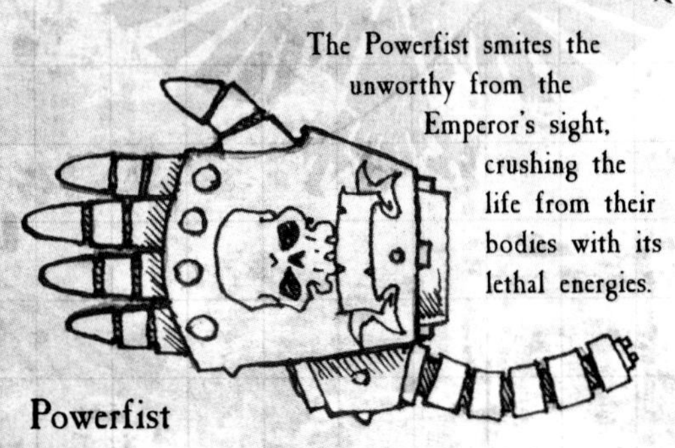

Powerfist

The sword, the axe, the mace and the glaive; all are equal in the aid they provide to those who carry out the Emperor's will. With them, the heretic, mutant and xeno shall be cleansed from the stars.

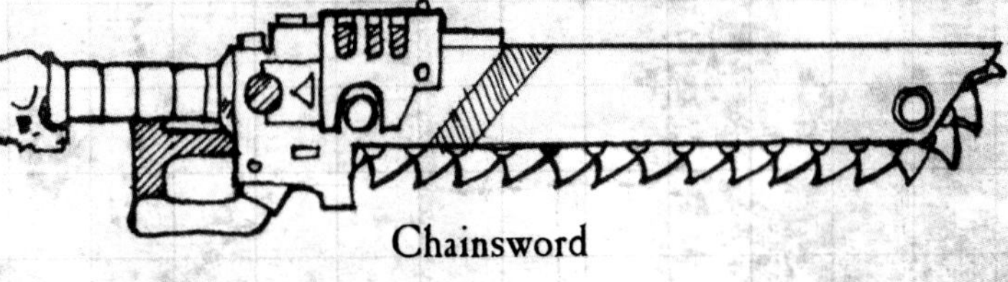

Chainsword

Flame weapons

Flamer weapons fire a holy mix of blessed chemicals that ignite upon contact with the air and burn the enemies of the Emperor in the cleansing fires. Carried extensively by the forces of the Emperor, they are particularly favoured by the Chamber Militant of the Ordo Hereticus. It is an honour to carry such a weapon of divine purification, though the warriors who carry them are often less than grateful for the privilege.

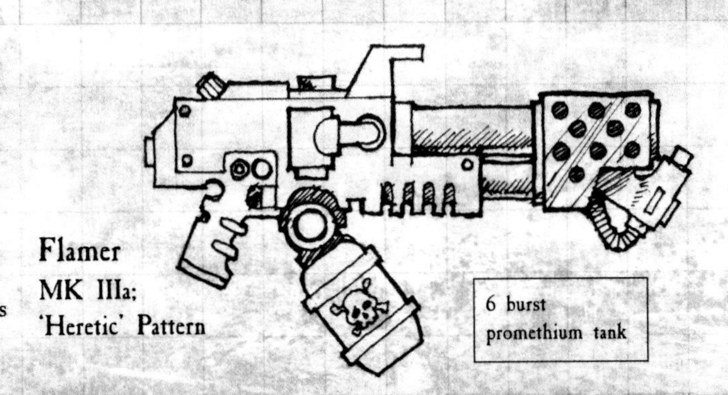

Flamer
MK IIIa;
'Heretic' Pattern

6 burst promethium tank

Las weapons

Cheap to manufacture and simple to maintain, las weapons are issued to the Imperial Guard and are readily available on most Imperial worlds. Many variants on the basic design exist, but all serve the same purpose – the destruction of the Emperor's foes.

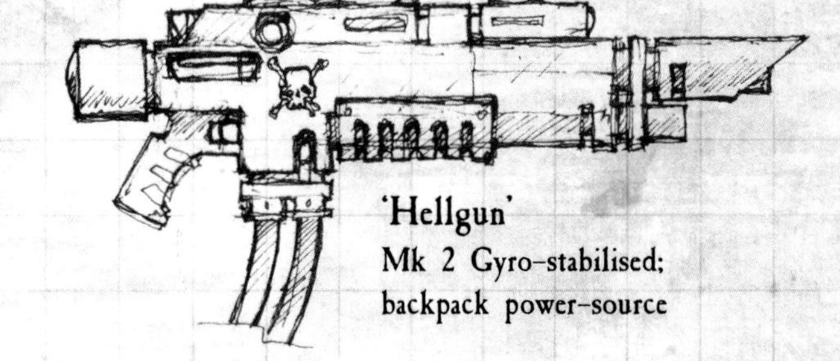

'Hellgun'
Mk 2 Gyro-stabilised; backpack power-source

Laspistol
Short pattern; Kantreal manufactured

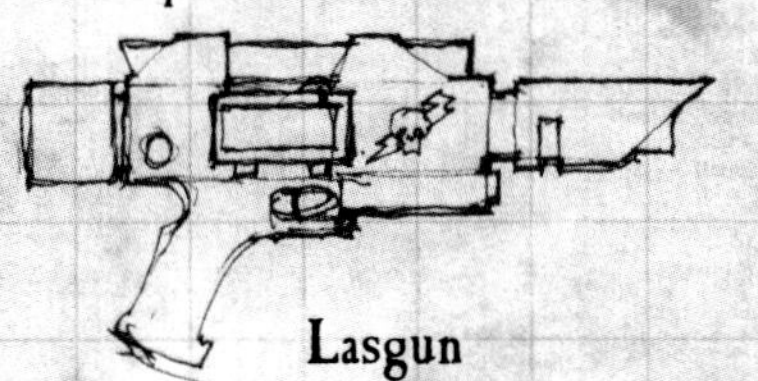

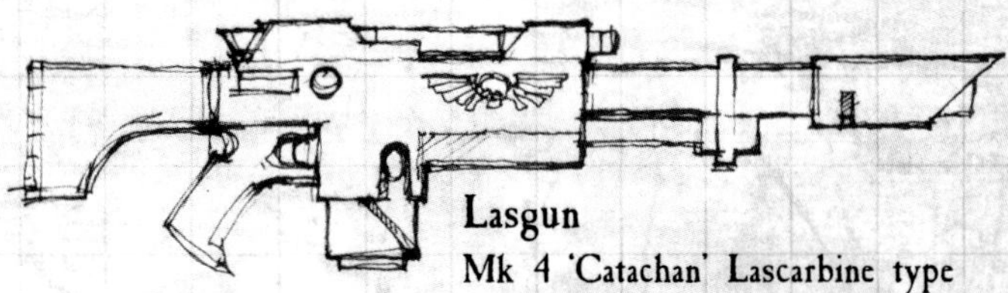

Lasgun
Mk 4 'Catachan' Lascarbine type

Lasgun
M36 Cadian issue Lasrifle with admantium bayonet

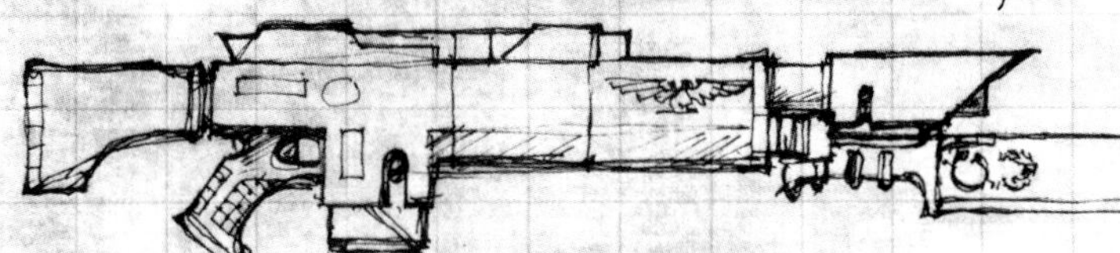

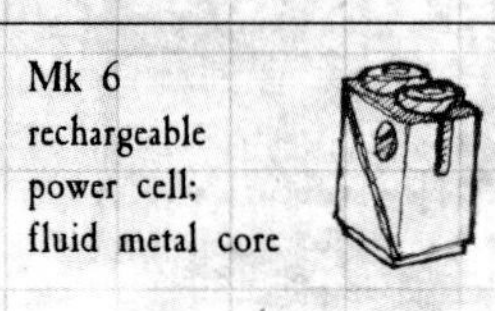

Mk 6 rechargeable power cell; fluid metal core

Solid slug weapons

Cheap and commonly available, such weapons fire a hail of bullets or shells and are often carried the Emperor's servants.

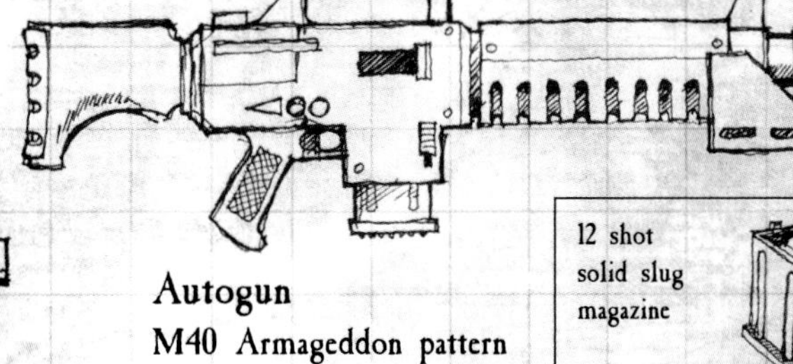

Autogun
M40 Armageddon pattern

12 shot solid slug magazine

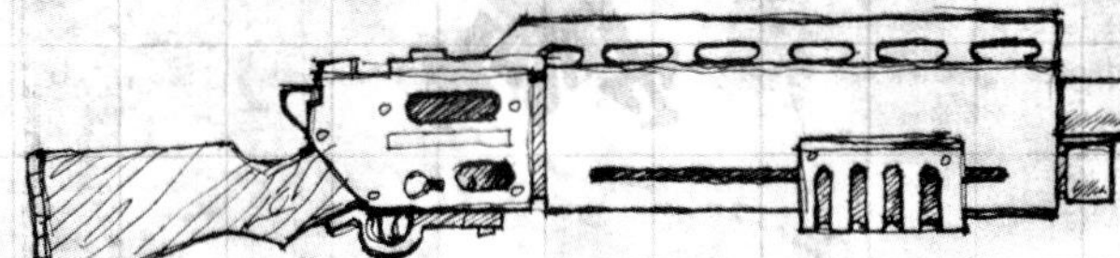

Combat Shotgun; Arbites Pattern III; 'Lawbringer'

Plasma weapons

Rare and devastating weapons, they are the burning light of the Emperor.

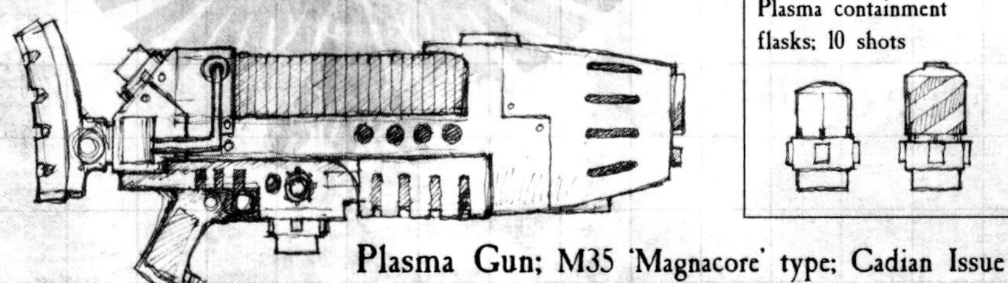

Plasma Gun; M35 'Magnacore' type; Cadian Issue

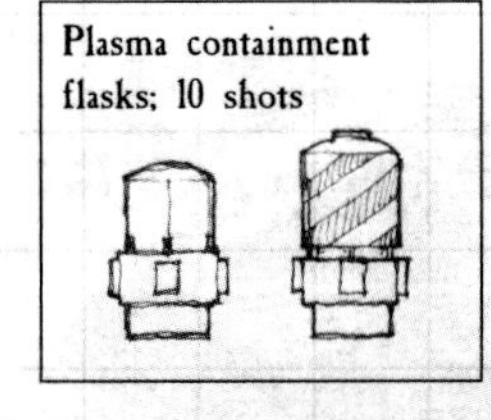

Plasma containment flasks; 10 shots

Plasma Pistol
MK III; 'Sunfury'

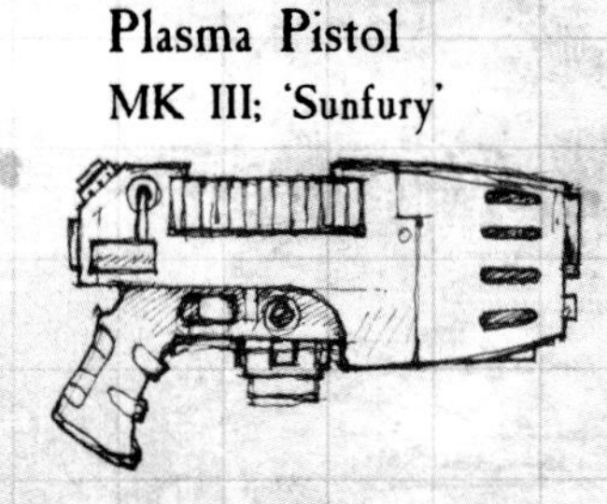

Melta guns

Melta guns use a two part injection system to force the pyrum-petrol gas into a sub-molecular state, which will vaporise just about any target, reducing it to a bubbling pool of molten slag. Many commanders issue such weapons to their most courageous soldiers, as they will be expected to put themseleves in harm's way most often, attacking tanks and storming enemy bunkers to employ their weapons to best effect.

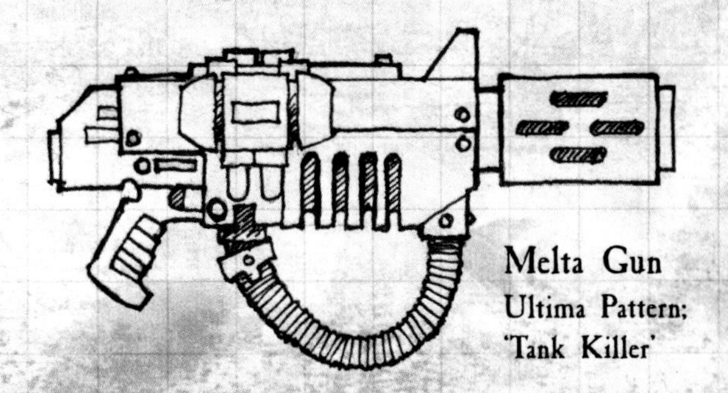

Melta Gun
Ultima Pattern; 'Tank Killer'

ASSAULT PHASE

***W**hile firepower alone may be enough to drive an enemy back from open ground or lightly held positions, shifting a determined foe from a fortified bunker or ruined settlement will need sterner measures. In an assault, troops storm forward, screaming their battle cries, eager to strike at their foes with knives, claws or gun butts in a desperate close combat.*

ASSAULT PHASE SUMMARY

RESOLVE CHARGES

1. **Pick a unit.**
2. **Declare charge with it.**
3. **Move the charging unit.**
4. **Repeat the above until all charging units have moved.**

RESOLVE COMBATS

1. **Pick a combat.**
2. **Fight Close Combat.** Troops fight in close combat. Models roll to hit, wound and take Saving throws as required in Initiative order.
3. **Determine Assault Results.** Total up wounds inflicted. The side which inflicted the most wounds overall in the combat is the winner.
4. **Loser Checks Morale.** The loser has to pass a Morale check or fall back. If the loser passes the test go to step 7.
5. **Breaking-off and Consolidation.** Units falling back from close combat must test to see if they successfully break off, if they fail they are destroyed. The winners may then engage a new foe or reorder their ranks.
6. **Pile In.** If units are still locked in close combat then any models not in base-to-base contact are moved 6" towards the enemy to continue the fight next turn.
7. **Repeat until all combats have been resolved.**

DECLARE CHARGES

In his own Assault phase, a player can declare a charge with any of his units that he believes are within assault range of an enemy unit and not already in close combat. Some especially bloodthirsty units are compelled to declare a charge if they can, as denoted in their special rules. Assault range is 6" unless specified otherwise. A unit assaults at the speed of the slowest model.

A unit may charge any enemy unit that can be reached by at least one of its models making an Assault move (avoiding obstructions such as impassable terrain, or other enemy units they do not wish to contact).

SHOOTING AND ASSAULTING

A unit that fired in the Shooting phase of the current turn may only declare a charge against the unit it shot at. An infantry unit that fired twice with pistols or which shot with rapid fire weapons or remained stationary to fire heavy weapons may not charge at all in the Assault phase.

***Note:** Some rare units always count as stationary when firing rapid fire weapons and some units can move and fire heavy weapons. Such units can charge after firing.*

A unit may charge multiple enemy units, but only if the charging unit can reach them all without losing unit coherency. Select one unit as the primary target and move to engage that one first as detailed opposite. If the unit fired in the Shooting phase it must start its charge by engaging the unit it shot at.

Units that are falling back (see page 48) or Pinned (see page 32) may not declare charges.

MOVE CHARGING UNITS

Charging units must now move into close combat with the unit (or units) they have declared charges against. Charging units must attempt to engage as many opposing models as possible with as many of their models that can reach the fight – no holding back!

Start the charge by moving a single model from the charging unit. The model selected must be the one which can reach the enemy by using the least amount of its available movement. Move the model into contact with the nearest enemy model in the unit being charged, using the shortest possible route. This is the starting point of the close combat. Next, move each model in the charging unit in turn up to their Assault move distance, toward the unit or units they have declared a charge on. Remember that if the enemy is not within the Assault move distance of at least one model, the charge does not happen.

After the first model in the unit has been moved, you can move the others in any sequence you desire. There are some constraints on their movement though:

• The most important one is that each model must end its charge move in coherency with another model in its own unit that has already moved.

• If possible, the model must contact an enemy model which is not already in base-to-base contact with a friendly model.

• If there are no such models in reach, then you must contact an enemy model already in base-to-base contact with one or more friendly models.

• If you cannot reach any enemy models, you must try to move within 2" of one of your own models that is already engaged.

• If this is impossible, then the charging model must just simply maintain unit coherency.

If you follow this sequence you will end up with all the models in the charging unit in 2" unit coherency distance of one another, having engaged as many enemy models as possible with as many chargers as possible.

In all cases, models may not move through friendly or enemy models and may not pass through gaps narrower than their base diameter. You may not move models within 1" of enemy models from any unit they are not charging.

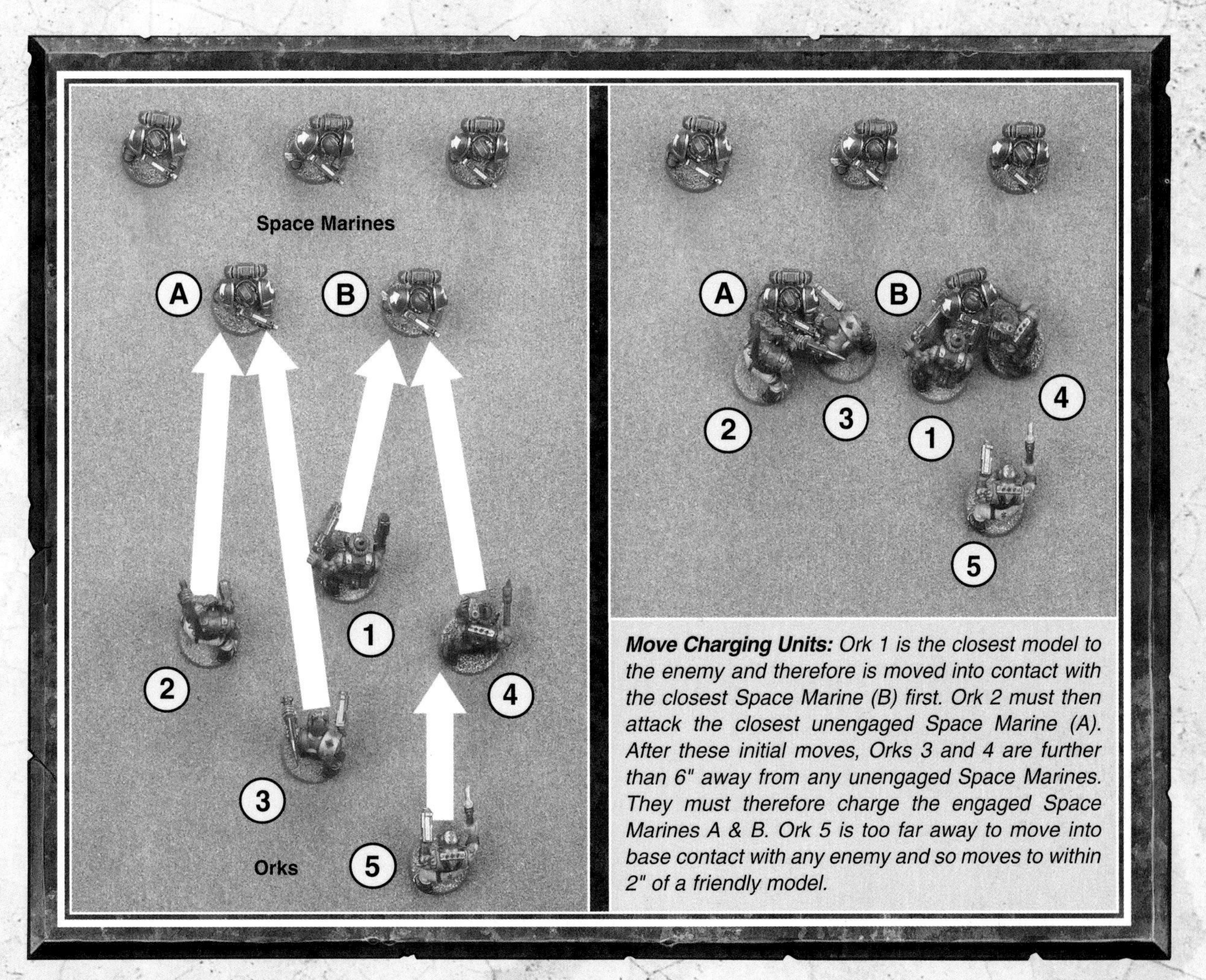

Move Charging Units: *Ork 1 is the closest model to the enemy and therefore is moved into contact with the closest Space Marine (B) first. Ork 2 must then attack the closest unengaged Space Marine (A). After these initial moves, Orks 3 and 4 are further than 6" away from any unengaged Space Marines. They must therefore charge the engaged Space Marines A & B. Ork 5 is too far away to move into base contact with any enemy and so moves to within 2" of a friendly model.*

Once a model is in base-to-base contact, or within 2" of a model from its own unit in base-to-base contact, with an enemy model it is said to be ENGAGED (as in engaged in combat). The unit that the models belong to is then said to be LOCKED (as in locked in close combat).

Move all the models in each charging unit before moving on to the next unit. The charging player decides the sequence in which his units will move. All the models in a charging unit make their Assault move subject to the same rules as in the Movement phase, but may be moved within 1" of enemy models they are charging.

TERRAIN EFFECTS

Models assaulting into, out of or through difficult terrain will be slowed down in the same way as models moving through it in the Movement phase. Make any Dangerous Terrain tests as appropriate.

DIDN'T MAKE IT?

If the unit's move is insufficient to reach at least one target unit then the charge does not proceed. The models are not moved and it is assumed they simply did not have time to engage, or thought better of it due to their poor progress. Enemy units that are not contacted are not considered to be 'locked' and are not involved in the combat in any way.

FIGHTING A CLOSE COMBAT

How good creatures are in close combat depends almost entirely on their physical characteristics, in other words how fast, strong, tough and ferocious they are. Armour remains useful for warding off blows and shots, but ranged weaponry becomes a secondary consideration – the best gun in the galaxy won't help if your opponent is bashing your brains out with a rock!

Space Marines

Tyranids

A B C

Engaged Models: *All Space Marines are engaged in combat. All Tyranids except A, B and C are engaged in combat, and may therefore attack and be attacked.*

In close combat, both players' models fight. How many blows are struck and who strikes first is detailed opposite. The rules are written assuming that there is only a single close combat occurring in the turn, though of course there may be several separate assaults being fought simultaneously in different parts of the battlefield. If this is the case, the player whose turn it is can choose what order to resolve the combats in, completing each combat before moving on to the next combat.

WHO CAN FIGHT?

Close combat is a swirling mêlée of troops leaping, spinning, hacking and slashing at one another. As well as fighting hand-to-hand, warriors will be firing at point blank range at any target that presents itself. The following models in a locked unit are said to be engaged in combat and can fight at full effect:

• Models in base-to-base contact with an enemy model.

• Models within 2" of a friendly model of the same unit, which itself is in base-to-base contact with an enemy model.

All engaged models fight with their full number of attacks and count the benefits of any special close combat attack forms they have. These are the members of the unit that can attack the enemy and be attacked by them. When determining which Weapon Skill and Toughness values count for the majority, and which models can be taken as casualties, only the engaged models are counted. The rest of the unit is Locked and is subject to the outcome of a close combat. They may pile in later to help their comrades, but only the engaged models can actually contribute to the fight.

WHO STRIKES FIRST

It's all in the reflexes when it comes to close combat – slow, lumbering opponents can be quickly dispatched by a faster and more agile foe. Unfortunately, many cumbersome opponents, such as Orks, are tough enough to be able to withstand a vicious pummelling and still come back for more.

In close combat, a model's Initiative characteristic determines who fights first. Work your way down the Initiative scores in the combat, starting with the highest and going down to the lowest. Models make their attacks when their Initiative is reached, assuming they haven't already been killed by a model with a higher Initiative. A model will only fight if it is still engaged when its Initiative rank is called. If both sides have models with the same Initiative, attacks are made simultaneously.

For example, a squad of Space Marines (Initiative 4) including a Veteran Sergeant with power fist (Initiative 1) is charged by a brood of Genestealers (Initiative 6) and a Carnifex (Initiative 2). The Genestealers strike first at Initiative 6, followed by the Space Marines at 4, then the Carnifex at 2 and the sergeant striking last at Initiative 1.

COVER

Troops who are defending in cover have a massive advantage in an assault. They can fire from their hiding place at the approaching enemy and then smite them as they struggle to get to grips with their foe.

Models that are charged while they are in or behind cover normally fight in close combat with an Initiative value of 10. This represents the advantage of cover – their improved Initiative accounts for not only close fighting but also shots against the enemy as they charge in. However, the cover does not affect hits or anything else in an assault. After the first round of close combat, fighting is assumed to have swept into the cover, so no further advantage is gained by models in it.

***Cover:** Space Marine A attacks first because his Initiative is increased to 10 due to being behind cover. Space Marines B & C fight simultaneously with the Eldar because the aliens' Initiative (4) is the same as the Space Marines' (4).*

Note that cover advantage applies only to models in cover that are being charged. Some units count as being in cover all the time because of psychic abilities or weird force fields, but these are of no benefit if the unit itself charges.

Sometimes, a model will only count as being in cover if assaulted from a specific direction from which the cover has an effect, eg, a Space Marine behind some oil drums is in cover if assaulted over the oil drums, but not if assaulted from the rear. If, before any assaulting models are moved, a direct line from the assaulting model to the enemy model passes through the cover then it is assumed to be enough of an obstruction to count. This expedient is used to ensure attackers can't 'run around' cover to negate its effects.

GRENADES

Grenades in Warhammer 40,000 are generally used as part of an assault. A well-placed barrage of grenades can help immeasurably in the vital last few seconds it takes to overrun an enemy and come to grips. What follows are some of the most common types of grenades used in assault. Any actual damage done by the grenade is assumed to be taken into account in the unit's attacks in close combat, but the unit using them gains the added benefit shown.

FRAG GRENADES

Fragmentation grenades can be thrown at opponents in cover to force them to keep their heads down during a charge. The lethal storm of shrapnel from exploding frag grenades will drive opponents further under cover for a few precious moments, allowing the attackers to close in unmolested. Models armed with frag grenades that are charging enemy in or behind cover fight with Initiative 10, so they strike blows simultaneously with the defenders.

PLASMA GRENADES

Rather than the crude fragmentation grenades used by other races, the Eldar employ plasma grenades to stun their enemies and drive them out of cover when they charge into close combat. The effects of cover on close combat are negated by plasma grenades, so all fighting is done in the standard Initiative sequence, the Initiative 10 bonus for cover being lost.

PHOTON GRENADES

The Tau employ a defensive grenade which blinds and disorientates their attackers with multi-spectral light and a sonic burst. Models charging against units equipped with photon grenades gain no bonus attacks for charging, but can still employ any special close combat attacks they gain when charging.

ATTACKS

Attacks in close combat work like shots in shooting – each attack that hits has a chance to wound. The wounded model gets a chance to save, and if it fails is (generally) removed as a casualty. Each engaged model strikes with the number of Attacks (A) on his characteristics profile. In addition, the following bonus attacks apply:

+1 Charge Bonus: Engaged models who launched the close assault that turn (ie, charged) get +1 Attack on their normal profile for that turn only.

+1 Two Weapons: Engaged models with two single-handed weapons (typically a close combat weapon and/or pistol in each hand) have an extra +1 Attack for every turn of close combat, including the first. Models with more than two weapons gain no additional benefit – you only get one extra Attack regardless of whether you have two or more single-handed weapons.

Example 1: *A unit of five Space Marines with bolters would roll five D6 for their attacks in close combat. If they were charging they would roll ten D6 (1 Attack +1 each for charging). Note that the Space Marines could not charge if they had used their bolters in the Shooting phase, as they are rapid fire weapons.*

Example 2: *A unit of six Hormagaunts with scything talons (two close combat weapons) would roll twelve D6 for their attacks (1 attack +1 for two weapons). If they were charging they would roll eighteen D6 (1 Attack +1 each for charging +1 for two weapons = 3 each).*

ROLLING TO HIT

To determine whether hits are scored roll a D6 for each Attack a model gets to make. The dice roll needed to score a hit on your enemy depends on the relative Weapon Skills of the attackers and their foes. Compare the WS of the attackers with the WS of their opponents and consult the To Hit chart to find the minimum score needed on a D6 to hit. Attacks should be rolled together where the same To Hit roll is needed, as this saves time and speeds up the game. In the example above, the Space Marine player would therefore roll all of his ten attacks together.

UNITS WITH DIFFERENT WS

Many units in Warhammer 40,000 contain models with different Weapon Skill values. Attacks against a unit are resolved using the Weapon Skill of the majority of the engaged models. If there is no majority Weapon Skill, use the lowest Weapon Skill of the models engaged. For example, a mob of 20 Grots (WS2) led by an Ork Slaver (WS4) are all engaged in a combat. While the Grots are in the majority, attacks against the unit are resolved using their WS of 2 – however skilled the Slaver is, he can't prevent the Grots getting hit in the first place.

When the models attack, they calculate their own To Hit values based on their individual Weapon Skill. So, when the Grots and Slaver mentioned above attack their enemies, the Grots' To Hit value will be based on a comparison of their WS2 against the enemy's WS, and the Slaver on a comparison of his WS4 and the enemy's WS.

WHO IS HIT?

We assume that the warrior is contributing his shots and blows to the swirling combat going on. This means we don't have to worry about whether an individual model strikes its respective opponent in base contact. When a unit inflicts hits, it may only affect enemy models that are engaged. These are the only enemy models able to strike back, so it is reasonable that these are the only ones who can be hurt.

ROLLING TO WOUND

Not all of the attacks that find a mark will harm the enemy. They may be deflected by equipment, parried at the last moment or merely inflict a graze or flesh wound. As with shooting, once you have scored a hit with an attack you must roll again to see if you score a wound and incapacitate your foe. Consult the Damage chart, cross-referencing the attacker's Strength characteristic (S) with the defender's Toughness (T). The chart indicates the minimum value on a D6 roll required to inflict a wound.

WHAT STRENGTH TO USE

In almost all cases, when rolling to wound in close combat, use the Strength on the attacker's profile regardless of what weapon they are using. Some (but not all) close combat weapons may give the attacker a Strength bonus – this is explained in Special Close Combat Attacks. In a unit containing models with different Strength values, roll their attacks separately (they'll quite often have different Initiative characteristics too). So, for example, in a unit containing Grots and an Ork Slaver, the Grots' attacks are made with their puny Strength of 2, but the Slaver's attacks use his more macho Strength of 3.

DIFFERENT TOUGHNESSES

If the unit being attacked contains models with different Toughness characteristics, use the Toughness of the majority of the engaged models. If there is no majority, then use the lowest Toughness among them. To continue the example above, the engaged Grots (T2) and Ork Slaver (T4) will suffer To Wound rolls using the Grots' meagre Toughness as long as they are in the majority. Once again, remember that this is figured at each Initiative step – if the unit was whittled down to just the Slaver remaining, the attacks at the next Initiative will be resolved at the Toughness of the Slaver.

ARMOUR SAVES

Models struck and wounded in close combat can attempt Armour Saves to avoid becoming casualties. Models usually get to save regardless of the attacker's Strength, but some especially monstrous creatures and powerful close combat weapons will punch straight through armour. If a unit takes enough wounding hits in one Initiative step to cause one or more wounds on every engaged model, the attacking player nominates one engaged model to make the first save. After this, all other Saving throws are made normally.

Cover does not provide protection in close combat as it does against shooting. This means that models do not get Cover Saves against any attacks made in the Close Combat phase.

Remember that models are allowed to make Invulnerable Saving throws even if Armour Saving throws would not normally be allowed. If the rules for a weapon or attack states that no Armour Save is allowed then only an Invulnerable Save may be made. Some especially exotic attacks may even ignore Invulnerable Saves (but not necessarily Armour Saves), and where this is the case it is noted in the appropriate Codex book.

As noted in the Shooting section, with a unit of multi-Wound creatures, whole multi-Wound models must be removed as casualties wherever possible.

SUFFERING WOUNDS & REMOVING CASUALTIES

All the rules for removing shooting casualties apply in close combat, in addition to the following:

When a unit inflicts wounds, they may only affect engaged enemy models. The player suffering the casualties selects which models die from those engaged. Casualties must be removed in such a way that the unit maintains coherency wherever possible. This represents the way that a unit can be whittled down to a tight knot of combatants.

It is possible that casualties may exceed the number of engaged models, in which case the surplus wounds are discarded. The check on which models are engaged is made at the start of each Initiative step, so some models may lose their opportunity to attack if all engaged enemies are slain at an earlier Initiative step – the unit has already slain everyone it can reach.

If a model becomes a casualty before it has an opportunity to attack, then it may not strike back. When striking blows simultaneously, you may find it more convenient to resolve one side's attacks and simply lie wounded models on their side to remind you that they have yet to attack back.

TO HIT CHART

Opponent's Weapon Skill (columns) / **Attacker's Weapon Skill** (rows)

	1	2	3	4	5	6	7	8	9	10
1	4+	4+	5+	5+	5+	5+	5+	5+	5+	5+
2	3+	4+	4+	4+	5+	5+	5+	5+	5+	5+
3	3+	3+	4+	4+	4+	4+	5+	5+	5+	5+
4	3+	3+	3+	4+	4+	4+	4+	4+	5+	5+
5	3+	3+	3+	3+	4+	4+	4+	4+	4+	4+
6	3+	3+	3+	3+	3+	4+	4+	4+	4+	4+
7	3+	3+	3+	3+	3+	3+	4+	4+	4+	4+
8	3+	3+	3+	3+	3+	3+	3+	4+	4+	4+
9	3+	3+	3+	3+	3+	3+	3+	3+	4+	4+
10	3+	3+	3+	3+	3+	3+	3+	3+	3+	4+

DAMAGE CHART

Toughness (columns) / **Strength** (rows)

	1	2	3	4	5	6	7	8	9	10
1	4+	5+	6+	6+	N	N	N	N	N	N
2	3+	4+	5+	6+	6+	N	N	N	N	N
3	2+	3+	4+	5+	6+	6+	N	N	N	N
4	2+	2+	3+	4+	5+	6+	6+	N	N	N
5	2+	2+	2+	3+	4+	5+	6+	6+	N	N
6	2+	2+	2+	2+	3+	4+	5+	6+	6+	N
7	2+	2+	2+	2+	2+	3+	4+	5+	6+	6+
8	2+	2+	2+	2+	2+	2+	3+	4+	5+	6+
9	2+	2+	2+	2+	2+	2+	2+	3+	4+	5+
10	2+	2+	2+	2+	2+	2+	2+	2+	3+	4+

*Note that **N** on the chart means the hit has no effect. A target with the Toughness indicated cannot be harmed by a hit of such puny strength.*

"Strike fast and suddenly. Attack without warning. Secure victory before the foe is aware of his danger. Remember always, a war is easily won if your enemy does not know he is fighting."

Maxims of Macharius the Second Lord General Solar, quoted in The Macharian Heresy by Lord Inquisitor Kryptman

DETERMINE ASSAULT RESULTS

Assaults are usually decisive, one side or the other quickly gaining the upper hand and forcing back their foe. Numbers and leadership can keep a side in the fight, but the casualties each side inflicts are usually the most telling factor. To decide who has won the combat, total up the number of wounds inflicted by each side. The side that causes the most is the winner, the other side is the loser and may be forced back if they fail a Morale check. Note that wounds which have been negated by Armour Saves do not count, nor do wounds in excess of a model's Wounds characteristic, only wounds actually inflicted.

If both sides score the same number of wounds, the combat is drawn and continues next turn.

MASSACRE!

If one side destroys the enemy it wins automatically – even if it sustained more casualties. They may consolidate.

LOSER CHECKS MORALE

Units that lose a close combat must take a Morale check to hold their ground. If they fail, they must abandon the fight and fall back. If they pass, the unit holds its ground and fights on – basically the combat is drawn and no further account is made of the unit's defeat (apart from some good-natured taunting by the winner!). Morale checks and the Fall Back rules are fully covered in the Morale section of the rules (see page 47).

SWEEPING ADVANCES & CONSOLIDATION

When a unit falls back from combat, the victors make a Sweeping Advance, attempting to cut down the falling back enemies, and can then make a Consolidate move. Some troops, such as Space Marine Terminators, are not allowed to sweeping advance – in such cases the unit just consolidates.

If the falling back unit unit no longer has any models in base contact with the victor, or if the victor has models still engaged in combat with other units which are not falling back, the victors do not get a chance to sweeping advance, but may still consolidate.

SWEEPING ADVANCES

The falling back unit and the winning unit compare their Initiative characteristic + the roll of a D6.

Note: *For Initiative values, always count the Initiative characteristic from the creature's profile without any modifiers. In a unit with mixed Initiative characteristics, count the majority value, or the lowest if there is no majority.*

• If the falling back unit's total is **higher,** they break off from the combat successfully. Make a Fall Back move for the losing unit. The winners can now consolidate as detailed below.

• If the winner's total is **equal or greater** they catch the fleeing enemy with a sweeping advance. The falling back unit is scattered. We assume that the already demoralised foe is comprehensively defeated, ripped apart and sent packing, its members left either dead, wounded, and captured, or at best fleeing and hiding. The destroyed unit(s) is removed immediately. No Invulnerable Save or other special rule (such as the Necrons' We'll Be Back special rule) can save the unit at this stage; for them the battle is over and they can take no further useful part in the fighting. The victorious unit may now make a Consolidate move. Note that this does constitute a 'Massacre!' result.

Designer's Note: *Initiative is used in this case, rather than Movement, to represent the reaction times of the units involved – a faster Movement rate will be useful once a unit has extricated itself from a combat, but won't help if the enemy pounces at their backs as soon as the unit attempts to turn around and break off.*

There is a fate reserved for those who betray the Emperor's trust. It is not death. It is not life. What is it when flesh and mind are taken into the body of the Golden Throne? What is it when organs are absorbed slowly into the flesh of the living machine? Is there a mind that suffers for eons as the Emperor suffers, or does the personality fade and melt away as the flesh that houses it dissolves into nothing?

CONSOLIDATION

The victors of a close combat may move up to 3" in any direction to consolidate their position and recover an effective formation, or even engage new opponents. Consolidation may not be used to embark on a transport vehicle.

If a unit is consolidating due to a 'Massacre!' result, it moves D6" instead of 3" – the sudden victory may leave its members flat-footed and dumbfounded or raring to storm onward according to the vagaries of fate.

Units making a Consolidate move are not slowed by difficult terrain and do not trigger Dangerous Terrain tests.

The move may be used to contact enemy units and lock them in combat, but the consolidating unit must maintain unit coherency and does not count as charging when combat is worked out next turn. Locked models may not, of course, be targeted or fire themselves in the Shooting phase.

Note: Sometimes a losing unit will only fall back 3" or less from a combat and it is perfectly possible for a consolidating unit to move straight back into contact with such slow-footed foes. Treat this as the falling back unit being subject to a new assault (though no charge bonuses apply) – see 'Assaulted While Falling Back' in the Morale section (see page 48).

If several close combats are being fought in close proximity, a unit which consolidates into a new close combat does not count as engaged until the next Assault phase and is effectively ignored. All the combats are assumed to be simultaneous.

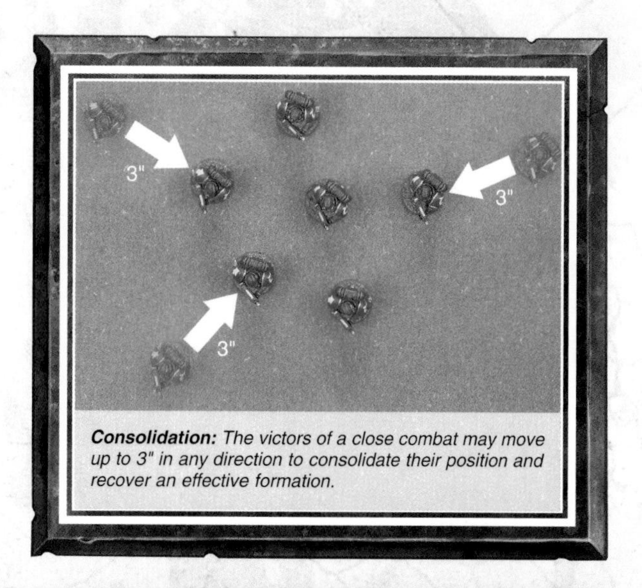

Consolidation: *The victors of a close combat may move up to 3" in any direction to consolidate their position and recover an effective formation.*

'PILE IN' MOVES

At the end of each Assault phase, models in units that were locked, but which are not themselves engaged in combat, MUST move up to 6" in an attempt to contact enemy that were in the same combat. This is done in the same way as moving chargers but is not slowed by difficult terrain and does not trigger Dangerous Terrain tests.

When making Pile In moves, the player whose turn it currently is moves first. A Pile In move may not be used to contact enemy units that are not currently involved in the assault. Once a unit is locked in combat it may only make Pile In moves and may not move in the Movement phase.

If, for some reason (mass carnage usually), the Pile In moves of the combatants are insufficient to allow them to get any models engaged, the assault comes to an end. Both sides may make Consolidation moves instead.

Pile In: *At the end of each Assault phase, models in units that are locked, but which are not themselves engaged in combat, MUST move up to 6" to contact enemy.*

SHOOTING INTO & OUT OF CLOSE COMBAT

Models belonging to units locked in combat may not fire weapons in the Shooting phase. Their attentions are completely engaged by the swirling mêlée. Likewise, while especially twisted and soulless commanders may wish their warriors to fire indiscriminately into the middle of close combats in the hopes of hitting the enemy, this is not permitted. The events in a close combat move too quickly and the warriors themselves will be understandably hesitant about firing on their comrades (they may end up in the same straits soon enough after all).

Locked models may not normally become casualties due to shooting. While Blast markers and templates may not be placed such that they cover any models locked in combat, they may end up there after scattering and will then affect friend and foe. Units that are locked in close combat do not have to take Morale and Pinning tests caused by shooting; they are considered to be much too focused on fighting to be worried about being shot at!

MULTIPLE COMBATS

When a unit is fighting more than one enemy unit, all such units are said to be involved in a multiple combat. Each unit's attacks must be divided between the enemy it is engaged with as follows:

• Models in base contact with the enemy must allocate their attacks against a unit that they are in base contact with.

• Models engaged but not in base contact must allocate their attacks against an enemy unit that another model from their unit they are within 2" of is in base contact with.

When determining assault results in a multiple combat, total up the number of wounds inflicted by each side to determine who is the winner. All the units on the losing side have to check their morale. Remember that winning units can only sweeping advance and consolidate if all of the units they are locked with fall back or are destroyed. Each winning unit that can sweeping advance makes a single roll and compares its total to each of the enemy unit's totals; any it equals or beats are destroyed. At the end of the Assault Phase, all units that were involved in a multiple combat must make Pile-in moves towards enemies that were originally in the combat.

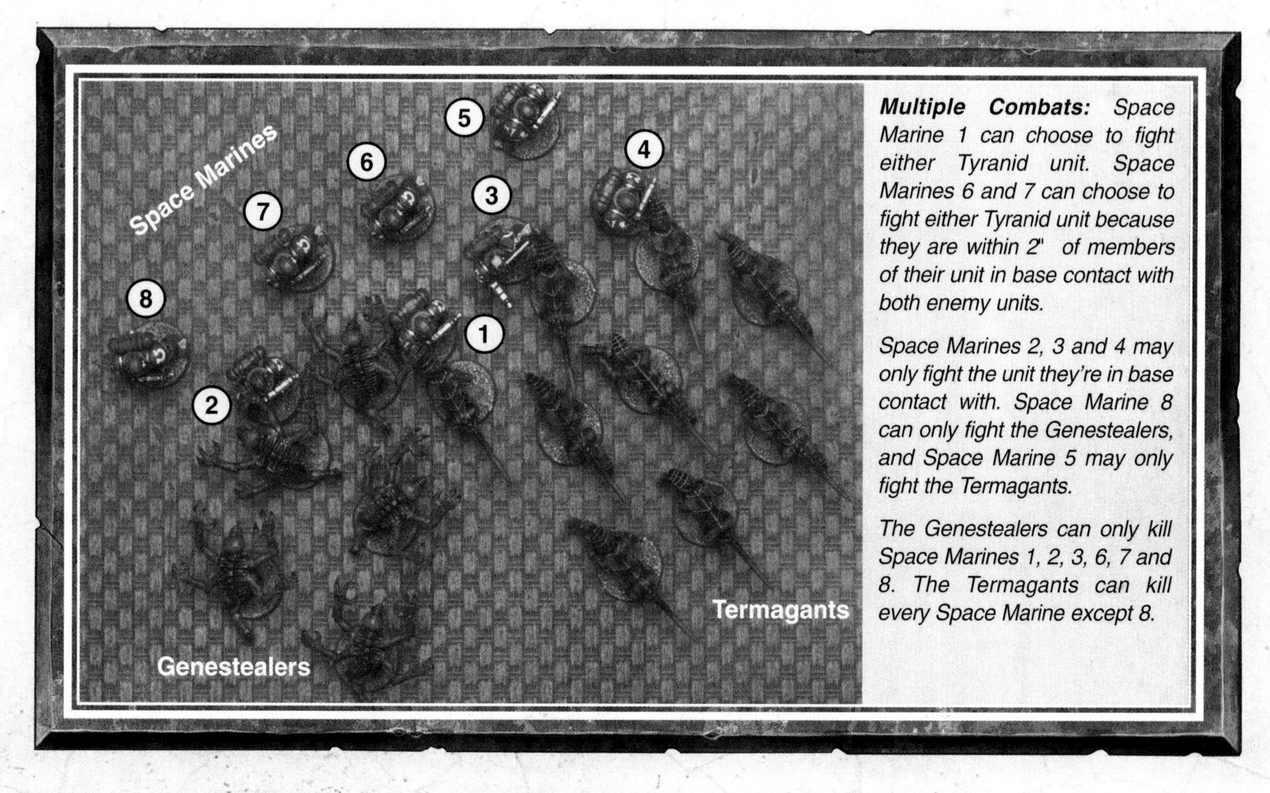

Multiple Combats: *Space Marine 1 can choose to fight either Tyranid unit. Space Marines 6 and 7 can choose to fight either Tyranid unit because they are within 2" of members of their unit in base contact with both enemy units.*

Space Marines 2, 3 and 4 may only fight the unit they're in base contact with. Space Marine 8 can only fight the Genestealers, and Space Marine 5 may only fight the Termagants.

The Genestealers can only kill Space Marines 1, 2, 3, 6, 7 and 8. The Termagants can kill every Space Marine except 8.

SPECIAL CLOSE COMBAT ATTACKS

Even though high-powered lasers and plasma weapons scour the battlefields of the 41st millennium, close combat remains commonplace – sieges, city fighting, boarding actions and tunnel warfare are noted more for the ferocity of the fighting than any strategic nuances. Seasoned warriors will often bear a deadly array of clubs, knives and frag grenades for close-quarter fighting. Assault troops will be even more ably equipped, taking pistols, swords and deadly power weapons into battle with them.

Some common close combat weapons are listed below. Models with special close combat attacks can choose not to use them and attack normally instead. A model might be equipped with more than one type of special close combat attack, eg, a power fist and a power axe. Only one special attack type can be used, so the player can opt to strike at his normal Initiative with the power axe, and use his power fist as an additional weapon, or can count his power axe as his additional weapon, and strike with his power fist at an Initiative of 1.

CLOSE COMBAT WEAPONS (CHAINSWORDS / AXES / PISTOLS, ETC)

There is a bewildering array of close combat weapons, all of which confer no bonus to the Strength of combatants. However, swords and pistols (or similar hand weapons) gain the wielder an additional close combat attack. A plasma pistol can be used as a close combat weapon, though it confers no Strength bonus or particular armour penetration advantages.

HEAVY CLOSE COMBAT WEAPONS

Heavy close combat weapons, such as the Ork choppa and the mighty chainaxes of Berzerkers of Khorne, are used to batter through an opponent's defences. No armour can completely protect its wearer against a direct blow from such a weapon. The maximum Armour Save that can be used against these weapons is 4+, even if it would normally be better.

POWER WEAPONS

A power weapon (typically a sword or axe, but sometimes a glaive, halberd or mace) is sheathed in the lethal haze of a disruptive energy field, eating through armour, flesh and bone with ease. Power weapons ignores Armour Saves, and some may even give a Strength bonus, or wound on a fixed dice score regardless of the enemy's Toughness characteristic (as detailed in the appropriate army Codex).

LIGHTNING CLAWS

Lightning claws are commonly used as matched pairs, as only a second lightning claw can provide an additional close combat weapon attack bonus for a model equipped with one. They consist of a number of blades, each a mini-power weapon, extending from a housing on the back of the hand. Lightning claws ignore Armour Saves and re-roll any To Wound dice that fail to cause a wound.

FORCE WEAPONS

Force weapons are potent psychic weapons only used by trained Psykers. They are treated as a power weapon, but can unleash a psychic attack that kills an opponent outright. Roll to hit and wound as normal, allowing any Invulnerable Saving throws the victim might have. As long as one wound has been inflicted, make a Psychic test for the Psyker against any one opponent wounded by the weapon. The normal rules for using psychic powers apply (see page 52), and you may not use another psychic power in the same turn. Passing the test slays the opponent outright, no matter how many Wounds it has (count the actual number inflicted for determining who won the assault). Force weapons have no special effect against targets that don't have Wounds, such as vehicles.

POWER FIST / CLAW

A power fist or claw is a powered, armoured gauntlet surrounded by a disruptive energy field. It doubles the user's Strength (up to a maximum of 10), ignoring Armour Saves. Only the user's basic Strength is doubled – any additional bonus for special abilities are added afterwards. A power fist is slow and cumbersome to use, so strikes with a power fist are always delivered at Initiative 1 (ignore any bonuses for special rules, cover, grenades or wargear, etc).

THUNDER HAMMER

Thunder hammers release a tremendous blast of energy when they strike. A thunder hammer counts as a power fist, with the addition that any model wounded but not killed by it is knocked reeling, and will attack with an Initiative of 1 in the next Assault phase. Vehicles struck by a thunder hammer suffer a 'Crew Shaken' result in addition to any other results.

WITCHBLADE

These psychically attuned weapons are often carried by Eldar psykers. They inflict wounds on a roll of 2+, regardless of the target's Toughness, though Armour Saves are taken as normal. Against vehicles, the wielder of a witchblade triples his Strength (up to S 10).

RENDING WEAPONS

A well-placed blow from a rending weapon can rip apart any armour. Any roll to hit of 6 with a rending weapon will ignore Armour Saves and automatically causes a wound. Against a vehicle, an Armour Penetration roll of 6 allows a further D6 to be rolled, with the result added to the total score. Note that if the additional roll is also a 6, no further dice are added.

POISONED WEAPONS

Poisoned weapons range from blades daubed in venom to hypodermic claws. They do not rely on a comparison of Strength and Toughness to wound – they will normally wound on a 4+. Some venoms are so lethal that the merest drop can kill – these wound on a 2+. Weapons with this type of lethal venom are described in the appropriate Codex.

MORALE

It's a fortunate commander who can rely on his troops always performing fearlessly. In the chaos and confusion of battle, troops can easily become demoralised, disorientated or simply terrified by the violence unleashed against them. To represent this element of the unknown, your units of troops have to check to see if their morale holds under certain circumstances. As you will have already gathered, certain events will require that your troops take a Morale check, and a unit in particularly dire straits may be forced to take several Morale checks in a single turn.

Note that Leadership tests are used for other functions in Warhammer 40,000, such as choosing a target. Morale checks are a very specific kind of Leadership test.

MORALE CHECKS

Units use their Leadership characteristic for taking Morale checks. This represents the grit, determination, élan or (sometimes) plain stupidity of warriors in action. Morale checks are taken by rolling 2D6 and comparing the total score to the unit's Leadership value. If the score is equal to or under the unit's Leadership value, the test is passed. However, if the score rolled is higher, then the test is failed and the unit will immediately fall back, as described below.

MORALE CHECK MODIFIERS

Certain circumstances can make Morale checks harder for a unit to pass. For example, a unit that has already suffered heavy casualties will be more inclined to give way than a unit that is at full strength. This is represented by applying Leadership modifiers to Morale checks, which can reduce the unit's Leadership value by -1, -2 or sometimes even more.

INSANE HEROISM

Occasionally, warriors will refuse to retreat even when faced with impossible odds or particularly harrowing experiences. Sometimes you can push someone just too far! A score of 2 on the 2D6 always indicates a unit has passed its Morale check regardless of modifiers.

TAKING MORALE TESTS

Units normally have to take a Morale check in the following situations:

- If a unit takes 25% or more casualties from shooting in the turn – test at the end of the Shooting phase.
- If a unit is defeated in close combat in the Assault phase – test once combat results are established.
- If an enemy unit performs a Tank Shock attack on their unit – test once the vehicle has moved.

Some units have special rules pertaining to Morale checks which are detailed in the appropriate Codex. For example, some particularly fanatical units may be immune to the effects of morale. Some units automatically pass Morale checks, while others automatically pass all Leadership tests. This is a subtle, but important difference, eg, units that automatically pass Morale checks will still have to test for Pinning and Last Man Standing.

A) SHOOTING CASUALTIES

A unit losing 25% or more of its current unit strength in models from shooting during a single Shooting phase must pass a Morale check at the end of the Shooting phase, with the appropriate modifiers, or else it will fall back.

A unit that is already falling back, is pinned or is locked in close combat does not have to take this test.

The Leadership test is modified by the following factor:

> -1 if the unit is below 50% of its starting strength (ie, the unit has fewer than half the number of models remaining than it had it when the battle started).

Example: *A unit of five troops suffers two casualties, so it takes a Morale check, which it promptly passes. Next turn, the unit, now three strong, suffers another casualty, so it takes another Morale check, this time at -1 Leadership for being below 50% of starting strength.*

B) LOSING AN ASSAULT

Units that lose a close combat (ie, they suffer more wounds than they inflict) must pass a Morale check at the end of the Assault phase, with the appropriate modifiers to hold their ground. If they fail, they must fall back.

The Leadership test is modified by the following factors:

-1 If the unit is below 50% of its starting strength.

-1 If the losing side is outnumbered by its opponents.*

-2 If the losing side is outnumbered 2:1 or more.*

-3 If the losing side is outnumbered 3:1 or more.*

-4 If the losing side is outnumbered 4:1 or more.*

* Only apply the highest of these modifiers.

Example: *An Imperial Guard squad has lost an assault. They would normally require a 7 or less to pass the Leadership test, but since they are below half strength (-1) and are outnumbered by a value of 2:1 (-2), they now require a 4 or less in order to hold their ground.*

The following rules are used to determine if a unit is outnumbered:

• Vehicles with a Weapon Skill count as 10 models if they have a front armour of 12 or more, or 5 models if their front armour is 11 or less.

• Monstrous Creatures count as 10 models.

• Other models with more than one Wound count as a number of models matching the Wounds value shown on their profile.

Count all the models in the opposing unit(s) once casualties have been removed, not just the engaged ones

NO RETREAT!

It's not uncommon for units to be immune to Morale checks for losing a close combat, or to automatically pass them for some reason. They may be Fearless, subject to a vow, a walker, or be affected by some other special rule. When such units lose a close combat, and are outnumbered by 2:1 or more, they are in danger of being dragged down or overrun despite their determination to hang on.

The unit in question will not have to fall back but suffers one additional wound if outnumbered by 2:1, two wounds if outnumbered by 3:1 or three wounds if outnumbered by 4:1 or more. Saving throws can be taken against these wounds as normal. Walkers (which do not have Wounds) instead suffer one glancing hit if they are outnumbered by 2:1 or more. Remember this rule only applies if the unit lost the close combat in the first place!

C) TANK SHOCK

Units that are driven at by an enemy tank may wisely decide it's time to abandon their position and fall back. If a tank reaches a unit's position then the unit must take a Morale check, with the appropriate modifier, to see whether or not it falls back. For a fuller explanation of how tank shock works, see the Vehicle rules later on (see page 58).

The Leadership test is modified by the following factors:

-1 If the unit is below 50% of its starting strength.

FALL BACK!

A fall back is a fighting withdrawal, not an out-and-out rout. Sometimes a fighting retreat in the face of overwhelming odds is the only option left. A withdrawal can give troops the chance to retire to a stronger position, to regroup and mount a fresh attack, or hold back the approaching enemy.

Units make a Fall Back move upon failing a Morale test, and in each subsequent Movement phase until the unit regroups or leaves the table.

Most units fall back 2D6". A unit falls back directly towards the closest point of the player's table edge or of the base line where the unit deployed/entered the table if it came on at a different place. Certain missions may also specify different rules regarding fall back direction. If possible the unit must remain coherent, with gaps of no more than 2" between models as they fall back.

A unit that falls back must move within a corridor lying between its most extended models as shown in the diagram on the left – but each model can move anywhere within this corridor, as you wish. If a unit is spread out such that its models are more than 2" apart, the models must be moved back into coherency as the unit moves. If the unit moves into, out of or through difficult terrain, the distance rolled on the dice is halved for a Fall Back move.

FIRING WHILE FALLING BACK

Troops who are falling back may continue to shoot, but are obviously moving.

ASSAULTED WHILE FALLING BACK

A unit that is assaulted whilst falling back must check to regroup immediately (see Regrouping below), before any charging models are moved. No modifiers apply to the check in this case and even units which would not normally be allowed to regroup are allowed to make the check.

If successful, the unit regroups and will fight the close combat normally. If it fails to regroup then the unit is scattered and destroyed. Note that this rule applies if a unit consolidates into enemies falling back too.

TRAPPED!

Sometimes a unit will find its Fall Back corridor blocked by impassable terrain and/or models (ignoring enemy models that have fought in close combat against the unit this turn but including friends). A unit falling back may move around any obstruction in such a way as to get back to their base line by the shortest route.

If a unit cannot perform a full Fall Back move in any direction, without doubling back, it is destroyed.

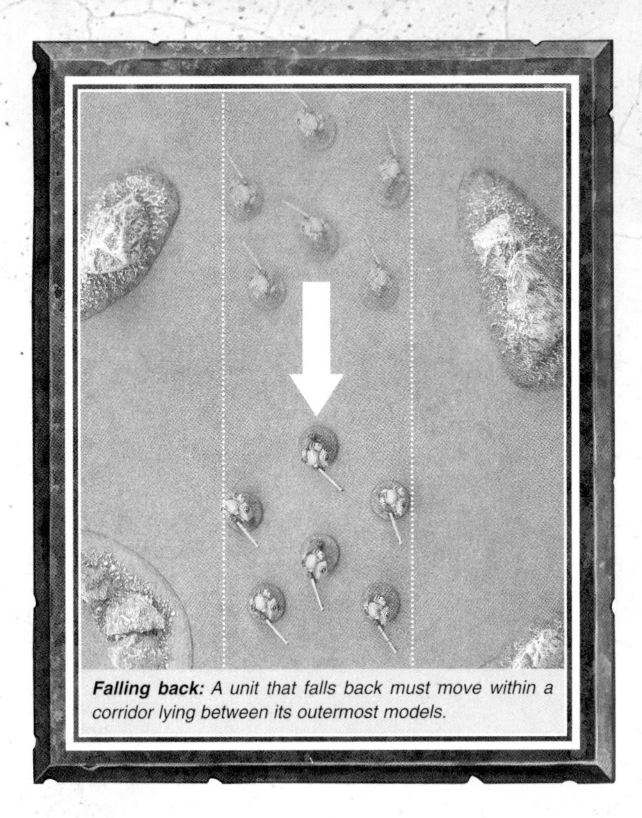

Falling back: A unit that falls back must move within a corridor lying between its outermost models.

Trapped: The Tau Fire Warriors cannot perform their full Fall Back move of 11" in any direction, because they are surrounded by either units or impassable terrain, and so they are destroyed.

FALLING BACK AND PINNING

As noted in the Pinning rules, Morale checks are not taken by units which are pinned. However, it is possible that a Pinning test may be required of a unit already falling back. Take the test and apply its full effects if failed. To make matters worse, a unit may not regroup while pinned either, unless they are charged (see Assaulted While Falling Back). When the pinned unit has missed a turn it will revert to falling back again, no doubt fervently hoping to get out of the mess they're in.

LAST MAN STANDING

Sometimes a unit will be almost entirely wiped out, with only a single member left. Such lone individuals must take a Leadership test at the start of each of their turns. If they pass they are filled with heroic fervour and continue to fight on single-handedly. If they fail, they suffer an outbreak of common sense and begin to fall back. Units that start the battle as a single model never have to take Last Man Standing tests as they're obviously used to fighting on their own.

REGROUPING

Just because a unit falls back doesn't mean it is out of the fight. Courageous officers will try to inspire their troops to rally. Warriors might regain their composure or their will to fight, perhaps out of a sense of honour, duty or sheer bloody-mindedness. A unit falling back can attempt to regroup by taking a Leadership test (with the appropriate modifiers) at the start of its Movement phase so long as:

1. It has left at least 50% of its original strength.

2. There are no enemies within 6".

3. The unit is in coherency.

The Leadership test for regrouping is modified by the following factor:

+1 If no enemy units are in line of sight.

If the unit successfully passes its Leadership test, it regroups. It cannot move any further during that Movement phase, except that models are allowed to consolidate (see page 44). Once a unit has regrouped it fights as normal. For example, it can shoot (though it does count as if it had moved on the turn it regroups) or launch an assault if it gets the chance. A unit forced to regroup before its turn was due – eg, by being assaulted by an enemy – can act normally in its next turn.

If the unit fails its Leadership test, (or cannot regroup because of the restrictions given above), then it must continue to fall back, and is moved a further 2D6".

LEAVING THE BATTLE

Once a unit reaches the table edge it is considered to have left the immediate battle and may not return. Note that there is no need for individual models in the unit to move 'off' the table – once a model reaches the edge, that unit has gone! The unit takes no further part in the battle and is removed, doubtless spreading tales of the unstoppable nature of the foes they were facing to their compatriots behind the front lines.

Designer's Note: *This is a purposefully harsh ruling to discourage players hugging table edges too closely with their forces instead of getting into the thick of the action.*

CHARACTERS

Nearly every race or power throws up exceptional individuals who stand out above the normal herd. Veteran warriors, brilliant officers, inspired prophets and ferocious war-leaders can take to the battlefield and make a difference. They inspire others to greater feats of heroism (or fiendish bravery as the case may be) and are often quicker, stronger and more powerful in combat. Some may wield fearsome psychic energies or channel unearthly powers to destroy their enemies. In Warhammer 40,000 these kinds of powerful individuals are called Characters and there are certain special rules that apply to them.

CHARACTERS IN BATTLE

There are two kinds of characters:

• Upgrade characters are fielded as part of units from the start of the game, representing a squad leader or unit champion. They are effectively another trooper in the unit with enhanced characteristics and usually a superior Leadership value, as well as a wide selection of weapon/wargear choices. The Character rules given here do not apply to them.

• Independent characters are represented by individual models, which fight as units in their own right. One of the most useful abilities of independent characters is to join other units in battle, so that they can move in to bolster the battle line where the fighting is fiercest.

In addition, various Codexes may also include independent models that only ever fight as units of one model. These are not independent characters, and the following rules do not apply to them.

THE MOVEMENT PHASE

Characters follow the Movement rules for models of their type, be it infantry, jump infantry or beasts/cavalry. In addition, characters can move through difficult terrain more quickly and safely than ordinary troops. All characters have the Move Through Cover and Skilled Rider special rules (see pages 75). This advantage does not extend to vehicles they may be travelling in.

CHARACTERS JOINING & LEAVING UNITS

Characters are allowed to move freely around the battlefield and can temporarily join other units. While a character is part of a unit, he must obey the usual Coherency rules until he leaves the unit, as detailed below. The combined unit moves and assaults at the speed of the slowest model while they stay together. In order to join a unit, an independent character simply has to move within the 2" coherency distance of the unit during his Movement phase and be declared as joining it. Note that a lone character cannot join another character to create a character unit.

• An independent character can leave a unit during the Movement phase by moving out of coherency distance with it.

• An independent character may only join or leave a unit during the Movement phase – once assaults are launched it is too late to join in or duck out!

• A character may not join or leave a unit while it is falling back – he/she/it must wait until the unit has regrouped.

• If the unit has been pinned, the character may not leave it until it is no longer pinned.

When an independent character joins a unit, it might have different special rules from those of the unit. Unless specified in the rule itself (like in the Stubborn special rule), the unit's special rules are not conferred upon the character, and the character's special rules are not conferred upon the unit.

In some cases though, the character or the unit may lose their special rules as a result of the character joining the unit. For example, if a character that does not have the Infiltrate special rule joins a unit of Infiltrators, the unit loses the Infiltrate rule. Such exceptions are addressed case by case in the Universal Special Rules section on page 74.

CHARACTERS AS LEADERS

One advantage of a character being part of a unit is that any Leadership tests the unit takes are then made using the character's Leadership value, if it is superior to the unit's. Remember, if a character is part of a unit that falls back he may not leave the unit until it regroups. Characters never need to take Last Man Standing tests, as they are used to fighting heroically on their own.

RETINUES

Some characters are able to lead a special retinue, bodyguard or other HQ unit in battle. Where this is the case it is specified in their Codex book entry. If a character is fielded with such a unit, he may not leave them and join another unit while they remain alive. Should the unit be destroyed, the character may once again move between units.

THE SHOOTING PHASE

Characters function in the same manner as normal troopers during the Shooting phase, though they will often have abilities superior to the press of men around them.

SHOOTING AT CHARACTERS

In the heat of battle it is often hard to distinguish individuals, and even harder to pick them out as specific targets. Characters who've joined a unit are considered part of that unit and so may not normally be picked out as targets. Characters that are not part of a unit can only be chosen as targets if they are the closest target to the firer. Characters that are Monstrous Creatures can always be picked out as separate targets unless they've joined a unit of monstrous creatures or a unit with special rules that offer them protection, such as the Tyranid Tyrant Guard.

CHARACTERS SHOOTING

All characters shoot just like ordinary troopers, although in many cases they will have better Ballistic Skills or exotic weaponry that sets them apart. Where this is the case, either roll for them separately or use different coloured dice to differentiate their shooting. Characters must still fire at the same target as any unit they are with.

THE ASSAULT PHASE

If a unit including a character charges into close combat, the character must charge in too – they cannot hold back like cowards! A character on his own can charge into close combat if within range of the enemy in the Assault phase.

Characters are treated as a separate unit when resolving close combats, following the normal rules for multiple combats (see page 45). This means that they **must** be in base-to-base contact with an enemy model in order to fight, and may not make attacks for being within 2" of another friendly model. If the unit they have joined is locked in combat with the enemy, the character is locked with them. However, wounds suffered by a unit never carry over onto a character that joined them.

This also means that only the enemy models that are engaged with the character may allocate their attacks against it and can be hurt by its attacks.

Characters in Close Combat: *The Chaos Lord is engaged with the Guardsman in base-to-base contact with him, and those within 2" of that Guardsman. Guardsman A is therefore not engaged with the Chaos Lord.*

Guardsmen B and C are engaged with both the Lord and the Chaos Marines unit, and can therefore choose to direct their attacks against either (provided they live long enough that is...).

SPECIAL CHARACTERS

In the Codex books, you'll find characters you can field as part of your army. As with squads of troops you can choose for your army, the character's profile tells you how tough he is and what weapons and armour he can have. It is left to you to name your heroes, and follow their illustrious careers across bloody battlefields.

Nonetheless, the 41st millennium is filled with famous characters renowned as legendary heroes or infamous villains. These individuals are called special characters and can be found in the Codex army books and in other sources, such as White Dwarf magazine. Special characters are highly skilled and dangerous individuals who have incredible traits or skills that make them particularly valuable to an army.

For example, Commissar Yarrick is without doubt the most respected Imperial Guard Commissar of the 41st millennium, his inspiring presence securing the world of Armageddon against two massive Ork invasions within the space of fifty years. An army led by him can expect great benefits in terms of morale and leadership. On the other hand, Khârn the Betrayer, an Exalted Champion of the Dark Gods, is a mad butcher and slaughterer of men with no thought for anything other than personal combat (at which, it must be granted, he excels).

Special characters represent unique individuals, past and present, that many players like to use in their games. In order to prevent such powerful characters dominating small engagements there are usually restrictions on their use to certain sizes of army, particular opponents and so forth. In some cases, with particularly legendary and celebrated (or infamous and reviled) characters, they may only be used in battles where both players have agreed to their use beforehand.

PSYCHIC POWERS

Some individuals are known as Psykers, characters capable of tapping the power of the Warp and manipulating its energies in terrifying ways. Some can send bolts of lightning arcing from their fingertips while others can hurl aside tanks with the powers of their mind, or rip their foes asunder with but a glance. However, in order to wield such power they risk eternal damnation, for the Warp is a nightmare realm inhabited by all manner of fell entities and daemons that can ravage the mind and body of the incautious Psyker.

Some army lists include characters who are Psykers, and who are allowed to use psychic powers. Psychic powers vary from race to race, so the effect of each power and when it may be used is included in their special rules. The rules below tell you how the Psyker can use his powers, and what can happen to him if things go wrong.

It requires intense concentration and inner calm for a Psyker to use his power, which is not always easy to attain in the midst of a firefight! In order to use one of his powers the Psyker must make a Psychic test by rolling equal to or under his Leadership on 2D6. If he fails, then his concentration has been broken and he cannot use the power that turn. A pass means the power may be used as described in the special rules for the Psyker in his Codex.

Unless specified otherwise, psychic abilities are subject to the usual Shooting rules, so the Psyker must be able to see the target, all attacks must be directed against a single target unit, etc. This is because Psykers find it hard to pinpoint the mind of an opponent with any clarity in the heat of combat; generally they all blur and merge in a confusing swirl. While most psychic powers are used instead of shooting, there are a number of other psychic abilities that may take effect in other phases. Most commonly these are minor psychic powers, subsidiary abilities of Psykers less potent than their major powers.

PERILS OF THE WARP

In order to use their psychic powers a Psyker must draw deeply upon the power of the Warp – a very risky and dangerous thing to do, for the Warp is inhabited by hostile entities that can attack an unwary Psyker during the few moments that he draws upon its power. To represent the dangers of the Warp, if a Psyker rolls a 2 or a 12 when taking the Leadership test to use a psychic power, he is attacked. The Psyker suffers one automatic hit at Strength 6 with no saves (of any sort) allowed – a Warp creature has tried to fry the Psyker's brain! Note that on a Leadership test roll of a 2 the psychic power still works, even though the Psyker has been attacked or killed.

UNIT TYPE RULES

As you will have seen in the descriptions of unit types earlier, the armies of the 41st millennium are remarkably diverse and include many specialist unit types. In this section, you will find the rules for each of these unit types. Unless stated in this section, these unit types will follow the rules for infantry.

BIKES

Troops mounted on bikes excel at hit-and-run attacks. They are able to use their high speed to strike deep into enemy territory, complete their mission and escape before an enemy is able to react. A skilled commander will recognise the benefit of having bikes at his disposal, and is able to use them for advanced reconnaissance, as well as to outflank a slower enemy. Indeed, in open ground, bikes are easily capable of outrunning all but the fastest vehicles. Riding through heavy terrain can be somewhat dangerous however, but many riders take great pride in their superior driving skills and daring. These warriors are often regarded as dangerously hot-headed risk-takers, but their effectiveness cannot be denied.

Bikes are treated like non-vehicle units rather than vehicles. However, in some respects they are treated slightly differently from other infantry troops. The exact changes are detailed below, divided between the different phases of the turn sequence.

MOVEMENT PHASE

Bikes can move up to 12" in the Movement phase instead of the normal 6" move. Bikes are not slowed down by difficult terrain. However, each model entering or moving through difficult terrain must take a Dangerous Terrain test (see page 17).

All bikes can use the Turbo Boosters special rule.

SHOOTING

Each bike in a unit may fire with one weapon for each rider on the bike. Thus a Space Marine attack bike with a driver and passenger in sidecar can fire with two weapons. If rapid fire weapons are mounted on a bike, then they are allowed to fire once up to maximum range even if the bike moved. In addition, rapid fire weapons and heavy weapons may be fired if the unit moves and the bike is still allowed to charge into close combat in the same turn.

ASSAULT

Bike assault moves are not slowed down by difficult terrain. However, each model entering or moving through difficult terrain must take a Dangerous Terrain test (see page 17).

MORALE

As bikes are so fast moving, they will fall back 3D6" after failing a Morale check, rather than 2D6".

ADDITIONAL PROTECTION

Bikes are large, solid constructions, and are often fitted with protective armour and shields to deflect and absorb incoming fire. Bike riders benefit from the protection offered by their bike, and increase their Toughness characteristic by 1. Note that this increase does not affect the model's Toughness when adjudicating Instant Death (see page 27).

JETBIKES

Jetbikes are powered by highly advanced anti-gravitational technology that allows them to hover a few metres above the ground and make powered boosts over obstacles. They are ideal for making raids on unsuspecting enemies, able to strike without warning from behind dense terrain, before using their superior speed and handling to escape. The Eldar are the undisputed masters of anti-grav technology, and their jetbikes are a swift moving force that is justifiably feared by any who have faced them.

Jetbikes are treated like non-vehicle units rather than vehicles. However, in some respects they are treated slightly differently from other infantry troops. The exact changes are detailed below, divided between the different phases of the turn sequence:

MOVEMENT PHASE

Jetbikes can move up to 12" in the Movement phase instead of the normal 6" move. Jetbikes may move over enemy and friendly units. They are able to move completely over difficult terrain, so that they do not have to take Dangerous Terrain tests. They may even end their move on top of difficult terrain, but if they do this they cannot claim any cover save, and will be as tall as the terrain for line of sight purposes.

Jetbikes may try to pass through Area Terrain, eg, woods and forests, rather than fly above them, in order to claim a Cover Save. If they do this, they are not slowed down by difficult terrain but each model entering or moving through the area must take a Dangerous Terrain test (see page 17). If they end their move within difficult terrain, they will be able to claim a Cover Save.

All bikes can use the Turbo Boosters special rule.

ELDAR JETBIKES

Eldar jetbike units are always allowed to move 6" in the Assault phase, even if they don't assault. When Eldar jetbikes move in the Assault phase and do not assault, then they treat difficult terrain just as jetbikes do in the Movement phase (and so can opt to move through it, or end their move on top of it).

SHOOTING PHASE

Each jetbike in a unit may fire with one weapon for each rider on the bike. If rapid fire weapons are mounted on a jetbike, then they are allowed to fire once up to maximum range even if the bike moved. In addition, rapid fire weapons and heavy weapons may be fired if the unit moves and the jetbike is still allowed to charge into close combat in the same turn.

ASSAULT

Jetbikes' assault moves are not slowed down by difficult terrain. However, each model entering or moving through difficult terrain when assaulting must take a Dangerous Terrain test. Note that jetbikes cannot opt to move over difficult terrain in the Assault phase as they can in the Movement phase, as the jetbikes are assumed to be close to the ground in order to initiate combat.

MORALE

As jetbikes are so fast moving, they will fall back 3D6" if they fail a Morale check, rather than 2D6".

ADDITIONAL PROTECTION

Jetbikes are solid and fast moving constructions, and are often fitted with protective armour and shields to deflect and absorb incoming fire. Jetbike riders benefit from the protection offered by their bike, and increase their Toughness characteristic by 1. Note that this increase does not affect the model's Toughness when adjudicating Instant Death (see page 27).

MONSTROUS CREATURES

Some creatures are terrifying beings that tower over their opponents, are capable of hurling tanks out of their path, and slaying a score of men with a single sweep of an arm. Greater Daemons, Eldar Avatars and the feared Tyranid Carnifex count amongst their number.

This unit type behaves differently on the battlefield to a normal infantry unit. The exact changes are detailed below, divided between the different phases of the turn sequence:

MOVEMENT PHASE

When moving through difficult terrain, monstrous creatures may re-roll the dice to see how far they move, as they smash aside anything in their path.

SHOOTING PHASE

Monstrous creatures enjoy the advantage of being able to automatically pass the Leadership test required to target enemy units other than the closest. They are large enough and scary enough to be able to casually ignore any foolish enemy bearing down on them!

FIRING MORE THAN ONE WEAPON

Monstrous Creatures can fire up to two weapons a turn.

ASSAULT PHASE

A Monstrous Creature is so huge and powerful that its attacks make a mockery of armour – foes wounded by Monstrous Creatures are hideously mangled and crushed. All wounds inflicted in close combat by a monstrous creature ignore Armour Saves.

Some Monstrous Creatures have weapons that augment their Strength (such as the Eldar Wraithlord's power fist) or work unusually (like the Dark Eldar Talos). Monstrous Creatures without such a special rule roll an additional D6 for armour penetration (2D6 + Strength) when attacking a vehicle, due to their weight and size.

JUMP INFANTRY

Some special troops use devices that allow them to move at great speed across the battlefield, making them especially good at assaulting enemy troops and outflanking enemy positions. The Space Marines use jump packs, which utilise high powered controlled bursts from turbines to make bounding leaps across the field of battle, jumping over terrain with ease. Other races tend to have their own particular versions, such as Orks (whose Stormboyz use rudimentary screaming jets to close with the enemy) and Eldar, whose Swooping Hawks soar elegantly on light wings supported by gravitic motors. Sometimes the technology will be more exotic, such as that used by Eldar Warp Spiders, who utilise short-ranged teleport devices for a similar effect.

This unit type behaves differently on the battlefield than a normal infantry unit. The exact changes are detailed below, divided between the different phases of the turn sequence.

MOVEMENT PHASE

Jump infantry can move up to 12" in the Movement phase instead of the normal 6" move. This is optional and they can choose to move as normal infantry if they wish. When using jump packs, movement is not reduced for difficult terrain, and jump pack equipped models can move over other models or obstacles freely. However, if they end their move in difficult terrain, they must take a Dangerous Terrain test.

SHOOTING PHASE

Jump infantry shoot like normal infantry units.

ASSAULT PHASE

Jump infantry assault 6" like normal infantry. This move is slowed by difficult terrain in the same way as other infantry, because the unit tends to cover the last few yards of a charge on foot.

MORALE

Jump infantry fall back 3D6", as they will always use their packs. They may, of course, move over any obstructions when falling back, but if they end their move in difficult terrain they will still have to take a Dangerous Terrain test.

JET PACKS

Some Jump Infantry are equipped with a special type of jump pack, referred to as a jet pack. The most frequent users of this technology are the Tau. Jet packs are designed to provide stable firing platforms rather than a means of getting into close combat. Jet packs differ from jump packs in the following ways:

In the Movement phase, they only move 6" when using their packs, but are allowed to move 6" in the Assault phase even if they don't assault. This allows them to put more distance between themselves and the enemy.

In the Shooting phase, models with jet packs are allowed to fire rapid fire weapons once at up to maximum range, even if the unit has moved. They are also allowed to declare a charge after firing rapid fire weapons.

ARTILLERY

Some weapons are so large and powerful that a single man could not hope to carry or operate them by himself. These weapons are more usually seen mounted on vehicles or as part of bunker emplacements, but they are sometimes utilised by infantry artillery teams, particularly on battlefields where the terrain might not be suitable for vehicles. Sometimes, these mighty artillery weapons are mounted on tracks or wheels and operate under their own engines, or in the case of some races, on highly advanced anti-grav platforms, as they are simply too heavy to lug across a battlefield.

This unit type behaves differently to a normal infantry unit on the battlefield. The exact changes are detailed below, divided between the different phases of the turn sequence:

Artillery is quite complex as it combines some of the features of vehicles with that of infantry. The unit consists of a number of crewmen models and the gun models themselves. The gun models are treated as vehicles with an Armour Rating of 10. Any penetrating or glancing hit will destroy a gun – there is no need to roll on the Vehicle Damage tables. If all the crewmen models are killed, the guns are immediately removed as well.

MOVEMENT PHASE

Artillery units move in the same way as infantry. They are slowed by difficult terrain like infantry, but gun models must also take Dangerous Terrain tests when they pass through it. There must be at least one crewman per gun to allow the unit to move – if there are fewer than this, then the unit may not move.

SHOOTING PHASE

In order to shoot with the guns in an artillery unit, there must be at least one different crewman within 2" of each gun firing. Artillery crewmen may never fire any other weapons as long as the unit still contains any gun models. Unless firing barrage weapons, there must be a line of sight to the target from both a gun model and a crewman within 2" of it. Ranges are measured from the gun model.

When template or blast weapons are fired at an artillery battery, the guns and crew can be hit as normal if they are under the marker/template. When other weapons are fired at the unit, randomise any hits between the crew and the guns themselves (so long as both types are still in the unit) – roll a D6 and consult the chart below:

D6	Result
1-4	Hits the crew
5-6	Hits a gun

ASSAULT PHASE

Artillery units may not declare charges if they still have any gun models with them. In an assault, enemy models attack as normal against the crew's Weapon Skill – randomise any hits using the table above while both crew and gun models remain engaged. If only gun models are engaged, the enemy will hit automatically and resolve their hits against the gun models. Only engaged crew models fight in an assault.

MORALE

Artillery units follow the normal rules for Morale for infantry units, with the following exceptions:

If an artillery unit does not have one crewman per remaining gun model and is forced to fall back, the gun models without crewmen are destroyed and the rest of the unit falls back as normal.

If an artillery unit is forced to fall back from close combat and the enemy is free to make a sweeping advance, then the artillery unit automatically loses the Initiative roll and is caught and massacred by the victor.

BEASTS & CAVALRY

As well as squads of warriors fighting on foot, and the armoured bulk of vehicles, many armies of the 41st millennium make use of fearsome predators and beasts, such as Warp Beasts and gigantic wolves, to augment their forces. Other warriors ride to battle on horses, grunting Cyboars, daemonic steeds and countless other strange creatures. When closing on their enemies, they are able to move at far greater speeds than warriors on foot, and as such are able to launch deadly charges and counter charges. Their speed also allows them to quickly react to the movements of their enemies, allowing them to rapidly redeploy to where they are most needed.

This unit type behaves differently on the battlefield to a normal infantry unit. The exact changes are detailed below, divided between the different phases of the turn sequence.

MOVEMENT PHASE

Beasts and cavalry are capable of making a faster move if they concentrate on moving, and do not take time to fire their weapons. They may use the Fleet special rule, as described in the Universal Special Rules section (see page 74). In all other respects they move as infantry.

SHOOTING PHASE

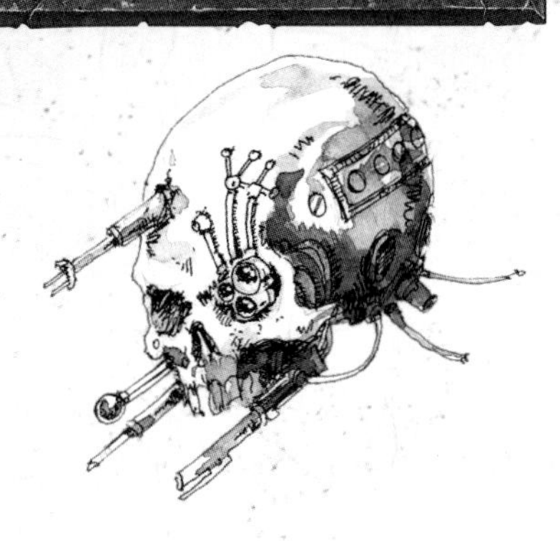

Although beasts generally do not shoot, cavalry frequently can. They follow the same rules as infantry when they do so.

ASSAULT PHASE

Beasts and cavalry are capable of making an especially fast charge to assault their enemies. When charging they move 12". They are slowed by difficult terrain – roll for the distance they can move just as you would for infantry, but double the result. Otherwise they assault exactly as infantry would.

MORALE

Beasts and cavalry fall back 3D6" due to their speed.

VEHICLES

This section of the rules describes how vehicles larger than bikes move and fight. Vehicle rules have to work differently from those for infantry in order to show their unique strengths and weaknesses. Vehicles can move swiftly and bring a tremendous arsenal of weapons to bear while infantry fire patters harmlessly off their armoured shell. That said, a determined infantry squad with the right weapons can use dense terrain to outmanoeuvre ponderous vehicles and can easily knock them out unless the vehicles have their own infantry to guard them.

VEHICLE CHARACTERISTICS

Vehicles have characteristics that define how powerful they are in a similar way that troops do. However, as vehicles do not fight in the same way as creatures of flesh and blood their characteristics are different. Vehicle characteristics are as follows:

	Type	Front Armour	Side Armour	Rear Armour	BS
Leman Russ	Tank	14	12	10	3

TYPE

Vehicles come in all sorts of different types, some are faster than others while some are able to fly or walk instead of driving along on wheels or tracks. Any special traits a vehicle has are described by its type. The different types are Fast, Tank, Open-topped, Skimmer and Walker. These traits can be combined to define, for example, a Fast Skimmer or an Open-topped Walker.

ARMOUR VALUE

The Armour Value of a vehicle tells you how hard it is to damage. Vehicles have separate Armour Values to represent their protection on their front, sides and rear. Armour Values typically range from 10 to 14, depending on which side of the vehicle is being attacked, usually with the lightest armour on the rear to represent vulnerable fuel cells, engine compartments, etc.

BALLISTIC SKILL

Vehicles have a BS value just like troops and it represents the accuracy of the crew as they blast away at their enemy with the vehicle's weapons.

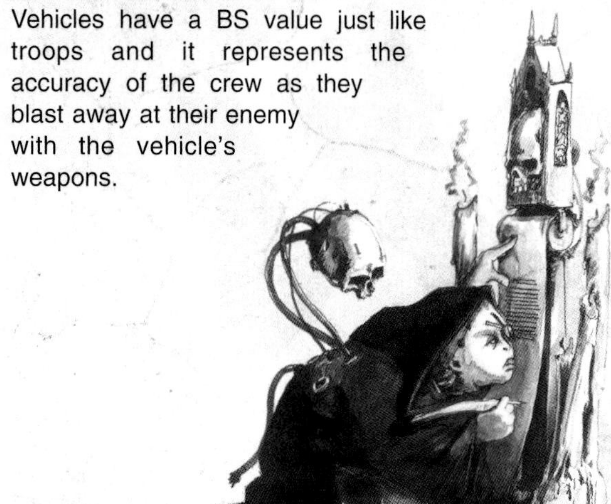

TRANSPORT CAPACITY

Some vehicles are capable of carrying infantry models inside them. The transport capacity tells how many approximately human-sized infantry can be carried.

FIRE POINTS

If a vehicle is not open-topped, the Fire Points characteristic tells you how many passengers can fire their weapons through slits or hatches while inside the vehicle.

ADDITIONAL CHARACTERISTICS

Some vehicles, most commonly Walkers, will also have a Weapon Skill, Strength and Attacks value representing its ability in close combat and an Initiative value denoting its reaction speed, in the same way as they would for normal troops. The profile for a Walker looks like this:

		Armour							
	Type	F	S	R	WS	BS	S	I	A
Dreadnought	Walker	12	12	10	4	4	6(10)	4	2

ACCESS POINTS

A vehicle's access points specify where passengers can embark and disembark from – typically via hatches or ramps shown on the model itself.

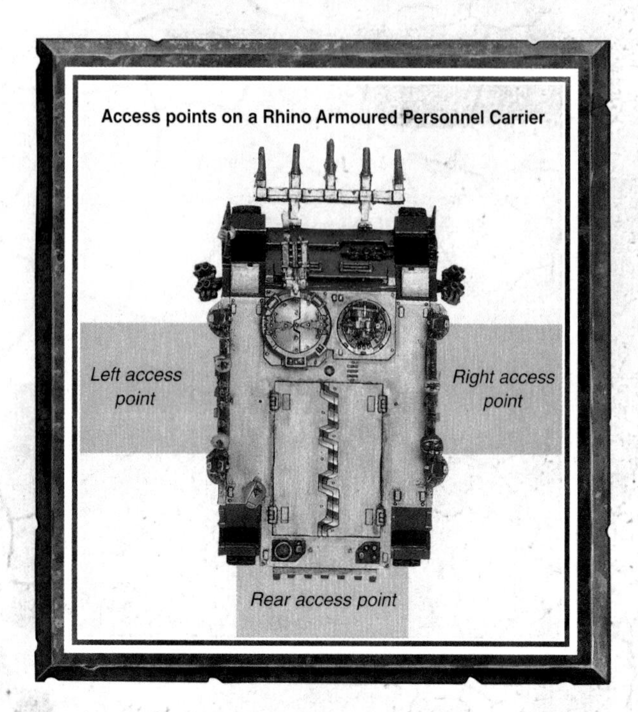

VEHICLE TYPES

OPEN-TOPPED VEHICLES

Some vehicles are not fully enclosed, but expose their crews to a hostile universe. There are many reasons for this – to give reconnaissance units a good field of vision, make embarking and disembarking passengers easier, or it may simply be impractical to enclose the crew. While crews and embarked passengers on open-topped vehicles have more freedom of movement and better arcs of vision, the lack of an enclosed crew space inevitably means that they and their vehicle are more vulnerable to incoming fire.

FAST VEHICLES

Most of the fastest vehicles on the battlefield are skimmers, such as Space Marine Land Speeders. These are able to avoid terrain which would slow down conventional vehicles. However, a few wheeled or tracked vehicles are also capable of high speeds and are classed as Fast Vehicles, mostly due to either their light weight or extremely powerful engines.

WALKERS

On any battlefield, there are places where conventional vehicles cannot go – built-up areas, dense forests, narrow tunnels, and so on. For this reason, many armies use vehicles that are propelled by two, or sometimes more, mechanical legs. These vehicles are usually capable of carrying as many weapon systems as a tank on a significantly smaller and lighter chassis. They combine the armour and weaponry of a tank with the manoeuvrability of an infantryman.

SKIMMERS

While most vehicles travel across the ground on wheels, tracks or legs, some advanced machines are fitted with jets or anti-gravity drives that enable them to swoop and hover a few metres above the battlefield. This is not true flight, but rather a limited version of it. Often skimmers will also be categorised as Fast but this is not always the case.

TANKS

Tanks are a common sight on the battlefields of the 41st millennium. Most races field some kind of heavily armed and armoured vehicle, whether it be the huge and lumbering Leman Russ battle tanks of the Imperial Guard, or the sleek and sophisticated grav-tanks of the Eldar. Tanks are often fitted for multi-role capability which will commonly include troop transportation, tank-hunting capability and infantry support.

THOUGHT FOR THE DAY: IF YOU CANNOT SPEAK WELL OF YOUR MASTER, BE SILENT!

VEHICLE MOVEMENT

Many armoured vehicles are fitted with powerful engines, allowing them to cover open ground more quickly than infantry, ensuring that their mighty guns can get to where they are needed on the battlefield. Other highly advanced vehicles are fitted with anti-gravity drives that allow them to skim swiftly over rough terrain to launch unexpected attacks, while some vehicles stride forwards on mechanical limbs, ploughing through densely packed terrain with ease in order to bring their weapons to bear.

Most vehicles can move up to 12" in the Movement phase. This is relatively slow, but it represents a cross-country speed rather than moving flat out. However, some vehicles will want to move even slower in order to use their weapons (see later). Normally vehicles can only move in the Movement phase, but walkers can move in both the Movement phase and the Assault phase just as infantry can.

Vehicles can turn any number of times as they move, just like any other model. Vehicles turn by pivoting on the spot about their centre-point, rather than 'wheeling' round. Turning does not reduce the vehicle's move, but once the Movement phase is over they can only make turns as described in the Shooting phase, to bring weapons to bear if they have not actually moved in the Movement phase. This means that a vehicle may combine forward and reverse movement in the same turn providing it does not exceed its maximum move.

FAST VEHICLES

Some vehicles are notably fast either because of their light construction or powerful engines – or both. Fast vehicles can move up to 24" in the Movement phase.

TERRAIN EFFECTS

Vehicles that move out of, into or through difficult terrain risk becoming stuck, bogged down or something similar. Skimmers and walkers are handled differently and are explained later. Other vehicles must make a Dangerous Terrain test. Note that when categorising terrain it is perfectly permissible to categorise terrain as being difficult, dangerous or impassable to vehicle units but not to non-vehicle units.

DANGEROUS TERRAIN TESTS FOR VEHICLES

These tests are taken whenever a vehicle attempts to enter difficult terrain or to move through or out of it. If the test is failed the vehicle halts immediately. If it was attempting to enter difficult terrain it stops just outside. If a vehicle has moved up to 6" the test is taken on a single D6, otherwise it is taken on two D6. If any dice rolls a 1 the test is failed and the vehicle is immobilised for the rest of the game (or until repaired where appropriate), while a 2-6 means it can carry on moving. If both dice roll a 1 the vehicle is tipped over or irretrievably bogged down and counts as destroyed (note: See the Damage tables for effects on passengers if any are carried). It follows then that a vehicle cannot be destroyed by a Dangerous Terrain test unless it attempts to move across difficult ground at high speed.

SKIMMERS

Skimmers are capable of making a powered boost to gain height and cross obstacles. As such, skimmers ignore terrain altogether when they move and can even end their move hovering over difficult or impassable terrain (but not over other models). Conversely, mobile skimmers never count obscured target benefits from terrain they are hovering over, instead relying on speed for their protection.

WALKERS

All walkers move in exactly the same way as infantry, so they can move up to 6" in the Movement phase and then charge up to 6" in the Assault phase if the enemy are within range. Difficult terrain affects walkers just as it does infantry – moving into, out of or through difficult terrain requires a roll of two D6, using the highest result as the maximum distance they may move that turn. If walkers fail a Dangerous Terrain test, they are immobilised.

ROADS

Vehicles – with the exception of walkers and skimmers – that follow a road for their entire Movement phase (including entering along it if coming from reserve) may add 6" to their maximum speed. They do not gain this benefit if any of the following apply: Difficult Terrain tests, shooting, embark or disembark passengers, performing Tank Shock, or the use of any vehicle upgrades (such as smoke launchers or searchlights). In essence the vehicle must concentrate on moving down the road and nothing else.

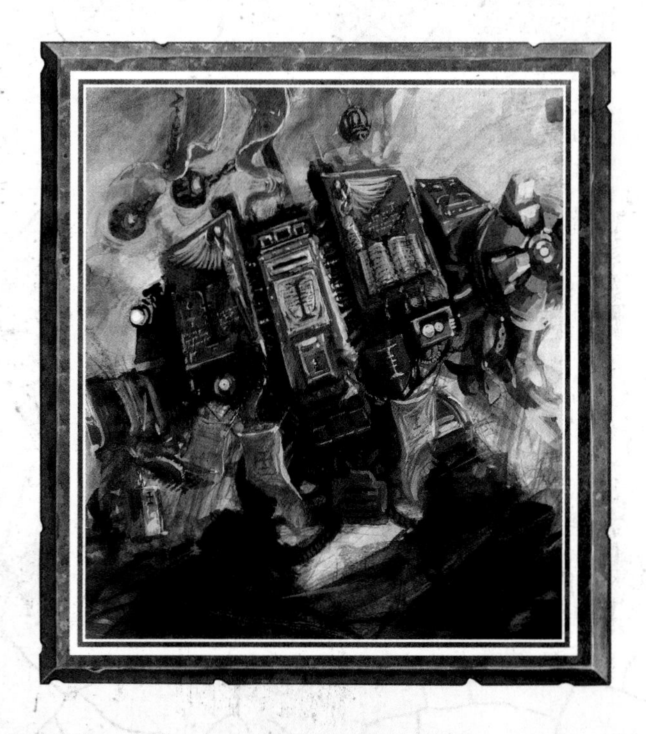

TRANSPORT VEHICLES

Some vehicles can carry infantry across the battlefield, and the advantages of being able to move a squad rapidly from one area to another under the protection of armour plate is obvious. The danger comes if the transport itself is destroyed before its passengers disembark, as they could become smoking corpses, burned alive inside the exploding vehicle.

PASSENGER CAPACITY

Each transport vehicle has a maximum passenger capacity which cannot be exceeded. Sometimes, there will be constraints on which types of models can embark on a particular vehicle. Terminators, for example, cannot embark on a Rhino or Razorback, although they may be transported by a Land Raider. Only infantry may embark in transports unless the transporting vehicle's rules specify otherwise.

WHO CAN USE A TRANSPORT VEHICLE?

Sometimes a unit entry in a Codex book will include a transport option, allowing a vehicle to be selected along with the unit. These transport vehicles are directly assigned to that particular unit and are known as dedicated transports. Other transport vehicles are chosen separately and occupy a Force Organisation chart slot (for example, Eldar Falcons), and can be used to provide ad hoc transportation to any unit that can embark on it.

Dedicated transports may only be used to transport the squad they are selected with plus any independent characters that have joined the squad (provided there is room in the transport, of course). An independent character may disembark and leave the unit still embarked, but if the unit disembarks then any independent characters must as well.

No more than one unit (plus any independent characters that have joined it) can be embarked on a transport. The entire unit must be embarked on a transport if any part of it is – a unit may never be spread across multiple transport vehicles.

ACCESS POINTS

Each vehicle capable of carrying passengers will have a number of 'access points'. These are the doors, ramps and hatches that passengers use to get in and out of the vehicle. The access points for all official vehicles on publication of these rules are given in the appendix. Open-topped vehicles do not have specific access points. Models can embark or disembark within 2" of any point of the vehicle.

EMBARKING & DISEMBARKING

Infantry may not voluntarily embark and disembark in the same player turn. However, they may embark and then be forced to disembark due to damage caused to their transport, or be subject to a special rule in their codex that permits them to do so. Models can only voluntarily embark or disembark in the Movement phase.

EMBARKING

A unit can embark onto a vehicle by moving each model to within 2" of its access points in the Movement phase. The whole unit must be able to embark or none of them can. If some models are out of range, their compatriots will have to wait until they can all embark together.

- If the vehicle moved before its passengers got aboard then it may not move any further or make any turns.

- If the vehicle has not moved before its passengers got aboard then it can move normally, as soon as the unit is on board.

DISEMBARKING

A unit that begins its Movement phase aboard a vehicle can get out either before or after the vehicle has moved. When the unit disembarks, each model must be deployed within 2" of one of the vehicle's access points, and within unit coherency.

- If the vehicle has already moved, the passengers move only far enough to deploy, and cannot disembark at all if the vehicle moved more than 12". Once the models have disembarked, the vehicle may not move any further or make any turns.

- If the vehicle has not yet moved then the passengers may move as normal after disembarking, the vehicle can then move off separately at up to full speed.

Passengers aboard a vehicle cannot disembark within 1" of an enemy model. If compelled to disembark (eg, because of the vehicle being destroyed), any models that cannot disembark because there is no room for them to disembark into are killed and removed from play as casualties. After disembarking, models may shoot (counting as moving) but may not assault unless the vehicle has 'open-topped' noted in its profile, is a Land Raider (or one of its variants) or did not move before the passengers disembarked.

When the unit embarks or disembarks, each model must be within 2" of one of the vehicle's access points, and within unit coherency.

VEHICLES AND SHOOTING

Many vehicles, particularly tanks, are able to bear massive weapons that are easily capable of smashing apart bunkers, annihilating enemy troops and making smoking wrecks of other vehicles. In terms of destructive power, vehicles are amongst the most powerful tools in a commander's arsenal. Nevertheless, some vehicles will need to sacrifice their speed in order to fully utilise their immense firepower, thus requiring some tactical forethought for effective use.

When a vehicle fires, it normally uses its own BS characteristic (representing the BS of the crew) and shoots like other units – all its weapons must fire at a single target unit. Vehicles can fire weapons on the move but they are limited in the number of larger weapons that they can fire.

VEHICLE WEAPONRY

Vehicles can mount a frightening array of weapons. These can be divided into four categories:

- Ordnance weapons
- Ordnance Barrage weapons
- Main weapons (Strength 7 or greater)
- Defensive weapons (Strength 6 or less)

Details of these weapons are as laid down in the Weapons section of the rules.

Any weapon of Strength 6 or below that is mounted on a vehicle is called a **defensive weapon**, whilst those of Strength 7 or greater are known as **main weapons**. If a weapon has a variable Strength rating, the Strength used that turn determines which category it belongs to. For example, a missile launcher would count as a main weapon if firing krak (S8) but as a defensive weapon if firing frag (S4).

How many main and defensive weapons a vehicle can fire in a turn depends on how fast it moves. The normal restrictions for infantry moving, shooting and assaulting don't apply to weapons fitted to vehicles (including add-ons like Hunter-Killer missiles and pintle-mounted guns). This means that vehicle-mounted rapid fire and heavy weapons always count as stationary even if the vehicle moves and don't prevent a walker that fires them from charging in the following Assault phase.

MOVING & SHOOTING VEHICLE WEAPONRY

The table below shows what weapons can be fired by each type of vehicle at each speed. Fast vehicles may not mount ordnance weapons and so may never fire them.

VEHICLES MOVING & SHOOTING

Type	Stationary	Up to 6"	Up to 12"	More than 12"
Any vehicle that is neither Fast nor a Walker	All main and defensive weapons OR 1 ordnance weapon OR 1 ordnance barrage weapon	1 main weapon and all defensive weapons OR 1 ordnance weapon	No weapons	Not applicable
Fast Vehicle	All main and defensive weapons	All main and defensive weapons	1 main weapon and all defensive weapons	No weapons
Walker	All main and defensive weapons OR 1 ordnance weapon OR 1 ordnance barrage weapon	2 main or defensive weapons OR 1 ordnance weapon	Not applicable	Not applicable

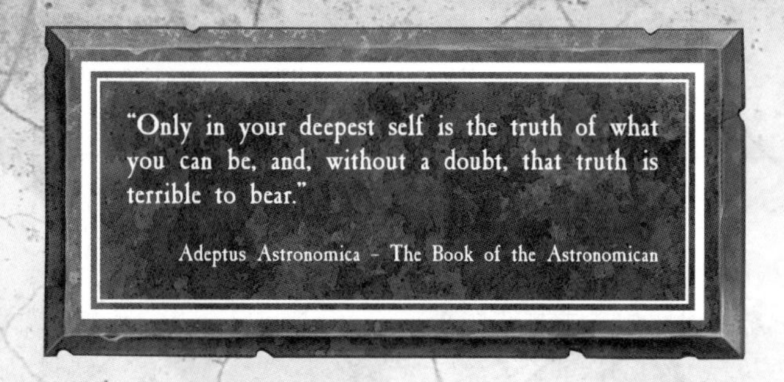

CHOOSING A TARGET

Vehicles enjoy the advantage of being able to automatically pass the Leadership test required to target enemy units other than the closest. This might be due to their additional height, better sights, sensors, tighter fire control or other targeting improvements.

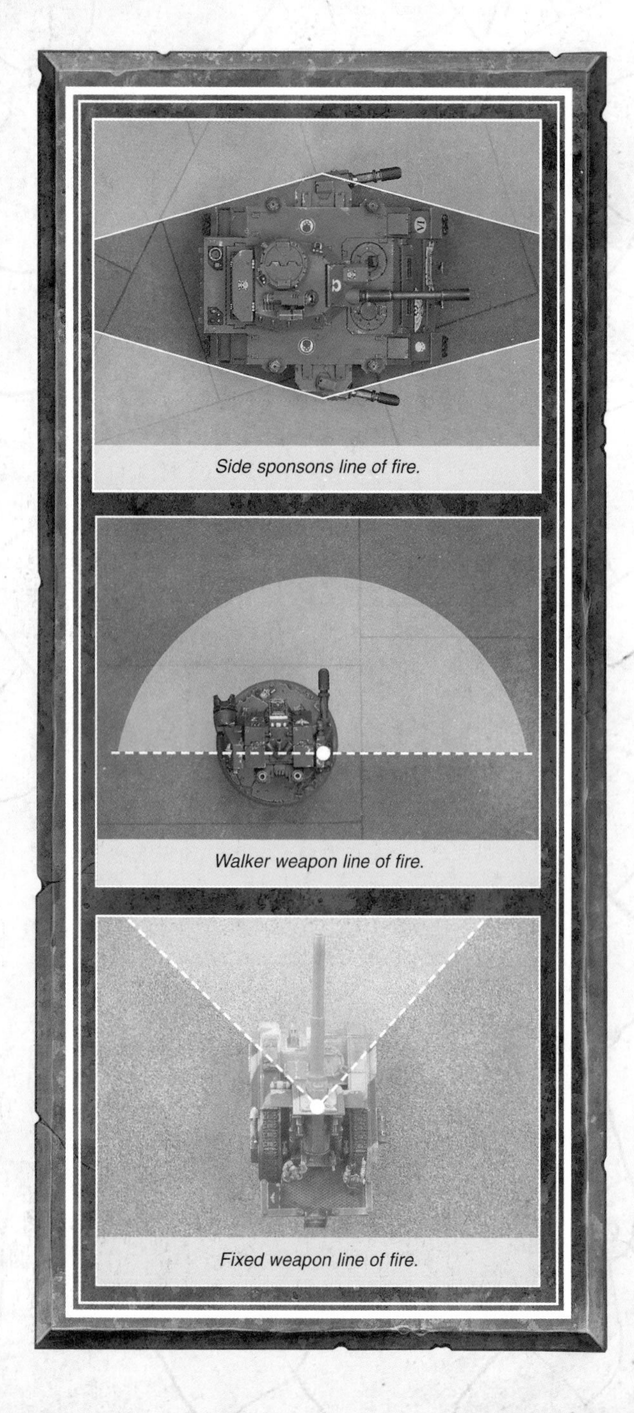

Side sponsons line of fire.

Walker weapon line of fire.

Fixed weapon line of fire.

TURNING TO FACE

Many vehicles have turrets that can swivel around to engage targets that the vehicle is not necessarily facing towards. Turrets can be turned to face without it counting as movement.

Any vehicle that is not immobilised, and did not move in the Movement phase, can pivot on the spot in the Shooting phase before they shoot without counting it as movement, so they can fire as if they were stationary.

FIRING MAIN & DEFENSIVE WEAPONRY

The rules for firing a vehicle's main and defensive weapons are the same as for firing the same types of weapons by infantry – you roll to hit, roll to wound and then make Saving throws as appropriate.

VEHICLE LINE OF SIGHT

Just like infantry, vehicles need to be able to draw a line of sight to their targets in order to shoot at them. Vehicles trace their line of sight for shooting directly from the weapon mountings. Weapons mounted on vehicles often have a limited arc of fire and may not fire on units that are outside this arc. Trace the actual line of fire from the weapon mounting to see if it will be blocked by terrain or other vehicles. Weapons mounted on walkers can fire in a 180º forward arc. Fixed weapons have a 90º fire arc from their mounting point.

FIRE POINTS

Each vehicle that can carry troops and is not classed as open-topped may have a number of fire points defined. A fire point is a hatch or gun slit from which one or more passengers inside the vehicle can fire.

INFANTRY FIRING FROM VEHICLES

Infantry aboard vehicles can fire from firing slits, hatches or over the sides of the fighting compartment if the vehicle is open-topped. All of the models aboard an open-topped vehicle can fire. Troops in a closed top vehicle, however, can only fire from designated fire points.

Infantry firing from a vehicle count as moving if the vehicle moves, and may not fire at all if the vehicle moves faster than 12". This means they may not fire heavy weapons from a moving vehicle unless normally allowed to fire heavy weapons while moving.

If passengers fire from a closed vehicle and any of them do not have a Saving throw of 2+ or 3+ (using the best of Armour Save and Invulnerable Save), then in the following player turn, enemy firing at or assaulting the vehicle count it as open-topped to represent the chance of hitting exposed passengers and the hits passing into the vehicle. This rule does not apply to the firing weapons built onto a vehicle, such as the Chimera's lasguns, or a pintle-mounted storm bolter, for example.

CHOOSING A VEHICLE AS A TARGET

Any of your units can choose the closest vehicle as a target. Just as when shooting at infantry, they may take a Leadership test to fire at one further away. When a unit fires at a vehicle it must direct all of its shooting at it. Often this means that some of their weapons can't damage it, so we assume that the other members of the squad are giving covering fire, bringing forward ammunition for heavy weapons or simply keeping their heads down. If one of your unit's shooting forces the passengers aboard an enemy vehicle to disembark during your Shooting phase, they may be shot at by units that have not yet fired in that Shooting phase.

Roll to hit against vehicles in the same way as you would against other units. If any hits are scored you then roll for each to see if they penetrate the vehicle's Armour Value, as explained later. Vehicles with a Weapon Skill characteristic that are engaged cannot be shot at.

VEHICLE ARMOUR VALUES

Not all vehicles are equally armoured. Some massive tanks are protected by countless layers of reinforced adamantium and ceramite plates, while other lighter vehicles rely more on their speed to avoid incoming fire. As such, each different type of vehicle will have different Armour Values, representing not just the thickness and slope of its armour, but also how difficult a target it is because of its size and speed, how tough and numerous its crew are, and so on. Armour Values for individual vehicles also vary depending on whether the shot comes from the front, sides, or rear.

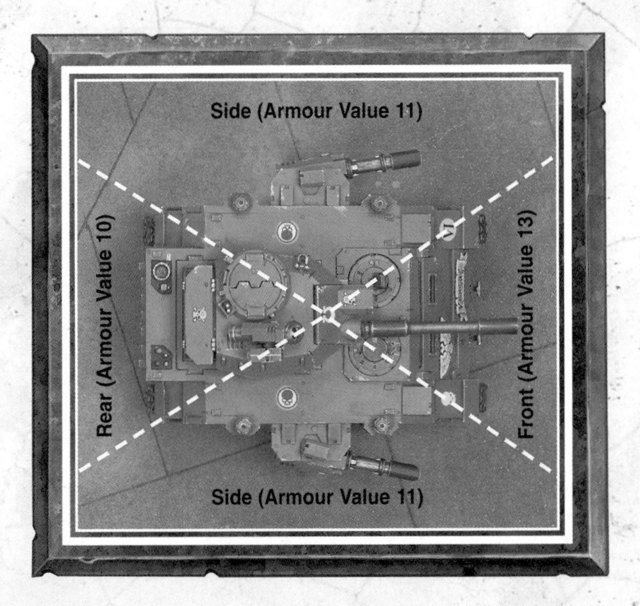

• If the hole in the middle of the Blast marker is not over the vehicle but the Blast marker is, then the Strength of the shot is halved (rounding fractions down).

• When a vehicle is hit by a non-barrage weapon with a Blast marker or Large Blast marker (including Ordnance), the shot is always assumed to strike the vehicle from the direction of the firer regardless of exactly where the marker is placed or scattered to.

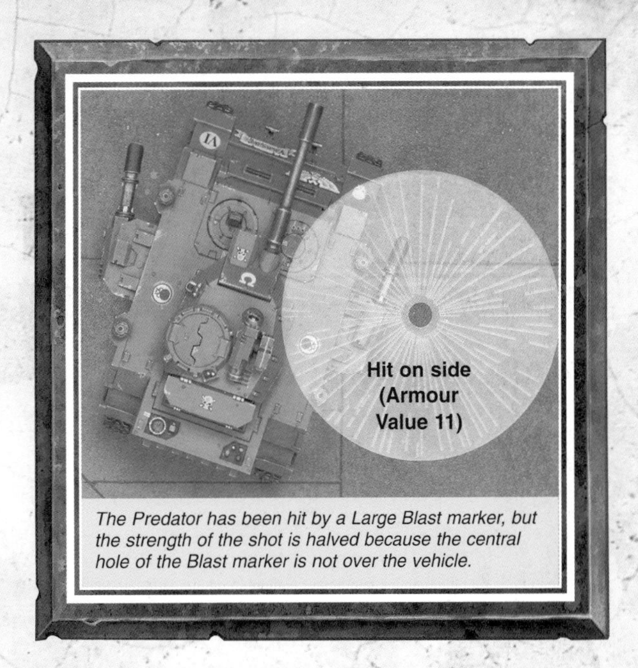

The Predator has been hit by a Large Blast marker, but the strength of the shot is halved because the central hole of the Blast marker is not over the vehicle.

• In the case of a barrage weapon of any kind, if the hole in the middle of the Blast marker ends over the vehicle, the shot is assumed to hit the side of the vehicle that faces the firer, otherwise the attack is assumed to hit the vehicle from the direction of the hole in the Blast marker. Thus a barrage shot landing behind a vehicle may hit the rear armour but will be at half strength.

ARMOUR PENETRATION

Hitting a vehicle is no guarantee that you will actually damage it. Once a hit has been scored on a vehicle, roll a D6 and add the weapon's Strength characteristic to it, comparing this total against the vehicle's Armour Value.

• If the total is **less** than the vehicle's Armour Value, the shot has no effect.

• If the total is **equal** to the vehicle's Armour Value, the shot causes a glancing hit.

• If the total is **greater** than the vehicle's Armour Value, the shot scores a penetrating hit.

Example: *A lascannon shot hits the front of a Space Marine Predator with an Armour Value of 13. Rolling a D6, the player scores a 4, and adds this to the lascannon's Strength of 9, for a total of 13. Because this equals the Armour Value of the Predator, the shot inflicts a glancing hit.*

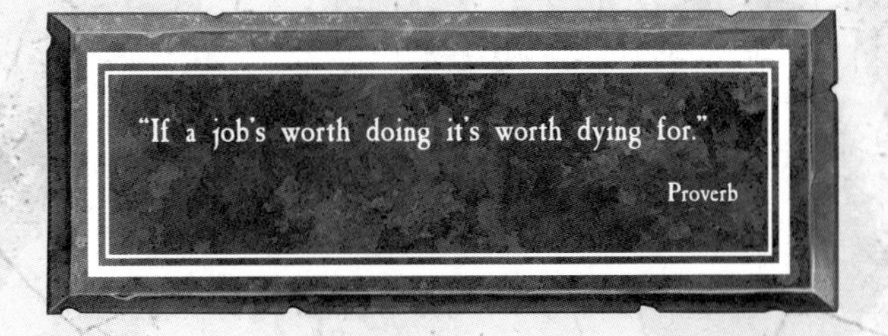

"If a job's worth doing it's worth dying for."
Proverb

"If I have strayed from the path of obedience it is only to follow the most sacred of all directions, those of the Emperor himself, for is it not written in the Book of the Astronomican, 'A true servant follows his Master if he listens to the heart and not the head.'"

The Trial of Sebastian Thor

ORDNANCE WEAPONS

Ordnance weapons fire such enormous projectiles that they can smash through armour or hit with such force that the target vehicle's crew are turned to mush. When you roll to penetrate a vehicle's armour with an ordnance weapon, you get to roll two D6 instead of one, and pick the highest result. Note that as Ordnance can be so destructively powerful, if these weapons manage to penetrate the armour of a vehicle you use the Ordnance Penetrating Hit table rather than the normal Penetrating Hit table.

'AP 1' WEAPONS & ARMOUR PENETRATION

Some weapons are so effective at cutting through armour that they will penetrate a vehicle's heavily armoured sides with ease. AP 1 weapons, such as multi-meltas, score penetrating hits even when they equal the target's Armour Value, instead of scoring glancing hits as normal. This can be still be reduced back to a glancing hit due to the target being obscured, (see Obscured Targets and Glancing Hits) or by a weapon's own special rules (for example, the Eldar Wraithcannon).

'AP -' WEAPONS & ARMOUR PENETRATION

While some weapons are especially good at cutting through heavily armoured targets, other weapons have great difficulty. A weapon shown as 'AP -' lacks the penetrating power to destroy a vehicle easily, and can only ever score glancing hits.

DAMAGE ROLLS

A hit on a vehicle can have a variety of results. A vehicle's armour could be completely pierced, yet merely result in giving the crew a nasty shock. Alternatively, a lucky shot could detonate ammunition held within the vehicle, resulting in an explosion of titanic proportions. If a vehicle's armour is breached, you need to determine what damage is caused. Roll a D6 for each shot that glanced or penetrated the vehicle's armour and look up the result on the appropriate Damage table below. Note that there are separate tables for glancing, penetrating and ordnance hits.

GLANCING HIT
(S+D6 ROLL EQUALS ARMOUR VALUE)

D6	Result
1-2	Crew shaken
3	Crew stunned
4	Armament destroyed
5	Immobilised
6	Vehicle destroyed!

PENETRATING HIT
(S+D6 ROLL BEATS ARMOUR VALUE)

D6	Result
1	Crew stunned
2	Armament destroyed & Crew stunned
3	Immobilised & Crew stunned
4	Vehicle destroyed!
5	Vehicle destroyed!
6	Vehicle explodes!

ORDNANCE PENETRATING HIT
(ORDNANCE BEATS ARMOUR VALUE)

D6	Result
1	Crew stunned
2	Armament destroyed & Crew stunned
3	Immobilised & Crew stunned
4	Vehicle destroyed!
5	Vehicle explodes!
6	Vehicle annihilated!

DAMAGE RESULTS

CREW SHAKEN

The vehicle is rocked by the attack, but no serious damage is sustained. The vehicle may not shoot next turn. Passengers may not shoot from within the vehicle next turn, but are otherwise unaffected.

CREW STUNNED

The vehicle is seriously knocked about by the attack, scrambling targeting information and temporarily losing control. The vehicle may not move or shoot next turn. Passengers may not shoot from within the vehicle next turn, but are otherwise unaffected.

Note: *Additional Stunned and Shaken results are not cumulative, so if a vehicle is shaken three times it is still only unable to fire in its next turn, not its next three turns.*

ARMAMENT DESTROYED

One of the vehicle's weapons is ripped off by the force of the attack. A weapon of S4 or greater (chosen by the attacker) is destroyed. If a vehicle has no eligible weapons left, treat this result as an Immobilised result instead. This can include vehicle upgrades that function as weapons, such as pintle-mounted storm bolters or Hunter-Killer missiles.

IMMOBILISED

The vehicle has taken a hit that has crippled a wheel, track, grav plate, jet or leg. It may not move for the rest of the game. An immobilised vehicle may not turn in place but its turret (if it has one) may continue to rotate to select targets, and other weapons retain their normal arc of fire. Further Immobilised results count as armament destroyed instead.

Skimmers that are immobilised immediately crash, and are destroyed if they moved more than 6" in their last turn, or are over impassable or difficult terrain. Otherwise they make a forced landing where they are and remain immobilised for the rest of the game, no longer counting as a skimmer.

Note: *A vehicle which suffers an Immobilised or Armament Destroyed result when it has no S4 or greater weapons left, and is already immobilised, counts the result as a Vehicle Destroyed! result instead.*

VEHICLE DESTROYED!

The attack critically damages the vehicle. The vehicle is destroyed and becomes a wreck.

VEHICLE EXPLODES!

The vehicle's fuel and ammo detonate, ripping the vehicle apart in a spectacular explosion. Flaming debris is scattered D6" in every direction, measured from the vehicle's edges. Models in range suffer 1 wound on a roll of 4+ (Saving throws are allowed), but other vehicles struck by this flaming debris are unaffected. The exploded vehicle is removed and should be replaced with an area of difficult ground representing scattered wreckage or a crater.

VEHICLE ANNIHILATED!

The vehicle is completely destroyed in an immense detonation, and red-hot fragments of armour, engine and weaponry are sent scything out in all directions. The resultant explosion will kill all passengers carried, with no Saving throws of any sort allowed. In addition, a 6" area is measured from the edges of the vehicle. Any models within range suffer 1 wound on a roll of 4+ (Saving throws are allowed), but other vehicles are unaffected. The annihilated vehicle is removed and should be replaced with an area of difficult ground representing scattered wreckage or a crater.

Note: *Vehicle drivers, gunners and other crew are considered killed if their vehicle is destroyed, explodes or is annihilated.*

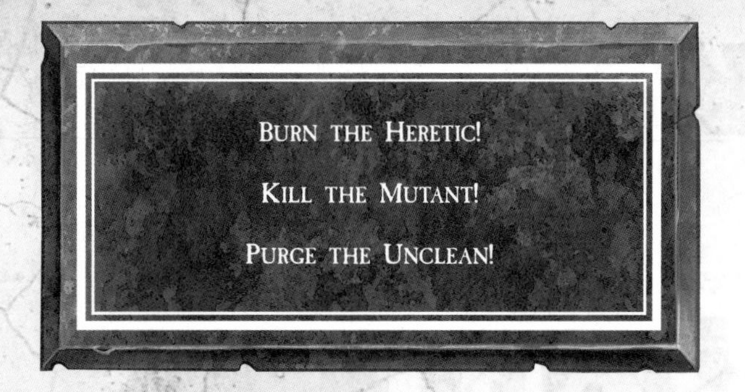

DAMAGE TO PASSENGERS

Passengers carried aboard a vehicle that is destroyed or suffers a Penetrating hit (no matter what the result) will try to get out of the steel coffin as quickly as possible. The passengers must make an immediate disembarkation move. In addition, they may also suffer casualties and/or be pinned as a result. This is explained in the table below.

ENTANGLED

Being involved in a vehicle crash due to weapons fire is extremely unpleasant. It will take the survivors some time to pull themselves clear of the wreckage and prepare to fight again. To represent this, an entangled unit is treated exactly the same as being pinned (see page 32). This applies to all passengers whether or not they could normally be pinned.

Once disembarked, passengers may be shot at by subsequent firing units and may be assaulted as normal.

WRECKS

Unless stated otherwise, a wrecked vehicle should be marked with some cotton wool smoke and flames and left on the table. It continues to block line of sight as if it were intact but counts as difficult terrain for infantry movement. It counts as difficult terrain for vehicles with a higher frontal armour but is impassable terrain for other vehicles. It provides a 4+ Cover Save for models on top of it or looking around it.

OPEN-TOPPED VEHICLES

Some vehicles are more vulnerable to damage than others because of their lightweight construction and the fact that their crew is exposed to enemy fire. A typical example of an open-topped vehicle is an Ork Wartrak or War Buggy. Whenever a Damage roll (glancing or penetrating) is made against an open-topped vehicle, add 1 to the Damage result. All open-topped vehicles have the Vulnerable to Blasts/Templates special rule.

OBSCURED TARGET & GLANCING HITS

A vehicle moving especially fast or behind cover, whether naturally or artificially generated, will be harder to destroy. Remember that successful firing at a vehicle effectively means carefully picking a target spot, and an obscured target denies this opportunity. The exact circumstances are detailed later.

EMERGENCY DISEMBARKATION TABLE

	The vehicle's last move was up to 6"	**The vehicle's last move was more than 6"**
Vehicle suffers a penetrating hit but does not explode and is not wrecked	Passengers do not suffer wounds. The disembarked passengers must take a normal Pinning test (see page 32).	Roll one D6 for each passenger. Each score of 4+ inflicts an automatic wound. Saves may be taken as normal. The disembarked passengers must take a normal Pinning test (see page 32).
Vehicle explodes or is wrecked	Roll one D6 for each passenger. Each score of 4+ inflicts an automatic wound. Saves may be taken as normal. The disembarked passengers are entangled (see above).	Roll one D6 for each passenger. Each score of 4+ inflicts an automatic wound. Any rolls of less than 4 must be re-rolled. Saves may be taken as normal. The disembarked passengers are entangled (see above).

SKIMMERS MOVING FAST

Moving skimmers are very difficult to hit squarely because they are more agile than other vehicles, and most shots are more likely to 'wing' them instead. Any hits that beat the Armour Value of a mobile skimmer moving more than 6" in its last Movement phase count as glancing hits instead of penetrating hits. In order to qualify as moving more than 6", the skimmer must end its move more than 6" from where it started the turn. Players may not claim their skimmers are 'circling' or moving 4" one way and 3" back. Skimmers are dependent on their speed and agility for avoiding enemy fire, and adequate velocity cannot be attained while circling.

OBSCURED TARGETS

Vehicles do not benefit from cover in the same way as infantry – their sheer size means that they will be relatively easy to hit. They can position themselves in such a way as to make it harder for the enemy to hit them in a vulnerable location. This is sometimes known as being 'hull down', and counts as an Obscured Target.

When firing on a vehicle, check that the firing models have a clear view of the whole surface (front, side or rear) of the vehicle that they are firing at.

If at least 50% of the side they are firing at is obscured by intervening terrain, or by other vehicles, artillery models, wrecks or Monstrous Creatures, then the target is classed as being obscured. Similarly, when the firer's view of a vehicle passes through an Area Terrain feature that is taller than Size 1, its view is also obscured.

If the target is obscured and a penetrating hit is scored, the vehicle's owner rolls a D6 – on a roll of 4+, the penetrating hit is downgraded to a glancing hit.

Obscured Targets: *The Predator is an obscured target and will downgrade any penetrating hits from the Vyper to glancing hits on a roll of 4+.*

SMOKE LAUNCHERS

Some vehicles have small launchers mounted onto them that carry smoke charges (or a more sophisticated equivalent in the case of some alien vehicles). These are used to temporarily hide the vehicle behind concealing clouds of smoke especially if it is moving out into the open.

Once per game, after completing its move, a vehicle with smoke launchers can trigger them (it doesn't matter how far it moved). Place some cotton wool around the vehicle to show it is concealed. The vehicle may not fire any of its weapons in the same turn as it used its smoke launchers, but any penetrating hits scored by the enemy in their next Shooting phase count as glancing hits instead.

After the enemy's turn, the smoke disperses with no further effect. Note that a vehicle may still use smoke launchers even if its crew are shaken or stunned.

VEHICLES AND ASSAULTS

Vehicles can be both very dangerous and very vulnerable at close quarters. On one hand, massively armoured vehicles can scatter infantry before them, as no one in their right mind would wish to be caught beneath the tracks of an eighty tonne tank bearing down on them! On the other hand, a stationary vehicle can often be very easily destroyed, as individuals clamber over it, attaching all manner of grenades and shooting into visions slits.

SKIMMERS

Skimmers can always choose to move over enemy troops and this neither impedes their movement nor harms the troops below. Enemy troops can attack skimmers in the Assault phase, as close combat takes into account close range shooting and grenade lobbing as well as actual hand-to-hand combat. Skimmer tanks can still choose to overrun an enemy unit and inflict Tank Shock in the normal manner.

TANK SHOCK

Tanks can overrun enemy units during their Movement phase. Having some monstrous metal behemoth coming straight at you is unnerving for anybody. During their Movement phase, a player can declare that a tank is going to attempt to Tank Shock an enemy unit. If the tank has sufficient movement to get into contact with the unit, the enemy must move aside and infantry may be forced to fall back.

To make a Tank Shock attack you must specify a direction before moving, and may not, after one initial turn, change direction during the move. Next, measure to see if any enemy units will be reached by the tank. If an enemy unit is not reached, just move the vehicle and no Tank Shock takes place. If a unit is overrun by a tank, and individual models would end up underneath the vehicle, they must be moved out of the way by the shortest distance (maintaining unit coherency), but otherwise the unit is unharmed. Vehicles with an equal or higher frontal Armour Value, or that are immobilised, do not have to move, and their presence will effectively stop a Tank Shock at a 1" separation distance. A vehicle that makes way can change its facing when it is moved back into position.

Remember that vehicles cannot move over friendly models, and may not be able to move over wrecks (see the rules for wrecked vehicles).

If an infantry unit has to move models in response to a Tank Shock, it must take a Morale check. Vehicles only have to 'give way' and no check is taken. If an infantry unit fails its Morale check it will fall back, see the Morale rules for details.

DEATH OR GLORY!
If an infantry unit passes its Morale check against Tank Shock, one of its models that is in the vehicle's path can stand and attempt to destroy it rather than move out of the way (this is potentially a rather suicidal thing to do!). Note that a walker can also attempt to halt a Tank Shock using Death or Glory, often with better odds of success. The model nominated for this heroic duty gets one attack at the tank as it heads towards him.

Only one attack is made, so even if the weapon used is Assault 3 or the model is normally allowed more than one Attack – only one attack is resolved in this instance. The attack can be either a shot from a weapon carried by the model, or a single close combat attack using any weapon carried, including grenades (such as krak grenades, melta bombs and haywire grenades). Whatever form it takes, the attack hits automatically, so resolve the hit against the tank's front armour immediately.

If the model **successfully** manages to stun, destroy, explode, annihilate or immobilise the tank, then it grinds to a halt directly in front of the heroic individual.

However, if he **fails** to stop the tank, then the brave (but perhaps rather foolish) glory merchant is crushed by the tank grinding over him – the model is killed regardless of Wounds or armour (invulnerable or not), or any other cunning way of staying alive they can think of. Walkers are crushed utterly (and removed from play) by the tank smashing into them if their Death or Glory attempt fails to stop it. The vehicle may then continue with its Tank Shock – the unit that attempted Death or Glory must give way.

INFANTRY ASSAULTING VEHICLES
Infantry can pose a grave risk to vehicles if they get close enough. With the right weapons, troopers can wreck a vehicle by shooting through vision slits, planting explosive charges on fuel tanks, tearing open hatches to attack crew members or committing some other equally imaginative act of mayhem.

Whilst vehicles can be assaulted by infantry, they cannot be Locked in close combat by them, so when the vehicle's player turn comes around it can simply drive off (unless damage prevents it). Alternatively, it could just remain stationary and blaze away with its weapons at the enemy around it, although this might be rather dangerous when using ordnance or blast weapons!

LAUNCHING AN ASSAULT
A unit can assault a vehicle by charging it in the Assault phase. The charge move is conducted just the same as when assaulting other enemy units. Individual models can only assault the side of the vehicle facing them at the start of their charge.

HITS
Models attack vehicles with the same number of attacks as they would if attacking any other unit – so, a model gets +1 attack for charging, models within 2" of a model in base contact also get to fight, etc. The roll to hit score needed is as follows:

Target	D6 roll needed
Attacking a vehicle that is immobilised or was stationary in its previous turn	Automatic hit
Attacking a vehicle that moved 6" or less in its previous turn	4+
Attacking a vehicle that moved more than 6" in its previous turn	6

A skimmer that is not immobilised always counts as moving more than 6" in its previous turn.

When assessing how far a vehicle has moved, only take into account the actual distance covered, moving forwards and backwards doesn't help!

ARMOUR PENETRATION IN CLOSE COMBAT
Armour Penetration is worked out as normal (D6 + the Strength of the attacker). Note that this means few troops can actually harm vehicles, as even the lightest combat vehicle has an Armour Value of 10.

RESULTS
At the conclusion of a round of close combat against a vehicle with no WS characteristic, there are no sweeping advances or Consolidation moves. The vehicle and the infantry are free to simply move away on future turns.

Models that have assaulted a vehicle with no WS are not classed as Locked, and can therefore be shot at (or through) during the Shooting phase, just bear in mind Blast markers and templates may well hit both sides.

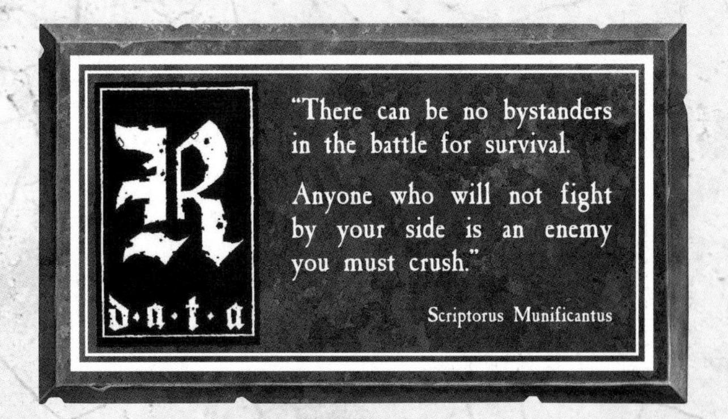

R
d·a·t·a
"There can be no bystanders in the battle for survival.
Anyone who will not fight by your side is an enemy you must crush."
Scriptorus Munificantus

GRENADES

A well placed grenade can often achieve a kill on a vehicle. Specialist tank hunting troops are frequently equipped with melta bombs – fusion based charges which can reduce a battle tank to a burnt-out wreck in milliseconds, or krak grenades, a special type of grenade designed to implode, shattering armour and (hopefully) stopping vehicles in their tracks. Exotic alien equivalents include Eldar haywire grenades.

Grenades have to be clamped or placed so as to inflict enough damage, so each model using them can only make one attack, regardless of the number of Attacks on their profile or any other bonus normally gained in an assault. Grenades can also be used in a Death or Glory attack against a Tank Shock. Against vehicles, grenades have the following Armour Penetration:

Frag/Photon	4+D6 AP
Krak	6+D6 AP
Melta	8+2D6 AP
Plasma	5+D6 AP
Tankbusta	6+(D6x2) AP

WALKERS IN AN ASSAULT

Walkers fight in an assault in the same way as infantry. However, any hits scored against them must roll for armour penetration and damage as for a vehicle. This means that while a walker is quite capable of tearing apart its enemies in close combat, only the specially armed (or monstrously powerful) will have any hope of destroying a walker up close. Models fighting a walker always fight against its front armour, as the walker is not a static target and rampages through the mêlée, turning to face its enemies.

immobilised, shaken and stunned walkers fight in close combat with one less attack than normal (down to a minimum of 1), but otherwise attack normally, no matter how many Immobilised, Stunned and Shaken results they have suffered.

Each roll made on the Vehicle Damage charts against a walker counts as a single wound for the purposes of working out who won the combat.

There is one very important difference about walkers in an assault; walkers never have to take Morale checks, and so will never fall back. If a walker loses a combat, treat the result as a drawn combat instead. The only way to win a close combat involving a walker is to destroy it. However, heavily outnumbered walkers may take additional damage as their enemies scramble all over them – see the No Retreat rule for details (page 48).

USING GRENADES AGAINST WALKERS IN CLOSE COMBAT

Grenades and melta bombs can be used against a walker. A model will only manage to score a hit with a grenade against a walker on a roll of 6. However, if a walker is already stunned or immobilised at the start of the Assault phase, then they attempt to hit based on the normal comparison of WS. Remember that models using grenades against vehicles can only ever make one attack.

PILE IN MOVES

At the end of the Assault phase, a walker must make a reinforcement move just like other models, unless it is immobilised.

SWEEPING ADVANCES & CONSOLIDATION

Walkers may only make a sweeping advance or Consolidation move if they are not stunned or immobilised.

DREADNOUGHT CLOSE COMBAT WEAPONS

Dreadnoughts are often armed with enormous close combat weapons – hammers, wrecking balls, claws, etc. If a Dreadnought is armed with a close combat weapon, it doubles its Strength in close combat (up to a maximum of 10) and ignores Armour Saving throws. A Dreadnought armed with two close combat weapons gains an extra attack, just like ordinary troopers armed with two weapons. If one of its weapons is destroyed, the bonus attack is lost. Further Armament Destroyed results do not affect the walker's Attacks characteristic, but will prevent it gaining the benefits of Dreadnought close combat weapons if that armament is destroyed (so, the Dreadnought will fight at its base Strength, and wounded enemies will be allowed to take their Armour Saves).

VEHICLE MORALE

Vehicles don't normally need to take Morale checks for any reason, whether they are clanking great behemoths or arrow-quick attack craft. It is assumed that in all cases the vehicle's crew has unshakeable faith in both their vehicle, and you as their supreme commander. Any occasional lapses that do occur are represented by shaken and stunned crew damage results.

VEHICLES IN A UNIT (SQUADRON)

Most vehicles fight as individual units and are represented as a single model. However, some vehicles, like Ork Wartraks and Eldar Vypers, often operate in units of more than one vehicle rather like infantry, usually referred to as squadrons, with up to three vehicles in each squadron.

MOVEMENT PHASE

When a squadron of vehicles moves, all mobile squadron members have to move at the same speed, eg, they all move up to 6" or they all move up to 12", etc. All the vehicles have to maintain coherency, just like ordinary troops, but vehicle squadrons need only to remain within 4" of each other to remain in coherency, rather than within 2".

If any of the vehicles in the unit are immobilised or stunned for any reason, the rest of the unit must remain within 4" of them, or choose to abandon them. Any vehicles that are abandoned are left behind and counted as destroyed. It is assumed their crews flee rather than acting as sitting ducks!

A unit of tanks may perform a Tank Shock. If so, move the vehicles one at a time and resolve each in turn. All must move in the same direction and at the same speed. Enemy units that have already passed a Tank Shock Morale test caused by the unit earlier in the turn will pass subsequent tests automatically (and may attempt Death or Glory). It is possible that the squadron may be unable to maintain unit coherency, as some members are stopped by Death or Glory and others aren't. At the end of the move, the owning player must abandon models until the squadron is in unit coherency.

SHOOTING PHASE

When shooting, a unit of vehicles fires all of its available weaponry at a single opposing unit. When a unit of vehicles is fired at, any hits are distributed evenly amongst the vehicles, starting with the nearest vehicle model. No vehicle takes more than one hit until all of the vehicles in the unit have each taken one hit. Once all of the hits have been distributed, roll to penetrate the vehicles' armour and make any Damage rolls as appropriate.

For example, an Ork Trukk fires its big shoota at a squadron of two Vypers, and scores two hits. This is divided between the Vypers, one hit on each, rather than both hits on a single Vyper.

The number of weapons that can be fired by the squadron depends on the movement by the unit as a whole. For determining how many weapons can fire, treat all the vehicles in the squadron as if they had moved at the speed of the vehicle that moved the furthest that turn.

ASSAULT PHASE

When engaged in close combat, enemy units must allocate their attacks between the members of a vehicle squadron, as if each vehicle was a separate unit. Use the movement of individual vehicles to determine how hard they are to hit – this reflects the vulnerability of immobilised and stunned vehicles, even when in a unit.

UNIVERSAL SPECIAL RULES

As the number of Warhammer 40,000 armies has increased through the years, it has become apparent that there are a large number of special rules that are not specific to just a single army, and that these universal special rules really belong here in the Warhammer 40,000 rulebook. The following unit special rules are the definitive versions, and replace special rules of the same name printed in full in Codexes.

The Special Rules marked with an asterisk (*) are automatically lost by an independent character joining a unit that does not have the same special rule. These rules are also lost by a unit that is joined by an independent character that does not have the same special rule.

AND THEY SHALL KNOW NO FEAR

Space Marines automatically pass Morale tests to regroup, and can take such tests even if the squad has been reduced to less than 50% by casualties, though all other criteria apply. If Space Marines are caught by a sweeping advance, they are not destroyed and will instead continue to fight normally. If this happens, then the unit is subject to the No Retreat! rule (see page 48) in this round of close combat and may therefore lose additional casualties if outnumbered. Usually troops that regroup may not move normally and always count as moving whether they do or not, but these restrictions do not apply to models with this special rule.

COUNTER-ATTACK *

Troops with this skill believe that attack is always the best form of defence. If charged, they will spring forward themselves and counter-attack the enemy. To represent this, unengaged models from a unit that has been charged by the enemy must move up to 6" to get into base-to-base contact with the enemy. Treat the counter-attack as you would an Assault move, so take terrain into account as normal. Models that counter-attack do not receive the +1 attack bonus for charging but will be able to fight with their full complement of attacks. You may not counter-attack if the unit was charged as part of a Consolidation move.

FEARLESS

Fearless troops never have to fall back and are assumed to automatically pass any Morale test they are required to take. They can never be pinned. This special rule is gained by any independent character joining a Fearless unit. Also, as long as a Fearless character stays inside a non-Fearless unit, he loses this special rule.

FEEL NO PAIN

Some warriors are so blood-frenzied that they can ignore injuries that would incapacitate even a battle-hardened Space Marine. If a model with this ability loses a wound, roll a dice. On a 1, 2 or 3, take the wound as normal, removing the model if it loses its final wound. On a 4, 5 or 6, the injury is ignored and the model continues fighting. This ability cannot be used against weapons that inflict Instant Death (those with a Strength double or more the model's Toughness) or against close combat weapons that allow no Armour Save (such as power fists, power swords, Dreadnought close combat weapons, rending attacks that roll a 6 to hit, etc).

FLEET *

There are many variants of this rule: Fleet of Foot, Fleet of Claw, even Fleet of Hoof. Title aside, all models with these abilities are treated similarly. In a turn in which models with this rule do not shoot or use a psychic power that replaces shooting, they can move an additional D6" in the Shooting phase, ignoring penalties for difficult terrain.

FURIOUS CHARGE

Models with this skill are known for the wild ferocity of their charges. In a player turn in which they charged into close combat they add +1 to both their Initiative and Strength characteristics. This ability does not affect sweeping advances.

HIT & RUN*

Models with this ability may choose to leave close combat. Declare this at the end of the Close Combat phase. The unit using the Hit & Run ability must be involved in a combat, and will immediately move 3D6" in a straight line in any direction, ignoring the units they are locked with. This move may not be used to move into contact with any enemy models. The break-off move is automatically successful and is not subject to sweeping advance. The enemy can consolidate normally, however.

INFILTRATE *
In the right circumstances, stealthy troops have the ability to work their way into a forward position on the battlefield. To represent this, units with the Infiltrate ability may set up in accordance with the Infiltrate special rule (see page 84) in any mission that uses this special rule (see Organising a Battle). If the mission does not allow troops to use the Infiltrate rule then the troops in question must set up normally with the rest of the army. The Infiltrate ability does not allow units that would normally be in reserve to deploy on the table. If a unit with this ability is equipped with a transport vehicle, it loses the Infiltrate ability.

MOVE THROUGH COVER
Some units of infantry are especially adept at moving through difficult terrain. Accordingly, roll an extra D6 when rolling to move through difficult terrain. In most circumstances this will mean that they roll three D6 and pick the dice with the highest score.

NIGHT VISION/ACUTE SENSES
Warriors in certain parts of the galaxy have developed nocturnal tendencies by fighting in perpetual night, or perhaps carry equipment that gives them such abilities. When the Night Fighting mission special rules are in use, such models may choose to re-roll the test to determine how far they can see, but must abide by the new result. Such troops make excellent sentries and, when used in this role, they have a spotting distance equal to double their Initiative rating.

Characters with this rule confer it onto any unit they join, as long as they are part of the unit. Units with this rule confer it onto any characters joining them, as long as they are part of the unit.

PREFERRED ENEMY
Some warriors are able to predict the moves of the enemies they are used to fighting. In close combat, they have developed special techniques that enable them to counter such enemies more effectively. Such troops will always hit their designated preferred enemy on 3+ in close combat, regardless of the comparative Weapon Skills. This ability will not help when attempting to hit independent characters, monstrous creatures or vehicles without a Weapon Skill characteristic.

SCOUTS*
Scouts are used to reconnoitre ahead and are always in the vanguard of the army. To represent this, any Scouts in the army may be deployed at the start of a battle, even in scenarios where they could not normally be deployed. For example, if you are using a mission variant with the Escalation special rule, then your Scouts would set up at the start of the battle instead of being placed in reserve. In addition to this rule, after both sides have deployed (including Infiltrators), any Scouts may make a 'free move'. The move happens before rolling to see who goes first. All of the normal Movement rules apply.

SKILLED RIDER
The model may re-roll the dice for Dangerous Terrain tests.

SLOW AND PURPOSEFUL
Models with this ability always move as if they were moving through difficult terrain (typically rolling two dice and choosing the best as their movement rate). In addition to this, they are always treated as stationary when shooting, and never receive a bonus attack when charging into close combat.

SMALL TARGETS
Being extremely hard to hit in cover, the unit's Cover Save is improved by +1 if they are in cover.

STEALTH
The ability to make maximum use of available cover has saved many a warrior from discovery and death. The unit's Cover Save is improved by +1 if they are in cover.

STUBBORN
Stubborn resistance against impossible odds is a feature of some races. Stubborn models function as Fearless, except that they still have to test for pinning as normal.

This special rule is gained by any independent character joining a Stubborn unit. Characters that are Stubborn confer the ability onto any unit that they lead, as long as the character is part of the unit.

SWARMS
Swarms represent creatures that are too puny to be an individual threat on the battlefield, but when operating as a sea of dozens of creatures they can destroy much larger enemies. All Swarms have the Small Targets and Vulnerable to Blasts/Templates special rules.

TANK HUNTERS

Tank Hunters are especially skilled at finding and exploiting weaknesses in the armour of enemy vehicles. They add +1 to their Armour Penetration rolls whenever they hit a vehicle (with any weapon), and automatically pass Morale checks caused by Tank Shock.

TRUE GRIT

Bolters have a 'pistol grip', allowing them to be fired with a single hand. This takes considerable practice and skill and is not normally encouraged. Units noted as having the True Grit skill in their army list, however, have trained how to use their bolters in this manner. In game terms, this means that they may count their bolter as a bolt pistol in close combat, and will therefore be allowed to roll an extra Attack dice as if they have been equipped with an additional pistol or close combat weapon. However, a model using their bolter in this manner does not receive the +1 attack bonus for charging, as a bolter is too unwieldy to be fired with one hand while simultaneously hurling yourself at the enemy. This ability is not usable with combi-weapons of any sort. It is usable with storm bolters, but only by Space Marines of the Grey Knights Chapter for whom this is a long-standing specialisation.

TURBO-BOOSTERS*

Units mounted on bikes and jetbikes may utilise turbo-boosters to move at extreme speed. When using their turbo-boosters they may move up to 24" in the Movement phase. Controlling their bike at such speeds takes all their concentration and skill, however, so they may not move through difficult terrain, shoot, launch assaults or move in the Assault phase in the same turn. In the following enemy Shooting phase, treat the bike's Armour Save as being an Invulnerable Save, to represent the difficulty of hitting such fast-moving targets. A unit using turbo-boosters must end its move at least 18" away from its starting position to claim this Invulnerable Save, as it relies on flat-out speed.

VULNERABLE TO BLASTS/TEMPLATES

Some units are especially vulnerable to blast weapons and template weapons. If the unit is a vehicle, then each hit counts as two hits. If the unit is a non-vehicle, each unsaved wound counts as two wounds rather than one.

MIXED ARMOUR

It's sometimes possible for some units to have models with different Armour Saves, and in these cases the normal casualty removal and Armour Save rules are modified slightly. The attacking player rolls hits and wounds for whichever unit he is attacking with as normal. However, when the player makes his Armour Saves, he must follow this procedure:

1. Count up the number of models that have each type of armour. Only count models that could potentially be casualties.

2. Determine which armour type is in the majority – if it is a tie then the worst type is assumed to be in the majority (it can be assumed that they are picked on by the enemy).

3. Apply the wounding hits to the majority armour type first.

Example: *In a Black Templar unit with six Initiates (each with a 3+ Save) and five Neophytes (each with a 4+ Save), the first six wounds must be allocated to the power-armoured Initiates before the Neophytes' lighter armour is used.*

4. If there are still more wounding hits to allocate, you can apply them to any remaining models. It is up to the owning player to decide who will save against which weapon. The only constraint is that the majority armour type must make saves before anyone else does.

Example: *A unit of Chosen of Tzeentch includes one model in Chaos armour (2+ Armour Save), eight in power armour (3+ Armour Save) and three Thrall Wizards (no Armour Save). It takes nine wounds; eight are saved against by the majority armour type (3+) leaving one wound. The Chaos player could use the Armour Save of the model in Chaos armour, which will probably succeed but carries the risk of losing a valuable model if it fails, or simply remove a Thrall Wizard.*

5. Incoming hits form 'sets', with a single set being all the wounds caused by the shooting of a single enemy unit, or by enemy models attacking the unit in close combat at a single initiative step. For each 'set' of wounds, every model must be allocated one wound before any of them can be allocated a second wound, all models must receive a second wound before any can take a third, and so on. Unsaved wounding hits must be applied against models with the same armour type that was used for the save. If a unit receives more wounds than it has models, then the wounds 'wrap around' and affect the majority type again.

Example: *If the Black Templar unit described received twenty wounds, six would be allocated to the Initiates, five to the Neophytes, six more to the Initiates and the remaining three to the Neophytes. The unit would therefore have to make twelve 3+ Saves with the Initiates and eight 4+ Saves with the Neophytes.*

If special close combat attacks come into play against a unit with different Armour Saves, it is up to the owning player to decide which models make saves against the special attacks, subject to the rules detailed above. If any model has an Invulnerable Save they are, of course, at liberty to use it against a special attack.

Example: *The Black Templars squad noted above suffers four power weapon hits and four normal hits in a single Initiative step. The six Initiates with a 3+ Save are in the majority so they must make saves first. The owning player decides to take the four normal weapon hits and two power weapon hits on them. The two remaining power weapon attacks are allocated to Neophytes.*

ORGANISING A BATTLE

Now that you've learnt the rules for moving, shooting and fighting with your army, we'll look at how to organise a game of Warhammer 40,000, including how to choose your forces, how to set up the battlefield and how to select a mission to play.

ORGANISING A BATTLE

1. Choose Forces
2. Prepare the Battlefield
3. Choose a Mission
4. Deploy Forces
5. Start the game!

"Now the past must unveil one of its darkest secrets, the story of the Plague of Unbelief and its most heinous vector Bucharis the Apostate Cardinal of Gathalamor. Never has the Imperium endured such a crisis of faith, not since the dark days of the Horus Heresy itself."

Galan Noirgrim Master of the Ordo Malleus
The Abominatus Cantos 13 the Libra Hereticus

CHOOSE FORCES

A game of Warhammer 40,000 can use as many models as you can collect. The army lists included in the Warhammer 40,000 Codex books specify the precise characteristics and abilities of each troop type, detail how many you can use and provide a points value for each. The better a combatant is, the more points it will cost. Normally a soldier will have a basic cost, which is then increased if you upgrade his equipment or abilities.

The most popular approach to playing a game of Warhammer 40,000 involves both you and your opponent selecting forces to a previously agreed points limit. A limit of 1,500 points per side produces a well-balanced game that can be concluded in a couple of hours. As you build up your armies and enter the ranks of the veteran gamer, you will no doubt crave opportunities to get your entire figure collection onto the battlefield and play with bigger points values. Don't be in a mad rush to play huge points limit games – it is far better to start small and gain familiarity with the rules rather than trying to master everything at once. You will inevitably make mistakes in your first few games, so it is better to play a number of small, quick games to learn the ropes before moving up to a full-size game.

As detailed in each army Codex, all the forces you can use are categorised broadly by type. These types are: HQ, Elite, Troops, Fast Attack and Heavy Support, and these categories tell you something about the role the troops in question play in the army.

HQ: A Headquarters unit might be a single heroic commander or powerful monster, possibly accompanied by personal guards or with a transport vehicle. These units are amongst the most powerful in the game, as leaders will generally have access to more special equipment than everyone else. They are not invincible but can provide a powerful spearhead for an attacking army, and a strong core for a defensive one. Every army will contain at least one Headquarters unit to command it.

ELITES: An Elite unit will normally be a powerful but rare option. Elite choices are often the best soldiers an army has to offer, but there are never enough of them. In some cases they will be specialists, while at other times they will be more experienced versions of the regular rank and file soldiers.

TROOPS: Troops represent the most commonly available soldiers in an army. This does not mean they are poor fighters though; the category includes such troops as Space Marines and Eldar Dire Avengers, both formidable adversaries. These are the warriors that make up the bulk of an army and, as such, every army will have at least two such units.

FAST ATTACK: Fast Attack units are generally (surprise, surprise!) faster than their comrades and are expected to fight in a more dashing and decisive way. Often they will be responsible for reconnaissance and scouting, while at other times they will be specialist assault troops relying on speed to strike at the heart of the enemy.

HEAVY SUPPORT: Heavy Support units are literally the big guns of the army. In this section you will find the heaviest items of equipment and the most powerful creatures. However, these units are also often the most expensive in points, so an over-reliance on them could see you being heavily outnumbered.

FORCE ORGANISATION CHART

The minimum and maximum numbers of each of these types of unit are detailed on a Force Organisation chart. One box on the chart allows you to make one selection from that part of your army list. Dark boxes are compulsory selections. As you can see from the Force Organisation chart opposite, which is used for all Standard Missions, you will always have to take at least one Headquarters selection and two Troops selections. These compulsory choices ensure that whatever else you select, your force will have a core within it that is representative of that army. This is rarely a disadvantage and many players often use the maximum number of Troops selections.

Sometimes a single choice on the Force Organisation chart will allow you to select more than one unit. This will always be explained in the appropriate Codex so be sure to read it carefully.

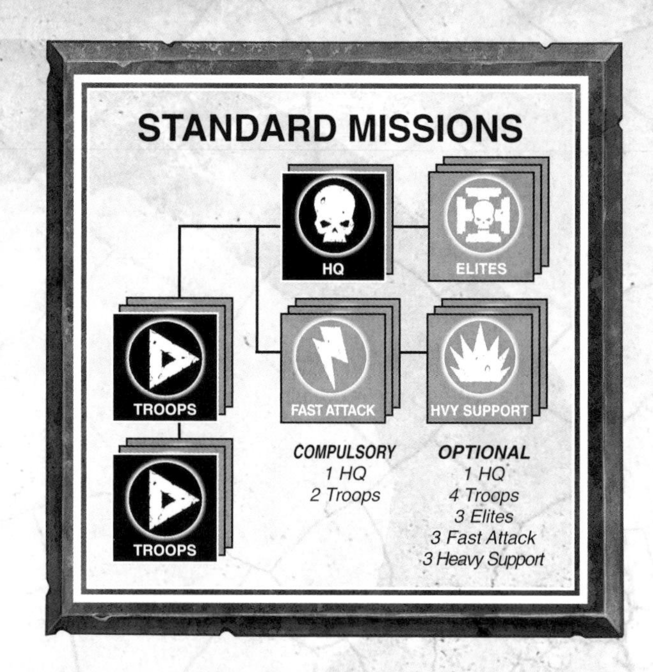

MULTIPLE DETACHMENT GAMES

As your collection of miniatures grows, the urge to use them all at once will become hard to resist. Above a total 2,500 points, the Force Organisation chart deliberately becomes a real limiting factor. The chart allows you to build the minimum sized force that can reasonably be expected to complete a mission. On a larger scale, an army will consist of many such detachments, each performing separate missions. If you want to play an especially large game then, as well as agreeing a points limit, you should also agree a maximum number of detachments. Each detachment will be a separate army, using its own Force Organisation chart.

PREPARE THE BATTLEFIELD

Setting up a well-modelled, interesting battlefield will enhance the enjoyment that you get from playing a game of Warhammer 40,000. Many players will happily collect several armies before even considering the possibility of investing some time and effort in producing good terrain. This is a shame, as a new set-up for your games can breathe fresh life into the most heavily used armies and missions. Adapting your tactics from fighting in rolling woodland to fighting in ruined hab-blocks is both challenging and fun.

It is best if terrain placement is done by mutual consent. A common convention is for the player hosting the game (or arriving first at the club) to set the terrain up, and for the other player to have choice of table edge. In the mission descriptions this player should be assumed to win the dice-off for table edge or quarter. In tournament play, terrain will often be pre-set by the organisers, in which case a dice-off for starting quarter or edge is still needed. In other circumstances the players should mutually set up the terrain, ensuring that the set-up is acceptable to them both.

> What is the terror of death?
> That we die our work incomplete.
> What is the joy of life?
> To die knowing our task is done.

HOW MUCH TERRAIN?

As a general rule, about a quarter of the total playing surface should have terrain on it, and there should be a good mixture of types. An equal division between terrain which blocks line of sight and provides cover (such as woods or ruins), terrain which provides cover but does not block line of sight (such as scrubland and low rubble) and terrain which blocks line of sight but provides little cover (such as gentle hills or ash waste dunes) makes for good tactical play, although this is entirely subject to the players' preferences. You may want to build terrain with this in mind.

Knowing that you need a certain amount of terrain to populate your gaming table means that you can build terrain 'sets', representing a particular planet or warzone. This could be as simple as a number of hills with rubble-strewn slopes, reminiscent of the quarries so beloved of low budget science fiction film-makers, or as complex as the domes of an Eldar craftworld. As long as you avoid building terrain guaranteed to give you a tactical advantage, you should get plenty of use out of each 'set' of terrain. The effect is analogous to building a movie set. Terrain pieces should convey some character and add possibilities to any game played using them.

TERRAIN SETS

To illustrate this point, let's consider a couple of terrain 'sets'. The assumption here is that if terrain pieces are roughly 12" by 12", then six are needed to fulfil the 25% terrain recommendation on a standard 6'x4' table (these dimensions are approximate and under no circumstances should terrain features, such as woods, be uniformly square. Irregular features look much better anyway).

For a fairly general wilderness set-up using large terrain features, what you need are a couple of features that, whilst not slowing movement, do block line of sight, such as hills. These will enable models to deploy and manoeuvre a bit without being shot at as well as providing good defensive positions. Next, you will need one or two features that provide some serious cover, such as woods. Woods also break up lines of fire and encourage manoeuvring, which is in the interests of a fun game.

Finally, the set can be rounded off with a simple rural farm, consisting of multiple buildings and an area of scrubland. The farm establishes the setting – in this case an Imperial agri-world – and provides a pleasing centrepiece for the 'set'. The scrubland provides a bit more cover whilst not further limiting lines of sight. Instead of scrubland, a field of crops will go well with the farm. A few minor pieces, such as an old piece of farm machinery or a water tank, can then be scattered around to add colour without getting in the way of the game. You may agree to ignore small scene-setting features of this sort for gaming purposes; the idea is to set the mood, not establish firebases.

One of the most important elements in building a terrain 'set' is to keep the terrain consistent with the board or surface you are playing on. It is the single largest area you'll be looking at when playing, so it's important that what you build will work with it.

The next example depicts a ruined Imperial city. Note that the board complements the rest of the 'set'. Here the six terrain features include a number of small pieces of wreckage and debris. The total area covered by these amounts to about two terrain features worth. They provide some relatively minor bits of cover and are great for dressing the set. There is also a single, much larger area of ruins that is raised, rather like a hill with rocky, rubble-strewn slopes. Finally, there are three ruined buildings, each providing good cover and blocking line of sight. With this 'set' it is likely the buildings will become vital strong points in any game, demonstrating that the way you design the 'set' has a big effect on the type of game you will get.

A player who builds distinctive terrain that makes for a fun game will find himself in much demand for games, and deserves as much kudos for his trouble as a player with a particularly well-painted army.

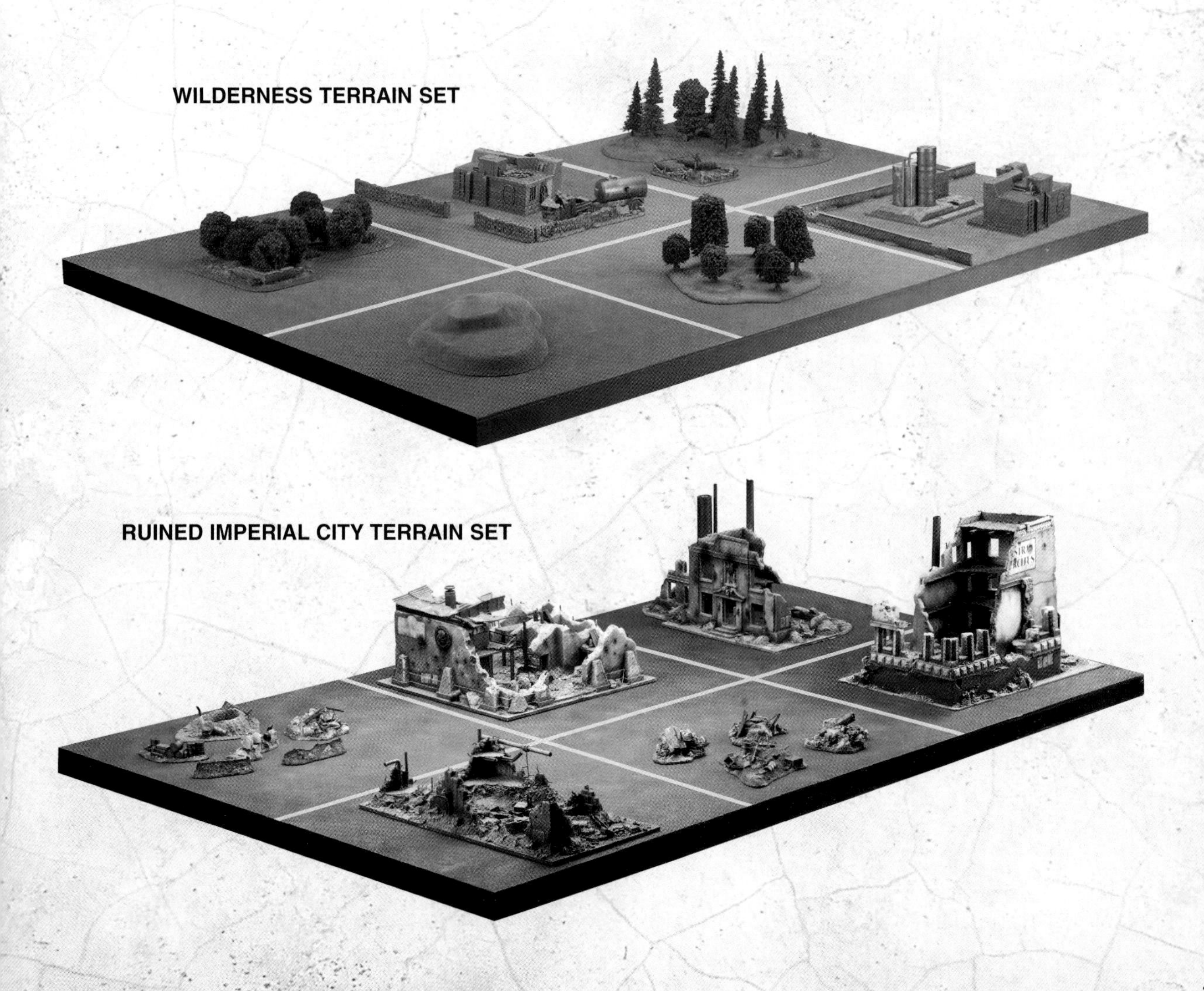
WILDERNESS TERRAIN SET

RUINED IMPERIAL CITY TERRAIN SET

CHOOSE A MISSION

Standard missions are the most common way Warhammer 40,000 battles are played. They are relatively simple, and do not require an army that is designed specifically towards a single style of play. There are a total of five standard missions to choose from. All of these missions use the standard Force Organisation chart. You can either agree with your opponent which mission to play, or roll D6 and consult the table below:

D6	Roll Mission
1	Cleanse
2	Secure and Control
3	Seek and Destroy
4	Recon
5	Take and Hold
6	Mission chosen by the player that wins the Strategy roll.

Each mission can be played at three levels: Alpha, Gamma and Omega. Each successive level adds more special rules, which change the way the mission can be played (this is detailed in each specific mission). Each version is just as tactically challenging as any other, and you can either agree which level of a mission to play or roll a D6. On the roll of 1 or 2 play an Alpha level battle, on a 3 or 4 play a Gamma level battle, or play an Omega level battle on a 5 or 6. See the mission specific rules to see what effect this will have on the game.

SCORING UNITS

This concept is central to all the missions presented here – at Alpha level, standard missions are won or lost entirely by getting more units onto the objective than the enemy. However, not all units count for this purpose (for example, a unit that is falling back cannot claim to be holding the objective) but those that do count for such objectives are called Scoring Units. At other levels, achieving these objectives will score you Victory Points. See the Victory Points table to see what counts as scoring units.

STRATEGY RATINGS

Some armies have elaborate command and control systems that allow them to react quickly to changing battlefield conditions. Others rely on applying pressure everywhere at once and lack the means to set the agenda on a given part of the battlefield. In Warhammer 40,000 these differences are reflected in the army's Strategy Rating. When a Strategy roll is called for, players roll a number of D6 equal to their Strategy Rating and then pick the highest result. The player with the highest result gets to choose the mission.

Strategy Ratings of the different armies in Warhammer 40,000 are as follows:

Army	Strategy Rating
Space Marines	3
Witch Hunters	3
Alien Hunters	3
Daemonhunters	3
Craftworld Eldar	3
Necrons	3
Chaos Space Marines	2
Dark Eldar	2
Imperial Guard	1
Tyranids	1
Orks	1
Tau	1
Other armies	1

DEPLOY FORCES

When deploying units or rolling for their arrival, the contents of one box on the Force Organisation chart is considered to be a single entity. In practice, a single choice on the chart may be several units. It might be a squad and their transport vehicle, an Imperial Guard infantry platoon consisting of a HQ squad and five infantry squads, or a brood of three Tyranid Zoanthropes. When deploying a single chart choice, the units that make up that choice may deploy separately from one another if you wish. When a single chart choice arrives from reserve, the units may similarly arrive separately from one another. Thus a squad does not have to arrive in its transport vehicle if you do not wish it to.

When deploying a unit or independent character on the table, you may specify that it is being placed inside a transport vehicle, subject to them being valid as passengers (see Vehicle rules).

When deploying an independent character on the table, you may specify that it starts the game already inside a unit and place it in coherency with it.

When deploying, players alternate placing units, and then alternate placing units with the Infiltrate special rule.

When all units are deployed, any that are entitled to a move before the game starts will make a move.

A note on secrecy. Your opponent cannot normally inspect your army roster, including asking you what is in each transport vehicle. Players are, however, free to share this information if they so wish.

START THE GAME

Once everything has been set up, you need to roll a dice to see who gets the first turn, and start the game!

CLEANSE

Both sides are attempting to sweep the area clean of opposing troops. Roving forces should be on the lookout to seek and destroy any enemies they encounter.

OBJECTIVE: TABLE QUARTERS

Both forces are seeking to clear the enemy from the area. This is achieved by controlling table quarters. The table is divided into four areas formed by drawing horizontal and vertical lines through the centre point. A 6'x4' table would have four 3'x2' quarters.

To control a table quarter there must be NO scoring enemy units and at least one scoring unit of your own in the quarter. A unit can only occupy one table quarter – if it is spread over more than one quarter, roll randomly to see which it is in.

In Alpha missions, the player that controls the most table quarters at the end of the game wins.

Victory Point rules are used in the Gamma and Omega missions. See the Special Rules section for details.

SCENARIO SPECIAL RULES

Alpha: None.

Gamma: Infiltrate, Deep Strike, Dusk & Dawn, Victory Points.

Omega: Escalation, Concealment, Infiltrate, Deep Strike, Dusk & Dawn, Victory Points, Random Game Length.

SET-UP

1 Divide the board into four quarters. Both players roll a dice, highest score picks which quarter to deploy in. The other player's deployment zone is the opposite quarter.

2 Starting with the player that scored lowest, the players take it in turns, deploying a unit at a time until both armies are fully deployed. Units are deployed in the following order: Heavy Support, Troops, Elites, HQ, Fast Attack.

No unit can be deployed within 18" of the enemy or within 6" of the centre of the table at the start of the game.

3 Roll a D6. Highest score may choose whether to go first or second.

RESERVES: *When available, reserves move on from the player's deployment zone board edge.*

GAME LENGTH: *The game lasts for 6 turns. The Omega game may last longer.*

SECURE AND CONTROL

The battlefield is strewn with discarded equipment, wounded comrades, supplies and the other detritus of war that, for various reasons, you wish to recover. You must fight off the enemy while scouring the field to secure as much plunder as you can.

OBJECTIVE: LOOT

The items to be secured are represented by a total of D3 +2 Loot counters. Each player alternates placing a Loot counter until they are all on the table. Toss a coin to see who places a counter first. A counter may not be placed in impassable terrain, nor may one be placed within 12" of a table edge or another counter.

At the end of the game you control a Loot counter if there is at least one of your scoring units, and no enemy scoring units, within 6" of it.

In Alpha missions, the player with the most Loot counters wins.

Victory Point rules are used in the Gamma and Omega missions. See the Special Rules section for details.

SCENARIO SPECIAL RULES

Alpha: None.

Gamma: Infiltrate, Deep Strike, Dusk & Dawn, Victory Points.

Omega: Escalation, Concealment, Infiltrate, Deep Strike, Dusk & Dawn, Victory Points, Random Game Length.

SET-UP

1. Place Loot counters on the battlefield, as described in Mission Objective.

2. Both players roll a dice, the winner chooses which of the long table edges to deploy in.

His opponent gets the opposite deployment zone, so both forces start along opposite long board edges.

3. Starting with the player that scored highest, the players take it in turns deploying a unit at a time in their deployment zone, until all their available models are on the tabletop. No unit may be deployed more than 12" from their own long table edge. Players must deploy their units in the following order – Heavy Support first, then Troops, followed by Elites, HQ and finally Fast Attack.

4. Roll a D6. Highest score may choose whether to go first or second.

RESERVES: *When available, reserves move on from the player's deployment zone board edge.*

GAME LENGTH: *The game lasts for 6 turns. The Omega game may last longer.*

SEEK AND DESTROY

There is only one objective in war – find your enemy, crush him utterly and take away his means to mount further resistance. The enemy must be sought out and eliminated; no prisoners, no mercy.

OBJECTIVE: ANNIHILATION

In Alpha missions, the player with the most scoring units left at the end of the game is the winner.

Victory Point rules are used in the Gamma and Omega missions. See the Special Rules section for details.

SCENARIO SPECIAL RULES

Alpha: None.

Gamma: Infiltrate, Deep Strike, Dusk & Dawn, Victory Points.

Omega: Escalation, Concealment, Infiltrate, Deep Strike, Dusk & Dawn, Victory Points, Random Game Length.

SET-UP

1. Both players roll a dice, the winner chooses which of the long table edges to deploy in.

His opponent gets the opposite deployment zone, so both forces start along opposite long board edges.

2. Starting with the player that scored lowest, the players take it in turns deploying a unit at a time in their deployment zone, until all their available models are on the tabletop. No unit may be deployed within 24" of the enemy or more than 15" from their own long table edge. Players must deploy their units in the following order – Heavy Support first, then Troops, followed by Elites, HQ and finally Fast Attack.

3. Roll a D6. Highest score may choose whether to go first or second.

RESERVES: *When available, reserves move on from the player's deployment zone board edge.*

GAME LENGTH: *The game lasts for 6 turns. The Omega game may last longer.*

RECON

Both sides are attempting to punch through enemy lines to establish forward positions and probe the enemy's strength in preparation for a major attack.

OBJECTIVE: ENEMY LINES

Both players must attempt to get units into the enemy deployment zone and overrun their lines.

In Alpha missions, the player with the most scoring units entirely in the enemy deployment zone at the end of the game wins. The deployment zones extend 15" from the long board edges.

Victory Point rules are used in the Gamma and Omega missions. See the Special Rules section for details.

SCENARIO SPECIAL RULES

Alpha: None.

Gamma: Infiltrate, Deep Strike, Dusk & Dawn, Victory Points.

Omega: Escalation, Concealment, Infiltrate, Deep Strike, Dusk & Dawn, Random Game Length, Victory Points.

SET-UP

1 Both players roll a dice, the winner chooses which of the long table edges to deploy in.

His opponent gets the opposite deployment zone, so both forces start along opposite long board edges.

2 Starting with the player that scored lowest, the players take it in turns deploying a unit at a time in their deployment zone, until all their available models are on the tabletop. No unit may be deployed within 24" of the enemy or more than 15" from their own long table edge. Players must deploy their units in the following order – Heavy Support first, then Troops, followed by Elites, HQ and finally Fast Attack.

3 Roll a D6. Highest score may choose whether to go first or second.

RESERVES: *When available, reserves move on from the player's deployment zone board edge.*

GAME LENGTH: *The game lasts for 6 turns. The Omega game may last longer.*

TAKE AND HOLD

You have to secure the battlefield prior to the arrival of much greater numbers of friendly troops for a decisive battle. The enemy are known to be moving with similar intent. You are the spearhead – smash the enemy aside, take the high ground and await reinforcements.

OBJECTIVE: FIELD OF BATTLE

The centre of the battlefield must be secured. In Alpha missions, the player with the most scoring units within 12" of the table centre point at the end of the game wins.

Victory Point rules are used in the Gamma and Omega missions. See the Special Rules section for details.

SCENARIO SPECIAL RULES

Alpha: None.

Gamma: Infiltrate, Deep Strike, Dusk & Dawn, Victory Points.

Omega: Escalation, Concealment, Infiltrate, Deep Strike, Dusk & Dawn, Random Game Length, Victory Points.

SET-UP

1 Both players roll a dice, the winner chooses which of the long table edges to deploy in.

His opponent gets the opposite deployment zone, so both forces start along opposite long board edges.

2 Starting with the player that scored highest, the players take it in turns deploying a unit at a time in their deployment zone, until all their available models are on the tabletop. No unit may be deployed more than 12" from their own long table edge. Players must deploy their units in the following order – Heavy Support first, then Troops, followed by Elites, HQ and finally Fast Attack.

3 Roll a D6. Highest score may choose whether to go first or second.

RESERVES: *When available, reserves move on from the player's deployment zone board edge.*

GAME LENGTH: *The game lasts for 6 turns. The Omega game may last longer.*

MISSION SPECIAL RULES

CONCEALMENT

If the Concealment rule is used in the mission, all non-vehicle units that are deployed at the beginning of the game are assumed to have made efforts to conceal themselves before the battle, even if in open terrain. If a concealed unit is fired at, the firers must determine if they can actually see their target using the Night Fight rules. If they cannot see their target, the unit may not fire (except for barrage weapons, which may fire at unseen targets but add an extra D6 to the distance scattered). Concealment is lost as soon as the concealed unit moves, shoots or uses a psychic power. If the Night Fight rules apply for that turn, these concealment rules are ignored (as troops will instead just rely on the darkness to conceal themselves). Concealment always ends after the first turn.

DEEP STRIKE

Some units are allowed to enter play via tunnelling, teleportation, flying, or some other extraordinary means. Where this is the case it will be noted in their special rules. Some units always have the option; others only have the option in missions where the Deep Strike special rule is in force. If you wish to use this option then the units in question begin the game in reserve – it does not matter whether the Reserves special rule is in force for the mission. Roll for arrival of these units as specified in the Reserves rules and then deploy them as follows:

Place one model from the unit anywhere on the table, in the position you would like the unit to arrive, and roll the Scatter dice. If you roll a HIT the model stays where it is, but if an arrow is shown this determines the direction the model is scattered in. If a scatter occurs, roll 2D6" to see how far the model scatters.

All Deep Striking models are arranged around the first model. Models must be placed in base contact with the original model in a circle around it. When the first circle is complete, a further circle should be placed with each model touching the circle inside it. Each circle should include as many models as will fit, and they may be facing in any direction. If the first model scatters off the table, the entire unit is destroyed. It is a good idea not to try to Deep Strike too close to a table edge! You may not place models within 1" of any enemy. If you are unable to complete a circle of models without any of them coming within 1" of the enemy, entering impassable terrain or going off-table, the surplus models are destroyed.

Troops arriving via Deep Strike may not move or assault on the turn they arrive. They may shoot as normal, but count as having moved.

DUSK & DAWN

Sometimes a battle may start before first light, or so late that dusk falls before an advantage is gained. After deployment, but before determining who has first turn, roll a D6. On a 1, the battle starts before dawn and the Night Fighting rules are used on Turn 1. On a roll of 6, the battle starts at dusk and the Night Fighting rules are used on Turn 6 and any subsequent turns.

ESCALATION

The Escalation special rule is always used in combination with the Reserves special rule. Escalation represents the situation where the battle begins reasonably quietly, with only infantry in the line, and suddenly explodes into action as reserves are deployed. In a mission using the Escalation rule, only basic infantry units that do not have dedicated transports (so no Monstrous Creatures, Bikes, Jump Infantry, Artillery, Beasts, etc) may be deployed at the start of the game, unless the mission rules state otherwise.

All units not deployed are in reserve and will arrive in accordance with the normal Reserves rules. Some units have special rules, such as 'Scouts', that allows them to deploy on-table. Such special rules apply as normal.

INFILTRATE

Any infiltrators deployed on the table at the start of the game are deployed after all other units. If both sides have infiltrators, toss a coin to determine who goes first and alternate deploying these units. Infiltrators may be set up anywhere on the table that is more than 12" from an enemy unit, if no deployed enemy unit can draw a line of sight to them. Alternatively, they may be set up anywhere on the table that is more than 18" from an enemy unit, even if they can be seen.

NIGHT FIGHTING

It is much harder to accurately identify enemy units at night; warriors must be sure of their targets before opening fire, and tend to be more cautious than normal. After selecting a target, but before a unit fires, a check needs to be made to see if the firers can see their target through the darkness. Roll 2D6 and multiply the result by 3, rolling once per unit only. This is the maximum range that any non-barrage weapon can be fired at. If the shooters have selected a target beyond this range they lose the right to fire, as they search the darkness for a target that never appears.

Normal barrage and ordnance barrage weapons may fire at unseen targets, but if they do, they add an extra D6 to the distance scattered.

RANDOM GAME LENGTH

At the end of the mission's stated number of turns, roll a D6. On a 4, 5 or 6 a further turn is played. Repeat this process at the end of every turn until either a 1, 2 or 3 is rolled, or three extra turns are played. If it is dark on Turn 6, it remains dark for these extra game turns.

RESERVES

Reserves are forces in the same sector as the troops on the battlefield who can be called in to reinforce them at relatively short notice. Units in reserve are not deployed at the start of the battle, but will become available in later turns of the game. Each selection from the Force Organisation chart is diced for separately at the start of the player's turn.

Reserves Table

	Turn 1	Turn 2	Turn 3	Turn 4+
Reserve unit arrives on:	N/A	4+	3+	2+

When a reserve unit arrives, it must move on as specified in the Reserves section of the mission description. If the reserves are able to use Deep Strike in the mission being played, then they may alternatively use this method. See the Deep Strike special rule for details. If a unit has a transport attached, roll for both together, though the passengers do not have to arrive mounted in the transport.

Note: *You must roll for reserves as soon as possible and must bring them onto the table as soon as they are available. You may not delay making the dice rolls or keep the reserves hanging around off-table until you decide you need them!*

VICTORY POINTS

At Gamma and Omega level, many missions are decided by Victory Points. In these missions, conditions for winning are modified from the method stated on the Mission sheet. Victory Points are gained first by damaging and destroying enemy units. A unit is worth as many Victory Points as its points cost. Thus a 250 point Land Raider would be worth 250 Victory Points to you if you managed to destroy it during the game. Sometimes merely damaging a unit will be adequate to score some Victory Points. See the Victory Points table to see what you score for inflicting casualties on the enemy.

In addition, achieving the mission objective will score Victory Points. It is possible to gain as many points from achieving the mission victory conditions as you can from destroying the enemy.

VICTORY POINTS TABLE

UNIT TYPE	CONDITION AT THE END OF THE GAME	DOES THE UNIT COUNT AS A SCORING UNIT?	WHAT VPS DOES THE OPPONENT GET?
Non-vehicle unit*	At least 50% strength	Yes	None
	Less than 50% strength	No	1/2 points value
	Destroyed, off-table or Falling Back	No	Full points value
Vehicle	Mobile	Yes	None
	Immobile	No	1/2 points value
	Wrecked, Exploded or Annihilated	No	Full points value
Dedicated Transport vehicle	Mobile	No	None
	Immobile	No	1/2 points value
	Wrecked, Exploded or Annihilated	No	Full points value
Vehicle squadron	At least 50% mobile	Yes	None
	Less than 50% mobile	No	1/2 points value
	All Wrecked, Exploded or Annihilated	No	Full points value
Independent character**	Unwounded	No	None
	Wounded	No	1/2 points value
	Dead, Off-table or Falling Back	No	Full points value
Artillery unit	At least 50% strength	Yes	None
	Less than 50% strength or all guns destroyed	No	1/2 points value
	Destroyed, off-table or Falling Back	No	Full points value

Note: *If any non-vehicle units include multi-Wound models, count wounds not models to see if a unit is above/below 50% strength.*

***An independent character always uses this line regardless of his unit type.*

UNITS WITH DISTINCT ELEMENTS

Some units consist of parts that deploy and operate separately, such as a squad of Space Marines and their Rhino transport vehicle, a Brood of Lictors or an Imperial Guard Infantry Platoon. Treat each element separately for Victory Points purposes. The same approach is taken when an independent character has a Command squad or retinue mounted in a transport. Each element is a separate entity when calculating Victory Points. Thus a Space Marine Chaplain with Command squad in a Rhino would be an independent character, a unit of Space Marines and a vehicle unit.

MISSION SPECIFIC OBJECTIVES

Objective: Table Quarters

If the mission objective is Table Quarters and the Victory Points special rule is being used, rather than deciding the mission purely on the basis of the number of Scoring Units in each quarter of the table, you score Victory Points both for enemy models damaged, wounded or destroyed as detailed above, and also by the number of table quarters you control.

• The table quarter your army deployed in is worth no Victory Points.

• The table quarters that are adjacent to your army's deployment zone are each worth 25% of the game's points limit.

• The table quarter that the enemy deployed in is worth 50% of the game's points limit.

Thus, in a 1,500 point game, your army scores 0 for its own quarter, 375 for each adjacent quarter and 750 for the enemy's quarter. The opposite of course is true for the enemy army.

Objective: Enemy Lines

If the mission objective is breaking through the enemy lines and the Victory Points special rule is being used, you score Victory Points equal to the points cost of those scoring units entirely in the enemy deployment zone, in addition to Victory Points for destroying enemy units.

Objective: Loot

If the mission objective involves securing Loot counters and the Victory Points special rule is being used, you score Victory Points for destroying enemy units and, in addition, each Loot counter is worth a number of points equal to the game points limit divided by the number of counters used. Thus, in a 1,500 point game with four Loot counters, each counter is worth 375 points.

Objective: The Field of Battle

If the mission objective involves securing the centre of the battlefield and the Victory Points special rule is being used, you score Victory Points for destroying enemy units and, in addition, score Victory Points equal to the points value of each of your scoring units entirely within 12" of the centre point at the end of the game.

Objective: Annihilation

If the mission objective involves annihilating the enemy and the Victory Points special rule is being used, you score Victory Points for destroying enemy units and, in addition, score Victory Points equal to the points value of each scoring unit you have left at the end of the game. This means that you must destroy as many of the enemy as possible, while avoiding heavy losses yourself.

MARGIN OF VICTORY

Comparing the total Victory Points you scored against your opponent's determines the margin of victory (or defeat). Obviously, this is only applicable in Gamma or Omega missions where Victory Points are used.

A difference of less than 10% of the points limit is a Draw. Anything greater is a win for the player with the highest Victory Point total. A difference of more than 10% and up to 50% is a Solid Victory. A difference of more than 50% and up to 80% is a Crushing Victory. A difference of more than 80% is a Victorious Slaughter!

The chart below summarizes these differences for the most common points limits.

In tournaments, the margin of victory may be used to determine how many Tournament Points each player scores. In a campaign, the scale of victory may result in different outcomes. For these purposes it is useful to define further categories based on the margin of victory.

GAME'S POINTS LIMIT				RESULT
500 pts	**1,000 pts**	**1,500 pts**	**2,000 pts**	
0-50	0-100	0-150	0-200	**Draw**
51-250	101-500	151-750	201-1,000	**Solid Victory**
251-400	501-800	751-1200	1,001-1600	**Crushing Victory**
401+	801+	1201+	1601+	**Victorious Slaughter!**

HOW TO USE THIS CHART: *Find the difference in Victory Points between the two players along the column with the appropriate points limit for the game played. Cross-reference with the 'Result' column to find out the margin of victory. For example, if a 1,500 point game ends with a difference of 472 points between the players, the 1,500 pts column shows that the result is a Solid Victory.*

Chaplain Mathis leads the scourging of the defiled basilica of Saint Dolan.

A GALAXY OF WAR

For ten thousand years, the Immortal Emperor has sat immobile on the Golden Throne, master of Mankind by the will of the gods and ruler of a million worlds by the might of his inexhaustible armies. Worshipped by untold billions, the sorrow and sacrifices made to sustain His divine corpse ensure the continued survival of the human race in the face of a hostile galaxy. From the blasted ruins of Terra, teeming with innumerable pilgrims and functionaries, the rule of the Imperium is maintained, but it is a dark time for the Imperium of Man. Beset on all sides by foes of such malice that it would sear a man's soul to know but a fraction of their blasphemies, only the strongest and most ruthless survive. Foes from within and without seek to overthrow the undying Emperor's rule, destroying in a moment that which took ten millennia to forge with the blood of heroes. The Great Devourer comes from beyond the galaxy, driven to consume all before it and Ork savages surge from their barbaric empires to pillage and slaughter. The vengeful Eldar cite prophetic visions as they raid and destroy, and an ancient evil arises from tombs sealed at the dawn of creation.

The denizens of the Warp, the nightmare realm that exists beyond the fragile veil of reality, constantly seek to enslave or destroy Mankind. Fallen warriors of legendary times return from the Eye of Terror to tear at their former master's realm, seeking vengeance for their long-ago defeat. Daemons of unimaginable power work through their willing servants amongst Humanity to achieve their terrible goals, and only those willing to risk their souls can stand before them. Against these multitudinous threats, the superhuman warriors of the Space Marines, the mighty ships of the Imperial Navy, the agents of the Inquisition and the incalculable power of the Imperial Guard stand as a bulwark against the darkness, but each year more worlds are lost. The Emperor's Light grows dim, the encroaching enemies of Mankind gather like carrion and a time of endless night presses in…

In the grim darkness of the far future, there is only war.

TEMPLAR

Imperius Dominatus

"The Revered Houses of the Navis Nobilite are one of the bastions upon which the Imperium is founded and the institution claims it can trace its ancestry back to the birth of our Great Empire.

The Great Families of the Navis Nobilite are uniquely composed of a particular form of human called a Navigator. Tech-adepts have speculated widely over the development and nature of the Navigators' unusual talents and many cast hints at shadowy genetic transmutation and interbreeding during the founding of the Navis Nobilite. Whatever their origins, the Navigators today are a glorious and esteemed organisation, loyal to the Imperium and stalwart in their faith. The peculiar powers of the Navigators can only be preserved by intermarriage; breeding with mundane humans eliminates the special abilities. This factor has led to the development of the closely-related Navigator families and the Navis Nobilite as a whole."

Preface – Historia Et Structura
Res Navis Nobilite

"For the warp is a strange and terrible place. You might as well throw a traveller into a sea of sharks and tell him to swim home as send him through the warp unprotected. Better it is not to let common man travel through the stars. Better still, let him not know such a thing is feasible."

Fra Safrane, 5th aide to Navigator Da'el.
Comment made prior to the departure of the second mission to search for the missing freighter 'Pride of Angelus'.

Imperial World | Inquisition Stronghold | Space Marine Homeworld | Cardinal World

And henceforth be it known that the Imperium shall be divided into five fleet zones to be known as the Segmentae Majoris. These shall each have a Segment Fortress, from whence the orders of his glorious magnificience, the Emperor, shall be enacted. Imperialis Command Decoriatum shall reside in each and with just duty be issued over the realms within their boundaries.

For the Segmentum Solar, this shall be Mars, World of the Adeptus Mechanicus and this Segment shall extend about Mars. Beneficent Emperor's Imperium. In the north of our most majestic domains shall be Segmentum Obscurus, being in fiefdom to the world of Cypra Mundi. To the South it shall make Segmentum Tempestus, with overlordship residing with the planetary estates of the hereditary Bakka.

To the West shall be Segmentum Pacificus, under the auspices of the Lords of Hydraphur. The most turbulent East, a region of much strife and dissension and of many lost worlds shall have its overlordship known as Ultima Segmentum, and its guarantor of safety shall be on the planetary Governor Kar Duniash. The Segment Fortress of the Imperial official of the Administratum shall be known as the Master of the Segmentum Solar. Lastly, the region of Segmentum Pacificus, and the Master of the Ultima Segmentum. In this the Emperor is most benevolent and thus shall the Emperor's charges be authority over such domains and reside with those who have the faith and temperament to dictate to the will of those others and take from them that which is the Emperor's due.

Ghoul Stars
Gates of Varl
Dominion of Storms
Ultima Segmentum
Kar Duniash
The Ymga Monolith
Attila
Mordant Zone
Tau Empire
Arch-arsonist of Charadon
Hive Fleet
San Leor
Pavonis
Macragge

UL01.01
Orb. Dist. 2.01AU
1.48G/Temp 23°C
Adeptus Astartes Home World
Tithe Grade: Adeptus Non
Aestimare: D0
Population: 400,000,000
Defeat of Hive Fleet Behemoth
(qf: Battle of Macragge 745.M41)

Quintarn Agri World
Calth Cavern World
Iax Garden World
Konor Ad. Mech. Research World
Macragge Ultramarines Homeworld
Tarentus Agri World
Talassar Ocean World
Parmenio Ultramarines Training World
Prandium *Dead World*
Masali Agri World
Talasa Prime *Inquisition Fortress*

Imperial Navy
Imperial Guard Homeworld
Forge World
Daemon World

THE IMPERIUM OF MAN

The Imperium of Man is the greatest stellar realm the galaxy has ever seen, stretching from holy Terra to the furthest reaches of the Eastern Fringe and the distant Halo Stars. A million worlds and innumerable souls to command, ruled over by the God-Emperor of Mankind. Entire armies of scribes attempt to collate how many humans inhabit the Imperium, but such a task is hopeless and without end, as the Emperor's realm encompasses every kind of world imaginable; sweltering jungle hells populated by club-wielding savages, ice-locked tundra with cities carved from glaciers, blisteringly-hot desert worlds, polluted industrial forge worlds, teeming worlds of unknown billions living in gargantuan hive cities and giant Cardinal planets where every building is given over to the worship of the Emperor. Such diversity of worlds breeds vastly varied, distinct cultures and humans from one world are likely to be completely different from one another, with wildly varying argots, customs and appearance.

Terra itself is a sprawling hive world, its surface utterly infertile and covered with dark, towering spires of iron, colossal, gothic cathedrals, ancient ruins and masses of pilgrims come to the cradle of Mankind to pay homage to the God-Emperor. Its oceans have long since boiled away, and beneath the countless layers of metal and stone that have built up over the aeons, Terra is a lifeless ball of rock. Hissing, verdigris-stained gargoyles vent steam into the polluted atmosphere and crumbling statues of angels stare blindly down on the teeming populace who mindlessly shuffle through the grinding business of simply existing. The object of these pilgrims' quest, the gothic majesty of the Imperial Palace, is a sight most will never see, having spent the majority of their life journeying to Terra only to be crushed by the mind-numbing scale of the queues of their fellow pilgrims. Even to tread the sacred surface of Terra is an honour most citizens of the Imperium can only dream of.

Far from the congested queues of pilgrims, a billion serried ranks of scribes and lexmechanics toil in the depths of Terra, locked in enormous, candle-lit scriptoria, gathering numbers and records of a thousand years ago, whose purpose and meaning has long been forgotten. Archives the size of continents delve deep underground in gloomy wings, their floors dusty with antiquity, sprawling with stacks of parchments, scrolls and data crystals that, in all likelihood, no one will ever read. Without insight or even the will to question what they do, these petty functionaries persevere through the same repetitive tasks each and every day because that is, was and ever shall be, their lot.

These scribes form part of the monolithic organisations known as the Adeptus Terra, a bloated, self-sustaining bureaucracy of petty functionaries and more senior ranking officials. The highest and mightiest of all are the High Lords of Terra, the supreme council of the twelve most powerful men in the Imperium who rule in the name of the Emperor. Their orders are passed to one of the five Segmentum commanders before reaching the sector and sub-sector lords. Thus do the Imperial Commanders of each world receive their orders and thus is the divine will of the Emperor enacted.

Of course, in practice the vast distances and delays in communication between worlds makes a mockery of such procedures and the sheer scale of the Imperium

Scribae

The entire surface of the forge world of Gryphonne IV is encrusted with massive machine shops and cathedral-like manufactorums. Factories the size of cities clank and hiss, belching pollutants into the ravaged atmosphere as rank upon rank of lobotomised servitors and devout Techpriests toil ceaselessly to churn out a constant stream of munitions and tanks. The Titans of the Legio Gryphonicus, bipedal god-machines with the firepower to level fortresses, tower over the scurrying factotums that form the lifeblood of this eternal machine, dwarfed in their turn by mighty edifices raised to the glory of the Omnissiah. Day blurs into night under the uncaring, soot-choked skies, the industrial landscape constantly ringing with the hymnals of eternal toil. To the Adepts of Gryphonne IV the concept of rest is a dangerous blasphemy, for the armies of the Segmentum Tempestus cannot function without the constant flow of war materiel from their iron-clad homeworld.

prevents any meaningful central control. The lack of communication between worlds often results in some falling into anarchy through simply being forgotten and slipping through the cracks of the Imperial bureaucracy. A plea for aid may come to the ears of the Imperium, but not be acted upon for centuries while the request makes its way through countless Adepts before finally reaching the hands of one who can sanction such action. Indeed, it is not uncommon for fleets and armies to arrive at a war zone to find that the war they were despatched to wage has long since ended.

The sheer scale of such a massive empire means that no method of control can ever be foolproof and as well as worlds that fall into disorder through neglect, there are some that purposefully defy the will of the Emperor, seeking to further their own ends. Traitors and malcontents, recklessly believing that they do not owe their continued survival to the Emperor, cast aside their oaths of loyalty and claim their worlds for themselves. Where ultimate authority is many light years distant, such subversion and insurrection is an ever-present danger, but the armies of the Imperium ruthlessly crush these revolts and execute the instigators before their heretical actions can spread further. There can be no mercy for such traitors, and only by such ruthless, oppressive measures can the Imperium survive; only by such drastic, unbending rules can Humanity defeat the myriad foes arrayed against it.

Further from Terra, there are vast expanses of wilderness space, where Imperial law is all but ignored and beyond the Emperor's Light, out towards the far-flung regions of the Eastern Fringe, there are whole tracts of space where the Imperium itself is nothing more than a half-remembered myth. There are many Imperial worlds in this far distant part of the galactic east, but so distant are they from Terra, that they can often go for centuries or more with no contact from the Imperium.

This region of space is truly the frontier of Imperial space, where the impossibly ancient Halo Stars can be seen as flickering wychfires beyond the furthest rims of the galaxy. The oldest stars in the galaxy, they are haunted, feared places and few who set out to explore them ever return.

Though more planets are lost and millions die every year, they are all nothing more than statistics, tiny embers lost against the backdrop of the stars and forgotten, obscured by newer, brighter lights by the time they are even noticed. Perhaps, in a thousand years, a lowly scribe on Terra may record such losses, but probably not...

THE ADEPTS OF TERRA

This is the Age of the Imperium, a time of war and bloodshed, where the promise of progress and enlightenment has been cast aside and the only constant is the Immortal God-Emperor of Mankind. Not only is the Imperium vast in terms of its physical scale, but also it is a monolithic organisation, the likes of which has never existed before, comprising billions of faceless servants who toil constantly in its service. Ruling over this colossal organisation are the High Lords of Terra, made up of representatives from the greatest branches of the Imperium, from the Navigator Houses to the Imperial Guard, the Adeptus Mechanicua to the Ministorum. The High Lords interpret the will of the Emperor and rule the galaxy in his stead, forming the very pinnacle of the Adeptus Terra.

Beneath them, billions of souls make up the ranks of the Adeptus Terra, from the lowly scrivener who fills the inkwells of the Scriptoria to the High Lords themselves. Like any huge bureaucracy, the Imperium is split into separate divisions, each a gargantuan organisation in its own right, and each with its own customs, practices and secrets. Every facet of Imperial life is, in theory, governed by these organisations, from planetary tithes, religion and military crusades. From the tiniest detail to decisions that affect entire star systems, the Imperium has an organisation whose entire existence is dedicated to it.

On Terra itself, the Eternal Guard of the Custodes keep constant vigil over the Sanctum Imperialis, the throne room of the Emperor himself. It is they, and they alone, who decide who may enter into the most sanctified place in the galaxy, and it is in their care that the future of Mankind is kept safe. Far beyond the pulsing, ancient machineries of the Sanctum Imperialis is the Hall of the Astronomican, where the psychic beacon utilised by the ships of the Imperial Navy to cross the vast gulfs of space is generated by thousands of psykers of the Adeptus Astronomica. Working in close conjunction with the Adeptus Astronomica are the psykers of the Adeptus Astra Telepathica, specially trained Astrotelepaths who can utilise their mysterious powers to communicate with others of their kind across the vast interstellar distances that separate the worlds of the Imperium. These psykers are not the only ones required to make the ultimate sacrifice, for the Emperor is no normal man and cannot take physical sustenance as one. Only the spiritual energies of those with psychic powers may sustain His immortal existence and though hundreds must die every day to nourish Him, the Preachers of the Ministorum teach that this is a small price to pay and those that must pay it do so gladly.

This eternal sacrifice has ensured that the Emperor is worshipped as nothing less than a god, and this has spawned a massively powerful organisation known as the

The Imperium contains over a million inhabited worlds, but even this is a fraction of the galactic whole. Huge tracts of wilderness space remain to be explored and the Eastern Fringe, where the light of the Astronomican does not reach, is also largely unknown. The exploration of these regions of space is often undertaken by Rogue Traders, flamboyant individuals granted the right to explore and claim new worlds in the name of the Imperium by ancient, hereditary Warrants of Trade. They venture into the unknown with ad hoc fleets of ships and the promise of unimaginable wealth. Many are highly pious, while others are little more than pirates, seeking merely to line their own pockets before returning to Imperial space, such as the infamous Jan van Yastobaal, who became little more than a desperado plundering whatever unsuspecting planet he and his band of cut-throats encountered.

Ministorum, a vast body of Adepts whose divinely-appointed task it is to interpret and promulgate His blessed will. To spread the word of the Emperor's divinity, the Adeptus Ministorum and the Missionarus Galaxia take His teachings to the farthest corners of the galaxy. Huge crusades of preachers, missionaries and holy warriors spread from Terra on great Wars of Faith, setting up shrines, cathedrals and basilica to the Divine Master of Mankind wherever they go.

Administering such massive undertakings and recording every detail of Imperial life is a colossal army of scribes, lexmechanics, record keepers and the like known as the Administratum. Occupying whole swathes of the Imperial Palace, itself covering much of the planet's surface, the Administratum assess and levy tithes, distribute Imperial resources and countless other functions. A similar role is undertaken by the Departmento Munitorum, but rather than the administration of the populace of the Imperium, its concern is its military might. It is the Departmento Munitorum that authorises raisings of the Imperial Guard and coordinates the logistical nightmare of supplying the ships of the Imperial Navy and the millions of soldiers at war throughout the galaxy.

While such organisations exist to teach the will of the Emperor and, in theory, facilitate the governance of his realm, there are many organisations that exist purely to enforce that will by force of arms. Sometimes, this will be the blunt instrument of the Imperial Guard, but there exists others that are more subtle, more secretive and more deadly. The Adeptus Arbites are grim-faced men and women, enforcers of the harsh Imperial Law, where failure and incompetence are crimes and the only punishment is death. Drawn from the most ruthless children of the Schola Progenium and stationed far from their homeworlds, the brooding presence of an Adeptus Arbites fortress-precinct has been enough to deter many an Imperial Commander from foolishly plotting treason and heresy against the Imperium.

Where a more insidious demonstration of the Imperium's might is required, the High Lords of Terra can call upon the services of the Officio Assassinorum, that secretive body specialising in assassination; the subtle knife or the shot in the dark. It takes the most highly skilled and lethal individual to become an assassin, and even then most will not survive the trials required to become one of these terrifying killers. Every aspect of the art of murder has been perfected and each of the Assassin Temples specialises in one such aspect; the shape-shifters of the Callidus, the snipers of the Vindicare, the abominations of the Culexus and many other, more esoteric, practitioners of death.

THE ORDERS OF THE EMPEROR'S HOLY INQUISITION

A dark and secretive organisation, the Inquisition moves in the shadows, investigating all manner of threats to the Imperium – alien plots, corruption, mutation, heresy, cults, rogue psykers or any other matter an Inquisitor deems worthy of his scrutiny. Nothing is beyond their authority, no one is exempt from their justice and entire worlds may be destroyed in the fires of Exterminatus. An Inquisitor has the power to requisition anything at all, be it entire armies, fleets of starships or even the resources of an entire world. Sometimes they will act alone, but frequently they surround themselves with retinues of trusted henchmen; deadly warriors, powerful psykers or anyone else the Inquisitor considers may be useful.

> "Some may question your right to destroy ten billion people. Those who understand realise that you have no right to let them live..."
>
> In Exterminatus Extremis

Though the Inquisition deals with every threat imaginable, there are inevitably those amongst its ranks who specialise in meeting and destroying particular foes. The Ordos Malleus, Hereticus and Xenos each combat the threats of the daemonic, the heretic and the alien respectively, and each Ordo maintains its own specialist warriors in the form of their Chamber Militant. The Chambers Militant train their entire lives to fight the threats their masters single out for destruction, and there are no more dedicated warriors in the entirety of the galaxy.

THE CULT IMPERIALIS

Following the ultimate sacrifice of the Emperor at the hands of the traitor Horus, the Imperium was swept by a general upsurge in adoration and worship for him. Visionaries and prophets appeared on every world and cults following these divinely inspired individuals soon formed. There was no central organisation, no control, and even on the same planet there could be hundreds of different denominations, each performing their worship in a different manner, every one of them interpreting the Emperor's will in a slightly different way. Although lots of worlds still have several different sects, other cults have managed to spread beyond the surface of their planet, their servants travelling to other stars and worlds to spread their own version of faith. Many of these sects still exist in the 41st millennium, some thriving, others small, shadowy cults that exist on the fringe of society.

As is the way of such things, the stronger cults grew and prospered while others were incorporated into the schemes of the larger sects. Compromises of interpretation were found and slowly many cults became united. The most successful of these was the Temple of the Saviour Emperor, which in the 32nd millennium was recognised as an Imperial organisation – the Ministorum, or Ecclesiarchy as it is generally known. Through its Preachers, Confessors, Missionaries and Cardinals, the Ecclesiarchy attempts to control the veneration of the masses, giving them an organised focus for their homage. It fights Wars of Faith to protect its beliefs, and sends the agents of the Missionarus Galaxia to distant worlds to spread the word of the Ecclesiarch.

The Imperial Creed of the Ministorum is open to much interpretation, from the Ecclesiarch down to the parish Preachers. Schools of thought exist within the Ministorum concerning certain strictures, passages from the Litanies of Faith and so on. Although these schools differ in opinion from each other, and often the Ecclesiarch, it is now rare for them to be declared heretic (though it is still known) unless they are of exceptional deviance. Often these different viewpoints are points of detail – matters of protocol, layout of shrines and architectural styles are all matters of contention. Often the Holy Synod rages for weeks with debate concerning matters the ordinary citizen would find trivial or, more likely, incomprehensible.

There is a fine line between enlightened, healthy debate and heresy, and throughout the Ecclesiarchy's long history there are individuals and sects that have crossed over. Of course, there are the blatant heretics – for instance, deluded fools who worship the Chaos gods. The guilt of these people cannot be

mendicanti

SPACE MARINE CHAPLAINS

The Space Marine Chapters do not adhere to the teachings of the Ecclesiarchy, and there has been much conflict between the Ministorum and the Adeptus Astartes in the past. On occasion, such as during the Reign of Blood, this has even reached the level of outright warfare. The traditions of each Space Marine Chapter are kept by the Chaplains, who oversee the spiritual education and well-being of their Battle Brothers. These beliefs vary wildly from Chapter to Chapter, worshipping the Emperor and their Primarchs to differing degrees. The Space Marines do not consider him a god in the same sense as that preached by the Ecclesiarchy, and instead worship the Emperor as a great, gifted man. His blood runs in their veins and he is considered the ultimate example of Mankind, but a man nonetheless. It is also a matter of debate whether the Space Marines are truly human at all. Their genetically engineered bodies are far superior to a normal human, enough to make them a separate race if one wished to interpret their differences so. How can any self-respecting Confessor or Cardinal relate to a monstrous giant who can spit acid, crush a man's skull with one hand and practices crude acts of blood sacrifice?

disputed and their execution is rightly justified. Their betrayal of Humanity and the Emperor cannot go unpunished and if such cults were allowed to flourish the Imperium would be doomed. However, a heretic is not always so obvious in his treachery. Often those who stray from the ordained path do not do so in one leap, but in a series of small steps. The heretic may begin to doubt the teachings of the Ecclesiarchy, allowing his own self-interest to overcome his duty of sacrifice to the Emperor and Mankind. He may disagree with certain proclamations of the Ecclesiarch. From this selfishness, the heretic may then start to work against the established hierarchy and organisation of the Imperium, twisting and corrupting the system for their own ends.

There can be no forgiveness for heretics, and execution is the only punishment for such deviancy. Depending upon the severity of the heresy, their death may be a quick, clean matter or a drawn out tortuous affair of agony and injury to purge their souls of the dark taint within. To even suggest that there can be peace with such people is to invite dissent and disaster. Only through the vigilance of its loyal citizens can the Imperium survive. To think otherwise is to court anarchy and the destruction of Mankind.

THE ADEPTA SORORITAS

Within the immense structure of the Ministorum is an organisation devoted to worship of the Emperor and yet also dedicated to wider pursuits. Due to its all-female membership, the Adepta Sororitas is often referred to as the Sisterhood, although some still call it by its original name, the Daughters of the Emperor. The Sisterhood is most commonly associated with the Battle Sisters of the Orders Militant, but war is not its only role in the Imperium. There are several other major Orders of the Adepta Sororitas and many others numbering perhaps only a hundred or so individuals each. All of the Orders of the Sisterhood are divided between the two principal worlds of Terra and Ophelia VII. However, for much of the time, members of the Sisterhood will not be occupying their convent but are dispatched across the Imperium in accordance with their various duties.

THE ORDO HERETICUS

At the end of the Age of Apostasy, the Inquisition formed a secret order within its ranks to watch the Ecclesiarchy more closely. While the Inquisition as a whole monitors every aspect of the Imperium, the Ordo Hereticus is primarily concerned that another Plague of Unbelief does not occur. Though the Ecclesiarchy regulates itself and its followers closely (primarily with the Adepta Sororitas), the Ordo Hereticus provides another line of defence to ensure that those in power within the Ecclesiarchy do not abuse their position to such an extent that it threatens the stability of the Imperium again. These Inquisitors watch Wars of Faith closely to ensure the objectives laid down by the Ecclesiarch are both justified and not exceeded by those actually fighting. They monitor the Frateris Militia to safeguard the spirit of the Decree Passive (if not its letter) and to ensure its prohibitions stay enforced. They also regulate the amount of wealth and territory claimed by individuals within the Ecclesiarchy and halt attempts by Cardinals trying to amass more power than the Ordo Hereticus deems appropriate.

The Battle Sisters seek perfection of their martial skills in order to purify their minds and dedicate themselves to the Emperor. Each Order is run by a Canoness and her Sister Superiors. They look after the training of recruits, the performing of regular prayer sessions (usually several a day) and the maintenance of their own affairs. Part of the puritan lifestyle of the Sisterhood is its isolation and it is generally only the Canoness and her most experienced Sister Superiors who will have dealings with outsiders – even Sisters of another Order. The Sisters are utterly dedicated to one task or discipline and brook no distraction from their studies.

ca. 200.M36

THE AGE OF APOSTASY

The greatest strength of the Imperium is its faith in the Emperor, but when that faith is subverted it can be a powerful weapon for evil. In the 36th millennium, the insane tyrant Goge Vandire usurped the positions of both Ecclesiarch and High Lord of the Administratum, using bribery, blackmail, coercion and murder; driving the Imperium into its bloodiest period since the Horus Heresy – the Age of Apostasy and the Reign of Blood. With such unparalleled power to command, Vandire sought to bring the Imperium under his heel and millions died in the Reign of Blood as the Ministorum was split asunder by dozens of bloody Wars of Faith.

The Reign of Blood was to continue for another seven decades, with millions more burning in the fires of Vandire's insanity. As the years dragged on, Vandire grew ever more psychotic, and it was to this madman that a lone messenger delivered the news that heralded the end of the Reign of Blood. On the world of Dimmamar, a sect known as the Confederation of Light had emerged and denounced Vandire as a traitor. Its leader, a man known as Sebastian Thor, spread his message of hope to a brutalised people, only too ready to throw off the yoke of oppression, and soon system after system joined Thor's cause.

Vandire's forces set out to crush Thor, but shortly after its departure it was destroyed by a terrifyingly powerful warp storm in an area of space still known and feared as the Storm of the Emperor's Wrath. Whole swathes of the Imperium now rebelled against Vandire, with scores of systems declaring for Thor and the Confederation of Light. An orator of supreme skill, Sebastian Thor swayed millions to his cause and soon turned the tide against Vandire. Though millions rallied to his call, it was from the Adepts of Mars and a force of Space Marines that final deliverance came. Uniting with Thor against Vandire, they assaulted the Ecclesiarchal Palaces from without, a Centurion of the Adeptus Custodes, the Emperor's praetorian guard, moving against Vandire from within. Vandire's bodyguards, the Brides of the Emperor, were shown the heresies of Vandire and, being pure of faith in their hearts, they executed the maniacal lord. And from the ashes of this terrible conflict a new hope arose – the Sisters of Battle, protectors of the faith.

OPHELIA VII

Oldest of the Cardinal worlds, Ophelia VII is second in sanctity only to holy Terra itself. Site of the Synod Ministra, its surface is covered in mile-high cathedrals and bell towers, linked by avenues lined with statues of the Imperium's thousands of saints. Voices raised in hymn and prayer echo the draughty corridors day and night, accompanied by the solemn tolling of bells. Deep beneath the gold busts and fine tapestries, the dungeons of Ophelia VII plunge deep into the bowels of the world. Here heretics are chastised and made to repent their sins in their hundreds, subject to such soul-cleansing attentions as Arco-flagellation, Death-masking, Soul-scouring and the Trial of Castigation.

LOGIS
DÆMONUM

MILITARY FORCES OF THE IMPERIUM

The galaxy is a hostile place and only by force of arms is the Imperium held together. It is a time of war and warriors, where only the strong and ruthless can hope to survive, where there is no peace amongst the stars and only by the deaths of millions can the Imperium endure. Enemies attack from all sides, every aspect of the Imperium geared towards the struggle for survival, and the galaxy echoes to the clash of weapons and the thunder of mighty guns. The armies of the Emperor can afford no mercy, no weakness and no respite from their unending wars.

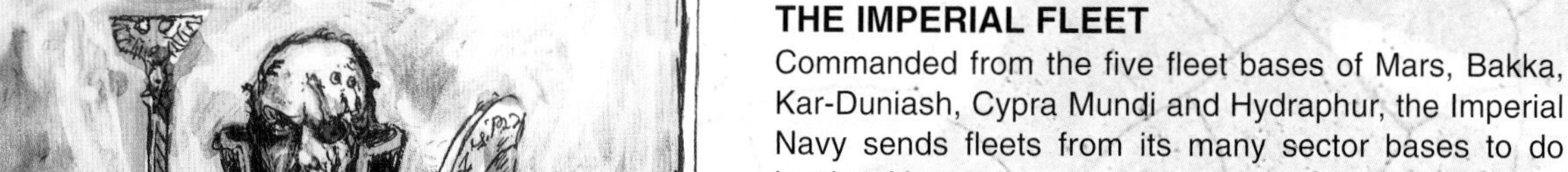

THE IMPERIAL FLEET

Commanded from the five fleet bases of Mars, Bakka, Kar-Duniash, Cypra Mundi and Hydraphur, the Imperial Navy sends fleets from its many sector bases to do battle. Vast, city-sized constructions, most Naval vessels are thousands of years old, ancient gothic leviathans with terrifyingly powerful weapons and whole squadrons of fighters and bombers within their hangar decks. Entire battlefleets cross the gulf of space to bring ruin upon the foes of the Emperor, destroying their ships and pounding their worlds into dust. The ships of the Navy also provide a forcible reminder to planetary governors of the might of the Imperium, and the arrival of but a single ship is often enough to bring a defiant world to heel.

As well as maintaining fleets of warships, the Imperial Navy is tasked with the sacred duty of transporting the Imperial Guard from war zone to war zone. Forbidden by ancient decree from maintaining their own fleets, the Imperial Guard is beholden to the Navy to ferry its regiments across the galaxy. Packed into colossal transports, tens of thousands of soldiers and their wargear are shipped to distant star systems to fight and die on planets most of them will never have heard of.

THE IMPERIAL GUARD

The vast armies of the Imperial Guard are the sledgehammer with which the enemies of Mankind are smashed asunder, covering the battlefields of the Imperium in their millions. The soldiers of the Emperor are as numerous as the stars themselves, and when the Guard goes to war, the very earth shakes with the rumble of tanks, the thunder of artillery and the pounding of marching feet. Raised from every world in the Imperium, the Imperial Guard is a hugely diverse organisation, with each regiment having all manner of special skills that they can bring to bear. The Catachan regiments come from one of the most lethal death worlds in the galaxy and are expert jungle fighters, the Tanith First and Only are stealth troopers without equal and the Narmenian Armoured brigades specialise in lightning-fast attacks with heavy tanks.

Every Planetary Governor within the Imperium must recruit, equip and maintain his own planetary defence forces from the local population. The number and type of these forces vary enormously from world to world and are, essentially, the Imperial Commander's personal

> Commissars are high-ranking officers of the Departmento Munitorum and form part of the strategic command of the Imperial Guard. Unlike Guard regiments, which are levied from their homeworlds when they are needed or tithed, Commissars are raised to serve the Emperor from an early age, and learn the highest virtues of honour and obedience in the harsh environment of the Schola Progenium. Rigid adherents to the Imperial Creed, Commissars are ruthless, fearless individuals whose dedication to the service of the Emperor overrides any compassion or mercy for the men they must sometimes lead in battle. In times of war, their role is to maintain the fighting discipline and honour of the Emperor's fighting troops and, if necessary, give their lives as an example to their comrades. The soldiers of the Imperial Guard regard Commissars with a mixture of fear and respect, given that they summarily execute any troopers (or officers) deemed to be giving less than his all.

army, ranging from feral, spear-wielding warriors, hive gang militia to forces indistinguishable from Imperial Guard regiments. These warriors never leave their homeworld and are the first line of defence when the planet is threatened, often bearing the brunt of any invasion. Though many Imperial Guard regiments look down on Planetary Defence Forces, their fighting spirit and courage is not to be underestimated.

The Imperial Guard undertakes vast crusades to liberate entire star systems or sectors from alien or rebel domination. Led by Warmasters, powerful men in whose hands the fate of billions rests, they fight on countless worlds, with crusades sometimes lasting generations and not stopping until victory is won, though the butcher's bill may cost the blood of every man fighting. Further down the chain of command are the Lords General Militant and the Colonels of each regiment, where command decisions are based on more immediate tactical concerns rather than the grand strategies employed by the higher echelons of command. To be a soldier of the Imperial Guard on the front line of battle is to be one among faceless billions, enduring the horrors of a deadly galaxy with nothing but a lasgun, faith and courage to call his own. Led by courageous officers and the feared Commissars, the soldiers of the Imperial Guard are truly the Armoured Fist of the Emperor.

THE ADEPTUS ASTARTES

Sometimes the Imperial Guard is too ponderous to react to developing war zones, and when a rapid strike is required, it is the Space Marines of the Adeptus Astartes who take up the fight. Organised into Chapters of roughly a thousand warriors, the Space Marines are the most supreme fighting force in the galaxy, angels of death who smite their enemies without mercy. Each Chapter maintains its own fleet of ships and armouries and, unfettered by the stifling bureaucracy of the Departmento Munitorum, is able to swiftly and decisively respond to an entreaty for aid, or to actively seek out and destroy threats to Mankind.

In battle, the Space Marines are the most devastating warriors the Imperium can muster. Stronger, faster and tougher than the greatest of normal men, their bio-engineered bodies can fight in any environment and survive the most traumatic of wounds, enabling a Space Marine to fight until his body has been utterly destroyed. In the depths of hive worlds, in bloody boarding actions and bitter street fighting, the Space Marines are at the forefront of the most dangerous warzones in the galaxy. The enemies of the Imperium fear many things – discovery, defeat, despair and death. Yet there is one thing they fear above all others – they fear the wrath of the Space Marines.

THE ANGELS OF DEATH

SPACE MARINES

Commander Cantor of the Crimson Fists, during the Rynn's World Reclamation

Genetically altered superhuman warriors created from the flesh of the Emperor Himself, the Space Marines are the greatest defenders of Humanity, standing resolute against the myriad horrors of a hostile galaxy. They are superior to normal humans in every respect, thanks to a brutal regime of genetic modification, psycho-conditioning and a life of strict discipline that only such enhanced warriors can endure. A Space Marine can survive wounds that would kill a normal man thrice over, fight in the harshest conditions imaginable, and has a depth of faith that is unquenchable in its force of belief. Armed with the boltgun, a weapon of divine wrath, and armoured in ancient, artificer-forged suits of power armour, the Space Marines are living embodiments of the Emperor's Will.

Space Marines are banded together in small, independent armies known as Chapters. Each Chapter is made up of a thousand Space Marines and is responsible for its own recruitment, training and indoctrination. Much more than soldiers, Space Marines are noble of spirit, stern of demeanour and fanatically devoted to their Chapter and the Emperor, fighting with a zeal and fervour no mortal man can match. Unable to muster the massive numbers of the Imperial Guard, the Space Marines fight on battlefields of their choosing; hard-hitting surgical strikes and lightning assaults. They are the Angels of Death and none can stand before them. With fire and steel they cleanse the stars of the xeno, purge the galaxy of the wicked and destroy the enemies of Mankind without mercy.

Logan Grimnar, Great Wolf of the Space Wolves

The Emperor's Champion

Commander Dante of the Blood Angels

Brother Tekisen of the Revilers Chapter

Brother-Sergeant Ezraen of the Crimson Fists

Brother Arikaas of the Salamanders

Scout Castus of the Imperial Fists

Clan-Brother Jogaten of the White Scars

Brother Kaelen of the Dark Angels Deathwing

Revered Brother Aristede, Ultramarines Dreadnought

ULTRA

The Ultramarines are strict adherents to the Codex Astartes, a holy tome of war penned by their Primarch, Roboute Guilliman. Here, the Ultramarines 2nd Company storm the walls of Corinth with support from Terminators of the 1st Company.

The Space Wolves are fierce, indepedent warriors who do not adhere to the strictures of the Codex Astartes, and are organised into Great Companies led by their Wolf Lords.

Watched over by their Chaplains, the battle-frenzied warriors of the Death Company have finally succumbed to the flaw that lies within the gene-seed of the Blood Angels.

Though staunchly loyal and stubborn in their defence of Mankind, the Dark Angels pursue their own agenda to atone for an ancient wrong that has shrouded them in mystery for ten thousand years.

The Black Templars are divided into many Crusades, spread across fleets all over the galaxy, taking the fight to the enemies of the Emperor. The zealous Novitiates and Initiates fight in mixed squads, allowing the newest recruits to learn quickly in the fires of battle.

HAMMER OF THE EMPEROR

Guardsman Heller, Shock Trooper and Sergeant Rawke, Kasrkin Grenadier, both of the Cadian 8th

The Imperium of Man is the greatest power in a galaxy wracked by endless war, locked in a daily battle for survival against the most horrific and implacable enemies imaginable. Its destruction is held at bay only by the might and courage of its inexhaustible armies, the brave soldiers that make up the ranks of the Imperial Guard. This mighty force is Mankind's primary and most numerous defence, numbering billions upon billions of soldiers raised as tens of thousands of Regiments from all the myriad types of world found in the Imperium. Regiments vary enormously across the galaxy and include all manner of warriors, from disciplined ranks of infantry, glorious cavalry, whole regiments of tanks and artillery to the leviathan-like super-heavy tanks and titanic Capitol Imperialis. They are the Imperial Guard – the Hammer of Emperor.

Each world of the Imperium is obliged to raise regiments of Imperial Guard, and these are shipped all across the galaxy to fight terrible wars in the Emperor's name. The Imperial Guard fights at every level, from a platoon assigned to defend a small frontier colony, to massive army groups fighting wars that stretch across dozens of star systems. Though its armies manoeuvre ponderously, the Imperial Guard can bring to battle an unending tide of infantry, supported by countless armoured vehicles and guns. With thunderous artillery barrages, roaring tanks and volleys of lasgun fire, the Imperial Guard crushes its enemies utterly, attacking in an unstoppable tide that reduces a war zone to a cratered hell. It is warfare at its most brutal, where individual soldiers are irrelevant and the advance of hundreds of thousands of men decides the fate of worlds.

Commissar Yarrick, Hero of Armageddon

Jarran Kell Regimental Standard, Cadian 8th

Ursarkar E. Creed, Commander, Cadian 8th

Kasrkin Sergeant Hursen, Cadian 8th

Sergeant Helvstok, Valhallan 93rd,Soldane Campaign

Guardsman Fulkerin, Armageddon Steel Legion

Sergeant Kolst, 211th Mordian, Capital Garrison

Trooper Barasq, 39th Cadian, Veldt fatigues

Corporal 'Burn It' Leafer, 113th Catachan

Sniper Poles of the 202nd Cadian recce Platoon

Trooper Alghuz, 12th Tallarn, Cursus War

The Cadians come from a Garrison World, drawing fighters from all of their society, from the Youth Armies to the elite Kasrkin. Here, the defenders of Bunker 135 prepare to meet the charge of the Black Legion head on.

The Valhallan regiments are often posted to the most inhospitable worlds, where the training on their harsh homeworld stands them in good stead.

The Tanith First and Only are a Light Infantry Regiment famed for their stealth skills, considered by most to be second to none in infiltrating behind enemy lines.

From the lethal Deathworld of Catachan, these Jungle Fighters are experts at laying traps and springing ambushes on their foes before melting back into the foliage.

The Steel Legion are well-supplied with tanks and weaponry from their homeworld of Armageddon and are renowned for their high proportion of armoured vehicles

SERVANTS OF THE EMPEROR

Sister Severine of the Order of Our Martyred Lady

Every subject of the Imperium serves the God-Emperor of Mankind, either in worship or in deed. From the lowliest scribe to the mightiest Space Marine there is not a single soul amongst his numberless subjects who does not serve the vast machine that is the Imperium. On a million worlds, the faithful give praise to the Emperor for their continued existence, gathering under the auspices of the Ecclesiarchy whose Preachers and Confessors spread the teachings of the Emperor to the masses. From their holy books and scriptures are the common citizenry of the Imperium warned of the dangers of heresy, mutation and witchcraft and the deadly punishments meted out to those who break faith with the Emperor. And they are also told of those servants of the Emperor who wage war upon such deviants; the agents of the Orders of the Emperor's Holy Inquisition.

Inquisitors are utterly ruthless individuals who hunt the enemies of the Emperor across every Imperial world and beyond, questing into the dark places of the galaxy for those who conspire against the Imperium. None are above their suspicions, and it is a brave individual who dares defy an Inquisitor, for their power is great and none who are cast within their nightmare oubliettes are ever seen again. They may call upon any to aid them and their servants range from battle-hardened Sisters of Battle, lethal assassins and Space Marines to monstrous beings of terrible power bound to the Inquisitor's service. The reach of the Emperor's servants is long and though the Imperium is the greatest stellar realm ever seen, no man or other creature is beyond their keen gaze.

Eversor Assassin of the Officio Assassinorum

Saint Celestine, Hieromartyr of the Palatine Crusade

Brother-Captain Stern of the Grey Knights

Lady Natalus, Inquisitor of the Ordo Hereticus

Sister Carmina of the Adepta Sororitas

Inquisitor Lord Fyodor Karamazov

Sister Helios of the Adepta Sororitas

Brother Jantine of the Grey Knights

When the threat is great, Inquisitors of the Ordo Malleus and Ordo Hereticus will often join forces to defend the enemies of Mankind. The Grey Knights and the Adepta Sororitas combine to formidable effect to defend the holy shrine of St. Capilene.

143–160.M41
THE GOTHIC WAR

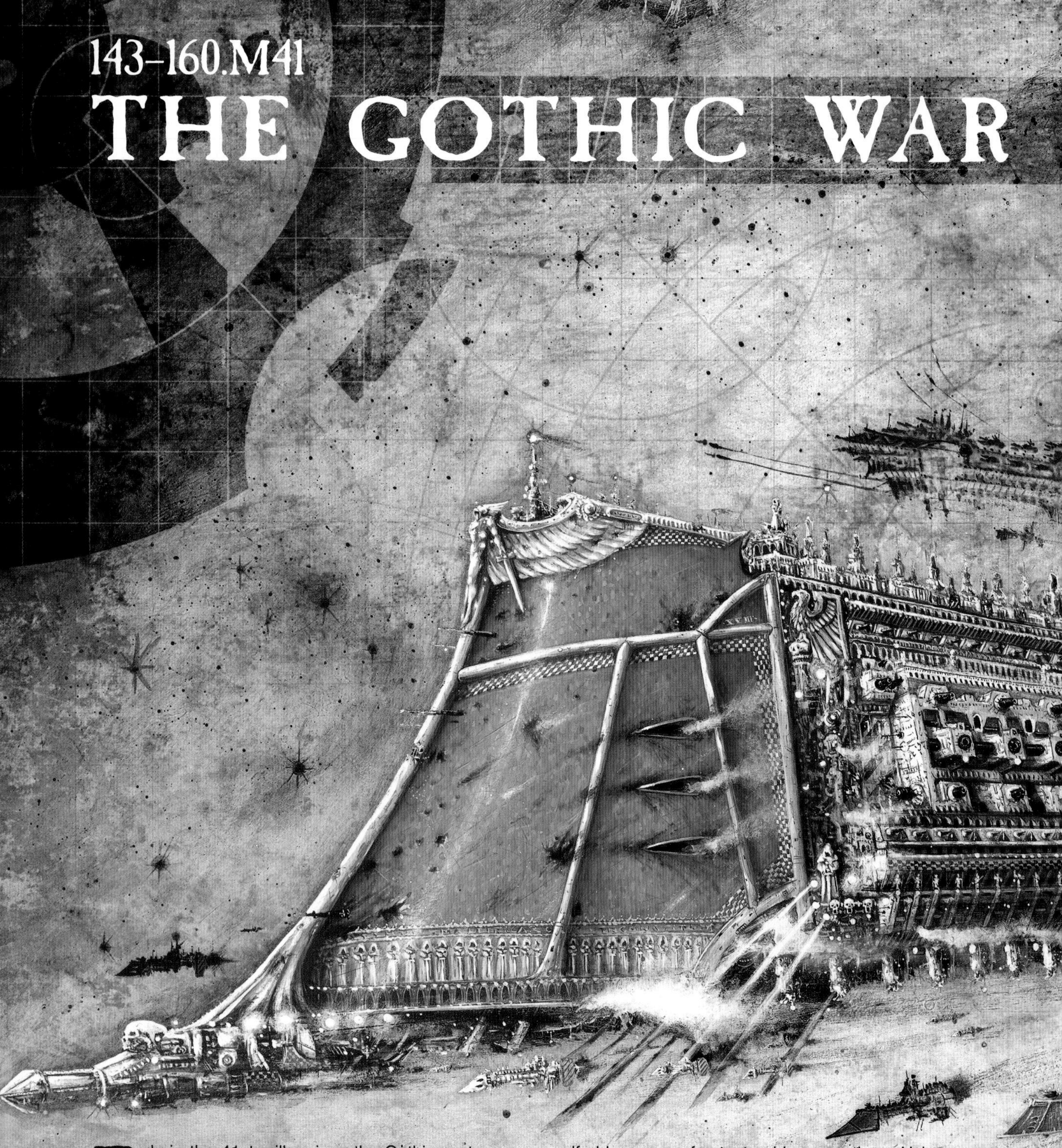

Early in the 41st millennium, the Gothic sector was engulfed by a war of catastrophic proportions. Using arcane means, Chaos Warmaster Abaddon the Despoiler led his forces from the Eye of Terror. A fleeting break in the warp storms that had embroiled the Gothic sector allowed Abaddon's massive armada to elude the monitor stations and garrison worlds of the Cadian Gate.

Imperial forces reeled under the sudden onslaught and Abaddon's followers conquered whole star systems in the first few weeks of the war. Isolated by the warp storms, the Gothic sector stood alone against Mankind's most hated foes. For nearly a decade the fleets of Lord Admiral Ravensburg did all they could to survive the repeated attacks, defending worlds and bases at tremendous cost. After years of suffering these depradations, Battlefleet Gothic under Lord Ravensburg won a great victory at the Battle of Gethsemane, breaking a large Chaos fleet asunder.

This victory turned the tide against Abaddon, who hastened forward his grand strategy. The entire war was an attempt to secure the ancient, monolithic weapons known as Blackstone Fortresses. These moon-sized artefacts date back to long before the Emperor rose to power, and Abaddon found the key to unlock their arcane secrets. One by one the Blackstones fell to Abaddon, and he unleashed their power against planets and even stars. It was thought that the last of the captured Blackstone Fortresses was destroyed as a combined Imperial and Eldar fleet pursued Abaddon from the Schindlegeist system, but the Despoiler was later to exploit their power during his attack on Cadia nearly a thousand years later.

PORT MAW

Port Maw is the capital of the Gothic sector and the headquarters of Battlefleet *Gothic*. It is ringed with hundreds of bastion-stations, monitor ships, defence satellites and minefields, and proved to be virtually impregnable to attack during the Gothic War. Faced with such awesome defences, the Chaos fleets were restricted to terror raids and sabotage missions, though the system was blockaded for almost the entirety of the war.

THE ADEPTUS MECHANICUS

Known by many as the Priesthood of Mars, the Adeptus Mechanicus develop and construct the weapons of war used by the Emperor's armies and it is their knowledge of arcane mysteries that maintains the technologies of the Golden Throne. The research and study of technoarcana, and the uncovering and protection of ancient knowledge from the Dark Age of Technology, are the goals of the Magi of Mars and their untold billions of servants spread across the galaxy. Through their painstaking mystic rites and ceremonies, intricately-phrased chants, meticulously prepared oils and unguents, the Techpriests sanctify Mankind's weapons with the blessings of the Machine God.

The Adeptus Mechanicus is centred upon Mars, but its influence stretches across the galaxy through its hundreds of forge worlds. On the forge worlds are billions of Techpriests toiling ceaselessly to fulfil manufacturing and research quotas, knowing the outside world only as a set of algorithms and pict-transfers. Their industry is carried out by an uncountable mass of servitors – half-man half-machine creatures whose minds have been partially programmed to perform specific duties.

THE CULT MECHANICUS

The Cult Mechanicus, or Cult of the Machine, acknowledges the Emperor as Master of Mankind, but does not recognise the authority of the Cult Imperialis. Instead, the Adepts of Mars follow their own dark and mysterious strictures.

According to the teachings of the Cult Mechanicus, knowledge is the supreme manifestation of divinity, and all creatures and artefacts that embody knowledge are holy because of it. Machines that preserve knowledge from ancient times are also holy, and machine intelligences are no less divine than those of flesh and blood. A man's worth is only the sum of his knowledge – his body is simply an organic machine capable of preserving intellect.

The Machine God, the Deus Mechanicus, is the ultimate object of the Techpriests' veneration. It is the Machine God that gave rise to all technologies and made them manifest

STANDARD TEMPLATE CONSTRUCTS

The Adeptus Mechanicus is driven by the quest for knowledge. This quest takes many forms, including research and exploration, but its ultimate embodiment is the search for ancient Standard Template Construct (STC) systems. These were created during the Dark Age of Technology to provide all the technical information needed to construct anything that settlers might need. Even the least technically-accomplished person could build a vehicle, aircraft or weapon given time. One result of the STC system and its pivotal place in human colonisation is that human material culture is very similar, even on worlds which are many thousands of light years apart.

Today there are no known surviving STC systems, and only a very few examples of first-generation texts. For thousands of years the Adeptus Mechanicus has pursued all information about the STC. Any scrap of information is eagerly sought out and jealously hoarded. Any rumour of a functional system is followed up and investigated in force.

A favoured servant or loyal functionary may be granted the honour of continuing to serve the Emperor after death. Engraved and gilded, their skulls are put to good use by the Emperor's devout followers.

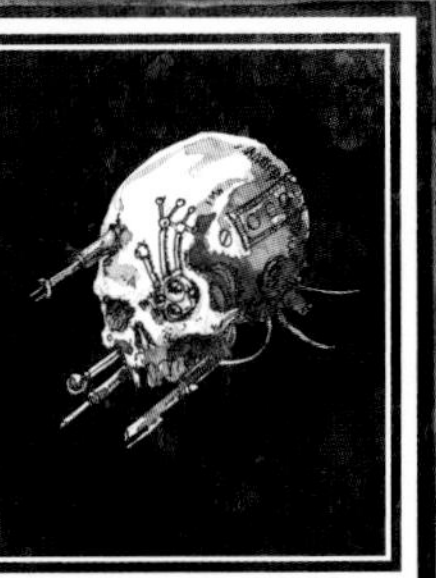

through his chosen illuminati among Mankind. To the Mechanicus, machines represent a higher form of life than that thrown up by the crude processes of evolution. The planned perfection of form and function embodied in a machine could only originate from a divine source, using biological or mechanical vessels to embody and pass on its great knowledge.

The ordinary cult membership of the Adeptus Mechanicus is composed of the Techpriests. They form a hierarchy of technicians, scientists and religious leaders. Techpriests provide the Imperium with its engineers and technical experts, serving aboard ships, in hives, at manufactoria and generatoria and wherever else their skills are required. The highest ranking Techpriests are usually found on the forge worlds themselves, and are the Magi. A Magos is dedicated to researching a sphere of particular knowledge, be he a Magos Biologis, a Magos Genetor, Magos Cybernetica, or an expert on one of dozens of other disciplines. The leader of the Adeptus Mechanicus is the Fabricator General of Mars. The Fabricator General is also a High Lord of Terra and one of the most powerful members of the Senatorum Imperialis. He is also the head of the Cult Mechanicus in his capacity as the Magos Mechanicus.

ARMIES OF THE MACHINE GOD

The bulk of the Adeptus Mechanicus' armed forces are forge guards known as Skitarii – human soldiers with basic bionic augmentations for communication, weapon links and sensory feeds. With the manufacturing power of the Adeptus Mechanicus behind them, the Skitarii are amongst the best equipped soldiers in the Imperium, rating alongside such forces as the Imperial Guard Storm Troopers and Drop Legions. Although most forge worlds maintain whole Regiments of Skitarii, their dominant role is to bolster the already considerable power of the gigantic war machines of the Titan Legions and crew the massive mobile support weapons of the Centurio Ordinatus.

Without the Titan Legions, few forge worlds would have survived the waves of heresy, corruption and alien attack that beset them during the Age of Strife. Titans are giant walking battleships capable of fighting in the most hostile conditions and carrying enough firepower to level city blocks. These behemoths of war are worshipped by the Mechanicus as god-machines, blazing seraphs of the Machine God. The Collegia Titanica is dedicated to maintaining the awesome fighting power of the Titan Legions, supplying them and repairing them on the field of battle, venerating and maintaining them in the brief respites between campaigns.

One of the most vital tasks of the Collegia is recruiting and training individuals of sufficient will to enter mind impulse links with the fierce and warlike machine spirit of a Titan. Only the strongest can survive such a link with their sanity intact, as they must be able to retain their sentience amidst the roaring, indomitable spirit of destruction that dwells within each of these adamantium giants. Recruits are taken from wherever they can be found among the Cult Mechancius or even beyond it, for it is a rare man that can ride to war in a Battle Titan.

THE IMMATERIUM

The galaxy is so vast as to defy comprehension by mortal minds, covering distances so enormous that they require centuries or even millennia to traverse. Under normal circumstances, such unimaginable gulfs would make a mockery of any attempt to establish a galactic-wide empire, but there exists a way to make such journeys without them taking centuries. The Warp, Empyrean or Immaterium as it is sometimes known, is an alternate dimension existing beyond the veil of reality that is a dark mirror of the material realm. It is a churning ocean of chaos, raw emotion and madness given form, where the laws of physics, time and nature are meaningless concepts and nothing is as it seems. Stirred by the thoughts and emotions of creatures in the material universe, it is inhabited by all manner of nightmare entities formed from the very stuff of chaos, ready to devour the unwary or incautious. The souls of mortals are as flickering fireflies in the Warp, pricking the darkness before fading into obscurity, though the souls of psykers are blazing torches, flaring like the brightest of beacons.

WARP TRAVEL

Starships equipped with warp engines are able to breach the invisible walls that separate the material realm and the Immaterium and traverse its hazardous expanse. Shielded from the destructive wrath of the Warp by the protective energies of a Gellar Field, ships that enter the Immaterium can complete a journey that might normally take centuries in a matter of months.. Only psychic signals can penetrate the barriers separating the material realm and warp space, and only the power of the psychic beacon known as the Astronomican is bright enough to cross the vastness of the galaxy. Originating on Terra, the Astronomican is projected through space from a vast, tiered chamber carved from a single mountain peak, where a ten-thousand strong choir of trained psykers is agonisingly leeched of their life energies to empower its divine light. The sheer quantity of such psychic energy generated is vast, and only the mind of the Emperor is mighty enough to direct such raw power. The prodigious amounts of energy required to maintain the Astronomican soon reduces these psykers to dry husks of withered flesh, and more must be brought forth every day to replace the corpses of those who have perished. Though their fate is a sad one, it is a necessary one, for without the Astronomican, there would be little or no space travel and the Imperium would soon collapse into warring factions.

In order to travel through the Warp, ships must have a Navigator, strange psykers that possess a unique sense, the Warp Eye that can see beyond the pitiful senses of most mortals. With the Astronomican as a reference point in the material universe, they enter a trance-like state and are able to chart the ship's journey with a greater degree of accuracy than would normally be possible. They can see the tides of the Immaterium, guiding a ship along the treacherous currents that carry a vessel towards its destination.

To traverse the roiling sea of chaos that is the Warp, Navigators must have a fixed point of reference to hold onto before risking such a dangerous undertaking. Though warp travel can drastically reduce the times required to travel between the stars, it is not without risk and there are many hazards inherent in such journeys. One side effect of such travel is that time passes differently in the Warp and while the crew of a starship may perceive days or weeks passing, months or even years may have passed in the material realm. Like a sea, the Warp is sometimes wracked by storms and these can throw ships wildly off course or vastly alter the effects of the time dilation.

As well as Navigators to chart a course through the Warp, starships require Astropaths to maintain contact with other ships and planets in real space. Astropaths are tormented, blind wretches with the ability to transmit dreams and thoughts to others of their kind across vast distances. Such communication is dangerous and never without consequence, and the unfortunate individuals cursed with such powers exist on the verge of madness, plagued by terrifying visions of blood and death, menaced by echoes of the future, their uncaring masters forcing them to cast their mind adrift the terrifying depths of the Warp. Astropaths also have powers of divination, able to glimpse fleeting hints of unwritten futures through readings of the mystical Emperor's Tarot or other, more barbaric, rituals such as the readings of entrails or the casting of bones. The use of these abilities inevitably takes its toll on the Astropath and only through the agonising ritual of the Soul Binding are they protected from the predations of the terrifying creatures that exist within the Warp. Such measures are never absolutely safe and the threat of possession or worse is a constant danger these individuals must live with.

PSYKERS

More and more psykers emerge throughout the Imperium and though they represent the future promise of Mankind, they are also its most deadly threat. Psykers draw their powers from the immaterial energies of warp space and their souls burn like the brightest flames in the darkness of the Warp, drawing terrifying Warp creatures to them like moths to a flame. The Inquisition constantly hunts down such individuals, executing those who are simply too dangerous to allow to live. The rest are taken by the Inquisition's Black Ships, some to feed the Emperor's voracious appetite, some condemned to join the choir of the Astronomican, while others, whose mental fortitude is great enough, may become battle psykers of the Imperial Guard or even Space Marine Librarians. These powerful individuals are capable of directing the energies of the Warp in hugely destructive ways, smiting their foes with bolts of psychic energy powerful enough to obliterate a battle tank. Space Marine Librarians are amongst the most terrifyingly powerful psykers in the galaxy, though it is only through a lifetime of discipline and training that they are able to use such abilities. Though, like all psykers, they walk a fine line between service to the Emperor and eternal damnation.

THE SOUL BINDING

No ordinary psyker could transmit a message through the warp, nor could he receive a telepathic message over such vast distances. Astropaths only gain this ability as a result of their many years training, culminating in a special ritual which combines some of the Emperor's own power with their own. This ritual, known as Soul Binding, brings the mind of the psyker close to the psychic greatness of the Emperor. In the process, some of the Emperor's vast energy is transferred to the Astropath.

The transference of energy is traumatic for the psyker – not all survive despite years of preparation, and not all those that survive retain their sanity. Even the survivors suffer damage to the sensitive nerves of the eyes, so that almost all Astropaths are blind. In fact their increased psychic skills tend to make up for this loss of sight, so that they would not appear blind were it not for their distorted, sunken and empty eye sockets.

THE PERILS OF THE WARP

Though it is the means by which Mankind has spread his empire across the stars, travel through the Immaterium is hazardous in the extreme. The tides of the Warp make the voids of real space seem familiar and safe, for its nature is fickle and perilous and to ply its shifting tides is to invite disaster. Storms thought sweep through this immaterial realm, spinning craft out of control for light years around, destroying all those embroiled in their merciless energies. In addition to the physical and spiritual peril of those caught in a warp storm, these maelstroms of energy obscure the signal of the Astronomican, making navigation in their vicinity difficult, if not impossible. Those that survive find themselves thousands of light years from their planned destination, or hurled into some distant time where all hope of returning home is lost. Some emerge horrifically changed, their craft melded into the drifting, haunted behemoths known as space hulks, conglomerations of ship and asteroid that wink in and out of the material realm spreading infestations of aliens and daemons wherever they appear. Most victims of these freakish storms do not emerge at all, trapped for all eternity as playthings of the denizens of the Warp.

Warp storms are not merely confined to the Immaterium, and can bleed into the material realm; shimmering, livid wounds in the fabric of real space that feed on the fears of those who witness them until they become raging tempests. Worlds can be cut off from the rest of the Imperium for months, years or even centuries. These storms appear from nowhere and can consign a world to a slow and gradual death, forcing it to devolve into barbarism and savagery. Ancient Terra itself suffered such a fate in the many centuries directly before the Emperor united Mankind and brought it back into the light.

Some hope remains for these benighted worlds, for warp storms sometimes recede for a few months, making travel possible though still highly dangerous. During these brief moments of calm the ships of the Imperium may arrive, demanding the Emperor's tithes and recruiting new warriors for its fleets and armies. Many such worlds are only barely aware of the Imperium's existence, a dimly remembered name or legend that tells of a mighty Emperor and his innumerable armies who stand in readiness for the day of judgement.

Warp storms are far from the only dangers within the Warp. Sentient energies and other immaterial lifeforms dwell within it; creatures formed from and sustained by

alpha bound

Enslavers travel on the currents of the Immaterium and are drawn to the psychic emanations of living creatures. Once a psychic host is found, Enslavers form a parasitic mental bond with it and bring about a sickening transformation. The host is distorted and twisted over a period of days to form a living warp portal, a pulsating arch of ruptured flesh that permits the Enslavers egress into the material plane. Once Enslavers have appeared on a world they seek out and transform more hosts so that more and more Enslavers appear. Once an Enslaver infestation has begun it is very hard to stop, short of the ultimate sanction of Exterminatus.

For a thousand days the great Black Ships of the Adeptus sailed towards Earth. In the thirteen holds, each as cavernous as a cathedral nave, our human cargo sent up a great wailing and moaning. I counted twenty thousand psychic souls bound for service. Men, women and children. Young and old. The sick and the sound. Only the children did not know, or could not guess, what lay at their journey's end. But I am a psyker like them and I sensed their pain and felt their chains as if bound to my own body. Already I could taste the fear of the weak and knew what fate held for them. Most would serve by giving their lives. The remainder would serve in more dangerous ways. Their powers would be trained to provide the Emperor's Psykers, Astropaths, and thousands of other functionaries. But the decision was not mine to make, to separate those who would live from those who must die. I am a guardian of the Adeptus. Souls such as these I carry to the Emperor's table.

the shifting energies of the Warp prowling the ether as sharks prowl the ocean. Emotions given form, these sentient entities range from gibbering dream-forms to ancient and terrible gods. Diverse and multifarious, at best they are mindless, but the vast majority are predatory and extremely hostile. Mankind has attempted to classify some of those that haunt the Warp – the Vampyre and wasp-like Psychneuein, the Astral Spectre, the bloated Enslaver – but attempting to impose logic on Warp entities is a fool's errand. These entities thrive on the thoughts and emotions of those who dwell in the material universe, nurturing their foul ambitions of power and conquest. Even to think of them is to risk their vile attentions.

Occasionally, the link between warp space and the material realm is weakened and energy from the Warp will burst through and create a vortex of power, destroying stars and planets. There are several such warp/real space interfaces throughout the galaxy, the largest of these being the Maelstrom and the infamous Eye of Terror. These regions cannot be traversed except by the most experienced Navigators, and such are the hazardous conditions that virtually no expeditions into these areas return. Those that do speak of a nightmare region where nature is anathema and madness and confusion reign. They speak of worlds whose skies burn with molten fire, of planets seething with rivers of ichor and blood, disc-shaped worlds slicing through seas of improbability, heavenly bodies with screaming faces and other far less comprehensible phenomena shaped by the mere whims of the Great Powers of the Warp. It would cost a man his mind, if not his soul, to list the inhabitants of these grim realms.

ALPHA-LEVEL PSYKERS

Perhaps the most dangerous human in the galaxy is an untrained psyker. If they are not controlled or purged, the erratic and awesome forces they can unwittingly unleash may destroy whole settlements or even worlds. Those cursed with an incredible level of psychic talent are codified by the Black Ships of the Inquisition as Alpha-level – the highest category a human psyker can reach. Alpha-level psykers can turn a man inside out with a glance. A mere flick of a wrist can snap a Battle Titan in two, or a muttered syllable turn an army upon itself in a frenzy of bloodlust. With such godlike power at their disposal, it is small wonder that Alpha-level psykers are amongst the most dreaded of foes that the Ordo Hereticus of the Inquisition must face.

The soul of one with such power burns like a supernova within the Empyrean, and all too frequently the denizens of the Warp flock to the uncontrolled mind like scavengers to a corpse, pushing through the veil into the mind of their prey. Such is the price of power, for the Warp does not give its gifts freely.

ca. M31

THE HORUS HERESY

The greatest and fiercest battle for Mankind's survival took place in the earliest years after the Emperor's rise to power. As the Space Marine Legions of the Emperor battled across the galaxy at the forefront of the Great Crusade, there were those amongst their number who were soon to commit the most despicable act of betrayal. Led by the Warmaster Horus, once most trusted of the Primarchs, fully half of the Legiones Astartes turned on the Emperor.

In an act of treachery so base that it has never been forgotten over ten thousand years, Horus bargained his soul to the Dark Gods of Chaos. He lured his unknowing foes into a trap on Isstvan V, massacring the loyal Space Marines as they landed. The few survivors who escaped brought word of the traitors' betrayal and the Imperium was split asunder by a galaxy-spanning civil war.

Battle-brother fought battle-brother on every world as the Legiones Astartes tore themselves apart. Horus himself besieged Terra and assaulted the Imperial Palace. Only the self-sacrifice of the Space Marine Primarch Sanguinius held Horus at bay, buying time for the Emperor to reach the Warmaster and slay him. Though Horus was destroyed, the Emperor was mortally crippled in body. Thus, in one vile act the Great Crusade was undone, the Emperor's plans thwarted, and the Age of the Imperium begun.

THE RUINOUS POWERS

Kor Phaeron of the Word Bearers, Master of the Dark Faith

For ten thousand years, there has been a canker at the heart of the Imperium. For ten millennia, the Traitor Legions have waged the Long War against the Emperor they once served. From within the Eye of Terror, the Chaos Space Marines sally forth to despoil and pillage, to destroy and conquer the worlds of the Imperium. Once the finest of the Emperor's warriors, at the forefront of the Great Crusade to conquer the galaxy, the Traitor Legionnaires have become twisted, hate-filled warriors intent on annihilating those who turned their backs on them and cast them into exile. Their dreams will not be achieved until holy Terra itself is reduced to a smouldering husk, bringing about the ruination of all that the Emperor sought to build.

Superhuman warriors invigorated and changed by the warping power of Chaos, these renegades are awesome killers whose abilities outstrip even those of the loyal Space Marines. With them come foul and terrifying Daemons, manifestations of Mankind's darkest horrors and ambitions. The ground trembles beneath the tread of clawed and beweaponed engines of destruction fuelled by the energy of the Warp. Led into battle by mighty Daemon Princes, horrific fighters with the power of Space Marine and Daemon combined, a force of Chaos Space Marines crushes any opposition with a swift and ruthless strike. Terror spreads before them, and devastation is left in their wake.

Khârn of the World Eaters, Betrayer of Skalathrax

Abaddon the Despoiler

The Daemon Prince Dhar'leth of the Black Legion

Hykal Ghon, Chaos Raptor

Morgaris, Chaos Terminator of the Night Lords

Sarisial of the Emperor's Children

Thousand Sons Warrior

Brother Kardon, World Eaters Berzerker

Refestus Plague Marine of the Death Guard

When the forces of Chaos unite under a powerful war leader, their invasions are a terrible thing to behold. Abaddon the Despoiler leads the hordes of Chaos in the destruction of the Cadian fortress at Kasr Partox.

THE TAINT OF CHAOS

Despite the myriad creatures of the Warp that swim through the Ether, the greatest threat to Mankind comes from within; from those who would consort with the Ruinous Powers or utilise the fell sorceries that can be wielded by tapping into the power of the Warp. Even a slight lapse in the harsh regime of discipline and vigilance imposed by the Adepts of the Imperium results in the spread of mutation, cultist and psyker activity and finally daemonic manifestation. Thus Imperial law is imposed with an iron hand – not only to control wayward subjects, but to prevent predators from another dimension entering the material realm. Faced with such threats, it is obvious why the edicts of the Imperium are enforced with lethal, uncompromising force.

Those who escape the scrutiny of the Imperium, and there are many skulking in the shadows, often fall prey to their own selfish pride and lust for power. They seek to bargain with the denizens of the Warp, to harness the might of the Empyrean in exchange for their obeisance. The sacrifice of human life, promises of service and arcane and superstitious ritual are employed by the heretic in his misguided attempts to gain the power of the creatures of Chaos. Ancient, unintelligible languages are chanted in barbaric ceremonies of desecration and treachery to bring forth the foul offerings of the Unnamed Gods. In most cases, such heathen efforts will go unanswered, as only the true student of the malevolent arts can really understand the circumstances that allow such creatures access to the material realm. In this way the cultist brings malignant entities forth from the Warp, and it is rare indeed that this does not cost him his soul. Such is the power and lure of Chaos, when its influence and servants are unearthed, the Inquisition must execute everyone even remotely in the vicinity lest its taint be spread further.

Accompanying the cultist down the path to ruination is the mutant. Mutation is a scourge upon all Mankind, a black reflection of the evolutionary process perverted into something far more sinister by the forces of Chaos. It nestles like a dark secret amongst even the most pious of Imperial organisations, and instances of mutation are becoming more and more frequent – a malignant epidemic threatening to turn Humanity into a race of degenerates.

Though it is rumoured the Eye of Terror harbours the walking dead and even mutant monstrosities that grow to the size of tanks, part of the difficulty in rooting out and destroying the mutant lies in the fact that these twisted individuals can often exist on civilised worlds by hiding their malformed parts from scrutiny. Mutation is a spiritual corruption as well as a physical; even the robes of an Ecclesiarchy Preacher could conceal a drooling mass of whispering, puckered mouths. In this way the taint of the mutant corrupts all levels of Imperial society, where it must be weeded out and purged by the Ordo Hereticus. Small wonder they have been known to put even those with the tiniest blemish to death, lest their shameful secret be the stigma of Chaos worship.

Some mutants do not bear any physical mark of their altered nature, for it is their minds that are altered, allowing them to wield unearthly power directly from the warp. Great power can be wielded by the psykers who are willing to risk their souls, but even greater is the danger they face by doing so. The minds of psykers act as portals for daemonic presences, appearing as bright flames in the ether. If a psyker is untrained, malevolent daemons will slide into his mind like cold, twisting knives. Ultimately, the psyker will be transformed into a portal through which streams of hellspawn begin to manifest, at first a trickle, then a flood as they pour unchecked into the material realm. Such breaches are uncommon, but each one causes untold destruction, strengthening the hold Chaos has upon the material realm. The armies of the Imperium are too blunt a weapon to combat this threat, unable to respond with the speed necessary to meet such foes. Inquisitors must take the most extreme measures imaginable to cut out such cancers wherever they are found, and if such measures mean hundreds of innocents must die, then that is a small price to pay for the Imperium's continued safety.

THE VILE PRESENCE

The malformed existence that a Dark Fiend will create within the material universe is based on a number of factors, not least being the perceptions of the individual or group entreating its presence. The intents and purpose of their Dark Master is reflected in their daemonic visage and appearance.

Those horrific beings conjoined to the ancient and terrible Lord of Skulls are dire warrior-things, dark of eye, blood-hued and bedecked with armour and weapons of brazen heritage. They are bloodthirsty, possessed of a supernatural bestiality, fury and rage, and excel in the arts of war and death. Their presence stirs men to bloodshed, their look turns the spine to ice with fear, and their bellows and war cries deafen those that oppose them.

The vile servants of the Prince of Misdeed are incarnate of the lascivious dreams and depraved imaginings of desperate malcontents. Their disgusting and foul nature is obscured by an aura of ecstasy and beauty, truly obscene in its falsity. Their grotesque conjurers are confronted by visions of unnatural serenity, charm and lustful suggestion, driving reason from their thoughts and causing unholy admiration and covetousness.

Those supplicants to the Architect of Fate who attract his supernal gaze will be gifted with bizarre, anarchic entities comprised of the raw magic of their master. They are a blaze of chaotic colour, shape-shifting and incorporeal. They are enveloped in an inconstant corona of energy, buzzing and shrieking with unearthly power, sparks of incandescence cascading from their bodies, piercing eyes seeing into souls.

Of all the nefarious devils that serve the Dark Masters, the corrupt minions of the Pestilent Beast are the most physically grotesque. Embodiments of decay and plague, their festering presence and unnatural stench is pervaded by a miasma of flies and nauseating putridity. Their swollen sores, exposed innards, wart-strewn and pus-slicked skin is sickening in the extreme.

Extract from the Liber Malificorum

The darkest emotions of Humanity given terrible form within the Warp, such daemons delight in spreading madness, putrescence and death throughout the mortal world. Although cataloguing the forms of the daemon would undoubtedly take a horrific toll on a man's sanity, the Ordo Malleus of the Inquisition has marshalled not only heretical texts that detail the servants of the Chaos gods in grotesque detail, but also compiled their own records from their millennia-long battles against these raw manifestations of Chaos. The most powerful of all daemons are those scions of the four Ruinous Powers: Khorne the Blood God, Nurgle the Lord of Decay, Tzeentch, the Changer of the Ways, and Slaanesh, the Dark Prince. The Inquisition knows the face of the daemon well, and from the most exalted Grand Master of the Grey Knights to the lowliest Explicator one fact is held true above all; the daemon must be exterminated wherever it is found if Mankind is to survive.

THE DREAD LEGIONS

Like a weeping sore on the verge of eruption, the stellar phenomenon known as the Eye of Terror has blighted Imperial space for ten thousand years. A permanent warp storm of unimaginable size, the Eye of Terror burst into existence after the galactic cataclysm that was the Fall of the Eldar. It serves as a constant reminder that Humanity's nemesis sits nestled within its very heart, bleeding the raw stuff of the Warp into the material universe, contaminating all that come near it with the infection of Chaos. It stains the heavens with its presence, dominating the stars with a smear the colour of infected blood. Across every system within ten thousand light years it can be seen clearly with the naked eye: a pulsing ocean of sickly purple from Cadia, a vast sore eating at the sky from Fenris, a baleful, glowering malignancy from Terra. Deadly warp storms surround it, making interstellar travel practically impossible without the most skilled of the Navis Nobilite at the helm. It is so massive that a full quarter of Imperial space sleeps under its malevolent stare, and though it may become faint or obscured by meteorological conditions or a stellar anomaly, it is nothing more than a brief respite. Those under its infected glare feel in their souls that they are under the constant scrutiny of their enemies. The Eye will never close, and its denizens will never cease to plot the downfall of the Imperium.

The Eye is known to be home to the darkest evils of the galaxy. Though it is infested by the countless perils that ride the tempests inside all warp storms, it also houses the most dangerous enemies of the Imperium; the Traitor Legions of the Chaos gods. During the Horus Heresy, fully half of the Space Marines renounced their allegiance to the Emperor. This was no mere rebellion; the Traitor Legions had willingly sworn their allegiance to the gods of Chaos. They readily sold their souls in exchange for an eternity in which to achieve their dreams and indulge their desires. To others, the Ruinous Powers spoke through Horus himself, promising justice against a distant Emperor who blindly demanded a lifetime of servitude and sacrifice with nothing in return. The whispers of the Dark Gods promised that the universe would be theirs for the taking; that they would be beyond reprisal.

With Horus defeated at the hand of the Emperor, the Traitor Legions were driven beyond the realms of Man into the Eye of Terror, seeking safety in the one place the vengeful fleets of the Imperium could not follow. Their damnation was sealed – twisted and bitter, they had become Chaos Space Marines, despised and feared as traitors and heretics throughout the galaxy. The immortality they were promised was nothing more than a hellish existence of bitterness and hatred. Daemonhood awaited those favoured by their unholy patrons, mindless servitude those that failed them, but all were bound to the whims of the thirsting gods of the Warp for the rest of time.

To this day, the dread legions of the Chaos Space Marines fight on, unrepentant and filled with an unquenchable desire to destroy the minions of the False Emperor and tear his corpse from the throne of Terra. Taking strength from a bottomless well of bloodlust and spite, the legions of Chaos harness the mercurial patronage of the Chaos gods and rage ceaselessly against the Imperium. They will wage the Long War without end until the Emperor is cast down and the Chaos gods rule over all.

More terrifying still are the Daemon Primarchs, dark and twisted reflections of the magnificent heroes created by the Emperor himself at the time of the Great Crusade. In ages past, each of these supreme warriors fought at the head of an entire Legion of Space Marines, venerated and adored by all who marched to war beside them. Since the fateful betrayal of the Horus Heresy they have become vile fusions of Primarch and

Daemon that tower over their countless minions: Mortarion of the Death Guard, gaunt and putrescent; Magnus the Red, cyclopean sorcerer of the Thousand Sons; Perturabo of the Iron Warriors, paranoid master of the siege; the many-limbed Fulgrim, once-perfect lord of the Emperor's Children; and Angron, bat-winged lord of the bloodthirsty World Eaters, to name but a few of their infernal number. Each rules over his own domain, a daemon world shaped by their mad desires, and it is on these worlds that the greatest foes of Mankind plot the downfall of the Imperium.

It is almost impossible to classify a daemon world, save that it defies all logic and is invariably an inhospitable hell that will either pervert or devour its inhabitants. Each and every one is radically different, wrought in a form pleasing to the ruler of each twisted planet. Although the daemonic require vast amounts of energy to exist outside the Immaterium, the Eye is a place of sanctuary for them. This peculiar inversion of natural law is echoed by the nature of each daemon world; none of the immutable strictures imposed by gravity and astrophysics within the material universe apply. What little is known about these worlds has come at great expense to the Imperium. Only the most powerful psykers dare attempt a vision-quest that enters the Eye and return with their minds intact; the weakest inevitably returning with something else entirely inhabiting their body. The Inquisition's Null-ships have also penetrated deep into the Eye, invisible to the scions of the Warp behind arrays of psychic shields – those who return from such a voyage do so with their hearts filled with hatred for the daemonic and their conviction renewed. Those who do not return damn themselves to an existence of physical and spiritual torture at the mercy of the sadistic denizens of the Immaterium.

THE ORDO MALLEUS

Meaning the Order of the Hammer in the High Gothic tongue, the Ordo Malleus is the division of the Emperor's Holy Inquisition concerned with destroying the physical manifestation of Chaos itself: the Daemon. Its members have pledged their every waking hour to the discovery and destruction of the daemonic wherever it is to be found. It is their role to hunt out and purge those who consort with the daemon and the hideous things they conjure before their blasphemous actions give rise to full-scale daemonic invasions.

Such is the authority of an Inquisitor and the magnitude of the threat posed by the Daemonic that no sacrifice is too great to combat this menace, and no force too strong to bring to bear against the horrific servants of Chaos. Even in victory those who have fought alongside a Daemonhunter may well be subsequently exterminated to prevent the taint of Chaos spreading further; Space Marines, too valuable to simply execute, are usually mind-scrubbed to eradicate the taint of Chaos, which can corrupt even the most faithful.

But there are times when the daemon bursts from the ether in such numbers that the Inquisitors of the Ordo Malleus need to call upon their own Chamber Militant - warriors even more powerful and devout than the Space Marines - to triumph. Times when ravening monstrosities pour into the material dimension in a gibbering tide, hungry for the souls of the innocent. Only one force in the galaxy has any chance of stemming such a daemonic infestation - the Grey Knights.

781.M31 – 999.M41

THE BLACK CRUSADES

Perhaps once in ten generations, a truly great Champion of Chaos will arise in the depths of the Eye of Terror. Through the power of his implacable will and the favour of the Dark Gods, this Champion brings about an unsteady alliance between the infernal scions of the Warp, drawing together a terrifying army of Chaos Space Marines, daemons, mutants and renegades. The daemon forges of the hell worlds echo with the clang of monstrous machines and dark industry, churning out armour and weapons for the chosen one's followers. Daemon engines are roused from their embittered slumbers with blood sacrifices and warring factions vie for command of the massed ranks of vengeful crusaders or are crushed into obedience.

When a Black Crusade is finally launched, the Eye of Terror vomits forth the diabolic hordes of Chaos: armies of daemons; rank upon rank of huge, twisted monsters; numberless masses of Cultists; wild tribes of mutants; ancient and terrifying Chaos Titans. Spearheading these nightmarish hosts are the Chaos Space Marine Legions, united behind their Champion in their desire to wreak untold destruction upon the hated Imperium. Twisted with bitter hatred for the Imperium that cast them out, the Chaos Space Marines seek to tear down the Emperor's realm in bloody vengeance for their long-ago defeat.

The most dangerous of these Black Crusades are those led by Abaddon the Despoiler, Warmaster of the dreaded Black Legion and heir to the Great Betrayer, Horus. Thirteen times has Abaddon rampaged from the daemon worlds of the Eye to unleash hell upon his mortal enemies, each time plunging into the Imperium like an envenomed blade, every attack a deeper wound than the last. Abaddon's Thirteenth Black Crusade was the most devastating yet, smashing aside the defences of the Cadian Gate and tearing the heart out of the entire Cadian sector. Whole sectors remain engulfed in war, millions have perished in the flames of battle and entire systems have been transformed into corpse-choked wastelands in the conflict. Mighty Cadia itself has been devastated, reduced to a smouldering ruin that bears little resemblance to the eternal bastion that once it was. Here, Abaddon's hate-fuelled forces battle for total control of the garrison world, and if victorious will be poised perhaps to make one final lunge toward Terra itself.

CADIA

The fortress world of Cadia stands upon the edge of the Eye of Terror, guarding the one stable route between the daemon worlds and the Imperium. A battlefleet of any size must rely on the Cadian Gate to escape the Eye of Terror, and thus Cadia and its surrounding systems are the most vital strategic objective in the whole Imperium. The people of Cadia have stoically resisted assault after bloody assault down through the millennia, their entire society, from the youngest to the oldest, geared for war and the defence of the Cadian Gate. Despite the carnage wrought by Abaddon's latest Black Crusade, the Cadians still valiantly fight against the tide and pray for eventual deliverance.

THE XENOS THREAT

The Imperium of Man is beset on all sides by aliens determined to enslave or destroy Mankind. Some of these races laid their claim to the galaxy whilst Mankind was in its infancy. To them, Humanity is an infestation to be scoured from the stars in a tide of blood. Yet others encroach upon the Imperium from without, carving their empires from areas of space Mankind has long fought to occupy. To them, Humanity is a lumbering, blind beast to be baited and put to death to make room for the propagation of their own species. Without waging a constant battle against the countless races with whom it shares the galaxy, the Imperium would quickly be pulled apart and destroyed.

There are alien races in the galaxy that Man has fought tooth and nail for countless aeons, no less deadly for the understanding gained about his ancestral foes. The mysterious Eldar, once lords amongst the stars, lost their empire to a galactic cataclysm millennia ago and have watched the Imperium's ascension with bitterness and hatred. Masters of technology, the remnants of this once-proud race wander the galaxy on giant craftworlds, striking with serpentine speed whenever Humanity strays upon their shifting domains and vanishing like ghosts before reprisal can be brought to bear. In stark contrast, the savage, green-skinned warriors of the Ork race stain the stars in numbers that, should they ever truly unite, would wash away all before them in an orgy of violence and death. The Imperium has culled the Orks time and time again, only to see them thrive and be strengthened by the very wars waged against them.

These ancestral foes, besieging human civilisation since it first took to the stars, pose the direst of threats to the future of Mankind. But the taint of the xenos has intensified without precedent over the last millennium. Even in the last few centuries several major alien races have revealed themselves and now wage war upon the Imperium, threatening to corrupt or destroy it once and for all. The most dynamic and vital of these are the Tau, whose empire on the Eastern Fringe of the Imperium is expanding at an alarming rate. Those worlds that refuse to swear allegiance to the Tau are obliterated by the alien race's incredible firepower. Beyond the sept worlds of the Tau lurk a far more

THE ORDO XENOS

The Ordo Xenos is one of the three major branches of the Emperor's Holy Inquisition and is entirely devoted to hunting down and destroying alien life. Though Inquisitors are held in awe and terror across the Imperium, it is the alien and those who dare to harbour it that need fear the focused wrath of the alien hunter. Equipped with the best wargear the Imperium can supply, possessed of extensive knowledge of their foe and blessed with a fiery hatred, the Ordo Xenos is the first and greatest of Mankind's defences against the alien. When the xenos taint is subtle, the Ordo's Inquisitors will cut it out with scalpel-sharp vigilance and determination. When the alien comes on in a great horde, the Deathwatch, elite warriors taken from amongst the Chapters of the Space Marines, will meet it head to head and purge it with fire and steel.

horrific threat; the hive fleets of the Tyranid race. Unthinking alien monstrosities from beyond the known galaxy, the Tyranids consume everything in their path in a flood of scythe-limbed beasts that think and kill as one. Most evil and insidious of all are the Necrons, immortal machines who have lain dormant since the dawn of time awaiting the call of their ancient star gods to begin the harvest of the living races once more.

Nevertheless, it is a fool who believes that the alien races of the universe can be numbered so easily, and in the dark corners of the galaxy countless alien races slither and dart. The infestations of the Hrud, the worm-like Drugh of Pyrus I, Lacrymole shape-shifters, hyper-violent Barghesi, the mind-eating Khrave are all but a tiny fraction of the xenos species haunting the stars and yet enough to gnaw at the worlds of Man until there is nothing left save depravation and ruin. No less lethal are those xeno-breeds who care nothing for civilisation or war, semi-sentient monsters that wish only to prey on the unwary – the Clawed Fiend, the crystalline Dracolith, the dread Ambull, the Devil of Catachan and countless others to whom Humanity is nothing but sustenance.

Despite the lethal array of hostile xenos races abroad in the Imperium, there are those who, in their ignorance, employ aliens as mercenaries or, worse still, utilise their arcane technology for their own ends. The lure of such actions is strong, as many alien races surpass Humanity in strength or technological achievement. The cannibalistic Kroot have fought alongside the armies of Imperial commanders, while winged and fickle Caradochians sell their services to the highest bidder. Concealed within the tallest spires of teeming hive worlds, xeno-tech is bartered as contraband by foolish nobles who know no better. In this way the taint of the alien spreads across the fringes of the Imperium, threatening to seep deeper into the fabric of its society until it can consume it from the inside as well as out. Truly it is said that the reward of tolerance is death.

"Contact with alien races always renews one's faith in Humanity. It is my belief that foreign travel narrows the mind wonderfully."

Helem Boesch

The Loxatl are sinuous, non-humanoid quadrupeds evolved from amphibian forms. Slighter larger than a standard human, they are extremely swift and dexterous, and use large dew-claws to give them purchase on any surface, allowing them to run up walls and across ceilings. Out of water, the vision, hearing and smell of these grey-skinned aliens is dull, and they rely on powerful taste and vibration sensing to hunt and corner prey.

The Loxatl use a weapon of alien design known as a flechette blaster. They carry these powerful weapons, along with ammunition bandoliers, on their torsos, mounted on mechanical armatures that fire the weapons via some unknown mind impulse device and leaves a Loxatl's limbs free for climbing. The blasters fire deadly shot-bursts filled with millions of razor-sharp filaments that shred grievous wounds in flesh and armour.

Loxatl are believed to operate in small, 'brood group' units of biological kin, communicating by vibration, subsonic calls and, when in close proximity, iridescent patternings that they are able to flash and move across their skins. Imperial Guardsmen have reported that nearby Loxatl activity can often be detected by a nauseating smell, a mix of rancid milk and crushed mint.

THE DYING

CRAFTWORLD ELDAR

Warlock Arquellia of Craftworld Ulthwé

Ancient and mysterious, the Eldar are enigmatic aliens who never speak openly of their terrible past. Long ago, when Mankind's ancestors had just crawled from the seas, their empire spanned the galaxy. Their whims decided the fate of worlds and quenched the fiercest suns. Now, they are all but extinct – the last fragments of a shattered civilisation plunged into constant warfare. They have been reduced to a scattered and nomadic race, as those who had retained enough sanity to flee before the Fall did so on mighty living vessels called Craftworlds. It is on these world-ships that the last remnants of the Eldar civilisation drift amongst the stars.

Millennia ago, the Eldar fell prey to sinful pride, then decadence, and finally depravity. From their waking dreams, an unimaginably sickening and obscene god was born. The psychic implosion of its birth-cries tore out the heart of their empire, leaving a pulsing, bleeding afterbirth of pure chaos in its place – the Eye of Terror. Only by rigid dedication and denial of their darker sides can the Eldar stave off the predatory god that still hungers for their souls, and in these dark times more and more Eldar turn to the Path of the Warrior.

Despite all they have lost, the incredibly advanced technology of the Eldar makes them a fearsome adversary on the battlefield. Sleek, graceful anti-grav vehicles glide effortlessly through incoming fire, laying down firepower that renders the thickest armour useless. Squads of elite Aspect Warriors strike at vital points in the enemy lines, destroying many times their own number. Without the skilled Aspect Warriors and the guidance of the powerful Farseers, the once-bright star of the Eldar race will dwindle and die out altogether.

The Phoenix Lord Karandras, The Shadow Hunter

Farseer Eldrad Ulthran, late of Craftworld Ulthwé

The Phoenix Lord Maugan-Ra, The Harvester of Souls

Lauthelias, Dire Avenger Aspect Warrior

Chauderia, Fire Dragon Aspect Warrior

Shiera, Howling Banshee Aspect Warrior

Icareane, Swooping Hawk Aspect Warrior

Taraq, Ranger of Alaitoc

Laconfir, Guardian of Biel-tan

Cimhaill, Guardian of Saim-Hann

Alarielle, Guardian of Iyanden

Led by the Court of the Young King, the Biel-tan Craftworld takes back those worlds lost in the Fall. This Swordwind Host surges from the webway to reclaim the world of Coriallis IV.

THE LOST

DARK ELDAR

Khalistas, warrior of the Kabal of the Sundered Blade

The Dark Eldar are utterly, irrevocably evil and corrupt in every sense. Not only do they enjoy the infliction of pain and suffering more than anything else, they also take gratification from the callous manipulation of the weaker beings they prey upon. When these twisted creatures emerge into the galaxy from their twilight realm of Commoragh, it is as piratical raiders, striking swiftly and without warning from their arrow-quick craft. A Dark Eldar raid is a horrific sight, merciless aliens slaughtering the majority of those they encounter and carrying the enslaved survivors back to their nightmarish domain.

The Dark Eldar delight in toying with their enemies, the full measure of their alien intellect given to the pleasure of playing upon their prey's fears. Their warrior sects strike swiftly and without warning, screaming into the enemy lines on baroque skiffs before leaping into their ranks so they may experience the joy of slaughter first-hand. Sprays of arterial blood and spasming corpses mark their passage, the deranged and cruel laughter of these murderous aliens ringing in their dying victims' ears as they search for new playthings.

To these depraved individuals, the sweet fruit of terror is as pleasing as the caress of a razor-sharp blade across soft flesh. They delight in breaking the bodies and souls of their captives, their tortures an art refined over long millennia. They revel in every nuance of anguish and woe until their captives are gibbering wrecks pleading for an end to their miserable existence – a mercy the Dark Eldar will never grant.

Lelith Hesperax, Leader of the Wych Cult of Strife

Urien Rakarth, Master Haemonculus

Drazhar, Master of Blades

Khastaphrax, Dark Eldar Scourge

Elsek Orinth, Archon of the Venomed Blade Kabal

Durabeli Arlehk of the Bloodied Claw Kabal

Yurnechaen, Reaver Jetbike pilot

Kesharq, Dark Eldar Warrior

Skechara, Dark Eldar Wych

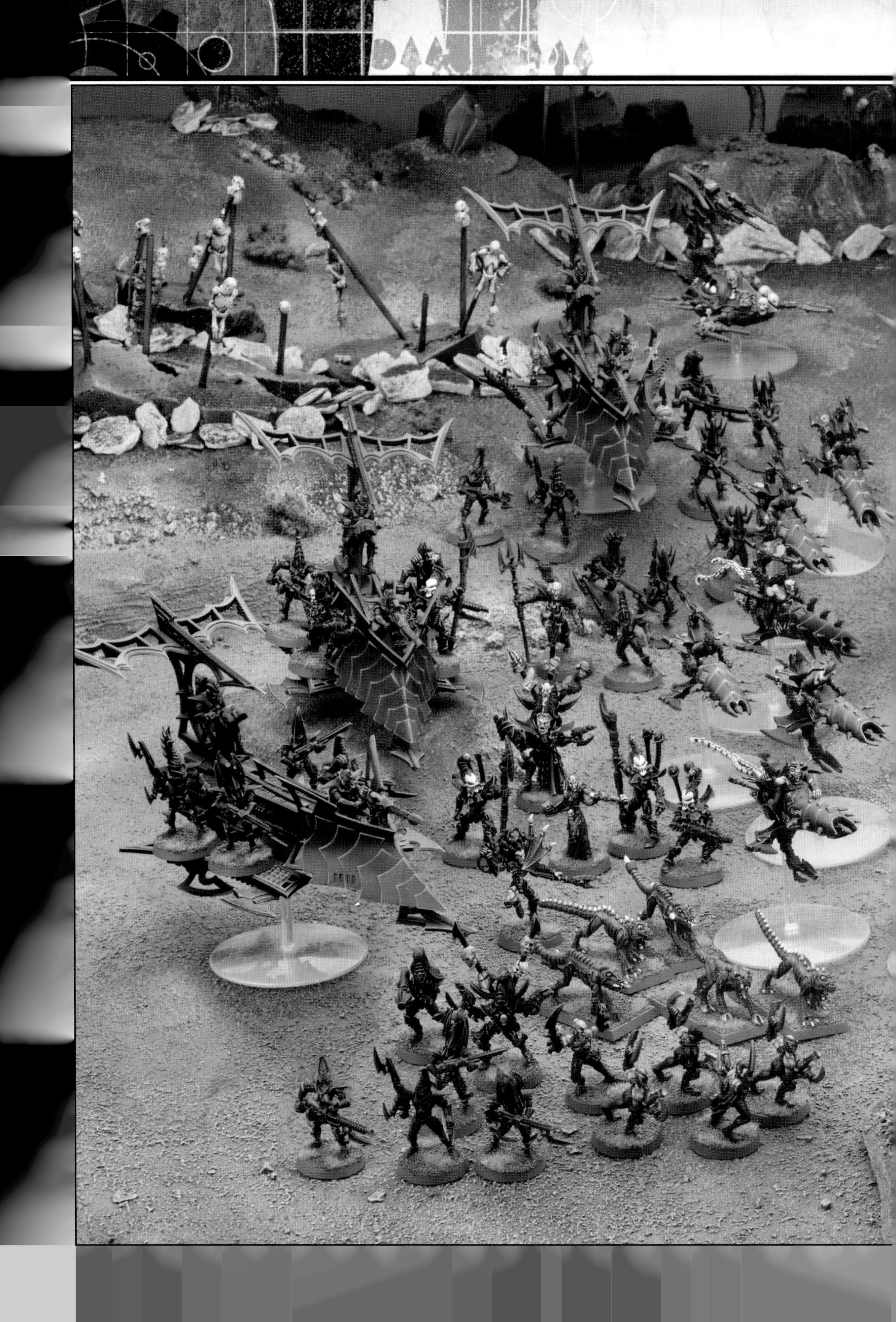

The Kabal of the Black Heart, subservient to the great Asdrubael Vect himself, launch a lightning-fast raid on the Imperial world of Trantor, hungry for slaves to take back to their pitiless ruler.

THE ANCIENTS

NECRONS

Necron Warrior, Designation Unknown

For sixty million years they have slumbered, awaiting the call from the star-gods. For an eternity they have lain dormant in stasis chambers deep beneath blasted Tomb worlds, far from the prying eyes of the lesser races. Unseen, but not unknown, they lie at the heart of the Imperium, anticipating the time to strike. Bitter souls encased in fleshless bodies, the Necrons have returned after their eons-long dormancy, and the bloody Harvest has begun again, their fleets hunting down mortal races for their masters to consume.

From huge Tomb ships and floating Monoliths, glittering phalanxes of Necron warriors stalk forth, their false bodies impervious to the weapons of their enemies. At the vanguard of their forces are the Necron Lords, their tattered shrouds flowing in an unearthly breeze as they wordlessly compel their skeletal warriors forward. Alongside them march the eldritch monstrosities and arcane war machines of their race, some miraculously fast and utterly lethal, some as ponderous and inescapable as death itself.

They strike without warning, slaughtering their prey and disappearing without trace, even their fallen mysteriously vanishing from the field of battle. To the Necrons, their foes are but cattle for their ever-hungry gods, and with each passing year the Tomb Fleets grow greater in size. Soon their eternal goal to eradicate all life will become a reality, and the galaxy will be turned into a barren wasteland.

Necron Lord

Necron Pariah

Flayed One

Necron Warrior

The Nightbringer, Master of Death

Necron Immortal

Tomb Spyder

Necron Scarab Swarm

Necron Destroyer

THEIR NUMBER IS LEGION, THEIR NAME IS DEATH

Risen from dusty sephulchres on worlds long thought dead, the Necrons arise to reclaim the realm of their ancient star gods. The newly-risen Nightbringer awakens his army from the dead world of Cthelmax to destroy the hated living.

THE BEAST

ORKS

Buzgob, Skarboy of the Goff Clan

Orks are the most brutal and warlike of all the alien races that plague the galaxy. These green-skinned monsters live only to fight, delighting in spreading carnage and mayhem. In fact, so great is their need for conflict, they will happily fight amongst themselves, indulging in bloody wars with their own kind just for the thrill of battle.

On occasion, a Warboss will arise from the ranks of the feuding warbands and unite them with his stirring vision of conquest. Under the dominating personality of their Warlord, as well as his intimidating physical presence, the Orks set off in search of a new enemy to fight – any enemy. As an invasion grows in size, attracting more and more Orks to the cause, it becomes a mighty Waaagh!

Such Waaaghs! are all but impossible to resist as hundreds of thousands of warriors hungering for battle descend on a world in a tide of Orkish malevolence. It is through these massive conquests that Orks have spread across the galaxy from the core to the outer rim. If ever the Orks united as a race, no force in the galaxy could resist them.

In battle, huge mobs of heavily-muscled Greenskins charge headlong with crude blades raised and guns blazing. Others scream towards the foe upon ramshackle bikes, buggies and battlewagons, while clanking war engines stomp forward, their roaring engines gouting oily smoke. Above them tower the mighty Gargants, huge mechanical effigies of the Ork gods, laden with guns and missiles capable of flattening a city. When the Orks are on the rampage, the galaxy trembles.

Mad Bazza, Goff Stormboy

Niblit, Gretchin sentry

Okbok, Deathskull Sluggaboy

Dagnazz, Goff Sluggaboy

Rogrok, Bad Moon Shoota Boy

Gorgoth, Burna Boy

Da Kan-busta, Ork Dreadnought

The Warlord Ghazghkull Mag Uruk Thraka

When the Orks go to war, they do so in a massive Waaagh! sweeping all before them in a tide of greenskinned bodies. The world of Armageddon suffered terribly during the invasion of the Ork Warlord Ghazghkull Thraka.

998.M41

THE ARMAGEDDON WAR

Armageddon is a world riven by war, first at the hands of Angron, Daemon Primarch of the World Eaters Legion, and then twice by the greatest Ork Warlord in the galaxy, Ghazghkull Mag Uruk Thraka. The third and most devastating war came fifty-seven years to the day after Ghazghkull's first Waaagh! was defeated. Ork Roks – mountain-like fortresses infested with Ork warriors and carrying immense war engines – smashed into the ash wastes like the pounding fists of an angry god. Millions died as Hades Hive, the site of Ghazghkull's previous defeat, was destroyed by immense asteroids dropped from orbit and hordes of Greenskins swarmed toward the Imperial defences. The earth shook to the tread of duelling Titans and Gargants alike, and Armageddon was set to fall.

But from the chaos of the first Ork invasion had arisen one of the most resolute heroes the Imperium has ever known, Commissar Yarrick of the Imperial Guard. Once more it was he who led the resistance against the Ork warlord, and when Ghazghkull heard that his nemesis stood against him again, he redoubled his efforts. Yarrick's tactics were masterful; the Old Man of Armageddon forged the Imperial forces into an unstoppable machine of iron and steel and drove Ghazghkull from the planet. Even though Ghazghkull withdrew with Yarrick in hot pursuit at the head of a crusade, the war rages still. The cost of this endeavour is measured in human lives, and the death toll spirals toward the billions. Whatever the cost, Armageddon must not fall.

ARMAGEDDON

The hive world of Armageddon is the lynchpin of the entire Armageddon sector. A polluted industrial wasteland of ash and metal, it is a vital node at the centre of the Imperium's navigational channels and its sprawling, clanking munitions factories supply arms and tanks to thousands of Imperial Guard regiments across the segmentum. Should Armageddon fall, whole systems would buckle and collapse under the terrible pressure of the Ork onslaught. The defenders of Mankind, however, will not stand idly by whilst the vital hive world is besieged, and uncounted millions stand ready to defend Armageddon to the last.

Fire Warrior Shas'O Vior'la Loresh of the D'yanoi Sept

Young and ambitious, united in their purpose, the Tau seek to bring enlightenment and unity to those who will join them. While the Imperium crumbles and is beset on all sides, the Tau Empire grows stronger and stronger. In the Eastern Fringe, far from the power of Terra, world after world has fallen to their dynamic advances. Yet there are those who fail to see the benefits of becoming part of the Tau Empire. Any resistance is swept aside, whether it is philosophical or physical, for the Greater Good can overcome any obstacle.

At the forefront of this rapid expansion are the warriors of the Fire Caste. Unfettered by Mankind's superstition and fear of technology, the Fire Warriors go to battle carrying weapons of immense power, encased in battlesuits that can withstand the fiercest attacks. Stealth and Pathfinder teams scout out the foe for the Hunter cadres to engage, using swift movement and immense firepower to destroy their foes from afar.

At the heart of the empire are the Ethereals, spiritual rulers of the Tau. Though rarely seen, their presence is felt on every Tau world. Many other races are part of the Tau Empire, such as the Kroot – mercenaries whose speed and strength make them natural fighters. Other aliens, some coerced or conquered, lend their own abilities to the Tau, united in their cause to bring the Greater Good to other worlds and peoples.

Shas'la Pathfinder

Shas'ui Fire Warrior

Tau Ethereal Aun'vre

Shas'la Fire Warrior

Shas'ui Pathfinder with Rail rifle

Shas'la Pathfinder

Shas'ui XV15 Stealth Suit

Shas'la Fire Warrior

Shas'vre XV8 Crisis Battlesuit

Gun Drone

Shas'vre XV88 Broadside Battlesuit

The Hunter Cadre of Aun'vre establish a landing zone prior to the reclamation of Nimbosa, accompanied by Kroot mercenaries, Hammerhead tanks and devilfish transports.

THE GREAT DEVOURER

Tyranid Warrior of Hive Fleet Behemoth

The Tyranids are the most alien of races to infest the galaxy. An elemental force, they mass in void-swimming shoals, remorselessly hungry and too numerous to stop. The Tyranids are believed to have migrated from beyond the known galaxy in search of new systems to consume, ravening swarms descending upon planets and stripping them of all life. Every living thing is consumed, brought back into the hive ships and dissolved into a rich biological gruel from which new Tyranid organisms are grown. When the Tyranids move on in search of fresh prey, they leave nothing but a ball of scoured rock in their wake.

Tyranids do not make their weapons and starships out of metal and plastic, but use gene-splicing and bioengineering to grow them from the living organic material harvested from the worlds they have devoured. Tyranid hive fleets consist of millions of sentient craft, each home to untold numbers of monstrosities evolved from the bubbling geno-organs of the ship's reproductive chambers. All these creatures are born to serve the single entity that is the ship, and the ship itself exists only as part of the horrific super-organism that is the hive fleet. Even when dead, they are nothing more than bio-matter to be reconstituted into new forms.

The Tyranids comprise many different creatures functioning as one, coordinated by the gestalt consciousness of the hive mind. At war they form a ferocious, unstoppable horde; chittering broods of scythe-limbed beasts race beneath lumbering bio-titans and fearsome Hive Tyrants in an avalanche of bioengineered killing machines. Totally, unrelenting, the Tyranid race represents an unimaginable threat, not only to Mankind, but to the entire galaxy.

Hive Tyrant, Hive Fleet Kraken

The Red Terror, Hive Fleet Kraken

Ripper Swarm, Hive Fleet Kraken

Termagant, Hive Fleet Harbinger

Hormagaunt, Hive Fleet Grendel

Genestealer, Hive Fleet Behemoth

Tyranid Warrior, Hive Fleet Kraken

A Tyranid invasion is a terrifying system-wide attack that transforms the world into a more easily digested biomass. The Tyranid invasion of Tarsus Ultra disfigured the landscape horrifically as millions upon millions of bio-engineered killers dropped from the skies.

745.M41 – present

THE TYRANNIC WARS

When contact was lost with a dozen worlds on the eastern fringes of Imperial space, the Imperium was slow to react. Unbeknownst to the Imperium, a deadly alien race had drifted from the void and was consuming worlds with horrifying efficiency.

The presence of this galactic threat came to light when Inquisitor Kryptman of the Ordo Xenos recovered a data-slate from the barren husk that had once been the Imperial world of Tyran. The alien fleets were composed of an innumerable tide of living craft, from biological attack vessels to gargantuan, tentacled hive ships – all cells in a single vast alien organism that threatened to devour the Imperium. Codified as Hive Fleet *Behemoth*, the initial Tyranid invasion led to one of the largest space battles of Imperial history around the rings of Circe. Both the Ultramarines and Battlefleet *Tempestus* suffered terrible casualties before the invasion was finally broken and destroyed.

But the Tyranids can never be truly defeated, for each time they are driven back, they evolve new ways to defeat and consume those in their path. Hive Fleet *Kraken* was all the more insidious and devastating, its approach covered by a wave of confusion and communications breakdowns. Blasphemous cults worshipping the Tyranid invaders as gods erupted across the worlds in its path, rebellion and civil war making planets easy pickings when Hive Fleet *Kraken* loomed from the void. Only the intervention and virtual destruction of the nearby Eldar Craftworld of Iyanden saved the worlds in Kraken's path from total disaster.

Now, the Imperium struggles against yet another Tyrannic invasion, that of Hive Fleet *Leviathan*, which is cutting a bloody swathe from below the galactic plane towards Terra. Only the future will reveal whether the primitive life forms of this galaxy can resist the Tyranid super-organism.

THE BATTLE FOR MACRAGGE

Macragge, homeworld of the Ultramarines chapter and the jewel in the crown of Ultramar, prospers under the rule of Marneus Calgar, Chapter Master of the Ultramarines. Heavily fortified and tenaciously defended by the Ultramarines and its planetary defence forces, Macragge famously held out against the vast, interstellar threat of Hive Fleet *Behemoth* until the combined fleets of Ultramar and Battlefleet *Tempestus* could engage and destroy the alien menace. On the surface, the hulking Terminators of the First Company crushed numberless aliens as they fought a bloody and gradual retreat through the labyrinths of their vital polar defence fortresses. Although it cost all of them their lives, the First Company held the alien menace in check long enough for their battle-brothers to return from the war in space and purge their homeworld of the xenos taint.

DARK MILLENNIUM

The main Warhammer 40,000 rules deal with the bare bones of how to play a tabletop game. However, they can only touch on some of the ways there are to play different kinds of battles. In this section of the book we're going to take a broader look at gaming in the 41st millennium and show you more ways in which you can add exciting elements to your games, as well as getting involved in the hobby. The reason we've separated things off in this way is because the rules for the Warhammer 40,000 game are to be found in the main rules section of this book and in the Codex army books. What follows is advice and ideas for use by players looking to expand their gaming horizons.

By far the most popular way of playing Warhammer 40,000 is for two players to each turn up with a 1,500-point army, roll a D6 to see which Standard Mission they will play, set up terrain in an even-handed manner, and then get to it. This approach has the major advantage that games can be arranged on the fly with little or no planning required beforehand. Many such 'pick up' games take place in Games Workshop's hobby centres, as well as in many independent stores and clubs. Many players find the challenge of collecting a 'standard' army that can meet all comers highly rewarding, and it is certainly a sign of a good general that his army has an equally good record against all-out assault forces as it does against firepower-heavy armies.

However, many players are part of a gaming group – a group of like-minded individuals who meet regularly and face each other's armies across the tabletop time and again. Amongst these groups, certain styles of play come to the fore, and many like to establish 'house rules' that cover unusual gaming situations they have encountered or additional rules they find enjoyable. Furthermore, through facing the same opponents on a regular basis, narratives and ongoing rivalries will develop, something that rarely happens in one-off games.

A major advantage of gaming in these tight-knit groups is that players can explore aspects of the Warhammer 40,000 game they would never find the opportunity to pursue during pick-up games, and that's what this section of the book is all about.

Dark Millennium looks at the hobby as a whole, expanding on the main rules by highlighting different ways to game, providing detailed advice on how to collect an army, and showing how you can really make your models your own by converting and personalising them. The philosophy behind Dark Millennium is that these elements are all interlinked, all essential to the complete experience of tabletop wargaming. Players should regard this section as a collection of resources and as a springboard for their own ideas.

COLLECTING

Collecting an army you can be proud of and fielding it on interesting and varied terrain is one of the greatest pleasures of the hobby. This section of Dark Millennium looks at approaches to collecting your force, from advice on choosing which army is right for you, to expanding your army. You'll find two examples of armies collected by veteran gamers, each including advice on how they planned, collected and painted their forces.

TERRAIN

Though games of Warhammer 40,000 can be fought across flat, featureless plains, these games soon become pretty dull, so in Dark Millennium we've put together a number of sections on terrain, from scenery that can be thrown together in no time at all, all the way to theming your terrain for campaigns set in specific locations and building really special, cinematic pieces for themed games.

COMBAT PATROL

Not all players have the time to play Warhammer 40,000 as often as they might like, so Combat Patrol provides a format for small, fast games that can be completed in, for example, a lunch break. This style of play has proved great for new players, as it allows them to get started with a small force that can be collected and painted very quickly, and as it limits the number of powerful units on the table, new players can start things off simple and work their way up to larger games, without needing to worry about facing too many scary foes. But Combat Patrol is not just about introductory gaming – it has also proved popular amongst veteran players who might like to collect a certain force, but don't have the time to collect an entire new army right away. So, if you're a Tau player with a longing to dish out the pain in close combat rather than be on the receiving end of it all the time, you might like to try a small Tyranid force. This keeps the hobby fresh, and you may even learn about tactics and other aspects of the game you've never had to consider before, by playing a completely different army every now and then.

Included in the Combat patrol section is advice on quick-painting techniques to help players get an army on the table in only a few hours, along with some useful tips for creating 'instant terrain'.

SPECIAL MISSIONS

'Special Missions' games are where players have arranged the kind of battle and forces to be used in advance in a mutually agreeable manner. Points costs may or may not be used to balance the forces, and we've given some examples of different missions like ambushes, raids and last stands where one side may be fighting against terrific odds or trying to achieve a tough objective. Special missions games are often a good change of pace from the standard missions in the main rulebook and remove some of their competitive pressure in favour of a more challenging, story-driven battle.

Most of the special missions benefit from the fact that they require the use of unusual types of scenery, such as bunkers, razor wire or tank traps, and so we've included advice on how to make these, along with plenty of examples to inspire you to make your own. Special missions are designed for those players looking to take their games to the next level.

KILL-TEAM

Kill-team is a set of rules that allow you to play skirmish level, narrative-driven games of Warhammer 40,000. These rules encourage you to go to town designing and modelling your small force, so we've included example Kill-teams made by some of the best painters and modellers around. The Kill-team section emphasises creative freedom in force selection, gaming, painting, modelling and terrain building.

CAMPAIGNS

This is where we tie together all the other aspects of Dark Millennium and provide guidance on how to plan and play your own campaigns. We consider campaigns to be one of the most rewarding and valuable aspects of the wargaming hobby, and so we've included as many examples of advice, rules, armies and terrain as we could cram into the book! The Campaigns section of Dark Millennium is aimed at those players who are looking to become truly immersed in their hobby, creating entire worlds as backdrops for their games and theming every miniature and piece of terrain in their collection to their campaign background.

COMMUNITY

Tabletop wargaming is, by its very nature, a social hobby, and the community extends way beyond your immediate group of gaming buddies to include Games Workshop hobby centres, local, regional and national events, such as Games Day, and of course the World Wide Web. This section tells you all you need to know about the larger world of hobby gaming.

ONWARD

We hope you find these pages informative and inspiring. You've seen the rules of the tabletop game, here you can see more of what the hobby is all about.

SHOWCASE

What better way to conclude Dark Millennium than with a showcase of some of the most spectacular miniatures, painted and converted by some of the world's most accomplished painters? Enough said.

The White Scars Chapter of Space Marines launch a lightning assault on the forces of the Black Legion during the Second Scouring of Urthwart.

COLLECTING AN ARMY

Mustering an army is easily both the most enjoyable and most challenging part of the hobby – in fact, it is probably the most important! As such, it can seem a fairly daunting task, but with a bit of forethought and planning it's possible to get your new force up and running with a minimum of fuss.

CHOOSING AN ARMY

As a general rule, the best way to choose which army to start collecting is simply to go for the one that appeals to you the most. You may be drawn to an army because you like the look of its models, the culture and ideology that drives them, or simply the way they perform on the battlefield. Either way, collecting an army is a long-term commitment so selecting the force that best suits you is very important! Once you've decided upon your allegiance, stick to your guns – it's all too easy to be distracted by new and interesting models and be drawn away from collecting your chosen army.

MUSTERING YOUR FORCES

As mighty oaks from little acorns grow, the best way to assemble your army is a little at a time. While you can go out and buy everything at once, this will invariably leave you with a large pile of grey and silver miniatures that never looks like it's getting any smaller, no matter how fast you paint. A far better way to go about assembling your host is to recruit a little at a time. In Warhammer 40,000 a good size army is normally between 1,500 and 2,000 points in size, so by collecting your force in blocks of about 500 points, you can spread both the cost and painting time over a series of weeks and months. If you challenge yourself to finish painting each block of 500 points before moving on to the next block, you will see your army take shape in sections that you can game with.

PREPARING TO PAINT

Before diving in and painting your army, it's always worth setting aside a little time to consider your colour scheme. Choosing the correct colours is a major part of getting your army's 'look'. The best way to ensure your chosen scheme works for you is to paint a few models as a test run. In this way you can iron out any problems you might have with your colour scheme before you've half painted an entire army in it. For more in-depth advice and practical help, refer to *How To Paint Citadel Miniatures*.

THE FIRST FIVE HUNDRED

The majority of games that you'll play of Warhammer 40,000 use the standard Force Organisation charts, which is shown in the Organising a Battle section. This means that you'll almost always need at least one HQ and two Troops choices in your army, so this is an ideal place to start. HQ choices are a fantastic place to start collecting your army; after all, an army without a leader is no army at all! In most cases these three selections will not fill out your 500 points, so you'll need to think about what else you want to add. The golden rule when adding to your army is much the same as when choosing your army in the first place: pick what appeals to you, not what you think that you *should* choose. When you've got your first 500 points up and running, it's time to play a few games…

MOVING FORWARD

Once you've played a few games with your fledgling 500 point army, you'll want to move onto your next 500 point block, the beauty being that as you've already fulfilled your minimum force organisation commitments, you have a fairly free rein with what you add. Before you know it, you'll have your second block of combatants ready to go and, before long, a fully-fledged army up and running…

Though 1,500 points is a common size for a Warhammer 40,000 army, few players stop collecting at this point. Many will go on to collect more units to add to their army, often choosing to collect at least one of each unit type available in the army list. This allows for variety and flexibility, meaning the army can be tailored to take on a variety of opponents in varying missions. By way of example, the Imperial Guard army on the facing page has been configured in three different ways, all of which are built around a core HQ and Troops choice.

The top picture shows the army set up as a balanced force, with a variety of units capable of completing many missions. The middle shows a more defensive force, with plenty of heavy weapons, while the bottom picture shows the army configured for a mission in which it will be expected to move, assault and hold an objective.

Imperial Guard Balanced Force

Imperial Guard Defence Force

Imperial Guard Assault Force

COLLECTING BLOOD ANGELS

A veteran Games Workshop staff member, Ted Williams has been collecting Blood Angels Space Marines for a grand total of fifteen years.

Ted: My obsession with Blood Angels started way back when Warhammer 40,000 was first published. I saw a squad of Blood Angels resplendent in red and yellow and I wanted a unit that looked just like it. I had a go at putting one together and the models became part of my very first Space Marine army. In fact, the army pictured below is my third, which says a lot about how much I'm into Space Marines. I began collecting my latest army in 1998 and have been adding squads to it ever since.

Although I enjoy the odd game, I'm much more interested in the army building process and owning a force made up of the coolest looking models available. This is pretty easy with the versatile Space Marine range. The models are always inspiring, and because of the large volume of plastic models in the range there are plenty of dynamic poses to try out.

My army really isn't a typical Blood Angels force. It's quite shooty, with more Tactical squads than Assault Troops – there's just something about the sight of rank upon rank of massed infantry. Even after all these years I still prefer the look of this kind of army. But, it's not like there are no close combat specialists in the force: the Death Company, grim and deadly in their black power armour, are amongst the most powerful assault troops in the entire Warhammer 40,000 universe. The Chaplain model accompanying them is one of my personal favourites and I even repainted him slightly to fit in with the Death Company. The rest of the models are a mix of metal and plastic models, which helps add to the diverse appearance and character of the squad. As any Blood Angels player knows, this squad is usually enough to give the enemy a real headache on its own.

My army is just large enough to fight a 1,500 point game, but I'd prefer to have 2000-2500 points of troops and vehicles to choose from. I'm currently looking to add more armour to allow me a greater choice when picking armies: a mighty Dreadnought or two, a few Predators fitted with different weapon configurations, and a couple of squads of Terminators, all in the same striking colour scheme.

In the stage-by-stage opposite, you can see how I painted the tactical troops in my army.

1

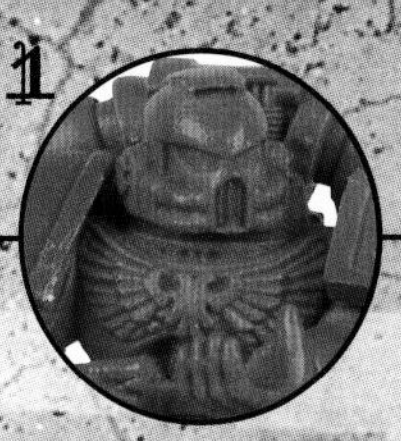

To begin with I paint the entire model Blood Red – I don't worry too much if this appears patchy as the following stage sorts this out.

2

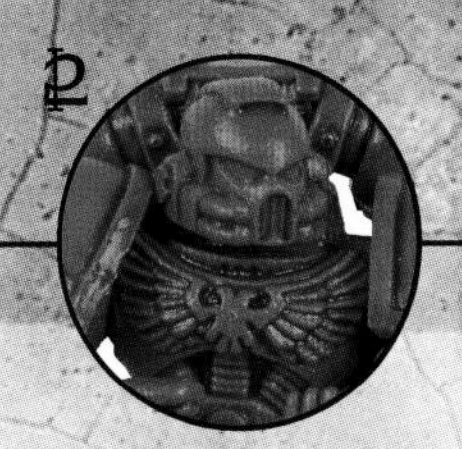

Using an equal parts mix of Chestnut and Red inks, I wash the entire model to create shading .

3

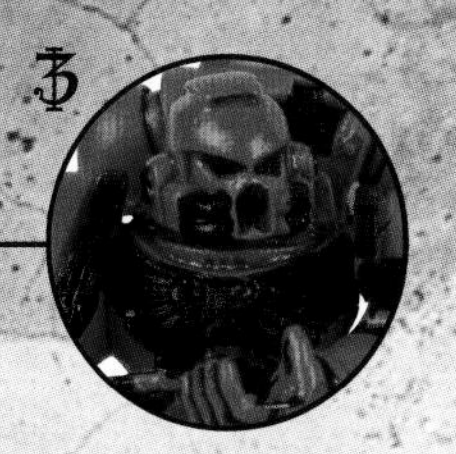

I then paint the armour edge bands, chest eagle, pipes, eye and earpieces, backpack vents, armour in-fills and divisions between the armour plates with Chaos Black.

4

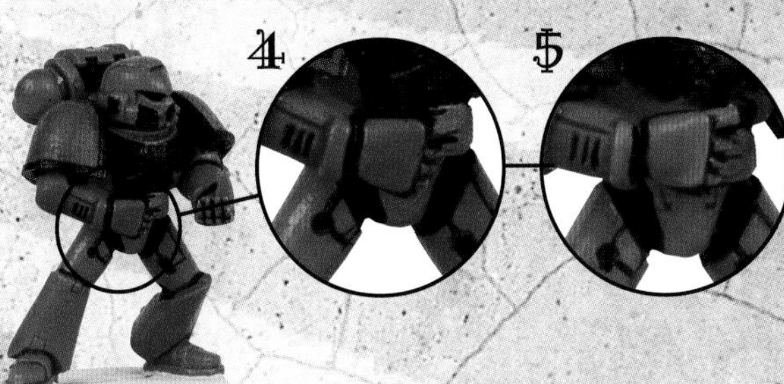

5

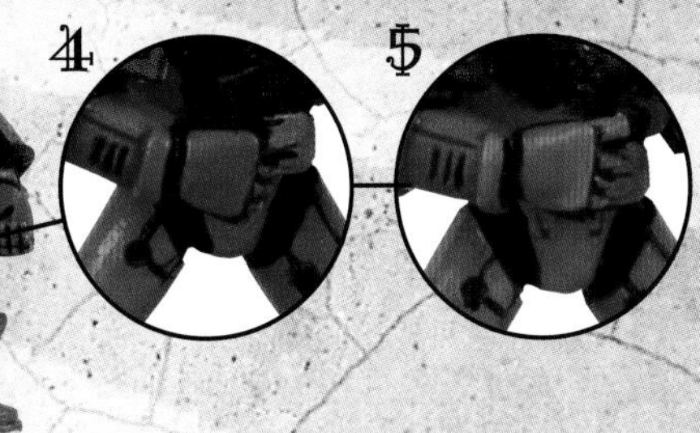

To finish the armour I paint on a mix of Blood Red and Fiery Orange, leaving the darker washed colour as shading in the recesses, where the armour butts against banding and so forth. I then work this up with the same mix plus a little Skull White, concentrating on the extreme edge highlights and the raised portions of the armour plates.

6

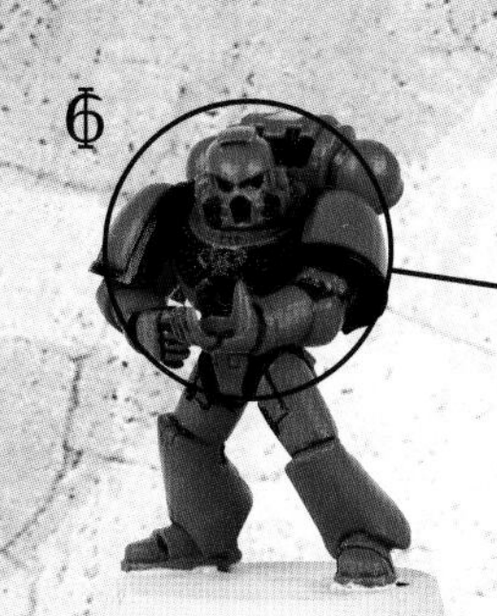

For the shoulder pads I paint the bands dark grey (a mix of black and white) leaving black around the edges for definition.

I use the same dark grey to overpaint the black detailing around the leg joints and on the chest eagle.

7

To finish off I mix a lighter grey and paint extreme edge highlights on the shoulder pads. I also use the same mix to overpaint the raised portions of the eagle and flexible leg joints.

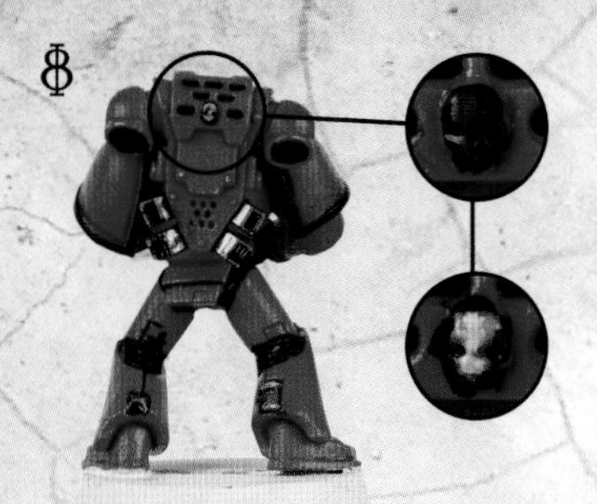

8

9

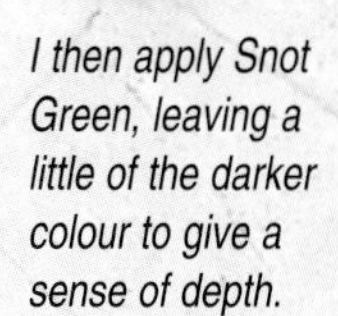

10

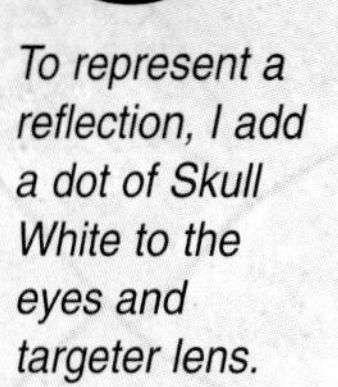

11

To paint the eyepieces I begin with Dark Angels Green.

I then apply Snot Green, leaving a little of the darker colour to give a sense of depth.

To represent a reflection, I add a dot of Skull White to the eyes and targeter lens.

I paint the skull insert on the backpack Bestial Brown and then layer on Skull White.

All the metal details – the helmet tubing, leg plate details, earpieces & backpack vents – I paint using Boltgun Metal.

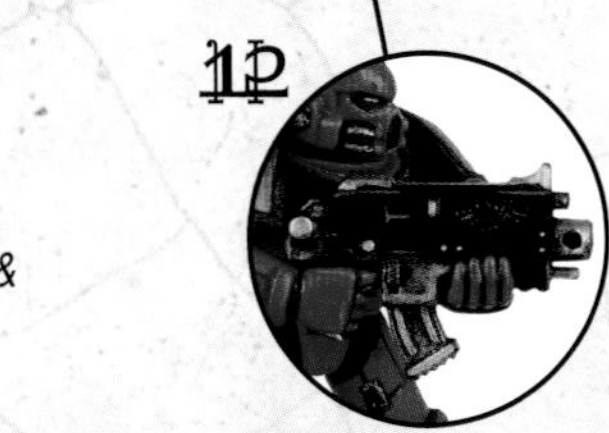

12

I paint the bolter Chaos Black and then fasten it to the model. The boltgun is painted in one go – I paint the metal areas Boltgun Metal and layer on Mithril Silver. I then paint the eagle and extreme upper edge highlight of the bolter Shining Gold. To finish off I apply Blood Red to the boltgun targeter lens.

13

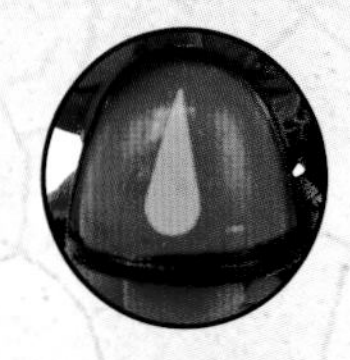

To finish off the model I apply the transfers – with no shading or highlighting added.

I prefer a brown base which sets off the strong red colour quite well. I've found this style of painting to be a very practical way of completing squads of Space Marines – the ink wash provides a good layer of shading which can easily be highlighted with a few layers of red paint.

COLLECTING TYRANIDS

Games Developer Phil Kelly started collecting Tyranids back when he was working for White Dwarf magazine. Initially a side project, his horde of Hive Fleet Jormungandr has grown quickly and steadily due to a simple but effective painting technique.

Phil: One of the first things to decide upon when collecting a new army is the colour scheme you're planning to use for it. Although a lot of armies, such as Space Marines, have set colour schemes, the Tyranids can be virtually any colour you fancy (although it's usually worth steering away from bright pink). I wanted my Tyranids to look as threatening as possible, and hence chose a colour scheme that, in the natural kingdom, means 'danger'; yellow and black. I wanted the Tyranid horde I was assembling to look like a swarm of angry, poisonous insects pouring across the table toward their prey. Not only that, but I wanted to put the minimum amount of effort into the paint job to get the maximum result, so black was always a good place to start.

That's where the dirty secret of this horde comes in – only one colour has been painted onto the models, the vast majority of the surface area is simply sprayed Chaos Black and then varnished. I reasoned that if I spent some time on getting one colour absolutely right, and concentrated it on the business ends of the Tyranid models – claws and teeth, mostly – then no one would actually look at the rest of the model. And, somehow, it works.

With that in mind I painted up a brood of Hormagaunts (OK, Hormagaunt claws and teeth), giving them two liberal coats of Purity Seal, so that the light highlighted all the bits that hadn't been given the paint job, and basing them with sand that is roughly the same tone as the painted areas. This two-tone approach always looks striking, especially from a distance.

Although this simple technique worked fine for the Gaunts, I wanted to put a little more effort onto the larger beasts in my army. I started to paint up a Carnifex's carapace with the pattern from the abdomen of a wasp to enhance the insect-swarm look, but sadly the execution of such a complex pattern went a bit wonky. I concentrated on keeping it symmetrical though, and, whilst applying the same idea to a Zoanthrope's carapace, I came up with the idea of using Rorschach patterns – those butterfly-like ink blot images – right the way across the large flat areas of all the big Tyranid creatures in the force. It's tricky to do, but it's not like there was much else to paint other than a blue tongue or bio-weapon here and there, and it draws the eye away from the largely neglected black areas. I'm really pleased with the results.

With the bases finished off desert-style, a whole brood of Phil's Hormagaunts looks extremely striking. The focus of the brood is its most deadly weapons, its teeth and claws, and goes to show that even the simplest colour scheme can look great when applied to a whole mass of models.

PAINTING TYRANIDS

On this spread I demonstrate the way I painted my Tyranid horde. As well as showing the minimal approach I took to painting the huge broods of Gaunts I have collected in my army, I also show how I made the larger models in my army, such as the Tyranid Warriors, look more striking. I did this by adding large symmetrical markings to the crests on their heads, as well as picking out more patterns on the legs and carapace.

1

After undercoating the model black, I paint the claws, teeth and the ridges on the Hormagaunt's back a basecoat of Snakebite Leather.

2

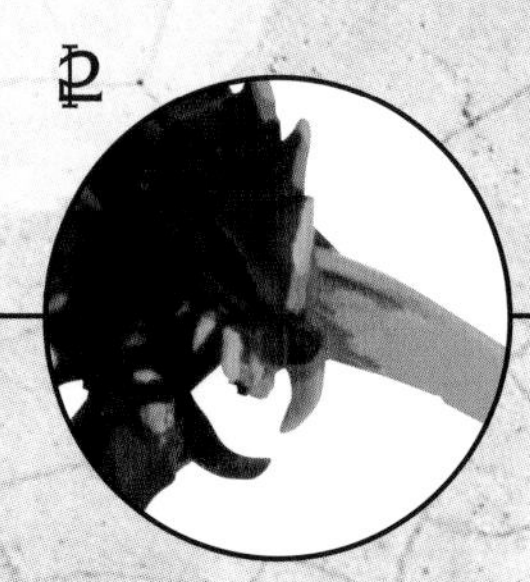

I then layer on three parts Snakebite Leather and one part Sunburst Yellow, leaving the basecoat showing in the deep recesses.

3

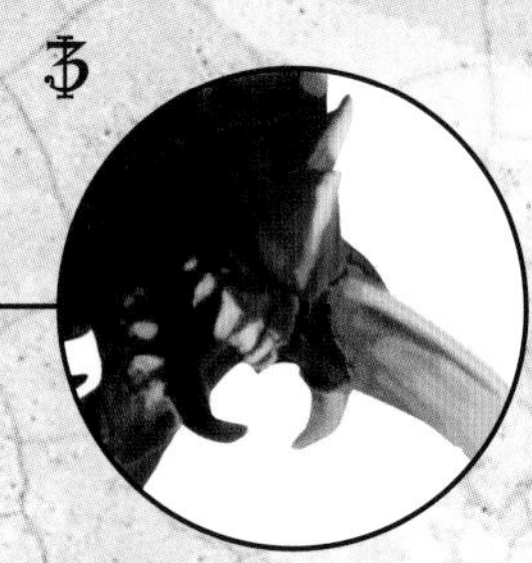

Leaving some of the previous layers showing, I apply a layer of equal parts Snakebite Leather, Sunburst Yellow and Skull White.

4

Adding more Skull White to the previous highlight mix, I carefully paint the edges and the tips of the claws and teeth.

For the final highlight I add even more Skull White to the edges, then paint the tongue Ultramarines Blue.

5

To highlight the tongue I add Skull White to the basecoat colour and apply that mix to the tip of the tongue.

I paint the eye Scab Red then thoroughly varnish the entire model, before finishing the base.

Here's how I add the markings to the large carapace plates on the Tyranid Warrior's heads.

To begin with I paint a roughly symmetrical design onto the carapace with a basecoat of Snakebite Leather.

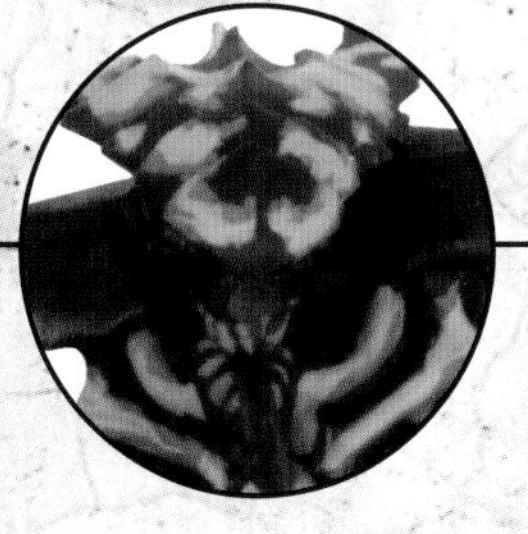

I define the markings with a layer of three parts Snakebite Leather and one part Sunburst Yellow, leaving a little of the basecoat showing.

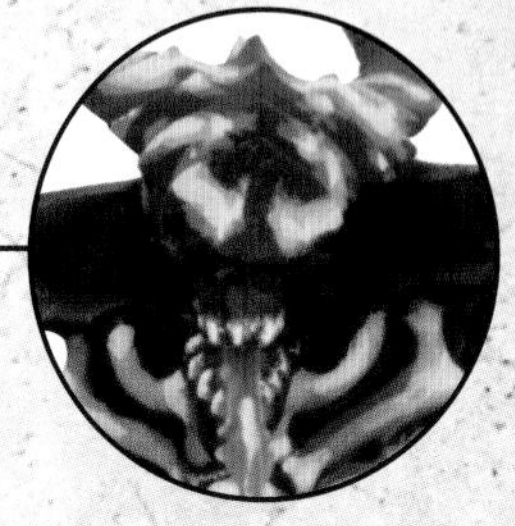

The final stage in refining the pattern is to apply a further layer of equal parts Snakebite Leather, Sunburst Yellow and Skull White.

TERRAIN BASICS

The subject of terrain, and how it can be made, could fill a book all by itself (in fact, it already does!). Here we look at three terrain elements which all require consideration before starting to make a gaming board. On the following pages we show you six different examples of terrain sets themed around different environments: urban, two different jungle boards, snow, ash waste and desert. If you are inspired to make more terrain for your board, How To Make Wargames Terrain shows you how.

THE TABLE

The most basic element in any collection of terrain is the gaming table itself. While you could make use of your own kitchen table or floor for this, most gamers will make their own, dedicated gaming board. While some will take an existing table and turn it into a permanent gaming table, most people prefer to use a baseboard, which can be placed on a kitchen table and stored out of the way when the game ends.

A good size for one of these boards is 6' x 4', which is big enough to stage all but the largest battles. Most gaming boards will be made either from polystyrene or wood and a good way to add a durable surface to the board is to apply a painted sand finish.

DESERT BOARD FINISHES

Sand boards can be painted and drybrushed different colours to create specific styles of gaming board.

1. *Apply a layer of glue to the board. You may find it useful to water down the glue to help cover the large area.*

2. *Pour on the sand. Once the surface is dry, knock off the excess sand onto a sheet of newspaper.*

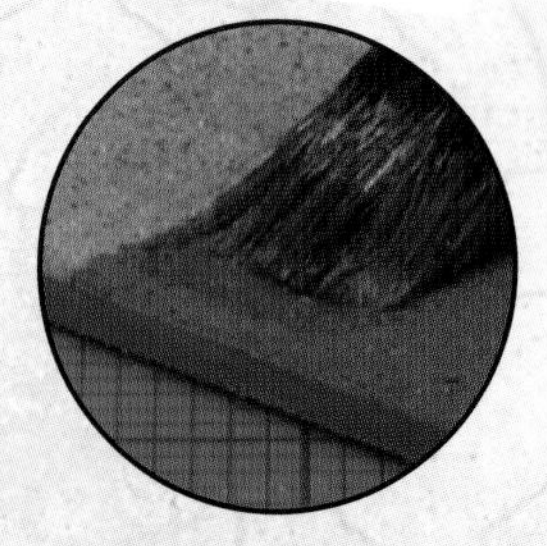

3. *Paint the surface with a mix of your chosen base colour, PVA/Woodworking glue and water.*

Ash Waste
Codex Grey
Bubonic Brown
Rotting Flesh

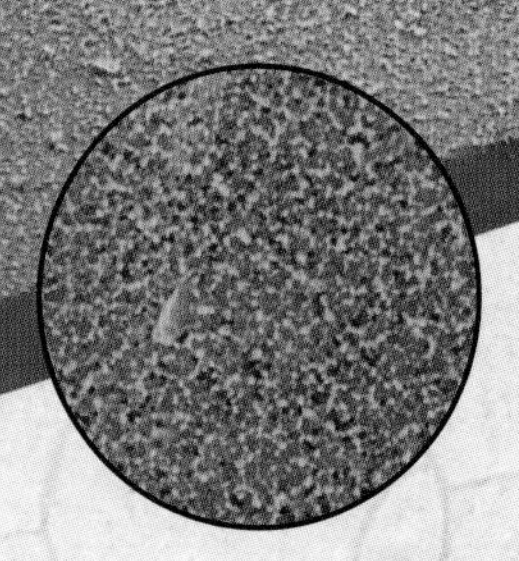

Sulphur Desert
Desert Yellow
Bubonic Brown
Bleached Bone

Red/Martian
Terracotta & Scab Red
Blood Red
Vomit Brown

Alien/Death World
Chaos Black
Codex Grey

WOODS

Using Games Workshop model trees, a set of woods is possibly the simplest piece of terrain to make. Just cut out an irregularly shaped base from card or wood, large enough for two or three trees, and paint it green. Once the base is dry, glue on the trees. Finish off the wood by gluing flock to the top of the base.

BARRICADES AND OBSTACLES

Simple barricades and obstacles can quickly be made from materials that you may already have. Rubble barricades can be made from polystyrene and card scraps, supplemented with any spare plastic parts you may have lying around. This fence was made from aluminium mesh, glued to bamboo skewers set into a foamboard base.

HILLS

While there is a variety of ready-made hills available, you can easily make your own from polystyrene to suit the requirements of your gaming area. For a simple hill, just cut two sheets of polystyrene to shape with a sharp knife or hot wire cutter, and glue them together. A layer of flock and gravel will help to blend the hill into its surroundings.

Ultramarines of the 2nd Company hold the breach in the defences of Yerelth Quay Spaceport against the forces of the Lost and the Damned.

SAMPLE BATTLEFIELDS

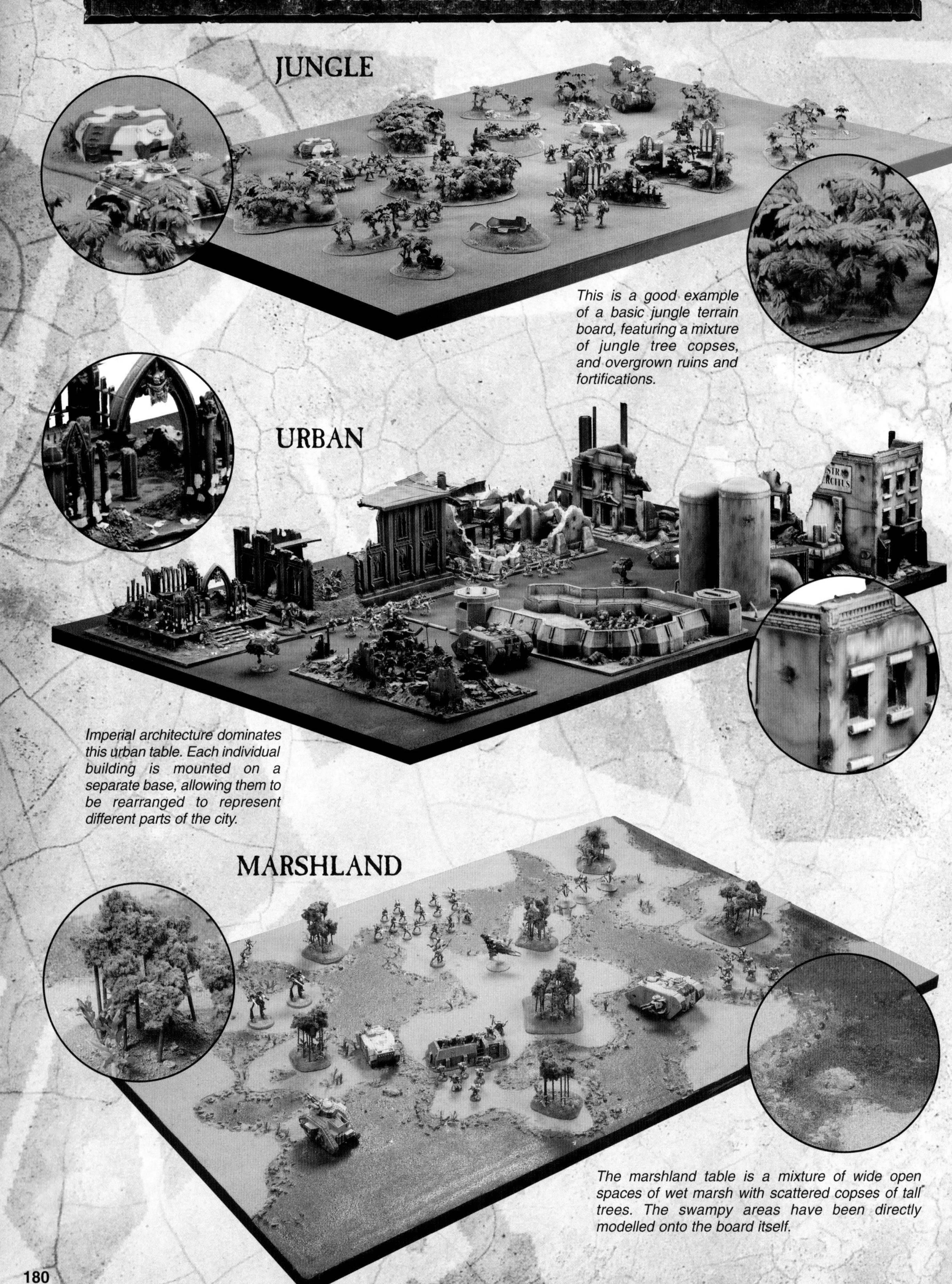

JUNGLE

This is a good example of a basic jungle terrain board, featuring a mixture of jungle tree copses, and overgrown ruins and fortifications.

URBAN

Imperial architecture dominates this urban table. Each individual building is mounted on a separate base, allowing them to be rearranged to represent different parts of the city.

MARSHLAND

The marshland table is a mixture of wide open spaces of wet marsh with scattered copses of tall trees. The swampy areas have been directly modelled onto the board itself.

SNOWSCAPE

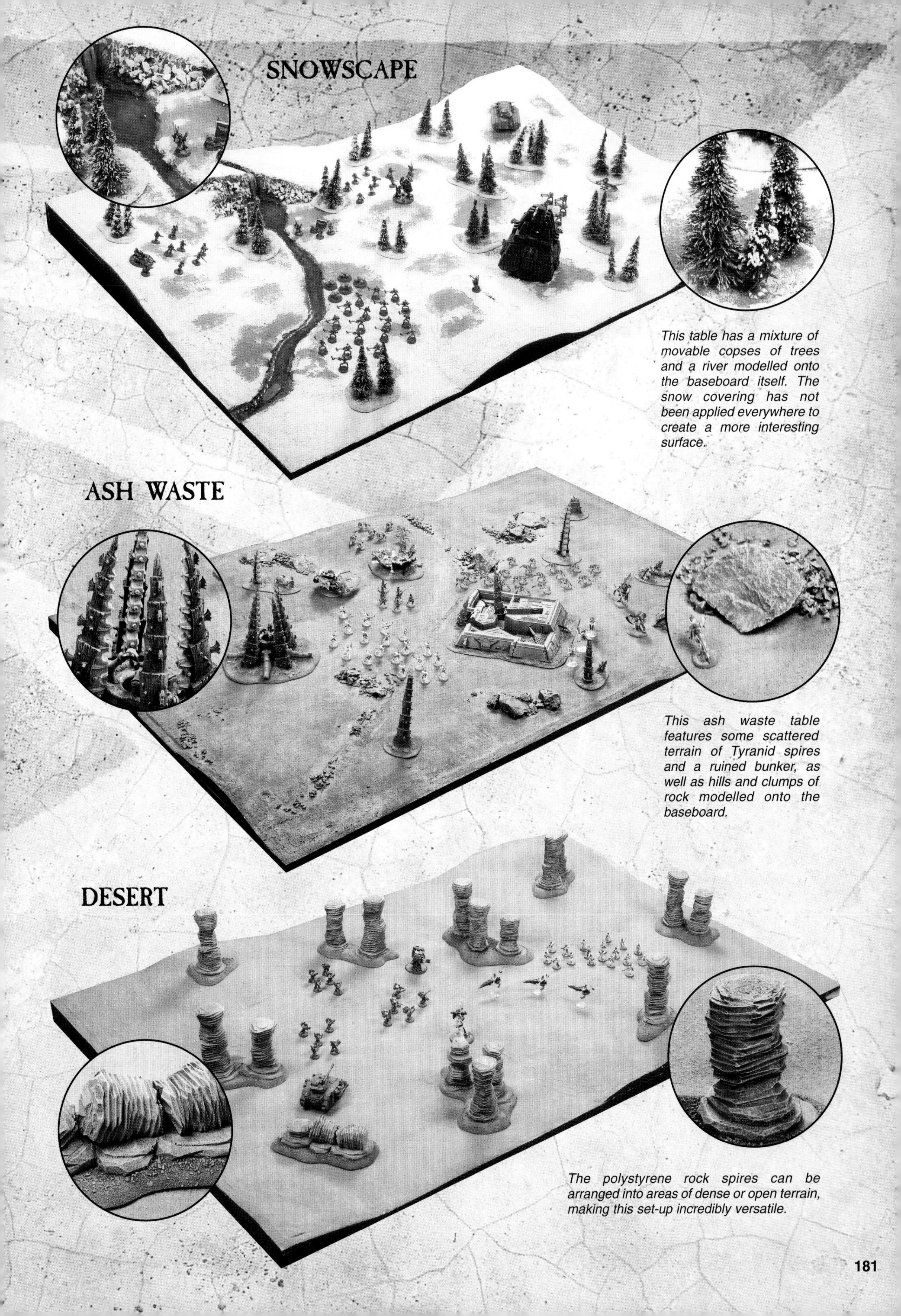

This table has a mixture of movable copses of trees and a river modelled onto the baseboard itself. The snow covering has not been applied everywhere to create a more interesting surface.

ASH WASTE

This ash waste table features some scattered terrain of Tyranid spires and a ruined bunker, as well as hills and clumps of rock modelled onto the baseboard.

DESERT

The polystyrene rock spires can be arranged into areas of dense or open terrain, making this set-up incredibly versatile.

COMBAT PATROL

Combat Patrol is short-form Warhammer 40,000 in which players command a small patrol of perhaps two squads and a light vehicle. The games are designed to take around forty minutes to play (or less) and are meant to be fast and fun. This set of rules is designed to help players get a regular game when time is the most limiting factor. This is not a 'light' set of rules but rather a fresh way to use the armies you already have.

RULES OF ENGAGEMENT

ARMY LIMITATIONS

Each player will need a patrol that conforms to the rules below:

- Armies are no more than 400 points.
- You must have one Troops choice.
- You may have one HQ choice, but no more than one.
- You may spend remaining points from anywhere in the Codex.
- No models can have more than 2 Wounds.
- No special characters.
- No 2+ Saves.
- No vehicles with a total Armour Value greater than 33. This is calculated by adding the Front, Side and Rear armour numbers (only count the Side once).
- No ordnance weapons.
- Games are played using the Combat Patrol mission (see next page).
- The Combat Patrol mission should ideally be played on a 4' x 4' area.

These rules do not necessarily cover every army – some exceptions will need to be made while still remaining true to the spirit of the game. For example, in Codex: Imperial Guard an Armoured Fist squad is a Troops choice, but you must take an Infantry platoon before you can take it. It is perfectly reasonable that a mobile unit like this would carry out patrols, so in Combat Patrol, the Armoured Fist squad can be taken on its own.

> "You are not free whose liberty is won by the rigour of other, more righteous souls. You are merely protected. Your freedom is parasitic, you suck the honourable man dry and offer nothing in return. You who have enjoyed freedom, who have done nothing to earn it, your time has come. This time you will stand alone and fight for yourselves. Now you will pay for your freedom in the currency of honest toil and human blood."
>
> Inquisitor Czevak – address to the Council of Ryanti

BEWARE ODDITIES

When you play Combat Patrol, it's important to remember that these games approach Warhammer 40,000 in a way that it was not originally intended to be approached. This means odd stuff might crop up that you need to sort out 'on the fly'. The best way to resolve these issues is to ask yourself the following:

- Is there any existing Warhammer 40,000 rule you can use as a precedent?
- What is the most reasonable thing that would happen in this situation?
- Agree on the two most likely outcomes and then roll a D6: 1-3 = Go with solution 1; 4-6 = Go with solution 2.

When it comes to army lists, you may, on occasion, find units with compulsory characters that break one of the above rules. If such a unit is the only Troops selection open to you, then simply leave out the offending character and don't pay the points for him. For example, a (3 Wound) Shaper is compulsory in a Kroot Carnivore Kindred, and Carnivores are the only Troops choice open to stand-alone Kroot Mercenary armies. In this case, don't count the Shaper as compulsory and go ahead and take the unit without him.

COMBAT PATROL MISSION

Both sides have unexpectedly collided with an enemy force whilst patrolling a disputed area.

SET-UP

1 Both players roll a D6; the player that scores higher gets to choose his deployment zone. Units must be deployed within 12" of the table edge. The player that scored the higher result now deploys one unit in his deployment zone. The players take it in turns deploying a unit at a time until both their entire forces are on the table.

2 Roll for who gets the first turn. Highest score may choose whether to go first or second.

SCENARIO SPECIAL RULES

Infiltrate, Victory Points

GAME LENGTH: *Six turns.*

MISSION OBJECTIVE

Both players must attempt to eliminate the enemy without losing too much of their own strength.

The player with the highest Victory Points total wins the game.

Ultramarine Scouts encounter the terrifying forces of the Necrons when exploring the ruins of a recently unearthed tomb complex on Angelis.

PAINTING PATROLS

While it's always rewarding to spend a long time patiently painting a model to a fine finish, sometimes you'll want to field a force more quickly. Troops painted for Combat Patrol are only one example of this, and there are a few techniques that are perfect for it. Here we look in detail at two of the most common techniques for creating shaded effects on your miniatures, followed by a look at three examples of forces painted for Combat Patrol.

DRYBRUSHING

The technique of drybrushing is both a fast and attractive way to add highlights to areas of raised detail. It can also be used to apply a fine texture to large flat areas such as armour plating, to create a realistic effect. A light drybrush over an entire model can give it an overall dusting that draws the colours together and gives a natural appearance.

Take a brush (preferably an old one) and mix up a light shade of the base colour – the paint needs to be fairly dense. If the paint is a little thin, let it dry slightly on the palette. Work the colour into the brush and then wipe any excess back onto the palette.

Now – most importantly – run the brush over a tissue or paper, or some similarly absorbent surface, until the strokes leave almost no mark, even when applied with pressure.

Begin by stroking the brush gently over the surface that you wish to highlight. Ideally, the brush should leave no discernable strokes, instead depositing a fine, even dusting of colour over the high points on the model. The drier the brush, the more the effect will appear as a dusting of even colour. Build up the highlights gradually – the longer you work at the result, the more intense the effect.

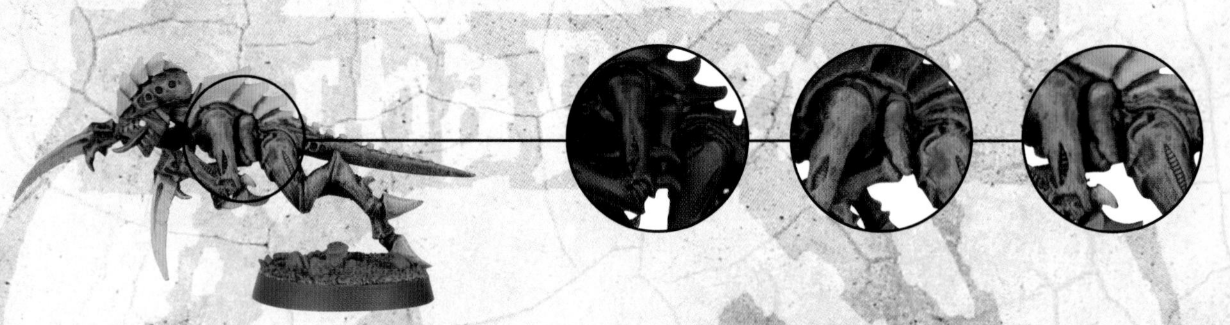

WASHES

Traditionally, a 'wash' is a mix of strongly coloured paint or ink and just sufficient water to give an overall fluid consistency. This mixture is applied over a light base colour and will tend to run into the cracks and crevices. The result is an overall 'stain' that is stronger in the recesses where the wash gathers. This introduces a level of naturally graduated shading onto the model and breaks up the overall colour into subtle patches of dark and light. The surface finish will be slightly mottled and therefore appears more natural in the case of organic surfaces, such as flesh, leather and cloth.

If you want to thin down an ink wash to reduce the intensity of colour then add water plus PVA/woodworking glue. The PVA/woodworking glue enhances the gathering qualities of the wash and produces a stronger contrast once dry. You will have to experiment to judge the effect for yourself. Conversely, if you want to reduce the gathering quality of an ink wash, producing a more overall tone, add a little liquid soap, such as washing up liquid. This breaks the surface tension so that the ink stains the surface more uniformly without forming patches.

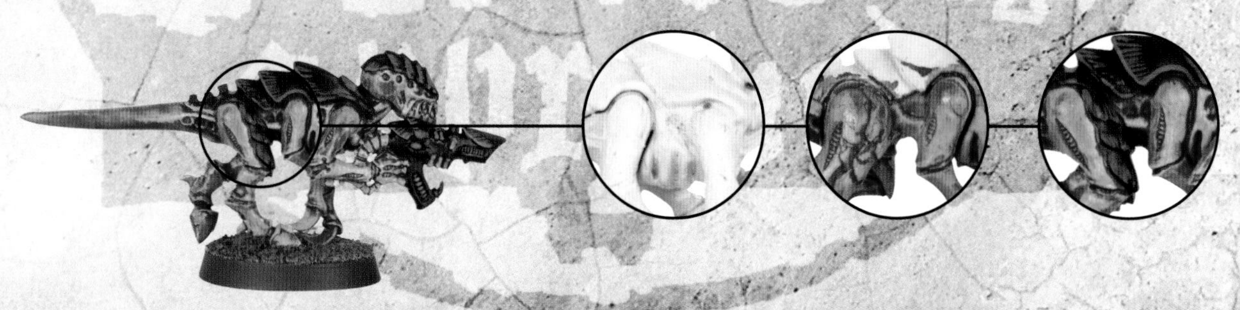

PAINTING A SPACE MARINE SCOUT PATROL

This small Scout force features an approach that was used to paint troops to a deadline – drybrushing the metal areas of the model first and then applying a very small number of flat colours to the cloth, armour plates and skin, working on all the models at the same time. As the focal point on the Scout models is the face, a little more time was spent painting them and finishing them off effectively.

The natural texture on the top of each base was drybrushed with Bleached Bone and then patches of static grass were glued on. A well-finished base is key to making any squad look good.

Once the undercoat is dry, all the metal areas, as well as the chest eagle and any decorative skulls, were drybrushed with Chainmail.

After repainting any pouches and holsters Chaos Black, the Scout's amour plates were painted Ultramarines Blue.

To create a nice bright contrast to both the armour plates and the metal, the areas of cloth were painted Bleached Bone.

A basecoat of Dwarf Flesh was used to paint the skin.

Chestnut Ink was applied to the skin to create deep shading.

The final stage for the skin was to apply a layer of Elf Flesh.

PAINTING A NECRON PATROL

There were two main parts to getting this Necron force up and running. The first and most important thing was to choose the colour scheme carefully. Half the battle can be choosing the right colours – in this case, red, black, and gold – and drybrushing the main colour onto the model, rather than painting it on. The second was the choice of giving the models a coat of gloss varnish. Normally, Necrons tend to be painted in metallic colours, but the deep red enamel finish on these models makes them stand out. The result is a group of models that look fantastic on the tabletop.

After the Necron was undercoated with Chaos Black, the model was drybrushed with Scab Red.

The joints, chest plate and gauss flayer were then picked out with Chaos Black.

To make the spine and gauss flayer workings stand out, they were painted with Brazen Bronze.

The finished model, complete with a coat of gloss varnish and the eyes picked out with Skull White.

To unify the red and bronze areas, a thinned down glaze of Flesh Wash was carefully applied.

PAINTING A TAU PATROL

This small Tau army was painted in less than a day, using simple techniques and a limited colour scheme. Tau are very easy to paint in a short period of time, as the miniatures feature large areas of flat armour that are simple to paint using only one or two colours. For this army, a 'production line' method was used, whereby each colour was applied to each miniature before moving on to the next. This method is perfect for turning out small armies, like those used in Combat Patrol, in no time at all.

After an undercoat of Chaos Black had been sprayed onto the miniature, any areas that the spray had missed were painted with a watered down wash of Chaos Black paint.

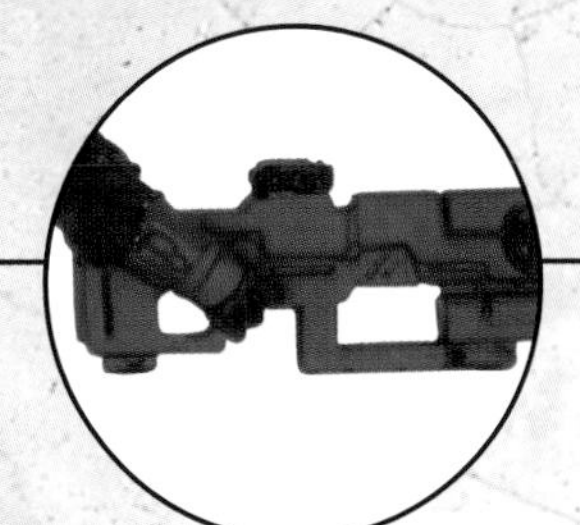

Catachan Green was then used as the main colour. When painting areas of armour it is ok to leave recessed areas black.

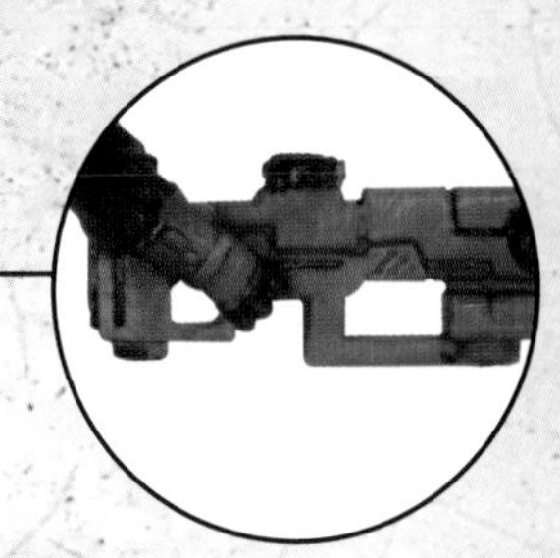

Next, the Catachan Green areas were drybrushed with Camo Green. The fabric visible on the Fire Warriors was first painted Scorched Brown, and then given a drybrush of Graveyard Earth.

Simple details, such as insignia, were picked out in Chainmail.

Waterslide transfers are great for adding striking detail to vehicle models, and take no time at all to apply.

INSTANT TERRAIN

If you want to put together a battlefield quickly, there are plenty of ways to do this, from buying terrain available in stores or using rapidly assembled buildings made from cardboard.

A CLOTH BATTLEFIELD

One of the quickest ways of making a battlefield with a landscape of rises and falls, is to use a large piece of cloth. You'll need to get hold of a piece of cheap cotton cloth to represent the ground – ideally green or brown – then spread it over the surface of the table. Place books, boxes, upturned bowls or something similar underneath to create hills and valleys. With a little care, it's possible to make the battlefield interesting by introducing cover that will restrict visibility and provide shelter. With the cloth in place, you can add further scenery, such as scrub, trees, buildings, and ruins, to complete the scene.

The different kinds of scenery you can add to a cloth battlefield include both everyday objects you find lying around and material you can buy. For instance, stones and gravel are freely available in whatever quantities you want. On the other hand, lichen and cork bark are both available to buy in model stores and craft stores. Lichen can be used to represent scrub and bushes whilst cork bark makes interestingly shaped rocky outcrops. Aquarium plants are also a useful addition and can be found in pet shops. All three can be reused time and again to create different table layouts.

Possibly the quickest alternative to building your own terrain is to buy it ready-made. Games Workshop's range of tabletop scenery includes trees, hedges, barricades and various set pieces, such as ruins and buildings.

Aquarium plants are available from pet shops and they are another great way to represent foliage, with an exotic, alien twist.

A RUINED CITY IN AN AFTERNOON

It's possible to create a whole set of city ruins in a single afternoon. All you need is stiff card, a ruler, a craft knife or scissors, adhesive tape, PVA/woodworking glue and the templates that we include here.

__1.__ Photocopy the template. Press a pin through the corners of the shapes, onto your card. When you remove the template, you will have a network of pinpricks: just join up the dots. Remember to mark on the dotted lines as well, as these show the position of the floors.

__2.__ Glue the lower floor to one wall.

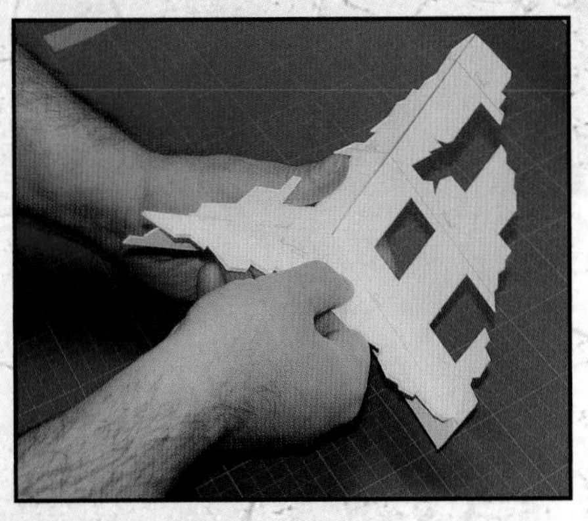

__3.__ Fold the other wall up and glue it in place.

__4.__ Glue in the remaining floors, leave to dry and then paint your ruin in the desired colour.

Don't throw away the waste card, you can use this to make a second building!

You can make the building look more realistic by gluing a few extra strips of card onto the surface, as shown in the finished building below.

__5.__ Repeat as necessary.

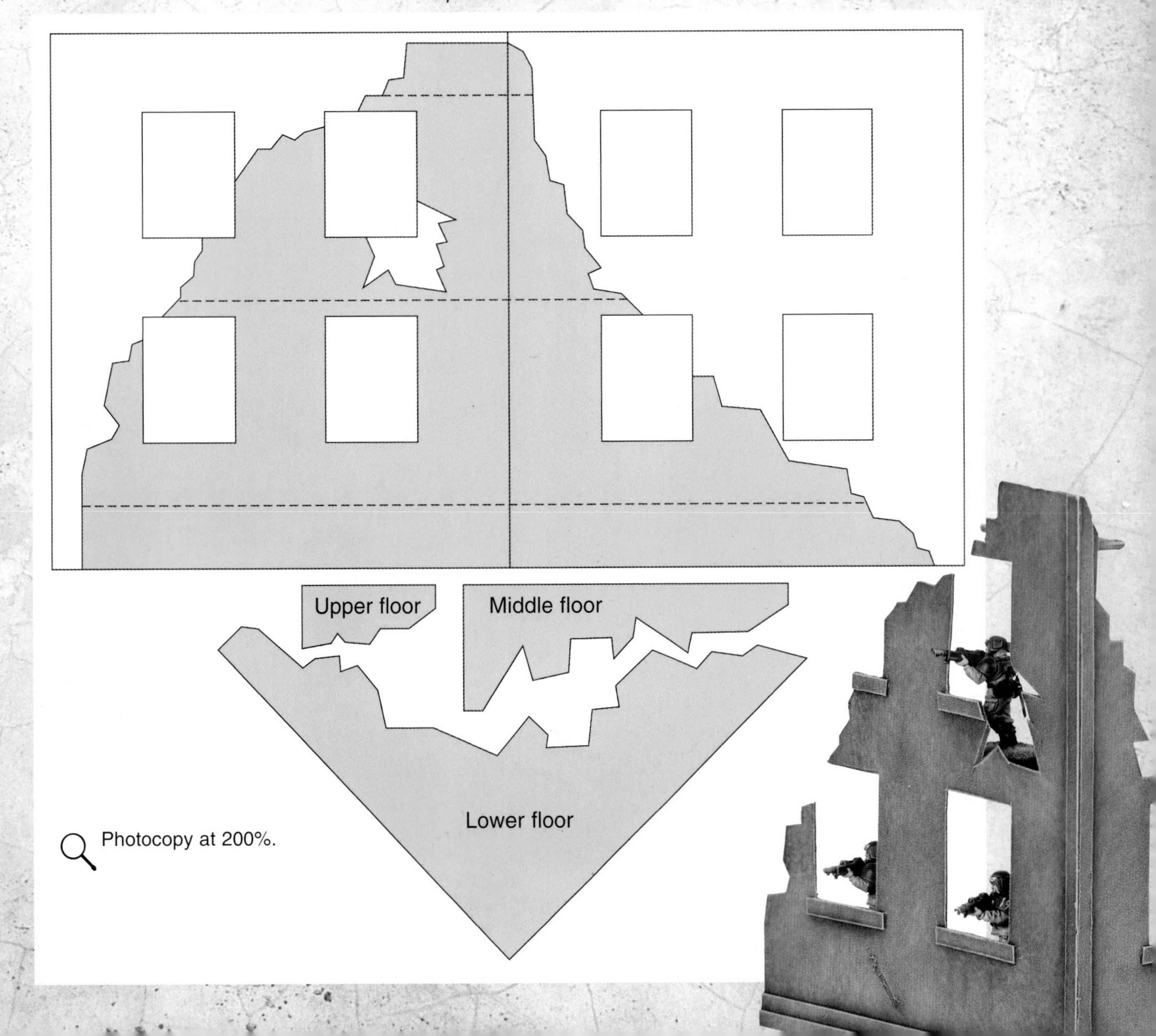

Photocopy at 200%.

SPECIAL MISSIONS

This section presents a collection of specialist missions. These represent unusual situations, ones with a story behind them, and provide unique challenges for beginners and veteran players alike. They often require a bit of preparation and may not always be perfectly balanced, but focusing on objectives and deployment allows such situations as ambushes and last stands to be played out by players really looking to test their gaming mettle.

If you are planning a campaign, you will find this section particularly useful as it consists of missions that can be dropped into your plans very easily, providing ready-made templates for whatever situations develop over the course of your games.

Players should feel free to adapt these missions to use in their own campaigns, or invent entirely new ones of their own devising.

The majority of these missions require some additional work in the form of building specialist terrain pieces, such as bunkers, obstacles, etc. The special rules for such pieces add great depth to your games of Warhammer 40,000, and we believe players should approach these games as opportunities to make great new terrain as much as to play new games. Throughout this section, you'll find guidance and inspiration for making the special terrain pieces needed for many of these missions.

RESCUE

Both forces are sweeping the area for something valuable – lost plans, maps or even an injured spy – when they clash near its location.

SET-UP

1 Before choosing table edges or deploying any forces, the players take turns to place six numbered counters, face down anywhere on the table, (without looking at the numbers on the counters!). Each counter must be no closer that 12" to another counter and no closer than 12" to any board edge.

2 Determine which one of these counters is the objective by rolling a dice. The counter with that number on it is the real objective and must be discovered by the armies during the battle.

3 Both players roll a dice, the winner chooses where he will deploy. He can choose to either deploy from a corner or a long board edge; he may not choose a short board edge. He may deploy up to 6" onto the board. His opponent gets the opposite deployment zone, so either both forces start in the corners or along either long board edge.

4 Both players roll a dice, the lowest dice roll deploys first. He may set up any or all of the units from his Troops allowance in his deployment zone. He does not have to deploy all his Troops, but he must deploy at least one unit. Any Troops not deployed are in reserve, as is the rest of his force. The other player then deploys his force.

5 Both players roll a dice, the winner choosing whether to take the first or second turn.

SCENARIO SPECIAL RULES

Reserves.

GAME LENGTH: *Six turns*

MISSION OBJECTIVE

The player in possession of the objective at the end of the game wins. If no one has the objective at the end of the game then it is a draw.

To reveal a counter, the player must move an infantry model into contact with it and halt the model's movement. Turn the counter face up and see which number it has on it. If the counter is the one with the number rolled at the start of the game, the model has located the objective, and it is now in that model's possession. If the counter is any other number, discard it and keep hunting.

If the model carrying the prize is killed or has to fall back then the counter is dropped and remains on the board. It may be picked up by any infantry model that moves into contact with it.

The model can pass the objective to another infantry model by moving into base contact.

Neither model may move after they have come into contact until their next turn, and the objective can only be handed off once per turn.

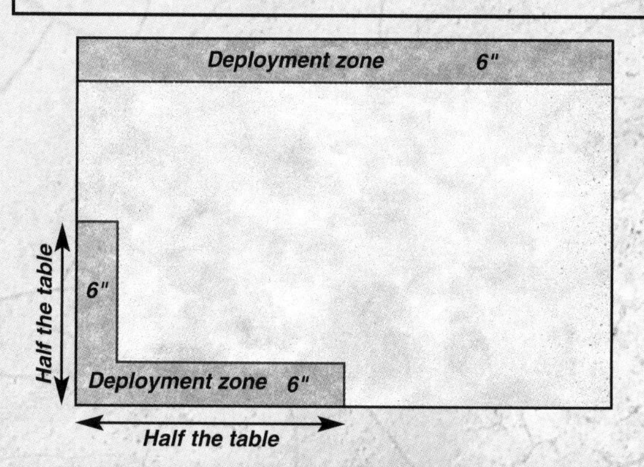

NIGHT FIGHT

Both sides have unexpectedly collided with an enemy force whilst moving forward at night. Muzzle flashes and tracer rounds criss-cross the battle as both sides attempt to locate and destroy the enemy.

SET-UP

1 Divide the board into four quarters. Both players roll a dice, highest score picks which quarter to deploy in. The other player's deployment zone is the opposite quarter.

2 Starting with the player that scored lowest, the players take it in turns deploying a unit at a time until both armies are fully deployed. Units are deployed in the following order: Heavy Support, Troops, Elites, HQ, Fast Attack.

No unit can be deployed within 24" of the enemy at the start of the game.

3 Roll a D6. Highest score may choose whether to go first or second.

GAME LENGTH: *Six turns*

MISSION OBJECTIVE

Both forces must clear the area of all enemies, securing ground as they go. The player that occupies the most quarters of the board at the end of the game wins.

To occupy a table quarter there must be at least one scoring friendly unit and no scoring enemy units in the table quarter. If a unit is in several quarters determine which it counts as being in randomly.

SCENARIO SPECIAL RULES

Night Fighting, Infiltrate.

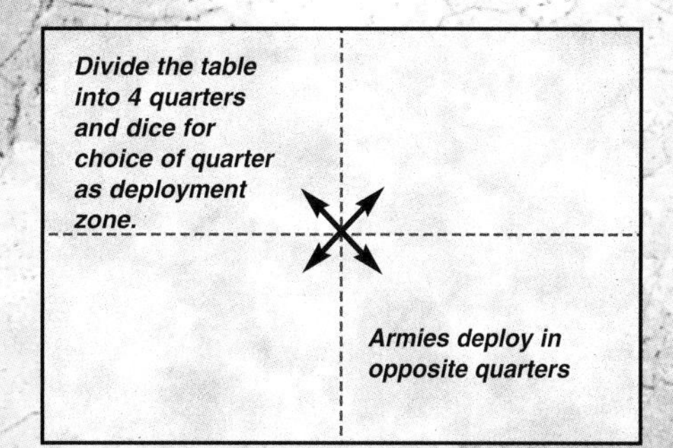

PATROL

You have been detailed to patrol no man's land and drive off any enemy forces encountered. Additional forces are near at hand to secure victory, but be warned – the enemy have their own reserves and will attempt to do the same to you.

SET-UP

1 Both players roll a dice, the winner chooses either a long board edge or a corner as his deployment zone. Units may be deployed up to 12" onto the board. If it is a corner then units may be deployed up to halfway along each board edge.

His opponent gets the opposite deployment zone, so either both forces start in opposite corners or along opposite long board edges.

2 Both players roll a dice, the loser deploys one unit of Troops, this is his patrol. The winner then deploys one unit of Troops in his deployment zone. The rest of their forces are in reserve.

3 Roll a D6. Highest score may choose whether to go first or second.

RESERVES: *When available, reserves move on from the player's deployment zone board edge.*

GAME LENGTH: *Six turns (Variable)*

MISSION OBJECTIVE

Both players must attempt to eliminate the enemy without losing too much of their own strength. The player with the highest Victory Points total wins the game.

SCENARIO SPECIAL RULES

Random Game Length, Reserves, Victory Points.

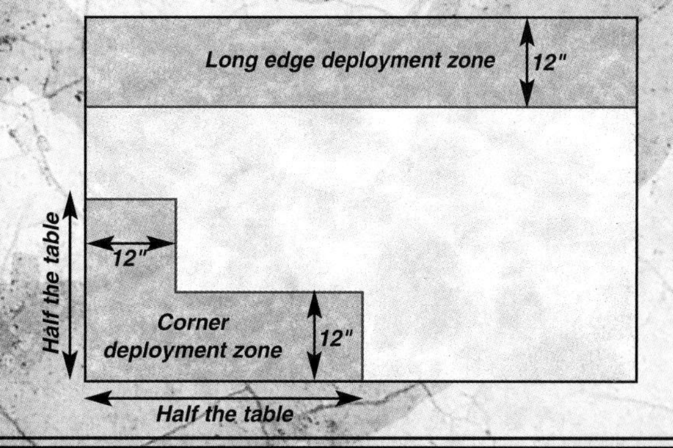

MAKING RESCUE MARKERS

Rescue markers represent the objectives in a Rescue Mission. They can be modelled as small pieces of scenery, and as such can be themed to one of the armies playing the mission, or to the terrain being played over.

These markers are very simple to make. Each is a 25mm round base painted to represent a 'blip' on an auspex screen. Once the target of the mission is discovered, a miniature is placed alongside the model that uncovered it, representing a rescue of an important individual who cannot be allowed to fall into enemy hands.

These markers represent supply canisters dropped onto the battlefield, and are themed to accompany an Imperial Guard Drop Troopers regiment. Once the marker is discovered, the small crate is placed next to the model that uncovered it, representing the trooper recovering a vital piece of equipment from the canister.

ALTERNATIVE FORCE ORGANISATION CHARTS

The standard Force Organisation chart provides enough scope for a varied army list. It may not always be appropriate though, and as part of the process of designing your own missions or establishing house rules for a campaign you may want to experiment with some alternatives. Reducing the number of Heavy Support choices will encourage more close combat, while reducing the number of Elites will ensure more points are spent on line troops and so on.

The alternatives shown here are included to show what can be done with Force Organisation charts. Below are some examples of Force Organisation charts appropriate for the missions presented on the following pages. Players are encouraged to alter these as they see fit for their games, and they should be taken only as examples of the forces that might be assembled for these types of battles.

When playing Battles, Raids and Breakthrough scenarios, models with the Infiltrate special rule may only deploy using it if they are on the attacking side. Infiltrators on the defending side have had no time to prepare for the battle, and so deploy according to the instructions for their army.

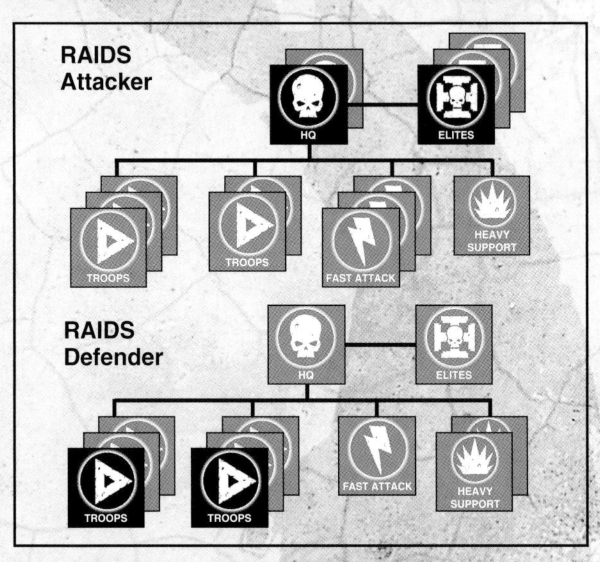

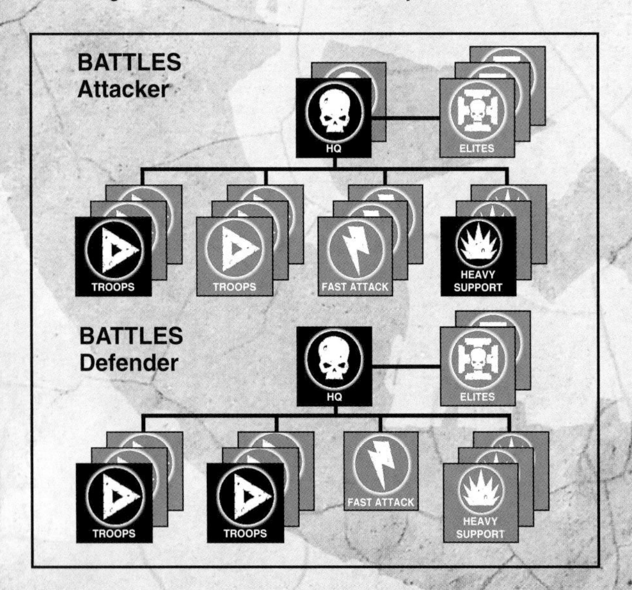

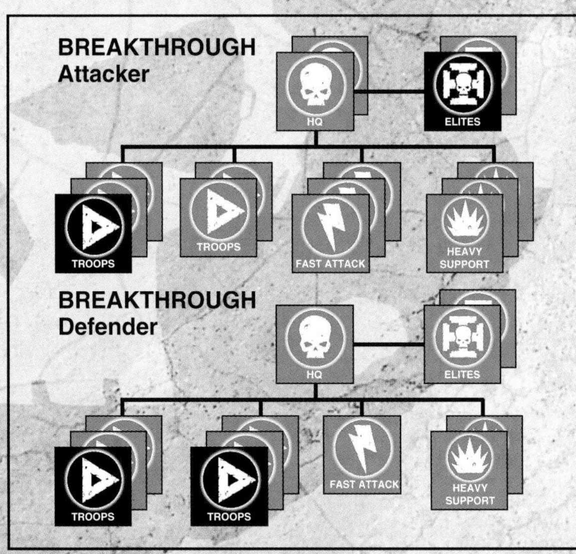

BATTLE MISSIONS

In battle scenarios, one player is the attacker and one is the defender. Battles may be fought to capture a vital objective or annihilate the enemy's forces in a sustained attack. As a commander, you will need a combination of tactical cunning and bloody-minded determination to overcome the foe.

FORTIFICATIONS

In some scenarios the defender may set up fortifications. All fortifications must be represented by a suitable model.

There are many forms of fortifications, but broadly they represent cover for the defender. Sandbagged positions, trenches, redoubts, makeshift barricades and fortress walls all count as fortifications. The defender may set up as many fortifications as he likes and the scenario set-up rules explain where these fortifications can be placed – usually in the defender's deployment zone.

A model in fortifications receives a Cover Saving throw of 3+, see page 25 for more information on Cover Saving throws.

BUNKERS

Bunkers in Warhammer 40,000 can take many forms – from fortified caves to plasteel fortifications. It is assumed that a bunker will consist of an enclosed structure no more than 8" across in any direction. It should have one access point and vision slits all around.

A bunker may contain as many models as will fit within it without overlapping bases. Each individual vision slit or 1" length of continual slit allows one model to fire out at targets visible from that slit. Units in bunkers may still only shoot at a single enemy unit.

If you are using more than one bunker in a game then you may use models combining several bunkers into one large fortification. In such complexes, the access points may open into other bunkers although the complex must have at least one external access point.

A bunker confers a Cover Save of 3+ on any models occupying it. In addition, they may not be assaulted while the bunker is intact.

A bunker is entered and exited by its access point in the same way as access points on vehicles (see page 62). An occupied bunker can only be accessed this way by troops on the same side as the occupying troops.

A bunker can be breached in one of two ways:

- Attacks aimed at the occupying troops may damage the bunker. In any Shooting phase in which a weapon of Strength 8 or more inflicts a casualty on occupying troops, roll a D6, and on a 6 the bunker is breached.
- Attacks can be aimed directly at the bunker. This includes not only ranged attacks but close combat attacks. For this purpose it is treated as an immobile vehicle with Armour Value 14 and any glancing or penetrating hit will breach it.

Once a bunker is breached, the Cover Saving throw of the occupants is reduced to 4+ and they may be assaulted normally, although they will still count as occupying cover.

Fortifications may be placed along the tops of bunkers and occupied by troops normally. Attacking troops may either shoot the bunker or the bunker's occupants or any troops on the roof. You may not claim to attack all three even if using blast or template weapons.

SUSTAINED ATTACK

Occasionally, the enemy will have an overwhelming superiority in numbers, with wave upon wave of foes hurling themselves forward. To represent the size of an attack like this, the player making the Sustained Attack can 'recycle' some of his units when they are destroyed. Recycled units are brought back into play to represent the almost limitless supply of reinforcements.

Any attacking Troops unit (ie, Troops choices on the Force Organisation table) that is wiped out may move on from the attacking player's own board edge or either of the short table edges outside of the enemy deployment zone. They move on at the beginning of the attacker's next turn.

Units of troops which are forced to fall back and reduced to less than 50% strength in models can be removed from the table immediately and reused as if they had been wiped out in their owner's next full player turn. They do not have to fall back off the table first.

Destroyed vehicles and HQ units cannot be recycled. Note that this includes transport vehicles for Troops units.

OBSTACLES

Fortifications are not the only form of defences. In some scenarios the defender may place obstacles. Obstacles are a hindrance to enemy movement and are split into two categories: razor wire and tank traps.

RAZOR WIRE

If the defender has suitable models then he may set up razor wire. Razor wire comes in 6" long sections. If the defender has obstacles then he gets D3+3 sections of razor wire to deploy at the start of the game.

Razor wire counts as difficult ground for all non-vehicle models. Vehicles can drive over razor wire with no effect.

TANK TRAPS

Tank traps also come in 6" long sections. If the defender has obstacles then he gets D3+3 sections of tank traps to position at the start of the game.

All vehicles, except skimmers, treat tank traps as impassable ground. Tank traps do not affect infantry movement, they can simply run around or clamber over them. Tank traps will provide cover for infantry.

Tank traps may be destroyed by enemy fire. They have an Armour Value of 10, and any penetrating hit destroys the section automatically. Glancing hits have no effect. They may be assaulted by infantry as if they were a stationary vehicle.

PRELIMINARY BOMBARDMENT

In a major offensive, the attacker will often attempt to soften up his target with a heavy bombardment before launching his attack. The barrage could come from artillery units far in the rear, close support vehicles like Basilisks and Whirlwinds, or from orbital barrages and air strikes. All races and armies have their own forms of artillery support and aircraft, be they Tyranid Biovores, Eldar Night Spinners, Chaos artillery, Ork Fighta-bommerz, or whatever.

A preliminary bombardment is unlikely to cause massive damage to a well dug in force, but it will make the enemy troopers keep their heads down and some of them will be so dazed that they only react slowly to the assault which follows. The huge ground-shaking explosions of the bombardment can also help clear the way for an attack by destroying fixed defences like razor wire and tank traps.

Roll a D6 for each enemy unit and each section of razor wire or tank traps on the tabletop. On a roll of 6, the unit or obstacle is hit. A squad takes D6 hits from the shelling, causing 1 wound each (make Armour Saves as normal), and must roll a Leadership test or be pinned in their first turn – see the Barrage section of the rules for details. Place a suitable piece of scenery under the squad if you have one available. A vehicle hit by a preliminary bombardment starts the game stunned (roll for each vehicle in a squadron independently). Troops that start the game in reserve cannot be hit by a preliminary bombardment.

A section of razor wire or tank traps is automatically destroyed by being hit, remove it from play.

Bunkers are not affected by a preliminary bombardment, (resisting long range shelling is what they are built to do), but you should still roll for troops inside them (some of the troops may have been caught in the open whilst running for cover).

BUNKER ASSAULT

The defenders have established a heavily fortified defensive line of bunkers, trenches and pillboxes. The attacker has been ordered to assault the strongpoints and capture or destroy them.

SET-UP

1. Both players roll a dice, the player that scores highest chooses which long edge he will deploy on.

2. The defender's deployment zone is up to 18" onto the board. He may set up fortifications anywhere in this zone and must include at least one bunker. Bunkers must be placed at least than 6" from any table edge.

3. The defender deploys any of his Troops and HQ units in his deployment zone. He does not have to deploy all these units, but must deploy at least one. All bunkers must be manned. Any units not deployed are in reserve.

4. The attacker deploys his entire army up to 12" onto the tabletop from his board edge.

5. The attacker resolves his preliminary bombardment.

6. Roll a D6. Highest score may choose whether to go first or second.

RESERVES: *The defender's reserves move on from his table edge.*

GAME LENGTH: *Six turns*

MISSION OBJECTIVE

Victory is determined by Victory Points and by control of the bunkers placed on table. Each bunker is worth Victory Points equal to the points limit of the game divided by the number of bunkers in play (so in a 1,500 point game with three bunkers, each bunker is worth 500 points). A bunker is held if it is occupied by at least one scoring Infantry unit and there are no scoring enemy infantry within 6" of it.

At the end of the game, add up Victory Points for enemy units destroyed and bunkers captured. The highest score wins.

SCENARIO SPECIAL RULES

Deep Strike, Fortifications, Infiltrate, Preliminary Bombardment, Reserves, Victory Points.

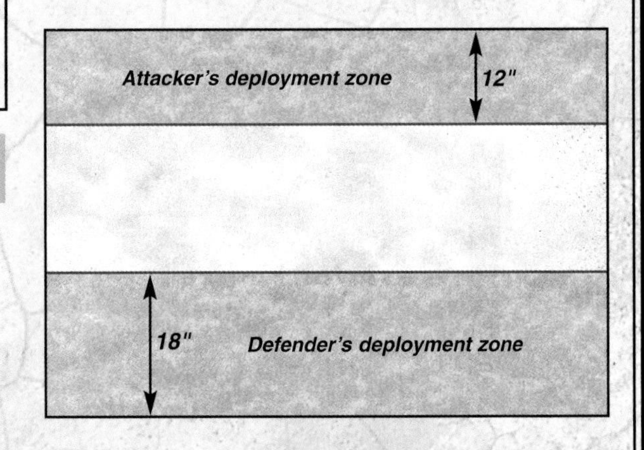

HOLD AT ALL COSTS

The attacker must eliminate enemy forces in the area and hold the objective against enemy counter-attacks. The defender must stop the objective falling into enemy hands at all costs.

SET-UP

1. Choose an objective as close as possible to the centre of the table.
2. The defender deploys any of his Troops and Heavy Support within 12" of the objective. He does not have to deploy all these units, but he must deploy at least one. The rest of his forces are in reserve.
3. The attacker may deploy his Infiltrators. The rest of his forces move onto the table at the beginning of turn one.
4. The attacker moves first.

RESERVES: *The defender's reserves move on from his table edge.*

GAME LENGTH: *Six turns (Variable)*

MISSION OBJECTIVE

The player that controls the objective at the end of the game wins the battle. To control the objective, you must have the closest scoring unit to the objective at the end of the game.

SCENARIO SPECIAL RULES

Deep Strike, Infiltrate, Random Game Length, Reserves.

MEAT GRINDER

The attacker has been ordered to annihilate all enemy forces, crushing them entirely in an all-out attack. The defender is badly outnumbered and must sell his forces dearly to blunt the attack, taking as many of his enemies with him as possible.

SET-UP

1. Both players roll a dice, the highest scorer chooses either of the long table edges as his deployment zone. He may deploy his forces up to 12" onto the board.

   The opposing player gets the opposite table edge. He may deploy his forces up to 12" onto the board.
2. Both players roll a dice. Starting with the player that scored lowest, the players take it in turns deploying a unit at a time until both armies are fully deployed. Units are deployed in the following order: Heavy Support, Troops, Elites, HQ, Fast Attack.
3. Roll a D6. Highest score may choose whether to go first or second.

LINE OF RETREAT: *Units which are forced to fall back will do so towards the nearest board edge of their deployment zone. Attacking units forced to fall back and reduced to less than 50% strength can be removed from the table and reused. They do not have to fall back off the table first. (See the Sustained Attack rules).*

GAME LENGTH: *Six turns (Variable)*

MISSION OBJECTIVE

To win the battle, the attacker must annihilate the defender's army. He wins the battle if, at the end of the game, the defender has no forces left. If the defender has any forces remaining at the end of the game, then he wins the battle.

SCENARIO SPECIAL RULES

Deep Strike, Infiltrate, Random Game Length, Sustained Attack.

Deployment zone 12"

12" *Deployment zone*

MAKING FORTIFICATIONS

Fortifications can include obstacles, such as razor wire, sandbags, wire fences, etc as well as defensive positions, such as armoured bunkers. The bunker below, which we show you how to build, is made using only a few simple tools and even fewer materials.

BUILDING A BUNKER

USING THE TEMPLATES

Photocopy the walls and roof templates on page 199 and use them as a guide to making the separate pieces of the bunker. To transfer the templates onto the foamboard, press a pin through the corners of the shapes onto your board. When you remove the template you will have a network of pinpricks. Then all you have to do is join up the dots.

YOU WILL NEED...

MATERIALS

- 5mm foamboard
- Textured paint
- Citadel Colour paints

TOOLS

- Modelling knife
- Metal ruler
- Pencil
- PVA /Woodworking glue

THE WALLS & ROOF

1. Using the front wall template as a guide, draw the outline of the wall and the two large firing slits on your 5mm foamboard. Cut out the wall and firing slit with your modelling knife: this is the outer wall. Draw the front wall shape once again, this time drawing on the smaller firing slits and then cut that wall shape out: this is the inner wall.

2. Glue the two wall halves together, making a complete wall section. Make the two side walls in the same way.

3. To make the back wall, draw and cut out the outer wall with the large firing slot and the door shape in the same way as for the front and side walls. Draw the inner wall in the same way using the smaller firing slot, only this time draw the outline of the interlocking door. Cut through the top layer of card to make the two halves of the door.

4. Glue these two parts together in the same way as the front and side walls.

5. You can then glue the side walls to the front and back walls to make the basic building shape.

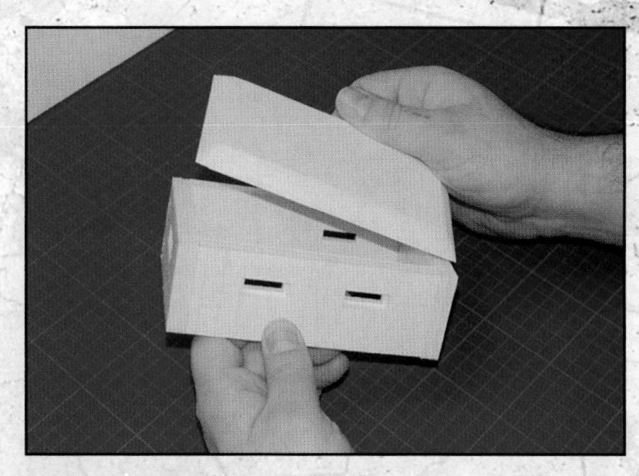

6. Copy the roof shape onto your foamboard twice and glue the two pieces one on top of each other. Mark another rectangle on the roof 10mm in from the edge and cut through the card layer. Peel this away, shape the foam to make a straight slope and then glue the roof in place.

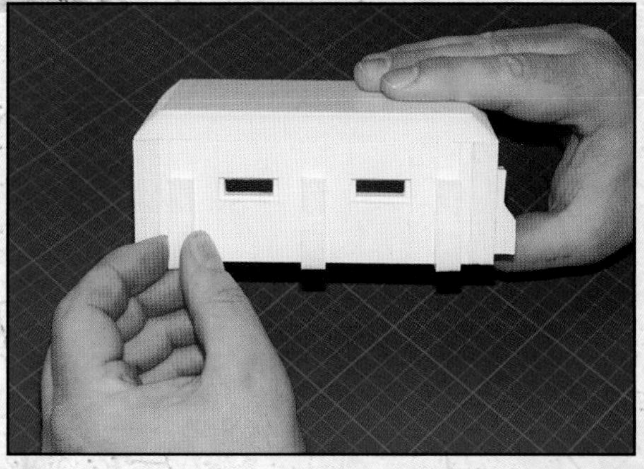

7. To finish off the bunker, cut out twenty buttress shapes, glue them together in pairs and then attach them to the outside walls. Use two on the side walls and three on the front and back. Use the dotted outlines on the wall templates as a guide.

PAINTING THE BUNKER

Apply a coat of textured paint to the bunker and then undercoat it black. Drybrush the walls with progressively lighter shades of colour.

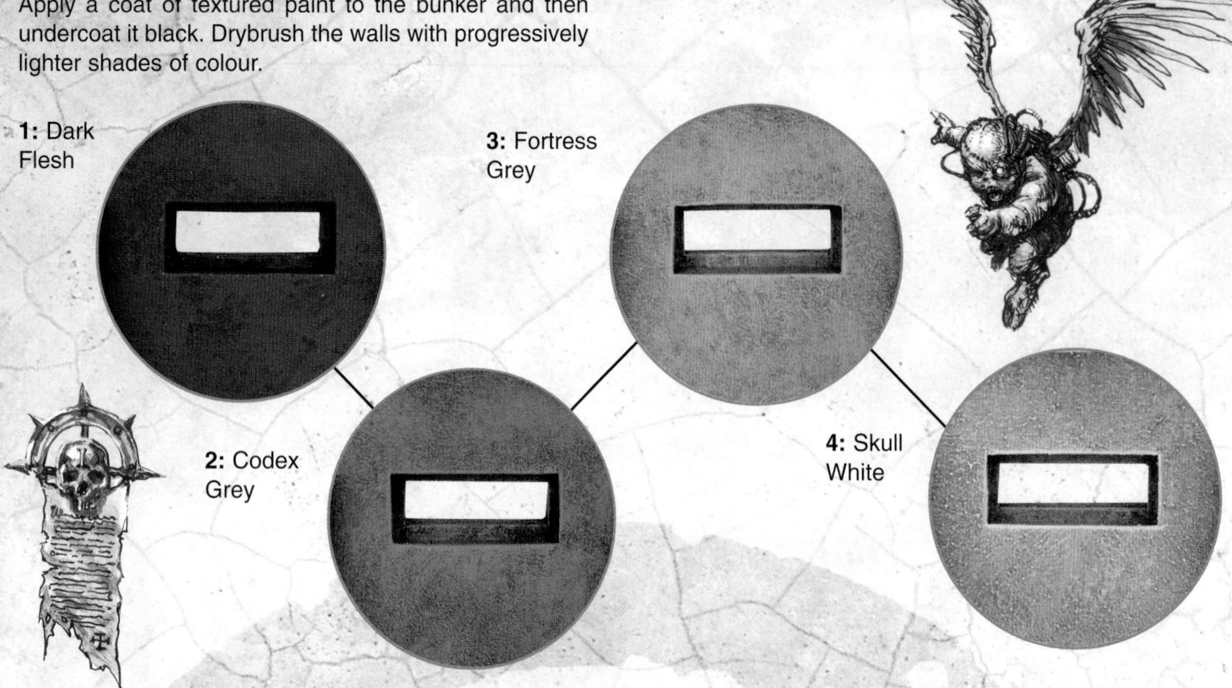

FINAL TOUCHES

Glue the complete model to a base. If you prefer, you can leave the roof unglued so you can place models inside the bunker. Here a rectangle of foamboard has been glued to the bottom of the roof to help it fit in place. A radar dish taken from the Land Raider Accessory sprue has been attached to the top of the roof and is used as a handle for removing the lid. You can also see how transfers have been applied to the bunker as a final touch.

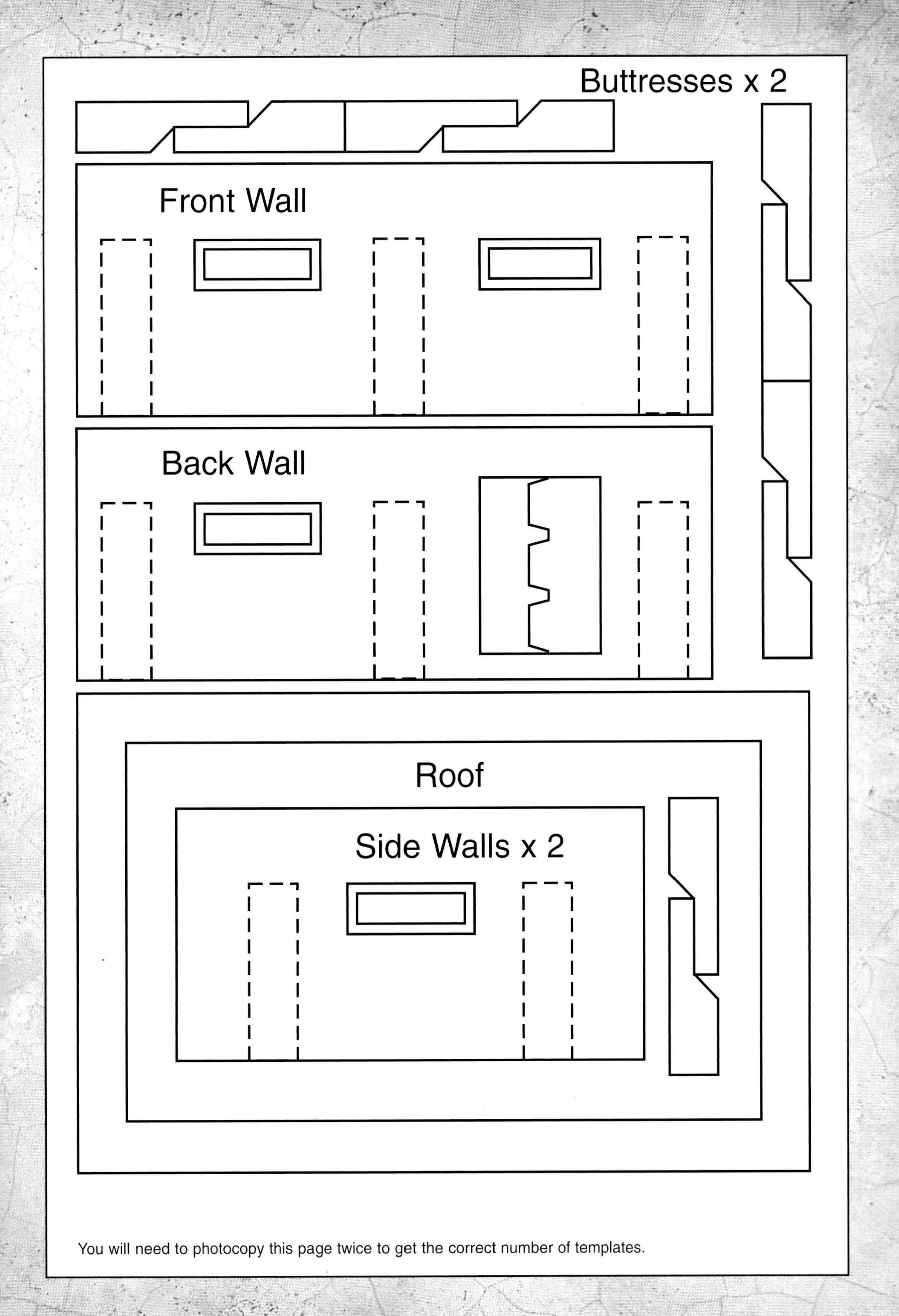

You will need to photocopy this page twice to get the correct number of templates.

MORE FORTIFICATIONS

Fortifications cover a range of scenery, including bastions, barricades, bunkers and tank traps. A defence line may be constructed from sturdy concrete, or may be nothing more than a hastily constructed barricade made from barrels and ammunition crates. This page shows more examples of different types of fortifications.

TANK TRAPS

BARRICADES

BUNKERS

The defences of Redoubt 783 are compromised when Nurgle's Rot strikes down the defenders, allowing Plague Marines of the Death Guard to breach its defences.

MAKING CRATERS

Adding craters to your table gives it an authentic battlefield look. They represent the effects of preliminary bombardments and provide essential cover to your troops.

First decide how big you want your crater to be. A useful guide for the interior is a 50mm round base. If you use one of these then you'll be able to get large miniatures, such as weapons teams, Sentinels and Dreadnoughts, inside the crater.

1. Draw around the base onto your foamboard then draw another outline 5mm or more around that to give some breathing room. You can then draw the outline of the outer edge of the crater – it's a good idea to make the base oversized then you can always trim it smaller.

YOU WILL NEED...

MATERIALS
- 25mm polystyrene
- 10mm foamboard
- Filler
- Pebbles and grit
- Textured paint and Citadel Colour paints

TOOLS
- Modelling knife
- Pencil
- PVA/Woodworking glue

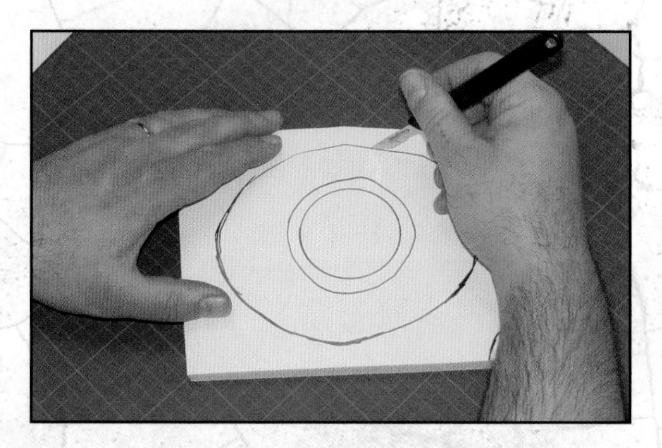

2. Once you've got the size of the model, cut out the base.

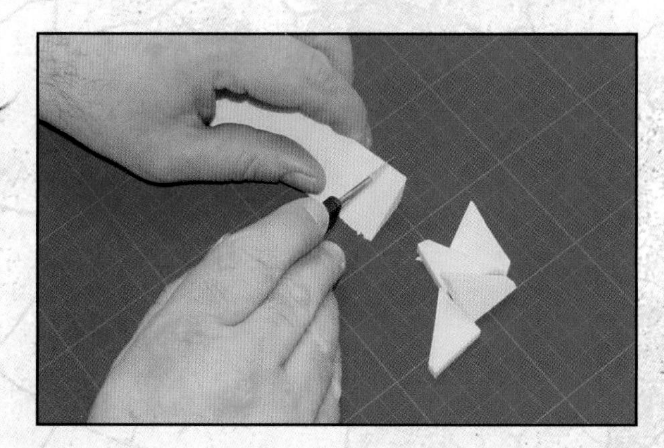

3. To build up the sides of the crater, you need to cut a large number of polystyrene triangles from polystyrene foam. Start by cutting a few triangular strips of foam of different thicknesses. Then cut individual triangles from the strips – it's a good idea to make more than you think you'll need.

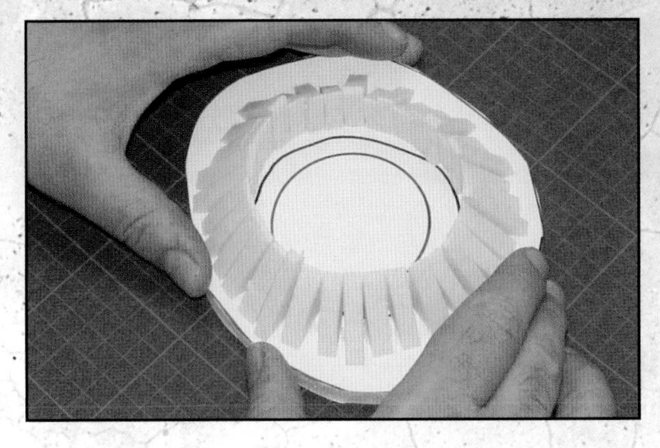

4. Arrange the triangles on your base to make the sloped sides. Once you're happy with how they look, glue them in place.

5. Once they are dry, shape the crater a little more with your modelling knife. You might want to trim your base to create a smoother slope. Angle your modelling knife to make a natural slope.

6. To finish off the crater apply filler to the gaps between the triangles to build up a smooth rounded shape.

7. Add some small stones and grit, then paint the model with a coat of textured paint. You can paint the model in a combination of browns and greys. Because of their earth-churned colours, craters look good on any colour of baseboard.

A whole set of craters can be built in very little time. To simulate the effect of cluster bombs you can even make two or three craters that overlap each other on a base.

Guardsmen of the Cadian 8th advance across the cratered hell of the battlefield of Kasr Gallan after a full day and night of bombardment.

RAID MISSIONS

In a Raid scenario one player will be the attacker whilst the other is the defender. Raids are lightning strikes against a specific objective, such as an ambush of an enemy column, a surprise attack on an important enemy strongpoint, or secret missions deep behind enemy lines.

SENTRIES

In certain scenarios the defender has set up sentries to keep a lookout for enemy activity. Sentries can be represented with card counters, but it is preferable to use spare miniatures of the appropriate type.

The number of sentries available depends on which army you are commanding and is given on the following list. These sentries do not cost any extra points.

Orks	12 Gretchin (Initiative 2)
Imperial Guard	10 Guardsmen (Initiative 3)
Daemonhunters, Alien Hunters, Witch Hunters	8 Inquisitorial Storm Troopers (Initiative 3) or 6 Sisters of Battle (Initiative 3, Witch Hunters only) (Witch Hunters only)
Tyranids	8 Termagants (Initiative 4)
Eldar	8 Guardians (Initiative 4)
Space Marines	6 Space Marines (Initiative 4)

Note: Chapters such as the Space Wolves with improved Initiative due to Acute Senses only use 4 Space Marines as sentries.

Chaos Space Marines	6 Chaos Space Marines (Initiative 4)
Dark Eldar	6 Dark Eldar Warriors (Initiative 5)
Necrons	10 Necron Warriors (Initiative 2)
Tau	Either 6 Gun Drones (Initiative 4) or 8 Kroot (Initiative 3)
Lost and the Damned	Either 10 Traitors (Initiative 3) or 10 Mutants (Initiative 3)

At the start of the sentries' turn, both players roll a dice for each sentry model (or marker). The player that rolls highest can move the sentry the distance indicated on the dice in any direction. If the rolls are tied then the defender moves the sentry.

Sentries do not have any Squad Coherency rules and operate independently.

SOUNDING THE ALARM

At the start of the game, the defending forces are not expecting combat. Instead they are resting, eating, servicing equipment, talking about the girls/bug-eyed monsters back home and so on. Because of this, only the sentries will be active to start with.

Until the alarm is raised, sentries move as described above and none of the defender's other units may move or fire. The alarm can be raised in several ways:

Spotting Distance. A sentry will spot any enemy model that is within his spotting distance at the end of any turn. This distance is equal to his Initiative characteristic in inches. For example, a sentry with an Initiative value of 4 would spot any attackers within 4" of him, regardless of whether the attacker is in cover or not.

Vehicles. If the attacker deploys any vehicles or bikes on the table then the sentries will spot them at the end of the turn. Tanks, Bikes, Dreadnoughts, armoured personnel carriers, etc, are all too noisy to avoid detection. Vehicles (including Infantry units with transport vehicles) and Bikes may therefore be kept in reserve and will arrive normally after the alarm has been raised.

Weapons Fire. The alarm is raised if the attacker fires any weapons except sniper rifles. If a sentry survives being hit by a sniper rifle he raises the alarm.

Close Combat. A sentry that is attacked in close combat will raise the alarm if he survives to the end of the turn. If the sentry is killed in close combat then the noise of the fighting may raise the alarm anyway. Roll a D6. On a 4+ the fighting was heard or the sentry screamed out and the alarm is raised.

Bodies. If a sentry is killed do not remove the model. Instead, leave it lying in position. If another sentry approaches within his Initiative distance of a dead sentry then he will find the body and raise the alarm.

Note that all the other defending models with an Initiative value count as sentries for purposes of sounding the alarm, they just can't move.

After raising the alarm, all sentries are removed and take no further part in the game.

If the alarm is raised during the attacker's turn, they finish it normally. The defender can move and shoot normally with all their forces in their next player turn.

If the alarm is raised during the defender's turn they begin a game turn immediately.

This first defender turn is the first turn of the game proper and counts as such for the purposes of determining game length and reserve arrival.

HIDDEN SET-UP

In some scenarios, forces have had time to conceal their troops and prepare booby traps and minefields to delay the enemy. When using Hidden Set-up you will need a Hidden Set-up marker for every unit in your force (including those in reserve or not starting on the tabletop for some other reason).

When forces are deployed on the table, the defender places Hidden Set-up markers instead of models. A marker may be placed on any terrain, as long as it can be moved over by the model it is representing, and is in the defender's normal deployment zone.

Each marker needs to be numbered so that you can note down which number corresponds to which unit – if you don't have any numbered markers simply make your own by tearing off some pieces of scrap paper and numbering them. Alternatively, the defender can draw a map of the tabletop and mark the location of each of his units on it.

HIDDEN VEHICLES

Vehicles must be hidden in appropriate terrain features. It is not possible to disguise a Leman Russ battle tank on an open plain, but it could be hidden at the edge of a wood, behind a building or behind a hill. Vehicles must be hidden behind or in a terrain feature which could conceivably hide the model. As terrain varies so much, it is impossible to give an exhaustive list, so apply common sense. Obviously, it's much easier to hide a buggy than a tank.

REVEALING HIDDEN TROOPS

Once the defender has placed all his Hidden Set-up markers the attacker then deploys his forces as described in the scenario set-up rules. Once the attacker's deployment is complete the defender reveals his Hidden Set-up markers and places the appropriate models on the table. For a unit of multiple models, one model is placed on the counter with the rest of the unit in 2" coherency as normal with no model more than 6" from the counter. A lone vehicle must be placed on the counter itself. Counters that are for units in reserve have a chance of being a minefield or a booby trap.

MINEFIELDS AND BOOBY TRAPS

If a counter is for a unit that is not deployed on the board, because it is in reserve or for any other reason, then there is a chance the counter represents a booby trap or minefield instead. When the counter is revealed or triggers (see below) roll a D6: on a 4+ it is a booby trap or minefield (defender's choice), otherwise it is just a dummy – remove it from the table.

Booby Traps: The player controlling the booby trap may choose to detonate it when an enemy model or unit is within 6" of the marker. As usual, the owner of the target unit chooses the model that takes the damage and resolves a single Strength 8 hit, Armour Piercing 2. Unlike minefields, booby traps only work once, so remove the marker once the attack has been made.

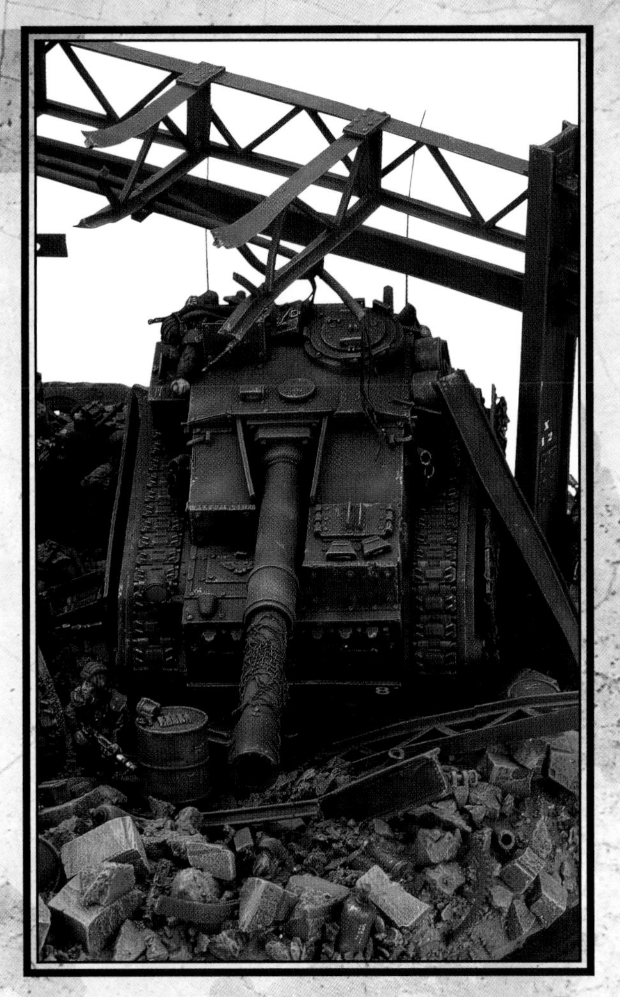

Minefields: A minefield is an 8" by 4" rectangle, centred on the hidden counter.

Any enemy model moving over a minefield triggers a mine on a roll of 4+, taking a Strength 6 hit with no Armour Piercing value. Vehicles take a Strength 6 hit against their rear armour, but all penetrating hits are treated as glancing hits only.

Skimmers and Minefields: Mines come in a variety of forms. Some contain specialised devices with proximity detectors, others will have the ability to leap upwards, or simply detonate in such a spectacular fashion that being a few metres in the air is no defence. Because of this, skimmers and troops with jump packs are affected by minefields just like ordinary troops and vehicles.

DIVIDED FORCE

This rule is used when a mission calls for an army to be split into an active part (that deploys in accordance with the Mission rules) and a passive part (that either begins the game in reserve or doesn't get used at all, as specified in the Mission rules).

The owning player splits his army into two separate forces, each must consist of at least 30% of the total army points value. A dice is then rolled to determine which force is the active force and which is the passive force.

SABOTAGE

The attacker is engaged on a surprise raid deep in enemy territory, his mission is to sneak through enemy lines and destroy an important installation.

SET-UP

1 Place the objective of the raid in the centre of the table.

2 The defender may set up any of his Troops and HQ units anywhere within 8" of the objective. He does not have to set them all up, but he must deploy at least one unit. Any forces not deployed are in reserve.

3 The defender's sentries are placed anywhere on the table that is not within 12" of a short table edge, and not in the defender's deployment zone.

4 The attacker chooses one of the short table edges as his board edge. If he has any troops that can infiltrate then he may deploy them up to 12" onto the board from his table edge in the area shown on the map.

5 The attacker takes the first turn, moving as much of his army as he chooses onto the board, and leaving the rest to come on as reserves.

RESERVES: *The attacker's reserves enter normally. The defender's reserves enter from a random board edge, as indicated on the map (roll a D6). Only begin rolling for the defender's reserves after the alarm has been raised.*

GAME LENGTH: *Six Turns (Variable)*

MISSION OBJECTIVE

For this raid, all the attacking forces have been issued with demo charges to destroy the objective and complete their mission. The objective cannot be destroyed by firing at it, only by non-vehicle models placing demo charges. To place a demo charge successfully, the model must assault the objective in its Assault phase and remain in contact until the end of its next Assault phase. At this point the charge is set and the objective is destroyed. Boom!

The attacker wins if he destroys his objective, otherwise the defender wins.

SCENARIO SPECIAL RULES

Infiltrate, Random Game Length, Reserves, Sentries.

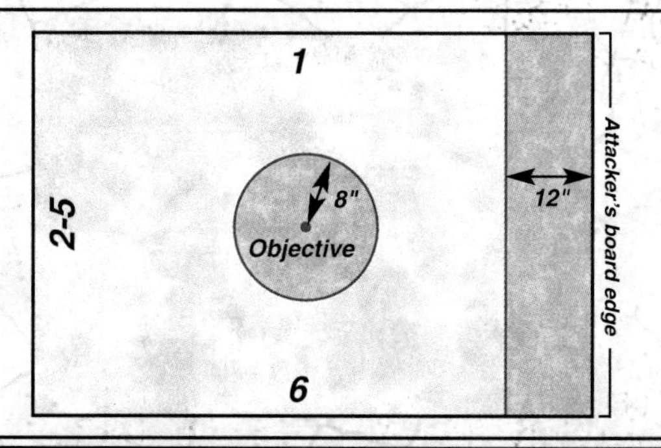

AMBUSH

The attacker's forces are lying in wait for a convoy of enemy reserves heading for the front line, hoping to destroy the convoy whilst minimising their own losses.

SET-UP

1 The defender chooses a short table edges as his escape route.

2 The attacker splits his force in accordance with the Divided Force special rule. The attacker sets up his active force using the Hidden Set-up rules, within his deployment zone. The attacker's passive force starts the game in reserve.

3 The defender places units one at a time. The front unit must be at least 36" from the short table edge that is the escape route. Each subsequent unit must deploy entirely behind the previous unit, creating a column of march.

4 The attacker has first turn.

RESERVES: *The attacker's reserves may enter the board from either of the long board edges.*

GAME LENGTH: *Six Turns (Variable)*

LINE OF RETREAT: *Attacking units fall back normally. Defending units forced to fall back do so toward the table edge opposite to that being used as the escape route edge.*

MISSION OBJECTIVE

The attacker must destroy as much of the enemy convoy as possible, whilst the defender must attempt to escape the trap.

Add the points value of each scoring unit the defender gets off the escape route board edge to his Victory Points total. Double the Victory Points awarded for destroying or damaging the defender's units. The player with the highest Victory Points total wins the battle.

SCENARIO SPECIAL RULES

Hidden Set-up, Divided Force, Random Game Length, Reserves, Victory Points.

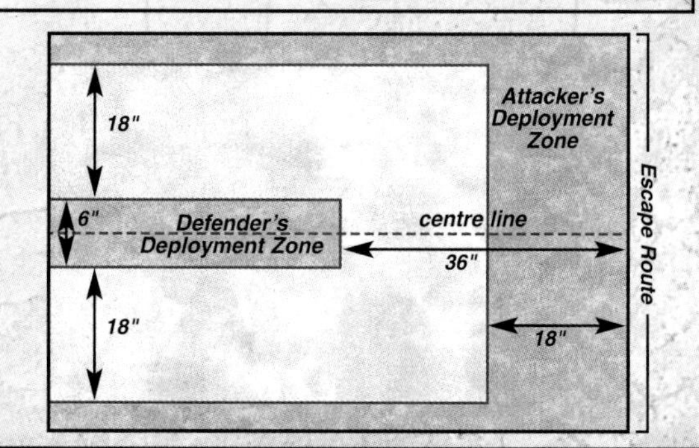

STRONGPOINT ATTACK

The attacker is to launch a surprise attack against an enemy strongpoint and eliminate it before enemy reserves can react. The defender's task is to guard the strongpoint and hold off any enemy attack until reserves can move up to support you.

SET-UP

1. Each player rolls a dice. The winner chooses a long board edge.

2. Mark a 24" square area central to the defender's edge of the board, as shown on the map. This is the defender's deployment zone.

3. The defender may position fortifications in his deployment zone, forming the strongpoint. He must include at least one bunker.

4. The defender positions his sentries, up to 18" from his deployment zone.

5. The defender places his obstacles, anywhere on the tabletop up to 18" away from the defender's deployment zone.

6. The defender deploys any of his HQ, Troops or Heavy Support units in his deployment zone. He does not have to deploy them all, but he must deploy at least one unit. Any units not deployed are in reserve.

7. The attacker's units must be set up at least 18" away from the defender's deployment zone. Any forces not deployed at the start of the game are held in reserve.

8. The attacker gets the first turn.

RESERVES: *When the defender's reserves arrive they move on from the defender's board edge. The attacker's reserves move on from any of the other board edges.*

GAME LENGTH: *Four turns after the alarm has been raised.*

MISSION OBJECTIVE

Victory is determined by Victory Points and by control of the bunkers placed on table. Each bunker is worth Victory Points equal to the points limit of the game divided by the number of bunkers in play (so in a 1,500 point game with three bunkers each bunker is worth 500 points). A bunker is held if it is occupied by at least one scoring Infantry unit and there are no scoring enemy infantry within 6" of it.

At the end of the game add up Victory Points for enemy units destroyed and bunkers captured. The highest score wins.

SCENARIO SPECIAL RULES

Deep Strike, Fortifications, Infiltrate, Obstacles, Reserves, Sentries, Victory Points.

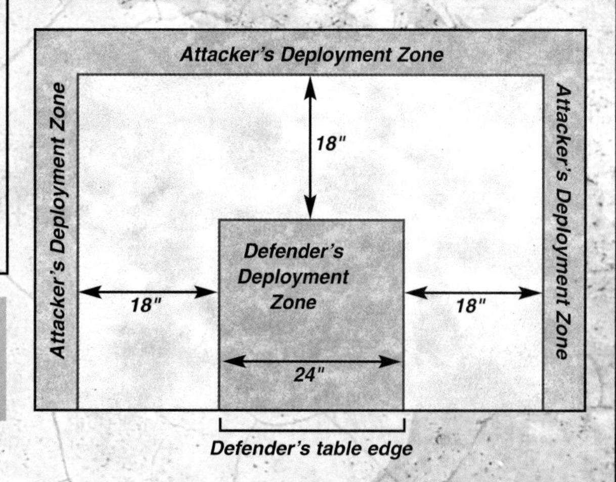

The doomed Guardsmen of Bunker Complex Delta call for their comrades to avenge them as they are finally overrun by the Lost and the Damned.

MODELLING SENTRIES

Sentries are used in the opening turns of missions such as Sabotage and Strongpoint Attack, and provide the modeller with an opportunity to produce a small set of characterful models that are themed to the army, but only used in special circumstances. On this page you'll find examples of sentries from different armies, all of which have been modelled as if they are standing guard against stealthy enemy intruders.

Turning these basic troop models into sentries was simply a matter of adding a few extra components to represent sensors, scanners or antenna.

HIDDEN SET-UP MARKERS

Hidden Set-up markers are used during deployment to indicate the presence of a squad, character, vehicle, booby trap or minefield. The markers themselves provide an excellent opportunity to create highly characterful pieces of terrain themed to your army, but even better, they can be used to psyche out your opponent, who will never know exactly what is represented by the marker until it is revealed. Markers can be made to represent hidden troopers, vicious traps or anything that you can imagine – they are essentially propaganda with which to prey on the fears of your enemy, so why not really go to town on them!

MAKING MARKERS

Booby traps are placed as part of the Hidden Set-up rule, and are a perfect opportunity to create some characterful terrain pieces themed to your army. Remember that your opponent will not know whether the marker represents a minefield or a booby trap, so let your imagination (and your opponent's) run wild.

Copper wire wrapped around thin pieces of twig cut to a point.

A plant covered with PVA/Woodworking glue with an arm from a Catachan heavy weapons sprue.

Gaunt scything claws, flesh hook and head.

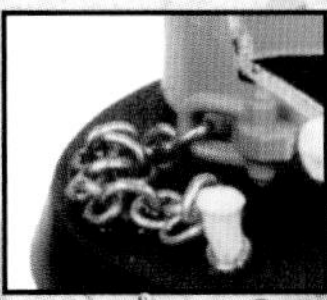

Fine chain attached to scratch-built metal jaws.

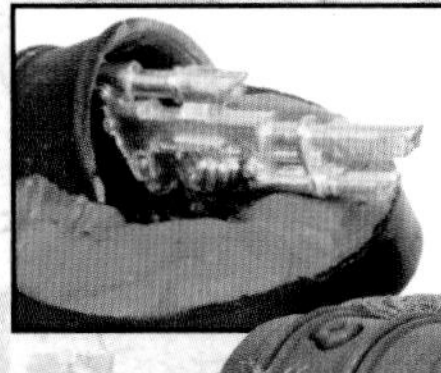

A sniper rifle glued inside a cut-down oil drum.

Bosspole from an Ork Warboss.

Ork head and slugga trimmed to fit a base painted to look like water with gloss varnish.

Ork shoota complete with gun sight covered with pieces of slate.

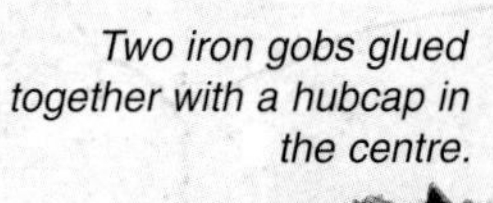

Two iron gobs glued together with a hubcap in the centre.

Half a wrecker ball with two Orc drumsticks.

Ork Nob's bosspole.

A militia model with a converted ripper.

Necron Warrior trimmed to emerge from plasticard rubble.

MAKING MINEFIELDS

These are deployed when an enemy model comes into contact with a Hidden Set-up marker that represents a minefield. The only stipulation rules-wise is that the minefield covers an area of 8" x 4" – beyond that you should feel free to theme the terrain piece to fit in with your army. Below are some examples of minefields constructed to tie in with a variety of armies.

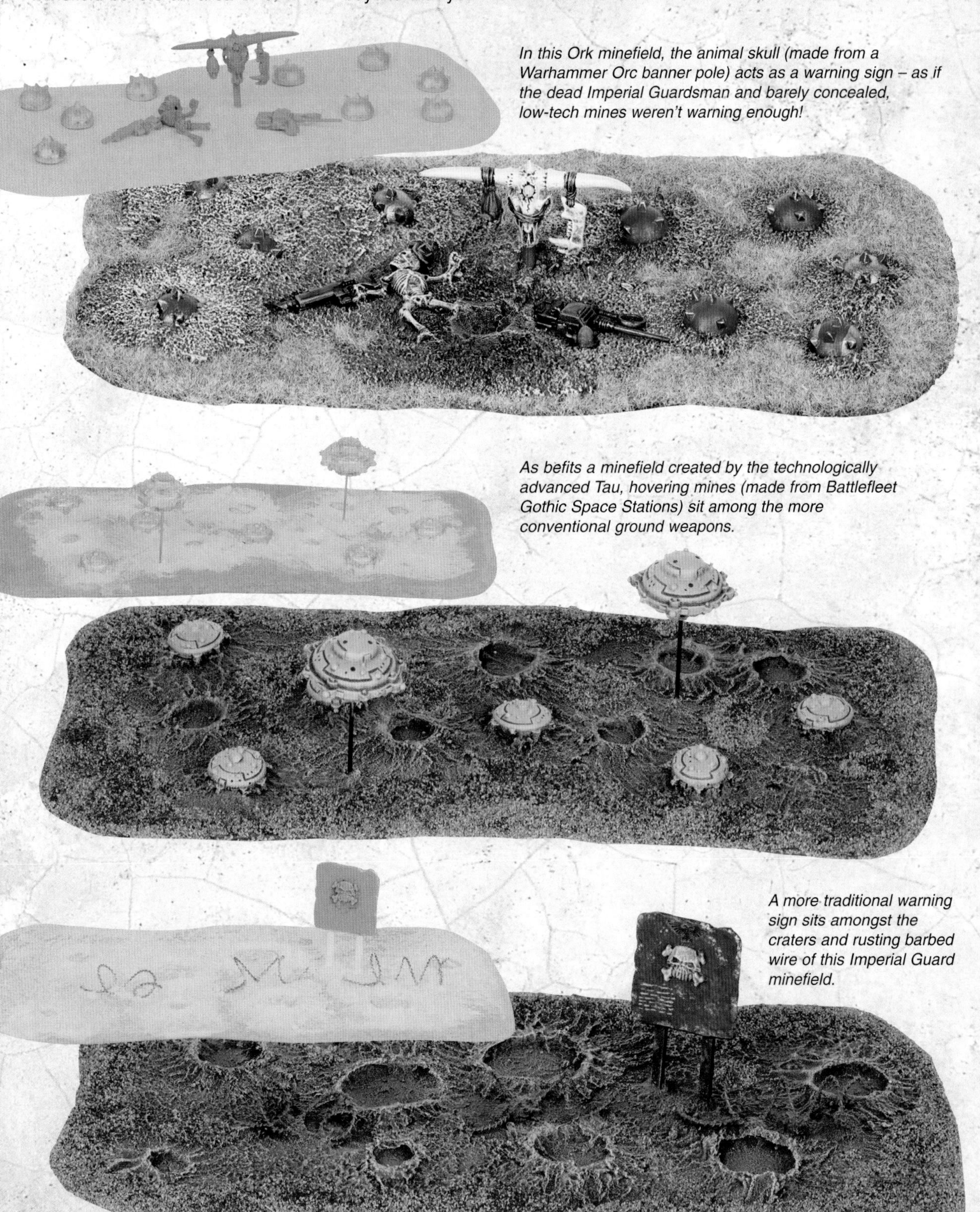

In this Ork minefield, the animal skull (made from a Warhammer Orc banner pole) acts as a warning sign – as if the dead Imperial Guardsman and barely concealed, low-tech mines weren't warning enough!

As befits a minefield created by the technologically advanced Tau, hovering mines (made from Battlefleet Gothic Space Stations) sit among the more conventional ground weapons.

A more traditional warning sign sits amongst the craters and rusting barbed wire of this Imperial Guard minefield.

BREAKTHROUGH MISSIONS

In these scenarios one player takes the role of the attacker whilst the other player is the defender. Breakthrough scenarios involve one force trying to punch a path through an opposing force. This might be because they are seeking to escape an encirclement, or to smash through the enemy's defensive lines in a major attack.

REARGUARD

The offensive is pushing the enemy back all along the front. The attacker must sweep aside any pockets of resistance as quickly as possible. The defender's army has been driven back by the enemy offensive, and needs time to regroup. The defender's force has been selected as the rearguard of the retreating army, and must stall the enemy advance as long as possible to give the rest of the army a chance to form a new defensive line.

SET-UP

1. Both players roll a dice. The winner chooses which long board edge to deploy from.
2. The defender splits his army in accordance with the Divided Force special rule. The passive part of the divided force plays no part in the game.
3. The defender's deployment zone is up to half way across the table. The defender deploys his active force in his deployment zone using the Hidden Set-up rules. He also places obstacles in his deployment zone. If he chooses he may leave any Deep Strike units he has in reserve.
4. The attacker splits his army in accordance with the Divided Force special rule.
5. The attacker takes the first turn. His active force moves on from his board edge on the first turn. He may hold Deep Strike units from the active force in reserve. Once the attacker's active force is on the board the defender reveals his Hidden Set-up markers.
6. All the forces in the attacker's passive force arrive at the beginning of Turn 4, and move on from the attacker's board edge.

SCENARIO SPECIAL RULES

Deep Strike, Hidden Set-up, Infiltrate, Obstacles, Random Game Length, Divided Force.

MISSION OBJECTIVE

The attacker must eliminate the rearguard forces quickly and keep the momentum of his advance going. The defender must stall the attack for as long as he can.

If the defender has any scoring units more than 12" from any table edge at the end of the game then he wins. If he does not and the attacker has at least one scoring unit left the attacker has won. Any other result is a draw.

RESERVES: *See the scenario special rules section for how to place Deep Strike units.*

GAME LENGTH: *Six Turns (Variable)*

Attacker's board edge

Defender's Deployment Zone

Half the table's width

Defender's board edge

BLITZ

The attacker's forces must quickly smash the foe aside so the units behind can drive deep into enemy territory.

SET-UP

1 The board is divided lengthways into thirds, as shown on the map.

2 The defender may place his fortifications and obstacles in the fortification zone.

3 The defender deploys any of his Troops, HQ and/or Heavy Support units in the fortification zone using the Hidden Set-up rules. He does not have to set up all these units but he must set up at least one. The rest of his forces are in reserve.

4 The attacker deploys all his forces in no man's land, up to 6" from his table edge (except for Infiltrators and Deep Strike units).

5 The attacker resolves his preliminary bombardment.

SCENARIO SPECIAL RULES

Deep Strike, Fortifications, Hidden Set-up, Infiltrate, Obstacles, Preliminary Bombardment, Reserves, Victory Points.

RESERVES: *When the defender's reserves arrive they move on from his board edge.*

GAME LENGTH: *Six Turns (Variable)*

MISSION OBJECTIVE

Victory is determined by Victory Points. In addition, the attacker must get as many units as he can into the defender's second line. He gets +100 Victory Points for each scoring unit in this area at the end of the game.

The defender gets +50 Victory Points for each scoring enemy unit in no man's land at the end of the game. If a unit straddles two areas, count it as being in the one further from its own table edge.

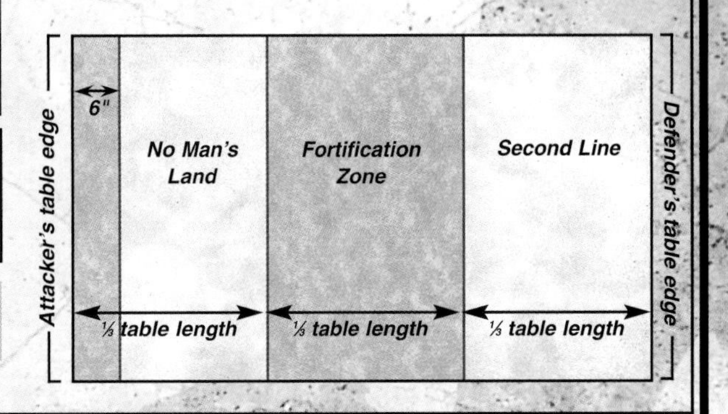

BREAKOUT

The attacker's forces have been surrounded and are facing annihilation unless they can break through the enemy lines. They must act quickly to escape before their foes can move up overwhelming forces to annihilate them.

SET-UP

1 Number the short board edges 1 and 2. The defender must split his force into two parts, one for each short board edge. Each force must include whole units, units may not be split between forces. Number these forces 1 and 2 to correspond with the short board edge numbers.

Forces chosen from the Elites section of the defender's army list do not have to be allocated to a force, they can be positioned in either force later.

2 The attacker deploys all his forces in his deployment zone.

3 The defender deploys his units. They may not be positioned within 18" of any enemy unit and must be closer to their allocated short board edge than the opposite short board edge.

4 The defender now deploys his Elite units, they can be placed anywhere on the board, but not within 18" of any enemy unit.

5 Roll a D6: on a 1 the defender gets the first turn, on a 2 or more the attacker gets the first turn.

SCENARIO SPECIAL RULES

None.

MISSION OBJECTIVE

The attacker must get as many units off the board as he can. If he manages to get half or more of the units in his force off either short board edge, or up to 12" along the long table edges from each corner, he wins. A unit with any survivors or a damaged vehicle still counts towards this. If the attacker does not manage this then the defender wins.

LINE OF RETREAT: *Defending units fall back normally. Attacking units forced to fall back do so towards the board centre. Once they reach the board centre attacking units automatically regroup regardless of numbers remaining, enemies in close proximity or anything else (the situation is desperate!).*

GAME LENGTH: *Six Turns*

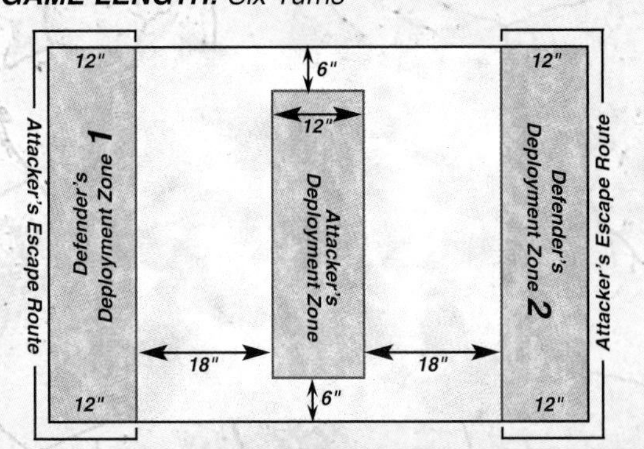

KILL-TEAM

The notion of this small-scale game is based on those movies we all know and love, where a crack team of experts (or desperadoes trained by a single-minded, double-hard drill instructor) go in and triumph against all the odds. We're all familiar with this formula due to good old Hollywood and the countless films that cover these themes.

WHAT IS KILL-TEAM ALL ABOUT?

The veterans amongst you will have spotted that this concept borrows heavily from the infamous Last Chancers of the Imperial Guard (the hard-bitten Colonel Schaeffer and his recruits from the Imperial Guard Penal Legions), but extends it into a games system for all races rather than just focusing on the Imperial Guard. In this way Kill-team can feature a team of Ork Kommandos sneaking into a Necron tomb complex, a pack of Kroot mercenaries using cover of night to 'liberate' a priceless Dark Eldar artefact from its twisted shrine, or a squad of Space Marine Scouts avoiding patrolling gun drones on their mission to assassinate a Tau Ethereal. It's a fair bet you'll have enough models in your collection to assemble at least one Kill-team, and the necessary forces you'll need to be the bad guys when it's your opponent's turn to be the desperadoes.

Kill-team is best thought of as small-scale, objective-based Warhammer 40,000, and is playable in an hour or less. If you've had a chance to try the 'Combat Patrol' system, this is also playable during a lunch hour. You'll need around ten models to play the good guys, although this varies slightly from race to race. The opponents, being mere grunts (or 'Brutes') as opposed to elite commandos, will have more: these are almost always the basic troop type for that race. So you'll find that if you regularly play a friend with Tyranids, you'll likely be infiltrating your way through patrols of Gaunts to dump a melta bomb in the central spore chimney, or some similar mission.

Players should make every effort to personalise their Kill-team, converting them to carry trophies or special gear and keeping tracks of who kills the most bad guys. A stetson or cigar (or squig and Iron Gob, etc) here and there can really get across the feeling of a gang of desperate but hardcore soldiers. We'll see some examples of Kill-teams converted in this way over the next few pages. You might even want to give them names, especially your Kill-team's leader, who will generally be kicking the most alien tail! You can complete the missions without Sarge, but it's an awful lot trickier.

Firstly, we'll cover the basic rules and throw a few ideas into the pot for you to get started with.

Colonel Schaeffer leads his latest team of murderers, thieves and assorted scum on a suicide mission.

KILL-TEAM BASIC RULES

SET-UP

• The good guys (the *Kill-team*) face off against the bad guys (the *Brute squads*) on a 4' by 4' table (or greater if you want an epic battle). The Brute squad player sets up the terrain – it's his territory after all. This should ideally feature a large and impressive scenery piece as the central objective. It's worth making sure the routes to the central objective are as difficult and treacherous as possible – you wouldn't want the Kill-team to have an easy time of it, after all.

• Mark a point (the *central objective*) that the Kill-team needs to reach in order to fulfil its mission (see 'Choose Objective', below); this should really be in the centre of the table or at least nearby, but you'll find the scenery piece will usually dictate this. It should also be elevated if possible so that bad guys can fall to their deaths onto spiked railings or into pools of radioactive waste, etc.

• The Kill-team player begins the game with one Kill-team, which will usually include a Sergeant or leader of some sort. Rules for creating Kill-teams are addressed later.

• The Brute squad player begins the game with a varying number of models dependant on what race he is taking. The Brute squad player may choose which race he fields. See the Brute squad player Forces table on the following pages for more details.

• The Brute squad player sets up his sentry models in groups of 3 anywhere within 12" of the objective. Each of these groups is called a Brute squad. No Brute squad can be deployed within 4" of any other. All Brute squads start the game deactivated (more on this later).

GOLDEN RULE

Kill-team is a relatively free and easy rules system. The rules allow players a lot of freedom to build an exciting and diverse Kill-team like the ones shown on the following pages, and if you feel the need to customise a rule or two to fit your circumstances, then feel free.

However, this freedom comes at a price – cooperation. If you want a competitive, tournament-style game then these rules aren't for you. Although the rules are flexible enough to allow some very scary Kill-teams, creating an indestructable killing machine that effortlessly destroys all before it isn't very rewarding for either player, and as you swap sides after every game, your opponent will be sure to have his revenge. Try to create Kill-teams that are characterful and fun, and keep the story in mind at all times. Basically, just keep it light-hearted, use your common sense and you can't go wrong.

Three unfortunate Brutes are distracted by the old 'Throwing the stone' trick! Notorious Flash Gitz mob 'Ghnaschnakoffz Boyz' have blown all their wealth on the biggest, shootiest gunz around. Unlike the other squads shown in this section, this mob is based exclusively on the Flash Gitz entry in the Ork army list: all of its members are from a single unit entry.

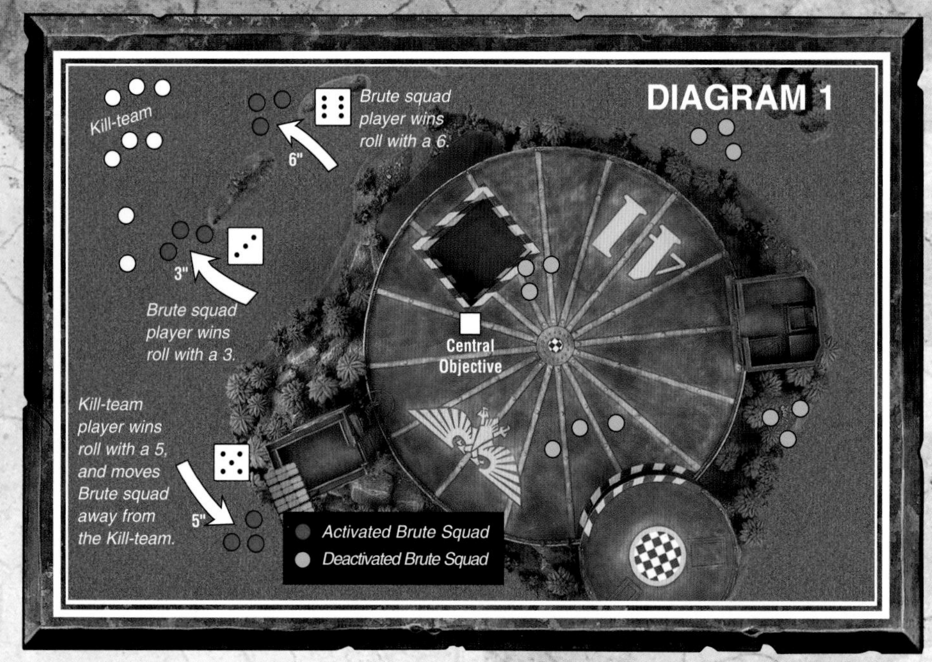

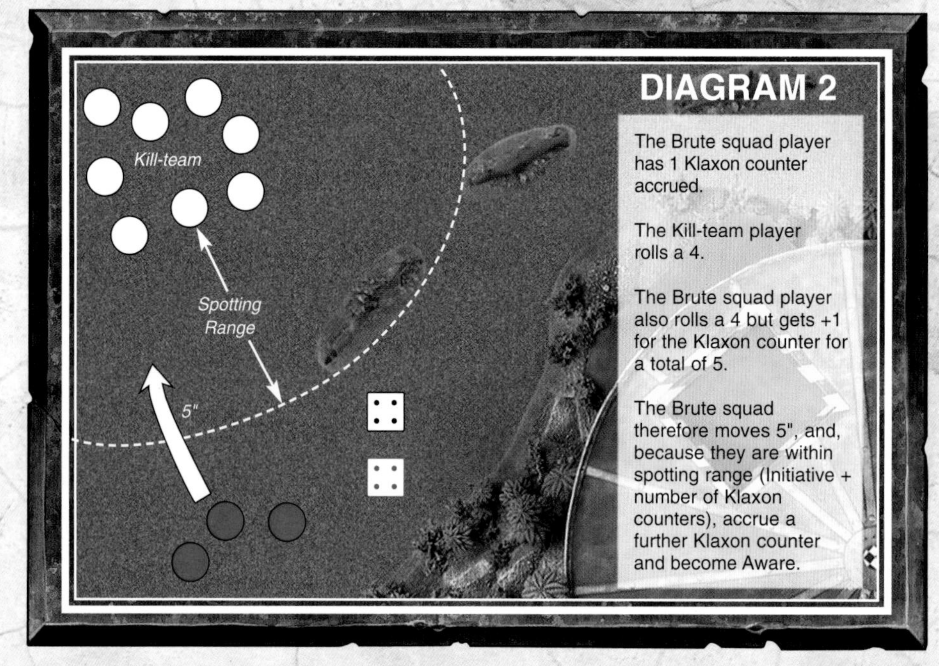

DIAGRAM 2
Kill-team
Spotting Range
5"
The Brute squad player has 1 Klaxon counter accrued.
The Kill-team player rolls a 4.
The Brute squad player also rolls a 4 but gets +1 for the Klaxon counter for a total of 5.
The Brute squad therefore moves 5", and, because they are within spotting range (Initiative + number of Klaxon counters), accrue a further Klaxon counter and become Aware.

PLAYING KILL-TEAM

- The Kill-team player may choose which table edge his Kill-team deploy from. They enter play from that table edge.

- The Kill-team player gets first turn and his Kill-team may act as normal, retaining unit coherency at all times.

- The Kill-team player must reach the objective by any means necessary and fulfil criteria determined by mission to achieve a victory. These criteria can be taken from 'Choose Objective' below or be agreed upon between the players. The Brute squad player must destroy the entire Kill-team to achieve a victory. All other considerations are irrelevant.

- The Brute squad player may *activate* or *deactivate* up to D6 Brute squads at the beginning of each turn. Only activated Brute squads can move (you might want to place a coloured dice or token by activated Brute squads). Bear in mind that although activated Brute squads can move, they won't necessarily move in the direction the Brute squad player wants. It is often advisable to leave the Brute squads nearest the objective deactivated (and therefore static) for the first few turns, so they don't wander off and leave the Kill-team a clear run at their objective. Deactivated squads remain

KLAXON COUNTERS

Klaxon counters simulate the alarms of the Brute squad's headquarters being raised and the sounds of battle bringing defenders scurrying to defend their territory.

Each time a Brute squad (activated or deactivated) comes within *spotting range* (its Initiative value plus the number of Klaxon counters accrued, in inches) of the Kill-team for any reason it has spotted the intruders and becomes *Aware.*

Aware units may act as normal from the start of their next turn; moving, shooting, and assaulting under the Brute squad player's control for the rest of the game. Whenever a Brute squad becomes Aware, for whatever reason, add a Klaxon counter to the Brute squad player's store. Also add a Klaxon counter whenever the Kill-team shoots. Units that are Aware may not accrue further counters – they have a Kill-team to worry about. It really doesn't matter what you use for Klaxon counters, but keep those you have accrued in a separate pile. Note that you get one Klaxon counter per squad, not per model, when a squad moves within spotting range.

Each Klaxon counter accrued adds +1 to the dice roll for controlling each Brute squad as well as +1 to their spotting range (note that it is the number of Klaxon counters accrued at the beginning of that turn that is taken into account). In this way, as the alarm is raised, Brute squads will quickly move to reinforce their brethren.

A Brute squad cannot accrue more than one Klaxon counter per phase.

in place, no doubt swapping stories about the girls/she-fungi/tentacled brood-beasts back home.

• In the Movement phase of the Brute squad player's turn, each activated Brute squad moves as if it were a single sentry. That means that during the Brute squad player's Movement phase, each player rolls a dice (the Control roll) for each Brute squad in turn: the player that scores highest moves the members of the Brute squad up to that many inches in the direction of his choice.

This dice roll is modified by the number of Klaxon counters the Brute squad player has accrued (see below). Brute squads can never move more than 6" regardless of their special rules (Fleet of Foot for example) due to the fact they are moving with caution. Brutes may never move off the table. See Diagram 1 for an example.

• If the result of the Control roll is a draw (taking into account any modifiers for Klaxon counters, etc) the Brute squad player moves the squad that number of inches, as even the thickest henchman has a brain and will act sensibly more often than not.

• Kill-teams are Fearless and hence will automatically pass any Leadership tests, whilst Brute squads test on their unmodified Leadership for all Morale checks, including regrouping. All other considerations for such tests are ignored (All On Your Own tests, enemy within 6", Drone leadership, etc).

• Kill-teams roll for difficult terrain as normal, whereas Brute squads ignore difficult terrain altogether: it's their territory and they know their way around pretty well.

• Kill-teams may only consolidate after combat; their mission is too important for them to go haring off after bad guys.

• Brute squads that fall back will do so towards the nearest table edge or toward the objective, whichever is nearest. They will automatically rally if they reach the objective and may act as normal from their next turn. Fleeing Brute squads cannot accrue Klaxon counters.

• Jump infantry may move 12" in the Movement phase as normal, but may not jump over enemy models. They may elect to move on foot instead of using their jump packs. In any round when they use a jump pack (or equivalent) they contribute a Klaxon counter to the opponent's store due to the amount of noise such devices make when used.

• Each Kill-team is equipped with frag grenade equivalents at no points cost (even alien units as Necrons and Tyranids – they are infiltrating defended positions after all). This is above and beyond the normal rules for that troop type.

• There is no turn limit, play until the Kill-team is dead or the objective is met. Then swap sides and let the Brute squad player use the Kill-team – he can even choose a different Kill-team race and objective if desired, or just play the same scenario over again and see if he can do better.

Wolf Guard Battle Leader Njarl Bloodhowl and his Kill-team of Thirteenth Company Space Wolves track their prey across the tundra of Glacia Prime. Note that most of this Kill-team is comprised of veteran Grey Slayers, but one of its number is one of the savage Wulfen – a warrior who is almost as much wolf as man. As you can see, Kill-teams can comprise of models from different units, although such departures from the normal rules of unit selection will award bonuses to the Kill-team's adversaries.

PLAYING KILL-TEAM

1. CHOOSE FORCES

The first step is to choose your forces. You can either choose a nice basic Kill-team to start with, or go the whole hog and customise up a more advanced Kill-team like the ones shown throughout this section, though this specialisation may cost you in the course of the game.

Kill-teams consisting of single units taken from a single unit entry are more numerous and therefore more forgiving, allowing beginners to make mistakes and still have a good chance of achieving their objectives. The more complicated Kill-teams, customised and sometimes even comprised of individuals from different unit entries, are for the more experienced player, and are extremely specialised. There are usually fewer operatives in such a Kill-team, so it's a lot more tricky to win with them – one lucky Brute can cripple your chances of achieving the objectives. You'll pack one hell of a punch, but specialists are only called in when the odds are high, and you're likely to be seriously outnumbered by a whole ton of bad guys… make no mistake, this isn't going to be easy.

You may choose any number of operatives within the points allowed, upgrades, wargear and options from the appropriate entry in that race's Codex, just as if you were choosing a squad for a normal game of Warhammer 40,000, up to a value of **160 points**.

Any and all special rules that affect a Kill-team are in effect, but if a rule proves to be too powerful or restrictive you might like to leave it out. For instance, a unit Deep Striking right next to the objective would make for a very short game. You should discuss with your opponent whether any special rules your Kill-team may employ would add to the fun or detract from it (see the Golden Rule at the start of this section).

There are several guidelines to bear in mind when choosing your Kill-team. These are divided into Immutable Laws, rules that cannot be changed without endangering the fairness and spirit of the game, and Mutable Laws, those which you can play around with or ignore altogether... at a price.

Some Kill-teams will consist of models from more than one unit type, for instance a Space Marine unit with a couple of Scout models in its number. When putting together a Kill-team in this manner, ignore all minimum unit size restrictions and treat all models purchased from your points allowance as if they were a single unit at all times (so they must retain unit coherency, etc).

As stated above, each Kill-team has **160 points** to spend, taken from the relevant Codex and subject to the following restrictions:

IMMUTABLE LAWS OF KILL-TEAM

These rules may not be ignored and must be abided by when constructing your Kill-team. The only exception is if your opponent gives his express permission for you to break one of these rules and you are playing a one-off game rather than a series of games linked together. If this is the case your opponent gets two extra Brute squads per rule broken and an extra 25 points to spend on his Boss Brute (more on these chaps later).

1. Kill-teams must be chosen from one Codex army list or its derivatives: they must all be from the same race. For instance, your Kill-team could consist of Eldar Rangers and Alaitoc Pathfinders, but not Eldar Rangers and Space Marine Scouts.

2. Kill-teams must consist entirely of one-Wound non-vehicle models – multi-Wound models, such as Tau Crisis Battlesuits, are just too big and noisy for covert operations, and HQ units and characters are too valuable to risk on do-or-die missions.

3. Models may not have a 2+ Save of any kind.

4. Kill-teams may have one weapon with either the Heavy or Template characteristic, but no more.

5. Kill-teams may not have psychic powers – such rare and talented individuals are too valuable to their commanders to risk on near-suicidal missions.

6. No model may spend more than 40 points in total on weaponry, wargear or special skills, such as Eldar Exarch Powers.

7. Kill-teams may choose only the weapon upgrades in the unit entry they are chosen from.

8. Bikes and Jetbikes of any kind may not be chosen, nor may anti-grav weapons platforms.

BRUTE SQUAD FORCES TABLE

The Brute squad player gets a number of 3-man Brute squads of the type specified, determined by the race chosen.

Brute Squad Type	Space Marines	Chaos Marines	Eldar Guardians	Ork Boyz	Dark Eldar Warriors	Tyranid Termagants	Tau Gun Drones	Necron Warriors	Imperial Guardsmen	Storm Troopers
Number of 3-man Brute squads	5	5	8	8	8	9	6	5	10	6

This Eldar Pirate Kill-team is extremely distinctive and has a definite sense of individuality for each of the models amongst its number. Even with a small amount of conversion work, the individuals making up the unit have plenty of character.

When on the field of battle most of the models act as Eldar Dire Avengers or Dire Avenger Exarchs, with the exception of Hlias Truestrike and Rhenuel who count as Eldar Pathfinders. It's perfectly acceptable to unite a Kill-team with a single theme, in this case Eldar Pirates, whilst at the same time incorporating models chosen from different units.

MUTABLE LAWS OF KILL-TEAM

These rules may be broken when constructing your Kill-team. However, every time you break a mutable law, your opponent gets an extra Brute squad and a bonus 10 points to spend on his Boss Brute.

So, for instance, if you wanted your Space Marine Kill-team to include two Space Marine Veteran Sergeants, you would be breaking Rule 1 once (the appropriate Unit Entry only allows one model to be upgraded to Veteran Sergeant, so you would be combining more than one squad to form your Kill-team) and Rule 4 once (the Veteran Sergeants both have the option of choosing wargear). When fielding this Kill-team your opponent would have two more Brute squads than usual and have a bonus 20 points to spend on his Boss Brute. If the same Kill-team included three Veteran Sergeants, your opponent would have an extra three Brute Squads and a whopping 30 bonus points to spend on his Boss Brute!

1. Kill-teams must be chosen from the same unit entry in the relevant Codex.

2. Kill-teams (or their composite parts) must obey all the normal restrictions for that unit type, barring the minimum unit size restriction. For instance, in a Grey Knight Kill-team one model must be upgraded to a Justicar as usual for a Grey Knight unit.

3. Kill-teams must number between five and twelve models.

4. No more than one model per Kill-team may have the option of choosing wargear.

5. No Kill-team weapon may have a Strength greater than 7 or be capable of firing more than two shots per turn – such heavy duty kit is usually reserved for full-scale war.

OK, now that you've assembled your Kill-team it's time to choose the nature of their mission.

2. CHOOSE OBJECTIVE

The next step is to choose a basic mission, either mutually agreed upon or randomly determined, from the list below. Alternatively, make your own up and go for it. Some are more difficult to win than others, so you might want to start with a simple Sabotage mission and work up to the trickier ones.

MISSION 1 – SABOTAGE

The Kill-team must infiltrate the enemy position and destroy an object of utmost importance to their overall battle plan.

Sabotaging Kill-teams count as being equipped with melta bombs at no points cost in addition to their usual equipment. The central objective, which can be represented by a pile of crates, a cogitator bank and so forth, must be destroyed in order for the Kill-team to win. The central objective counts as an immobile AV 14 vehicle that ignores glancing hits but is destroyed by any penetrating hits.

You might like to increase the difficulty of the Sabotage mission by incorporating more than one objective that must be destroyed for the Kill-team to succeed.

MISSION 2 – ASSASSINATE

The Kill-team must find an individual key to the enemy's strategy and ensure his death in any way they can.

The central objective is an individual of utmost importance to the enemy's strategies. They must be killed quickly and cleanly. You will need an appropriate miniature. For game purposes this model will have the following profile:

	WS	BS	S	T	W	I	A	Ld	Sv
Target	3	3	3	4	2	3	1	10	6+

The Target is equipped with two close combat weapons. It may not move, but will act as normal if attacked in any way. The Kill-team must kill this individual to achieve a victory.

MISSION 3 – ESCAPE

The Kill-team have fulfilled their objective, and must get the hell out of Dodge with as many of their number alive as possible…

There is no central objective in the Escape mission. Instead, the Kill-team must cross to the opposite side of the board from

The mutated desperados of the Hooked Claw cleanse and burn their way through a ruined building defended by Space Marines, intent on finding the Astropath they protect and killing him before he can send for reinforcements. The Kill-team is attempting the Assassinate mission detailed above – once they've fought their way past the Brute squad on the stairs, that is…

These conversions show how repositioning of a model or a combination of parts from two different plastic sets can allow you to build a really unusual and characterful Kill-team.

which they entered. They may not move off any point within 18" of any table edge. If any members of the Kill-team manage to move off that portion of the board edge for any reason, they automatically win.

MISSION 4 – LAST STAND

Though the Kill-team has fulfilled its mission, the alarm has been raised. Stealth has to be replaced by brute force if the Kill-team are to survive.

In the Last Stand mission, the roles are reversed. The Kill-team starts on the central objective, and the Brute squads start no further than 12" away from any table edge. The Brute squad player starts the game with one Klaxon counter.

The Kill-team must kill all of the Brute squad player's Brute squads or die in the attempt. It's going to be bloody...

This mission can also follow on from the Sabotage and Assassinate missions.

MISSION 5 – HIT AND RUN

The Kill-team must reach a predetermined point on the battlefield and achieve a set objective before getting back to base.

The central objective in this mission must be reached by the Kill-team (touched by at least one model) and have a model in contact with it for a full player turn. The objective can be assaulted. The Kill-team succeed in their mission if they subsequently manage to move at least one member of the team off any table edge.

MISSION 6 – RECONNOITRE

The Kill-team must thoroughly assess the enemy's capabilities and military capacity without alerting the enemy to their presence.

There is no central objective in a Reconnoitre. The Kill-team must cover the board, determining information. They achieve their objective if they manage to traverse a circuit around the central point whilst coming no closer than 6" to it, and have at least one model return to the board edge that they started from. This is one to play nice and stealthily...

Captain Leonatos

Brother Tranio

Brother Cloten

Brother Lysander

Brother Proteus

Brother Palamon

This Kill-team is really a force to be reckoned with. It's based on the heroes from the Bloodquest graphic novel about a team of disgraced Blood Angels Space Marines led by the heroic Captain Leonatos in their quest to redeem their honour. This warrior band is a great example of how a Kill-team can be based on your favourite story or movie. Woe betide the brutes who stand in their way...

Personalised Kill-teams like this are great for playing linked missions, and as the individual members distinguish themselves or get put out of action you might even consider sculpting trophies and battle scars onto them to show their progress.

3. CHOOSE STORYLINE

Below are some ideas for the narrative behind your Kill-team game. Naturally, these are not to be strictly adhered to, they are merely suggestions that you might like to adapt depending on what you have in your model and scenery collection.

MISSION 1 – SABOTAGE

The Kill-team must:

- Trigger the eruption of a volcano.
- Destroy a vital datacube at the centre of a complex electronic array.
- Cripple a spaceship's warp drive so that the enemy cannot escape.
- Disable a force field generator on a forest moon.
- Destroy a blasphemous shrine to Chaos in mid-ritual.
- Take out an enemy artillery position.
- Detonate the power conduit at the heart of a Necron tomb complex.
- Blow a hole in the side of a spaceship during warp travel.

MISSION 2 – ASSASSINATE

The Kill-team must:

- Kill an enemy commander on his way to the front lines in his personal transport.
- Kill a double agent of the same race as the Kill-team before he imparts vital information.
- Take out a Tyranid Node beast to collapse the nearby hive mind synapse web.
- Put a doomed companion out of the misery inflicted by his torturers, taking as many bad guys down as possible on the way.
- Put a bullet in the skull of a corrupt governor during a grand address from his balcony.
- Destroy a revered prophet, crippling the enemy morale.

MISSION 3 – ESCAPE

The Kill-team must:

- Reach the edge of a cliff and activate their grav-chutes, flying to freedom.
- Stay one step ahead of the alien tide or face a gribbly death.

Dane

'Buffalo'

Sergeant Dutch

Dublone

Axe Man

Winter

Kill-teams comprised of Imperial Guard are great fun to personalise, and fit the old template of a team of low-down and desperate specialists who triumph against the odds. It's also fun to model each with a specialisation in mind – we have a flamer specialist, a comms expert, the hard-as-nails leader, a sniper, the heavy-weapon toting bruiser and the machete-wielding scout. All they need now is a good storyline and some brutes to kill...

• Get inside the basement vault before the demolition charges take out the building.

• Climb out of an alien-infested trash compactor before the Kill-team becomes wafer thin.

• Reach their ship and get into space before the Exterminatus begins.

The traitorous General Rutgher Kaine, staring down from the lip of the active volcano housing his secret laboratories. Will the Kill-team reach him and bring him to justice before the rivers of lava cut them off and allow Kaine to escape?

MISSION 4 – LAST STAND

The Kill-team must:

• Face the consequences of destroying a massive Tyranid brood-beast.

• Rampage through an infested hive city killing everything they find.

• Cleanse and burn an enemy headquarters to cripple the enemy command structure.

• Take down as many of the enemy as possible before the plague finishes them off.

• Fight for their lives after a teleporter malfunction drops them into the heart of enemy lines.

• Revenge their fallen brethren whilst preventing their bodies from being defiled.

• Take as many of the enemy with them as possible as the space hulk's denizens realise their presence on the ship.

MISSION 5 – HIT AND RUN

The Kill-team must:

• Place a teleport homer in the middle of an enemy encampment so the reinforcements can arrive.

• Start a landslide to bury an enemy column and get out before it takes the Kill-team out too.

• Access data from an enemy command cogitator and get it back to base.

• Place a chronodetonator on the foundation pillar of an enemy temple.

• Kickstart a doomsday device that the enemy were planning to deploy in battle.

• Poison the enemy's water supply.

• Place a beacon so that the ensuing orbital strike is as accurate as it is lethal.

MISSION 6 – RECONNOITRE

The Kill-team must:

• Escort a data-drone around a precious facility currently in enemy hands.

• Complete a dark ritual that comes to fruition only once they have sown the soil with a circle of blood.

• Plot a route for the main advance through enemy territory.

BOSSES & SPECIALIST KIT

It can really add to a game of Kill-team to have a large and self-important bad guy (or Boss) at the centre of things, especially if he meets an appropriately grisly end…

The Boss will differ depending on race. Use the table below to determine the appropriate bad guy.

The Brute squad player in a game of Kill-team automatically has 20 points to spend on his Boss. This will usually only cover the cost of the upgrade to Sergeant status (or equivalent) and add some basic wargear – he starts with none at all.

However many points the Kill-team player spends on specialist kit (see later) can be added to the points spent on the Boss, or spent on defensive equipment. Points are also garnered every time an opponent breaks the rules of Kill-team selection. Make sure the Kill-team player lets you know how many bonus points his Kill-team selection entitles you to. These can be spent on specialist kit or abilities for your Brute squads, or on weaponry, wargear and psychic powers for your Boss. This can mean the Brute squad player's head honcho can be anything from a simple squad upgrade to a fully-kitted out killing machine. Simply choose the Boss's options, wargear and weaponry as usual for that Codex.

Bosses never have retinues or suchlike, they simply replace a Brute in one of your Brute squads.

RACE	BOSS
Space Marines	Veteran Sergeant
Chaos Space Marines	Aspiring Champion
Eldar	Exarch
Orks	Nob
Dark Eldar	Sybarite
Tyranids	Mutant Gaunt (Weapon-beast)
Tau	Shas'ui
Necrons	N/A*
Imperial Guard	Junior Officer
Inquisitorial Storm trooper	Veteran Sergeant

** Necrons, being essentially animate machines, find it impossible to scale the dizzying peaks of Brute-hood. Instead they add D3 models to one Brute squad after deployment.*

A specially modelled Boss to lead your Brutes (or use them as human shields) like the one above can really give you the feeling of playing the storyline's bad guy.

SPECIALIST KIT

It is typical for the members of a commando team to have specialist gear with them to successfully accomplish their mission. This might vary from simple silencers to holo-projectors and blind grenades. Likewise, it's not unheard of for enterprising bad guys to fortify their strongholds with all manner of traps and alarm systems.

• A Kill-team can choose one of the upgrades listed below. The points listed do not come from the Kill-team's 160 point allowance, but are awarded to the Brute squad player to spend on his own equipment. It may choose an additional upgrade per successful mission it has completed – a Kill-team that has successfully completed two missions may take three upgrades from the Specialist Kit listed below. If the Kill-team is wiped out to a man, the opportunity to take further upgrades is lost and they must start afresh.

• Keep a record of what specialist kit your Kill-team has accrued over the course of its career, along with a total of how many points it has spent on its kit.

• No upgrade can be taken more than once unless specifically noted.

• Any points spent on upgrades are rewarded to the Brute squad player in the same way as those points awarded due to unusual Kill-team selection. In this way, no matter who is playing the Brute squad player, you should never have an easy fight on your hands.

• The specialist pieces of kit you can field as the Kill-team player or Brute squad player are as follows:

KILL-TEAM SPECIALIST KIT

BACKSTABBERS . . . . 10 PTS

One or more of the Kill-team's operatives excel at the art of the silent kill, their blades cutting off the enemy's screams before they can alert their comrades.

Whenever the Kill-team assaults a Brute squad and kills them all in that single round, then roll a D6: on a 1, a Klaxon counter is added to the Brute squad player's store as usual. On any other result, no Klaxon counter is added.

CAMO GEAR . . . . 10 PTS

The Kill-team has refined their camo tactics to the point that they can hunker down and become almost unseen even when in the open. Combined with the patience of the hunter, this can considerably enhance the Kill-team's stealth capabilities.

In any turn in which the Kill-team does not move, shoot or assault, the Brute squad player must discard a Klaxon counter at the beginning of his turn.

CHANGE OF GUARD . . 10 PTS

Having staked out the enemy territory for some time the Kill-team has ascertained exactly when the sentries go off their shift and change guard, striking at just the right moment to benefit from resultant confusion.

Play the change of guard at any time when the Brute squad player has no Klaxon counters in his store. All activated Brute squads become deactivated, and vice versa. Continue the turn as normal.

CUNNING DISGUISES . . . . 15 PTS

The Kill-team has disguised itself in some manner, whether by donning enemy uniforms, covering themselves with the pheromonal signature of the foe, using sophisticated holographic technology or some other means. In theory, with a little luck and a lot of nerve, they can simply walk past the enemy soldiers and onto the central objective.

There is a chance that enemy Brute squads will mistake a Kill-team with this upgrade for one of their own units. Every time a Brute squad would normally gain a Klaxon counter by spotting the Kill-team, roll a D6. If the result is higher than the Brute squad's total spotting distance, then no Klaxon counter is added to the Brute squad player's store, and the Brute squad does not count as having spotted the Kill-team. Of course, the Brute squad player can have another go next turn if he is still within spotting distance, and the longer the Kill-team has to bluff it out, the less chance of success there is. If the Kill-team shoots or assaults at any point this benefit is lost for the rest of the game.

DISTRACTION . . . . 20 PTS

The Kill-team have spent considerable resources ensuring that a loud and startling event takes place on the other side of the enemy compound, drawing enemy forces away from their posts at the critical time and allowing the Kill-team egress into the enemy grounds.

The distraction can be played at any time in the Brute squad player's Movement phase provided he has less than 3 Klaxon counters in his store. Roll a D6. The Kill-team player may move that many Brute squads 6" in the direction of his choice, regardless of whether they were activated or not. However, the Brute squad player gets to choose which squads are affected in this manner. This counts as their movement for that turn, so do not roll for control afterward.

GUNG-HO . . . . 20 PTS

There comes a time in many covert operations when stealth goes out the window, and the only option is to go hell-for-leather at the objective. Needless to say this invariably leads to the enemy swarming over their position like flies around grox dung.

The Kill-team may assault 6+D6" rather than the usual 6" in the turn this is used, and will strike first in close combat regardless of any other factors on any turn in which they charge. The enemy automatically gains an additional Klaxon counter when this effect is played.

REDSHIRT . . . . 5 PTS

The Kill-team has been lumbered with an extra member against their wishes, and it's entirely possible that this inexperienced rookie will get himself killed in a gory and spectacular way at the first opportunity...

The Kill-team has with it an additional model with the profile below:

	WS	BS	S	T	W	I	A	Ld	Sv
Redshirt	3	3	3	3	1	3	1	7	5+

The Redshirt has no equipment. In the unlikely event he survives the game, the Kill-team will gain an extra upgrade free of charge for their next game. If he dies he does not come back next game.

SCALING LADDERS & GRAPNELS . . . . . 10 PTS

The Kill-team have coiled ropes, telescopic ladders and grapnels with them, enabling them to make their way up the outside of buildings, cross digestion pools and negotiate other hazardous obstacles.

The Kill-team may treat impassable terrain as difficult ground.

This sinister Kill-team of alien warriors, dubbed the Night Stalkers by the terrified Imperial Guardsmen they prey upon, stalk forth from the shadows once more. Such a diverse Kill-team would allow the enemy considerably more Brute squads than usual and a fully tooled up Boss, but with Scarabs, Wraiths and hideous Flayed Ones amongst the Kill-team's number, they're going to need all the help they can get.

SCRAMBLER.......................30 PTS
The Kill-team have with them a powerful scrambling device that disrupts enemy communications and temporarily disables their alarms.

The Kill-team may use the scrambler at any time, but only once per game. The Brute squad player must immediately discard D3 Klaxon counters.

SILENCERS......................10 PTS
The Kill-team have had their ranged weapons specially modified so that the first salvo they fire makes little or no noise. This enables them to take out a full team of sentries without alerting their fellows to the incursion.

The Kill-team is not nearly as likely to trigger the alarm with the silencers fitted. When the Kill-team opens fire for the first time, roll a D6: on a 1, a Klaxon counter is added to the Brute squad player's store as usual. On any other result no Klaxon counter is added.

SMOKE OR BLIND GRENADES.......10 PTS
The Kill-team can use this equipment to mask their approach, making it extremely difficult for enemy squads to pinpoint them in the artificially generated haze.

Once per game, after either Movement phase, the Kill-team can declare that it is using the smoke or blind grenades. They count as being in cover in all respects, and have a 5+ Cover Save until the beginning of their next turn.

SPANNER IN THE WORKS ......5 PTS EACH
As the enemy sentry approaches, one member of the Kill-team picks up a discarded tool, rock or other hard object and hurls it into a nearby cluster of machinery, barrels etc, momentarily distracting the patrol whilst they slink away.

Declare when a spanner is being used before control for a Brute squad is determined. The Kill-team player may add +2 to their result for this roll only. The spanner may only be used once per game.

STUMMERS......................15 PTS
Stummers, devices designed specifically to deaden noise and make detection that much more difficult, can cut out one of the sentry's main tools of the trade; a sharp pair of ears.

The Kill-team can employ the stummers once per game, declaring their use after the Brute squad player has determined which squads are activated or deactivated for that turn. For the rest of that turn only, all the Kill-team player's rolls for control of Brute squads count as being a 6.

WIRE CUTTERS ....10 PTS
The Kill-team have come well prepared for penetrating the thickest defensive terrain, toting wire cutters and electrocharges that can disable or cut through light obstacles.

The Kill-team rolls 3D6 for determining the distance it can move through difficult terrain, picking the highest result.

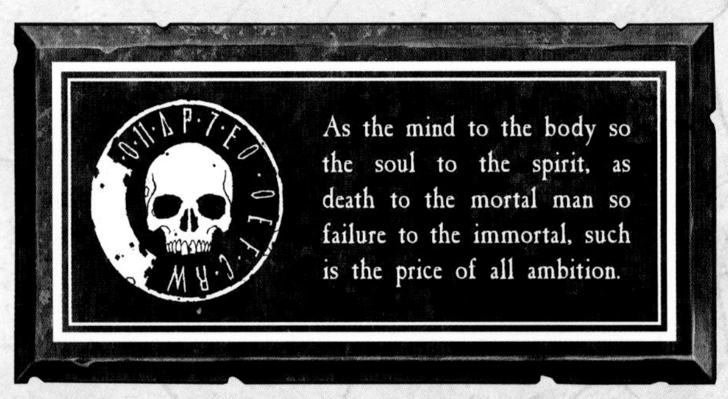

As the mind to the body so the soul to the spirit, as death to the mortal man so failure to the immortal, such is the price of all ambition.

BRUTE SQUAD SPECIALISED KIT

LAS-TRAPS.......................5 PTS
The Brute squad players have rigged the area surrounding the central objective with a series of sophisticated traps and alarms.

When setting up the scenery, the Brute squad player may place D6 pieces of 6" long red cord or thin strips of card anywhere on the table. If any member of the Kill-team touches one of these markers at any time, a Klaxon counter is added to the Brute squad player's store.

REINFORCEMENTS ....40 PTS
The game is up, and those Brutes just keep on coming! The Kill-team will have to be either very lucky or very capable to get out of this one alive...

When the Brute squad player has accrued three Klaxon counters, he will gain a fresh Brute squad each turn. This squad appears on the table edge of the Brute squad player's choice at the beginning of his turn, and will move in the same way as a normal Brute squad.

GET 'EM LADS!...................15 PTS
The Brute squad players have finally located the interlopers and, their morale bolstered by the presence of their comrades, charge in with every intention of ripping the Kill-team to pieces.

This upgrade may be used whenever more than one Brute squad spots the Kill-team in one Movement phase. Provided more than one Brute squad charges the Kill-team in the subsequent Assault phase, all Brutes gain +1 attack for the duration of that Assault phase in addition to other modifiers.

EXTRA BRUTES ....VARIABLE PTS
Having been forewarned of an enemy attack, there are more bad guys than normal around the central objective. This is going to be a tricky one!

Buying this upgrade entitles the Brute squad player to field an extra Brute squad. This upgrade may be taken multiple times. The price of this upgrade varies on race. The prices are as follows:

RACE	COST
Space Marines	45 pts
Chaos Space Marines	42 pts
Eldar Guardians	24 pts
Ork Boyz	24 pts
Dark Eldar Warriors	24 pts
Tyranid Termagants	21 pts
Tau Gun Drones	36 pts
Necron Warriors	48 pts
Imperial Guard	18 pts
Inquisitorial Storm Troopers	30 pts

DOOM SQUAD ....15 PTS
One of the Brute squads has been trained extensively until they are masters of close quarters warfare, usually entrusted with the security of the central objective.

Nominate a Brute squad as the Doom squad after set-up. That Brute squad has a spotting distance one higher than normal, and will have +1 Strength, Initiative and Attacks on any turn it charges. This also applies to any Boss Brute that joins the Doom squad.

Many of the models in this Kroot Kill-team, The Red Maw Kindred, have been converted to fulfil specific battlefield roles: a sniper with an extended gunsight; a tracker scenting the enemy from his fingers; the knife-wielding assassin; and the towering Krootox. The unifying features of all the models are the overall skin colour and the bold warpaint. This has only been applied to the head of each miniature: the face is painted black and the jaw a contrasting red.

ALL POINTS BULLETIN .... 10 PTS

The bad guys have been alerted to the fact that there are enemies in the perimeter, and appraised of their rough location. This can only be bad news for their prey.

Only usable once per game. Once the Brute squad player has determined how many squads are activated for that turn, he may use the All Points Bulletin. He may re-roll the Control rolls for his Brutes for the remainder of that turn. He must abide by the result of the second roll.

STILL NOT DEAD .... 10 PTS

Despite the fact that he has been gutted, burned, mangled and crushed, the Boss somehow manages to surge to his feet and go for a last ditch kill. No doubt this will be short lived, but he might take a couple of the good guys with him screaming to hell...

Should the Boss die, leave him on his side at the place of his death. He may be resurrected and stood back up at the beginning of the next Brute squad player turn and may act as normal during that turn, at the end of which he is removed as a casualty.

DOOMSDAY DEVICE................ 20 PTS

With the alarms raging, the Boss knows that it is only a matter of time before the Kill-team succeed in their mission and escape. Determined to prevent this from happening, he triggers an explosive mechanism that will take down the entire complex, killing everyone nearby. If you've gotta go, go in style.

If, at any point, there are more Kill-team operatives than Brutes left on the table and the Boss is still alive, he will automatically trigger the Doomsday Device. At the beginning of every subsequent Brute squad player turn (even if all Brutes have been killed, but the mission still remains to be completed) roll a dice: on a 1 the game is ended as everything on the board is vaporised in a cataclysmic explosion.

AND THERE YOU HAVE IT

Well, that little lot should keep you Kill-team raiding and sabotaging for a long time to come. And remember, even if the bad guys get lucky and end up with the Kill-team's heads on the trophy wall, it'll be your turn to play the Brute squad player next, and revenge is a dish best served cold....

KILL-TEAM TERRAIN

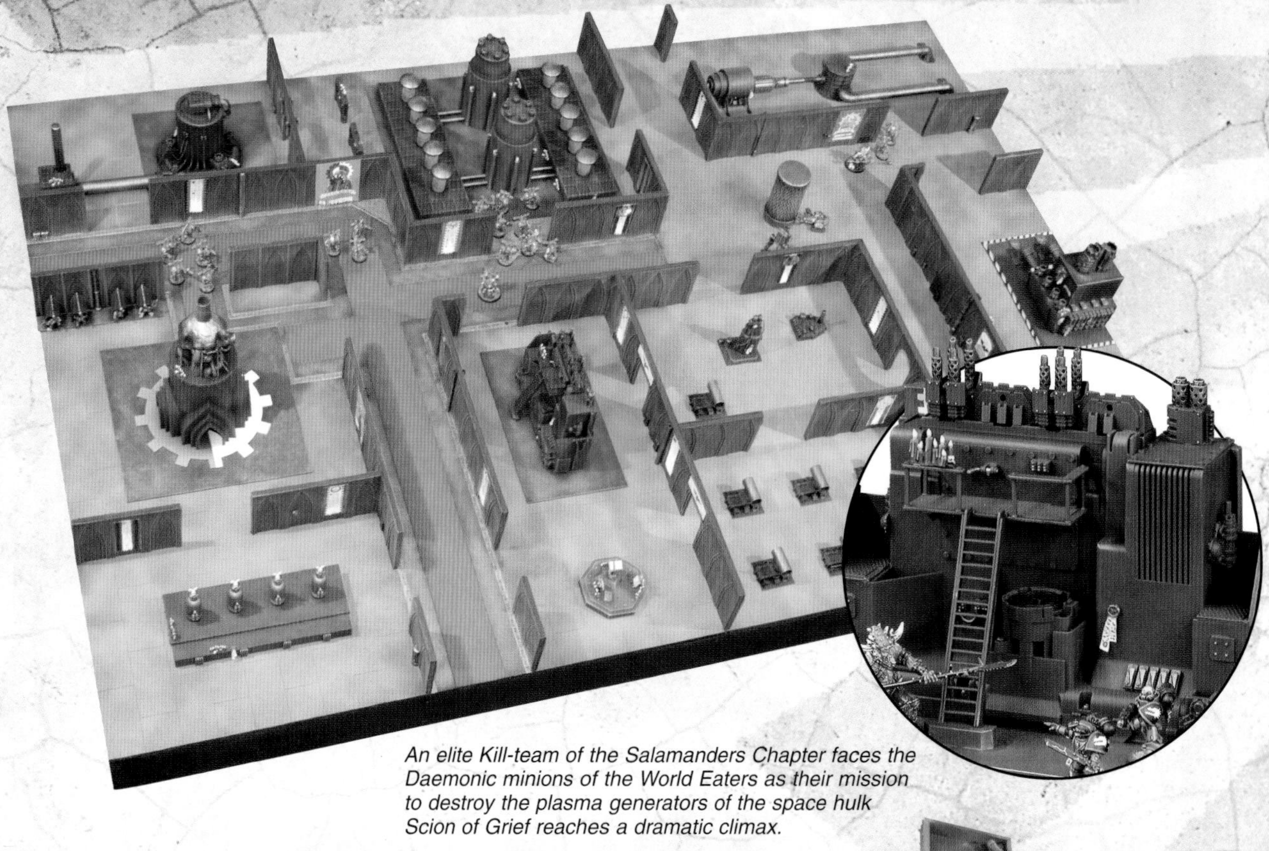

An elite Kill-team of the Salamanders Chapter faces the Daemonic minions of the World Eaters as their mission to destroy the plasma generators of the space hulk Scion of Grief reaches a dramatic climax.

Within the twisted mould-glades of Liberty V is the scene of a heroic last stand by an Imperial Guard Kill-team cornered by Eldar Raiders.

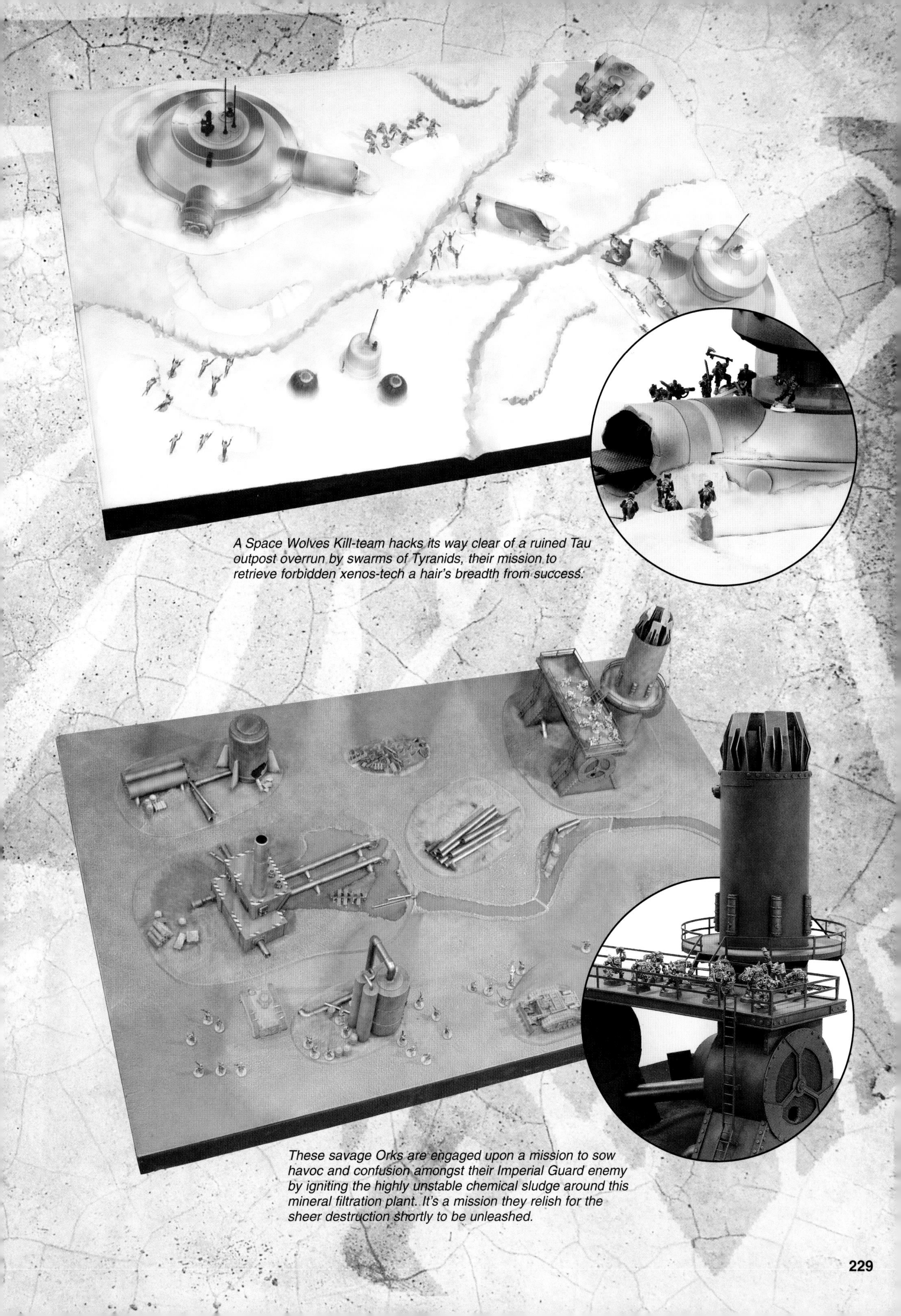

A Space Wolves Kill-team hacks its way clear of a ruined Tau outpost overrun by swarms of Tyranids, their mission to retrieve forbidden xenos-tech a hair's breadth from success.

These savage Orks are engaged upon a mission to sow havoc and confusion amongst their Imperial Guard enemy by igniting the highly unstable chemical sludge around this mineral filtration plant. It's a mission they relish for the sheer destruction shortly to be unleashed.

CAMPAIGNS

Whilst fighting individual games is an utterly absorbing pursuit in itself there comes a point when the urge to take part in a campaign becomes an unbearable itch you just have to scratch. Campaigns provide a context that makes an individual battle far more dramatic. Knowing what is at stake creates a narrative for the game that a standard mission brief cannot do.

There are many ways of conducting a campaign. At one end of the spectrum are campaigns moderated by a referee featuring rules for supply, hidden map-based movement, weather and so on. Such campaigns are a lot of work to set up and require careful bookkeeping. Because it is important to synchronise moves it is vital that all the players give the campaign their full commitment. On the plus side the campaign becomes a game in itself in which the strategic skills of the players are tested as much as their tabletop gaming skills. At the other end of the spectrum are pure narrative campaigns in which a sequence of games are played, sometimes using special missions devised purely for the campaign, often with each game's result having consequences for a later game. There is not really a strategic element to this type of campaign as it focuses on getting games of Warhammer 40,000 played. Both approaches have their virtues.

The most important thing though is adding context, drama and excitement to the game. Strategically valuable positions are heroically seized, hopeless positions are defended to the last, and troops become grizzled veterans as they learn how to survive the maelstrom of battle.

In this section you will find guidance on running different types of campaigns, and an example of a simple node-map campaign in the form of the Battle of Phoenix Island. This format will often be used when campaigns are detailed in Codexes and White Dwarf articles. Furthermore, you will find rules for units accumulating Experience Points and earning battle honours that make them more formidable and skilled as the campaign progresses, the effects of units being defeated, and what happens when a unit changes its weaponry or gains a new commander.

These elements are presented in the following section to provide you with a set of resources from with which you can tailor your campaign to suit your own tastes. Perhaps you decide that you will play a node-map campaign, using the full Experience Points system with each player drawing up a 5,000 point master roster. Or maybe your style is more suited to an open-ended narrative approach, using the Experience system but not worrying about master rosters, etc. The choice is entirely yours.

One last note before we get into the rules. Remember that you can vary the types of game played throughout a campaign. For example, you could kick things of with a 'prologue' mission in the form of a fast and dirty Kill-team game. This could be followed by games using the normal rules or those for Combat Patrol. The beauty of playing a campaign is that each game can be tailored to the tastes of the players in a way that one-off games never can.

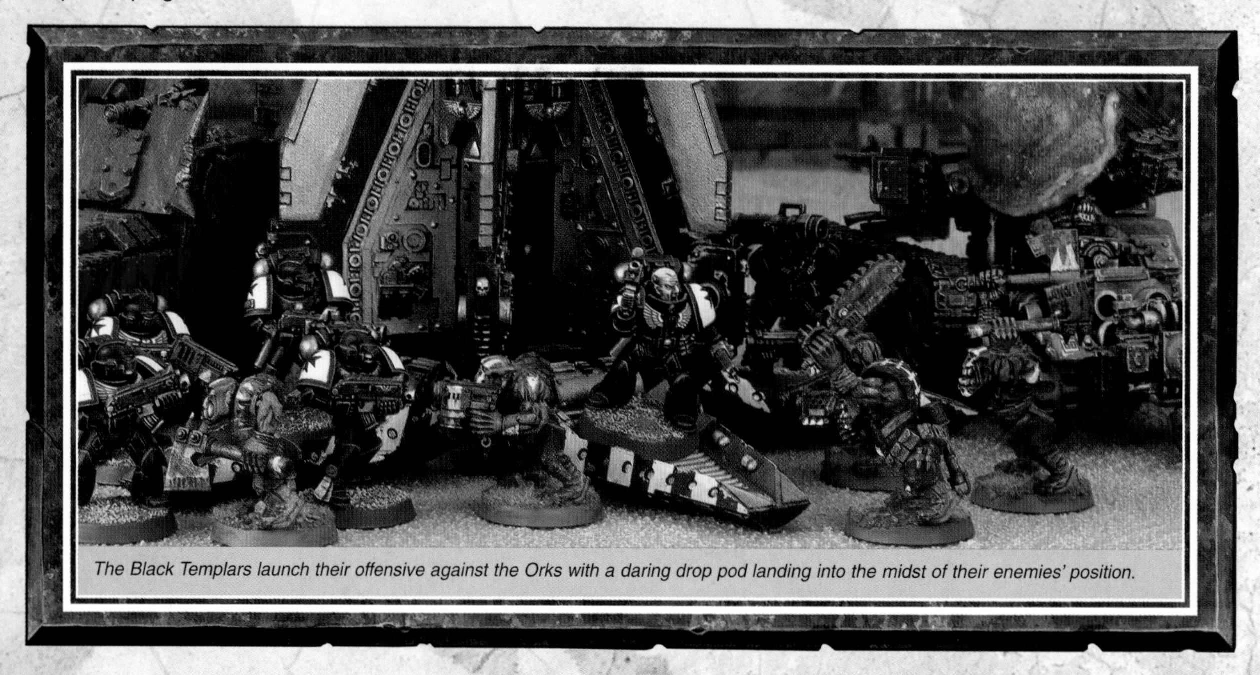

The Black Templars launch their offensive against the Orks with a daring drop pod landing into the midst of their enemies' position.

The Ultramarines stand resolute against the planet-scouring power of a newly launched Ork Waaagh!

NARRATIVE CAMPAIGNS

Probably the easiest form of campaign to play that doesn't require a great deal of planning beforehand is a narrative campaign. As the name suggests, this type of campaign relies on the players or a referee (if you have someone willing to step into the breach and play the part of evil overlord of the campaign) deciding after the game how the narrative develops based on the result of the battle. The first game should be a balanced affair that doesn't particularly favour one side over the other, but allows for different developments of the narrative depending on who wins. For example, a narrative campaign could revolve around the Daemonhunters attempting to discover the whereabouts of a Chaos cult in order to prevent them from summoning a Greater Daemon.

The first mission might be a simple Take and Hold mission that the Daemonhunters need to win in order to gain valuable intelligence regarding the disposition of enemy forces. If the Daemonhunters prevail, then the referee might decide that there could be advantages in deployment in the next game or they might find an approach to the enemy headquarters that's perhaps not as heavily defended as the others, allowing the Daemonhunters to take extra points into the next battle. The result of this mission will lead onto others and it's up to the referee to decide what will follow next, and the more dramatic and exciting the better. As each game is played, more and more possibilities will suggest themselves and the narrative can continue for as long as the players and referee desire or until it comes to a natural conclusion.

Narrative campaigns are great fun for both the players and referee and allow you to really use your imagination to come up with all manner of bizarre inventions and fun scenarios. You also shouldn't feel that you have to stick doggedly to the missions in this rulebook, you can invent all manner of missions to play in your campaigns.

TREE CAMPAIGNS

Another simple form of campaign that requires a little work beforehand, but is very simple to run once you've put in the initial work, is a tree campaign. The battles you fight in a tree campaign follow a predetermined path depending on the result of previous games, rather like a flow diagram. In a tree campaign, you start from an initial battle and the result of the first game will tell you which path to follow from there to the next game, and so on.

The paths of the diagram can intersect, overlap and even loop back on one another as you invent sub-plots that can further influence the campaign. Just remember not to go too far overboard and overload your campaign with so much detail that it collapses under the weight of its own worthiness.

Before the campaign starts, draw up a diagram showing the different battles that the players must fight as they progress through the campaign.

One such campaign ladder could involve Witch Hunters attempting to recapture a world that has fallen to heretics and who have taken control of the governor's palace. The premise of a campaign need not be overly complex to work; it just needs some thought as to what might be involved in it. For example, the campaign mentioned above starts with a Sabotage mission involving the forces of the Witch Hunters attempting to destroy a generator facility in order to prevent ground based lasers from firing on the strike cruisers of their Space Marine allies as they move into low orbit to bombard the planet's surface. If the Witch Hunters are successful and manage to wrest the objective from its defenders this then leads to a Take and Hold mission where they have to hold out until their allies can arrive. Should they fail however, this means that they are wiped out (or at least forced from the building) and the Space Marines must fight a Blitz mission, perhaps with the defender allowed to pick an additional Heavy Support slot to represent the extra firepower he can bring to bear. Each of these missions has a path to follow based on who wins the mission and you simply follow the correct path leading from each mission until you reach the end and one player is victorious.

SAMPLE TREE CAMPAIGN

A mighty Ork Warlord clashes with an Iron Father of the Iron Hands Chapter, and the fate of a world hangs in the balance.

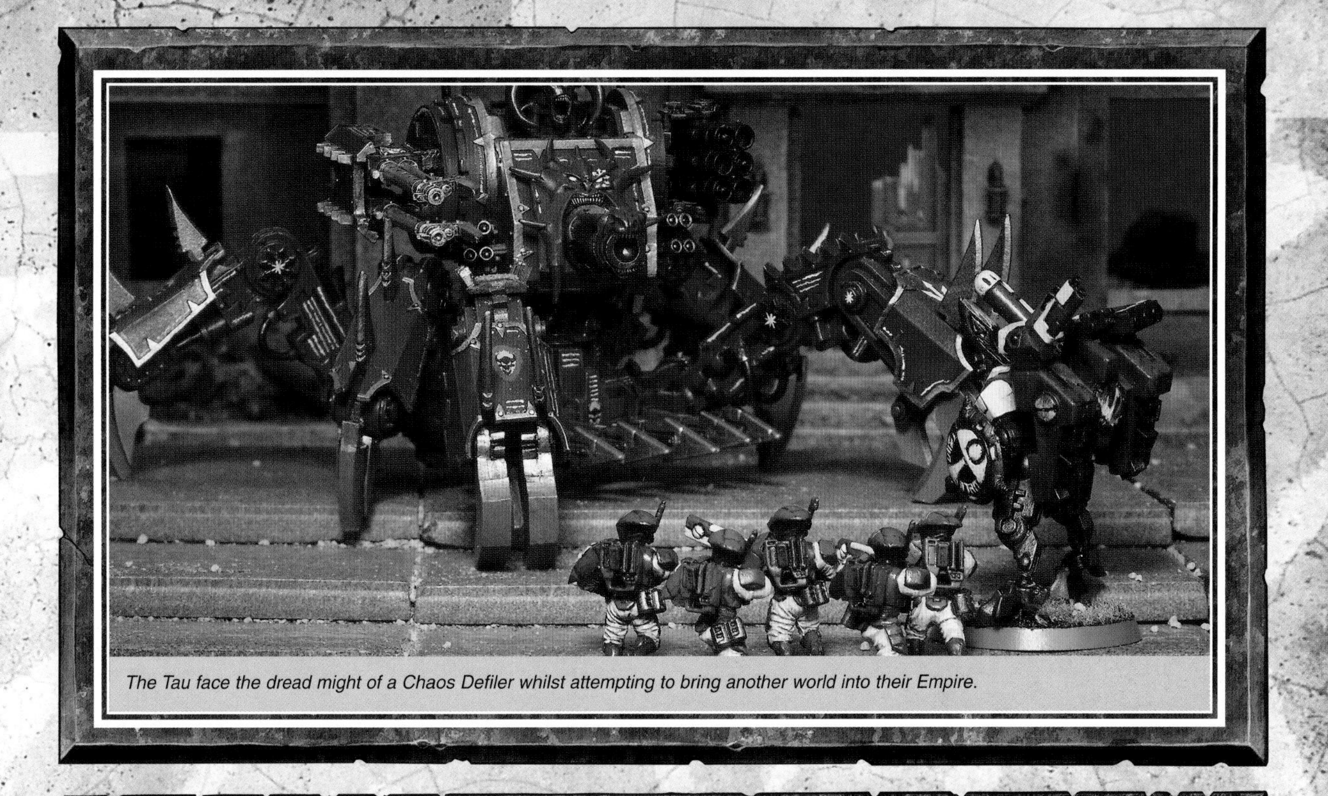

The Tau face the dread might of a Chaos Defiler whilst attempting to bring another world into their Empire.

MAP-BASED CAMPAIGNS

Some of the most successful campaigns are map-based, and that's no coincidence. Although they require a bit of expenditure of time and effort, and ideally a computer with at least rudimentary desktop publishing capabilities, they are well worth it and add so many new angles to the gaming experience that the games themselves can become events within a larger and far more intriguing master game.

THE CAMPAIGN CO-ORDINATOR

Someone will need to step into the role of campaign coordinator (or Games Master), the person who generates the map, rules and guides the campaign along, but don't worry, you'll probably end up playing just as many games as the other participants, if not more (see Launching the Crusade overleaf).

A map-based campaign, where all players have their forces placed on a communal map and the movement of their forces determines who they play (and often steal territory from in the event of a win), is usually quite lengthy. Alone amongst the varieties mentioned here, this is the one with the real trump card: a strong visual element. Once the map's sorted out, the majority of the work is done, all you have to do then is decide on a simple rules system allowing the players to pick on each other. Perhaps you might want to break the campaign into weekly or fortnightly 'phases' and allow each player one move per phase, giving them a chance to invade their neighbour's territory. When two players' markers clash, it's time for a game.

Although it sounds simple enough, it's important to get each stage of your preparation right before you start. Here are a few guidelines:

THE MAP

Unless you're feeling really ambitious it's easier to download a map from the internet or go to a library and photocopy one that you can scrawl all over rather than try to draw your own. You might want to use an old map of a city, for instance, or a mountain range or sewer network, or just look around for something that captures your imagination. Next, divide the map into sections, using natural boundaries (the borders of a park, a copse, a market square, or a building) to define each location, and then write an evocative name over that section. Do this for the whole map and you have your campaign setting.

When choosing starting places for your players, don't put everybody right next to each other, packed together like sardines; leave a little room for them to expand into without having to fight tooth and nail from the very beginning. This also ensures a fairly easy 'first phase' to get everyone used to the system. Make sure there are plenty of unclaimed/GM-controlled spaces on the map so that you get the odd game in or your players can make a non-confrontational move.

THE RULES

Although this might seem like the complicated bit, provided you keep it simple the campaign will practically run itself. Remember that provided everybody is using the same rules and there is an even spread of juicy locations, nobody will have an advantage they haven't earned.

Make a simple ruling so you can tell who's winning. This could be as simple as the player with the most territories, or a system where you assign Victory Points to certain key locations and the player with the most after a certain number of turns is the winner. It could even be something outlandish, such as recovering weapons from supply dumps scattered around the battlefield, which can be used by the troopers that claim them. If you're feeling thorough it's often a great idea to pick out the really key locations on your map and write a bit of text for them, even applying a special rule if you like. It will give a great background to the battle and indicate the scenery you should use: there will be a storyline in place even before a single dice has been rolled.

LAUNCHING THE CRUSADE

Make sure the map is placed somewhere central where everybody can gather round to plot and conspire, such as the wall of your gaming area. Get hold of some pins, stickers, or some other kind of markers, and give each player a set of them. They can be colour-coded with a guide to what colour belongs to whom alongside the map, or they can bear the initials of each player: just have in mind they are going to be moved around a lot, and that you will need plenty of spares.

Hand out copies of the campaign rules and a small version of your map to all players well before the campaign starts, in a 'campaign pack'. Then get everyone together around the map just before the campaign begins for a final briefing where people can ask any questions they have, throw challenges at each other and plan their initial moves. Write a brief newsletter-style journal for the campaign every so often and stick it up next to the map. This is a great place to chronicle hard-fought victories and ignominious defeats and it makes the players feel they are making history instead of just pushing miniatures about. Seeing your hero's name in an invented newspaper or diary that describes his banishment of the diabolic minions of Chaos is good fun. It makes the games feel like they really count, and after all, that's the whole essence of a campaign. Aim for one newsletter every phase if you can, or every other phase if that proves too much of a tall order.

Encourage plotting and scheming. A Dark Angels commander and Space Wolves Wolf Lord may have to join forces against a particular heinous threat, only to turn on each other once the battle is won. The forces of Slaanesh might turn on their Khorne allies, because they want to take their enemies alive. A noticeboard near the map is a great forum for your players' threats, wanted posters and challenges.

One of the golden rules of a campaign is that once it has run for a couple of months, and it looks like it could wrap up soon, make sure that it does. If it drags on too long people will begin to lose interest, and it's much better if they are left with good memories rather than the impression that the campaign has gone stale. A good way to do this is to stage a vast finale game. This might be a clash between two rival commanders and their armies across the walls of a city, an army mobilised to take down a ravening sea of daemons about to consume a settlement, or a full-scale storming of a powerful Ork warlord's fortress. The grander the better; you can even make it a multi-player game if you fancy it.

The Eldar repulse the forces of Chaos from the sacred ground of a lost Maiden world.

 THOUGHT FOR THE DAY: THE JUSTICE OF YOUR ACTION IS MEASURED BY THE STRENGTH OF YOUR CONVICTION.

EXAMPLE MAP-BASED CAMPAIGN

THE BATTLE FOR VOGEN

The Vogen Campaign works on a simple system of Victory Points, with each location worth a certain number of points based on its importance and proximity to the centre of the city. At the heart of the city is the Palace of Peace, the seat of government of Vogen and ultimate prize of the campaign. Worth a whopping 10 Victory Points, whoever holds it at the end of the campaign will probably be the winner. As well as Victory Points, some locations have special rules or scenarios. For example, in the centre of Angel Square there is an imposing statue of Sanguinius, the Blood Angels Primarch – should it fall into Chaos hands then every Imperial player in the campaign will suffer a -1 to their Leadership for the following battle.

Each player is allocated a location on the map as their home base and, once a week, they get to place a coloured pin (representing their force) in a location adjacent to one they have control of. In this way each player's territory can expand and offer them more potential routes towards the centre of the city and the Palace of Peace. If players opt to place a pin in an occupied location then those two players fight a battle, and whoever wins will control the location and win the Victory Points. If a player finds himself in the unfortunate position of having no territories left then he is defeated and unceremoniously removed from the campaign.

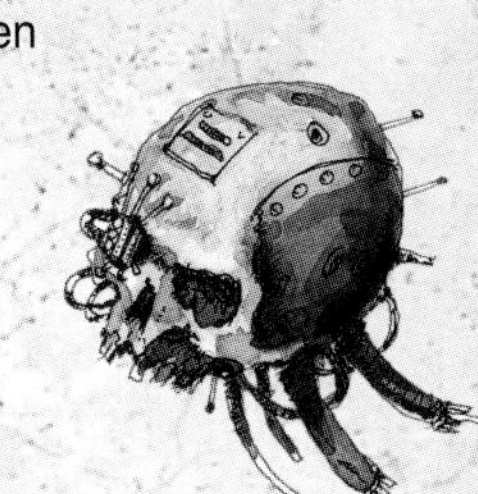

GIBBET HILL

Situated on an exposed and windswept rocky island to the northeast of the city walls, Gibbet Hill has always had associations with death. Convicted murderers were once hung by the neck until dead here, but now it is a fortified gun emplacement.

5 VICTORY POINTS: If you control the arsenal of laser silos on Gibbet Hill you may use preliminary bombardment in every game you play.

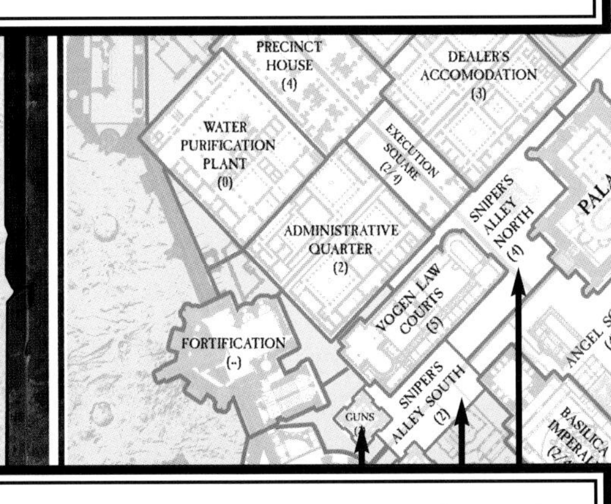

GUN TOWERS AND SNIPER'S ALLEY

These heavily armoured gun towers changed hands many times over the course of the war, their strategic location overlooking the Basilica and law courts making them ideal vantage points for snipers.

2 VICTORY POINTS per gun tower location: Each of the gun towers has both lascannon and heavy bolter sentry guns, set on point defence mode. They are elevated 8". Once the location is claimed, they will fire upon the nearest enemy target every turn.

2 VICTORY POINTS for Sniper's Alley South.

4 VICTORY POINTS for Sniper's Alley North: A Vindicare Assassin is operating in Sniper's Alley North and may be used by Imperial players in any game played here at no additional points cost.

SPACEPORT COMPLEX

The reason for Vogen's continued dominance of planetary affairs, the sole spaceport on the planet, is where all Vogen's imports and exports arrive and depart. The landing fields and warehouse complexes stretched far to the north of the city and Imperial forces were forced onto the defensive as Traitor units attempted to wrest control of the facilities.

0 VICTORY POINTS: Any forces with a pin in the Spaceport Complex may place their new pins in any unnamed location on the map (it does not need to be adjacent to a square occupied by that player). They may not place a pin in a named location. They may also Deep Strike any units they wish to keep in reserve if the scenario uses the Reserves rules.

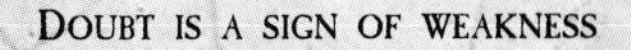

ROLLING CAMPAIGNS

'Rolling Campaigns' are a way of representing the 'bigger picture' of just what a game of Warhammer 40,000 is portraying. It would be a mistake to assume that the two armies fighting it out across the table are the only forces in the area, that an immortal star-god is taking time out from slaying worlds to lead a small patrol. In general, a game of Warhammer 40,000 represents the focus and culmination of a far larger battle. Imagine, if you will, that the armies' lines extend as far as the eye can see in either direction, and that there are many thousands of reinforcements waiting to take the places of those who should fall in this one battle.

Players of the Epic system will be familiar with the concept of formations and firefights, and in many ways a single game of Warhammer 40,000 represents such a firefight occurring between two formations, each drawn from a far larger army.

By playing a rolling game, you get to determine each army's part in the larger battle; the ground they took, the positions they overran, the counter-attacks launched against them and all the other events that are too big to be represented in a single game of Warhammer 40,000, but are also smaller in scope than a larger campaign.

A rolling game is fought as a series of linked games – between three and five being ideal. As the overall objective is to take ground, the best mission to use is a Recon mission.

The first game is set up and played as normal. However, at the end of the game sketch a basic map of the tabletop, showing the terrain and the extent of the ground taken by the winning side.

In the second game, the terrain is 'rolled' up, with the extent of the winner's advance becoming the front line of their deployment zone, and new terrain placed in the new area.

By using this simple system, you can represent the overall progress of a larger battle, by breaking it down into a number of smaller actions. This allows for the capturing of ground, and makes certain terrain features into strategically important objectives, as capturing them will put the attacker in a more favourable position in the next game.

As each game is played, you might like to add a strategic value to the victories earned. One way to do so is to allow each side a set points value of reinforcements, with the winner earning more: so in a 1,500 points game, the winner may earn 500 points to spend on reinforcements, while the loser earns 250. Another way is to draw up a Master Roster of, say 5,000 points, with 1,500 being fielded per game. This way you only field as many troops as you have on your roster – once they're gone, they're gone. Once all the games are fought, the side with the most victories, or which has attained a pre-agreed objective, has won.

Left: *At the end of the first game, the Space Wolves force has defeated its foe and captured the settlement in the enemy deployment zone.*

Right: *At the start of the second game, the settlement is set up in the Space Wolves' deployment zone, and the remainder of the table laid out in the normal manner.*

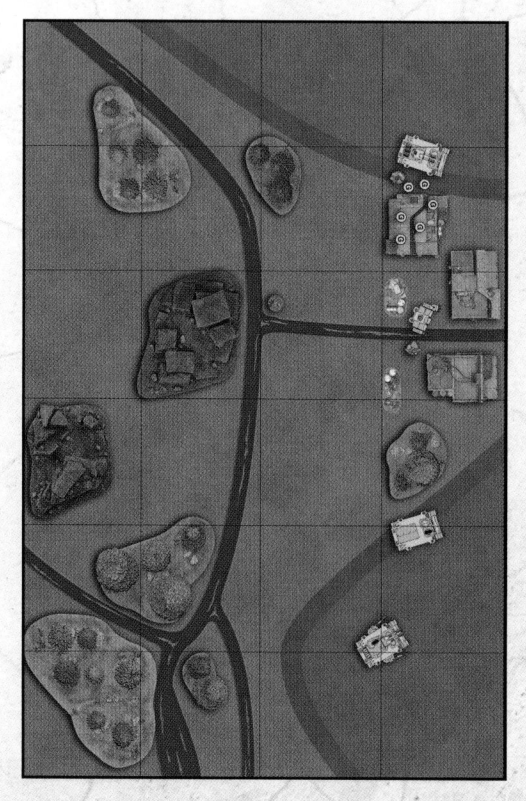

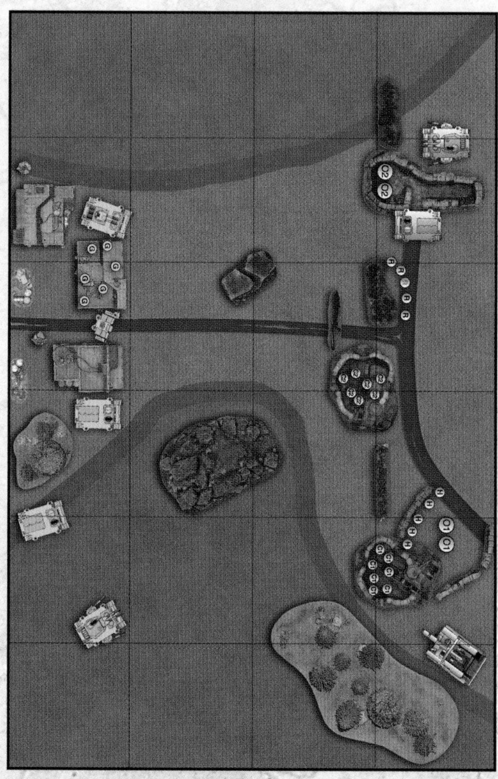

NODE CAMPAIGNS

Node-map campaigns are a mixture of the map and tree systems, and an example of one is included later in this section, in the form of the Battle for Phoenix Island. In essence, the tree is superimposed over the map, with strategically important points on the map forming the nodes, over which battles are fought. The normal way of deciding the winner is when a pre-agreed number of nodes have fallen to one player, that player has won the campaign.

Each node may have a particular type of mission associated with it. For example, if the node represents a vital installation, such as an ammunition dump or command centre, appropriate missions might be Strongpoint Attack, Sabotage or Take and Hold. It's a good idea to provide some variety in what missions are played at each node, so that players do not become tired of playing the same missions at certain bottleneck nodes.

You can also associate certain terrain with individual nodes. Some nodes may represent particularly built up areas, whilst others may be deep in the toxic ash wastes between hive cities. You could draw up your own terrain generator, tailored to your own terrain collection, and you could use the rules for fighting in cities found in Codex: Battlezone Cityfight when laying siege to a city.

As each node is joined to one or more others, you can determine how easy or difficult crossing the intervening terrain might be. If, for example, a highway joins two nodes, armies will have no trouble moving from one to the next. But should that highway cross a bridge that the enemy has mined (perhaps in a previous Sabotage mission) then you could state that the player wishing to use the route must roll equal to or over a given number on a D6. You can use this method to encourage sneaky players to attempt to use short cuts between otherwise distant nodes, although there is of course the risk that their army may become mired and not move at all.

Another option when it comes to using routes between nodes is to allow certain types of armies a bonus to the roll to cross difficult routes. For example, an Imperial Guard army mounted entirely in Chimeras may receive a +1 bonus to the dice roll, whereas a Space Marine army deploying entirely using their Drop Pods special rule may circumvent the route entirely and not need to roll at all.

When it comes to determining what happens during the 'Campaign phase' of a node-map campaign, the same advice applies here as to map-based campaigns. Each player makes a move, and the resulting battles are fought. You can add tension to this process by requiring each player to roll to see who gets to make the first move each phase, using their army's Strategy Rating.

One last point in node-map campaigns: they are very easy for two players to design between them without the need for a referee, as all the rules are agreed and the nodes planned out before the campaign begins. Of course, having a referee design the campaign means that he can build in some nasty surprises for the players, just to keep them on their toes...

CAMPAIGN ROSTERS

An additional quirk that can be introduced into your campaigns is for each side to write up a master roster with more points available than are needed for any one game. The size of the master roster may vary depending on the planned length of the campaign, so, for example, a campaign of three to five games may use master rosters of 50% more than the points limit for each game, where as a campaign of indefinite length may use master rosters of many thousands of points.

Used in conjunction with the rules for Experience Points (see later), changing units and units missing battles while they recover from damage, players will soon get a real feeling for their army, and learn to husband their finite resources from one game to the next.

The master roster does not have to conform to the Force Organisation chart so it is possible to have three HQs for example. You will however be limited to the Force Organisation chart when picking an army for a game.

*With this system in effect it pays to decide early on which units **have** to be involved in particularly gruelling missions so that they can be kept safe until they are needed. Alternatively, you can throw them in from the start in the hope that they will have a useful battle honour for the pivotal battle. Often the best way to design a master roster is to include several units of approximately the same points so they can be switched at will depending on the mission.*

The added kudos of your most successful units winning battle honours is considerable, and using this system you will soon find that your army list becomes populated by units with character and history, whose fate you really do care about.

CAMPAIGN ARMY – THE BLACKFANG TASK FORCE

The Blackfang task force represents part of the 11th Great Company of the Space Wolves. They are currently assigned to the planet Kollace in the Gothic sector, assisting in the struggle against the Ruinous Powers. Kollace has little strategic importance, but the Blackfangs use it as a convenient training ground and a staging post from which to launch their hunts.

The Blackfangs are an incredibly mobile battlegroup, able to reach threatened zones swiftly. All three infantry squads have assigned transport units, while Land speeders and Dreadnoughts provide the heavy firepower. The array of purity seals and trophies adorning the vehicles and Dreadnoughts show the experience and resolve of the Blackfangs over many successful campaigns.

	Unit	Wargear
	Kjalter Stormcrow – Rune Priest	*Runic armour, runic charm,runic staff, Chooser of the Slain, Belt of Russ.*
	Sundvik the Ancient – Venerable Dreadnought	*Plasma cannon, heavy flamer, smoke launchers.*
	Squad Arvo – 6 Grey Hunters	*Bolters, close combat weapons,1 plasma gun, 1 power fist. Mounted in a Razorback (lascannon, extra armour, smoke launchers).*
	Squad Reijo – 8 Blood Claws	*Bolt pistols, close combat weapons,1 power fist, 1 power weapon. Mounted in a Rhino (extra armour, smoke launchers).*
	Squad Teuvo – 6 Grey Hunters	*Bolt pistols, close combat weapons,1 power fist, 1 power weapon. Mounted in a Razorback (multi-melta, extra armour, smoke launchers).*
	Land Speeder	*Multi-melta.*
	Land Speeder	*Multi-melta.*
	Ingiga – Dreadnought	*Plasma cannon, heavy flamer, smoke launchers.*
	Torvald – Dreadnought	*Twin-linked lascannon, missile launcher.*
	Skaldheim – Dreadnought	*Twin-linked lascannon, missile launcher.*

CAMPAIGN ARMY – WAAAGH! GAZBAG

Waaagh! Gazbag has wreaked havoc across much of the Armageddon sector, its Warboss's reputation growing with each victory. Over a period of months, several Adeptus Astartes task forces have been tasked with its destruction, but each has found itself crushed beneath a brutal tide of Greenskins. Over the course of these engagements, Gazbag has come to develop a taste for combat with the Emperor's chosen. He has taken great care to retain a trophy from each combat as a way of recording of the Space Marine Chapters that he has defeated. Gazbag's Boyz themselves are veterans of brutal close-quarters streetfights, and prefer to fight with their feet on the war-scarred earth, rather than from trukks and battlewagons that can get bogged-down in rubble-strewn streets.

	Unit	Wargear
HQ	Warboss Gazbag	*Mega armour, kombi weapon: shoota/skorcha, mega boosta, iron gob.*
	Gazbag's Bodyguard	*3 Nobz (slugga, choppa & 'eavy armour), 2 Nobz (slugga, 'ugé choppa & 'eavy armour), 1 Nob (slugga, power claw & 'eavy armour).*
Troops	Nagruk's Skarboyz Mob	*1 Nob (slugga, choppa, frag stikkbombz & iron gob), 3 Boyz (burnas), 12 Boyz (sluggas & choppas).*
Troops	Gogruk's Shoota Boyz mob	*1 Nob (big shoota, choppa, iron gob & bosspole), 3 Boyz (big shootas), 17 Boyz (shootas).*
Troops	Hazrok's Skugga Boyz mob	*1 Nob (slugga, power claw, 'eavy armour & iron gob). 2 Boyz (burnas), 20 Boyz (sluggas & choppas).*
Troops	Skuzbag's Tankbustas Mob	*1 Nob (rokkit launcha, choppa, 'eavy armour & iron gob), 3 Boyz (rokkit launchas), 6 Boyz (sluggas & choppas), all have frag stikkbombz & tankbusta bombz.*
Heavy Support	Killer Kan Mob	*3 Killer Kans (Dreadnought close combat weapon, big shoota & armour plates).*
Heavy Support	Big Gunz Battery	*3 lobbas, 9 Grots, 1 Slaver (Squig Hound & grabba stick), 1 Mekboy (slugga, choppa & Mekboy's tools).*

EARNING EXPERIENCE POINTS

Over the course of many battles, soldiers may acquire tricks of the trade, learn from experience and the teachings of old hands. Units can earn Experience Points in a number of ways (and can also lose them if they perform badly). The charts below list the different ways in which Experience can be gained and lost.

TRANSPORT VEHICLES

A transport vehicle that has been chosen as a unit's transport vehicle (for example, a Space Marine Tactical squad's Rhino, or an Imperial Guard Armoured Fist squad's Chimera) cannot earn Experience Points or gain battle honours of its own. Vehicles that are chosen as a unit in their own right (a Space Marine Land Raider chosen as Heavy Support, or an Eldar Falcon for example) earn Experience Points like any other vehicle, and roll on the Vehicles table for any battle honours they earn.

INDEPENDENT CHARACTERS

Some characters do not have to be part of a particular squad, such as Space Marine commanders and Eldar Phoenix Lords. These characters earn Experience Points in the same way as units. If they earned any particular Experience Points having joined a unit they will earn the same amount of points as the unit as a whole. If the character has a bodyguard or retinue of any type, it is counted as part of that unit for the purposes of gaining Experience Points and battle honours, and all results apply to the character and unit as a whole.

EARNING EXPERIENCE

FOUGHT IN BATTLE .... +150

For every battle the unit takes part in, it earns +150 Experience Points.

ON WINNING SIDE .... +50

If the unit is on the side that won the battle it gains +50 Experience Points.

BROKE AN ENEMY IN ASSAULT .... +100

If the unit forces an enemy unit to fall back after an assault, or if it wipes the unit out by destroying all models in the unit, or if it destroys them as a result of a Sweeping Advance, or if it destroys a vehicle in an assault, it earns +100 Experience Points.

REDUCED TO HALF STRENGTH/VEHICLE DESTROYED .... -D3X100

If the unit is reduced to 50% or less of its original numbers, or is a vehicle that suffered lasting damage (ie, it has been immobilised or had a main or ordnance weapon destroyed), then it loses a number of Experience Points equal to a roll of D3 multiplied by 100. This is deducted from the Experience Points earned from this battle but does not reduce the unit or vehicle below the Experience it had prior to the battle.

WIPED OUT/VEHICLE DESTROYED .... -100 FROM TOTAL

If the unit is wiped out, or falls back off the table, or is a vehicle that is destroyed, then it gains no Experience from the battle at all. In addition, the unit loses 100 Experience Points from its total at the start of the battle (which may take it to below 0 Experience Points).

ACTING BEYOND THE CALL OF DUTY .... +D6X10

At the end of the battle, each player can nominate one unit in his army that he thinks has performed particularly admirably. The unit receives +D6x10 Experience Points, and a nice shiny medal/squig/gemstone or whatever.

REGROUPING .... +50

A unit that passes a Leadership test to regroup after having failed a Morale check earns +50 Experience Points ("he who fights and runs away, lives to fight another day!")

ACHIEVING MISSION OBJECTIVES .... +100

Most missions determine the winner by adding up the number of 'scoring units' who have achieved their objective (see the scenario special rules section on page 85). If the unit is counted as a scoring unit for the purposes of determining the winning side, it gains +100 Experience Points.

All of these Experience Points awards are cumulative with each other. For example, a unit is on the winning side and earned 100 Experience Points by achieving the mission objective, but was reduced to half strength doing so. In addition, the player decides the unit's courageous actions have earned it the award for 'acting beyond the call of duty'. The unit would have earned the following Experience Points:

EXPERIENCE POINTS	
Fighting	+150
Winning	+50
Achieving mission objective	+100
Half strength (if D3x100 result equals 200)	-200
Acting beyond the call of duty (D6x10 equals 40)	+40
Experience Points for battle	+140

EFFECTS OF EXPERIENCE POINTS

As a unit gains or loses Experience and its status changes, it will gain certain benefits or suffer penalties. For every 1,000 Experience Points a unit earns, it gains a battle honour. Each battle honour is represented by a bonus, depending on the type of unit. For every battle honour a unit gains, make one D6 roll on the appropriate Battle Honours table.

Just as units gain rolls on the Battle Honours tables by accumulating Experience Points, they can lose those battle honours they have earned by losing Experience Points. Should a unit's Experience Point total drop below a 1,000 Experience Point threshold, it will lose one randomly determined battle honour. This represents the unit losing experienced soldiers and grizzled veterans who possess those skills.

For example, Squad Morlok, an infantry squad of the 8th Valhallan Imperial Guard regiment, has earned a total of 2,050 Experience Points and two battle honours, Street Fighters and Grizzled Veterans, throughout a long and gruelling campaign. Following a particularly costly defeat, during which the unit took heavy casualties and fell back off the table, it lost 100 Experience Points, reducing its total to 1,950. As this takes it below a 1,000 Experience Point threshold, the players agree that on a roll of 1, 2 or 3 the Street Fighters battle honour will be lost, and on 4, 5 or 6, the Grizzled Veterans battle honour will be lost. The owning player rolls a 4, and the unit loses Grizzled Veterans.

BECOMING ELITE

A unit from the Troops, Heavy Support or Fast Attack sections of the army list with 3,000 or more Experience Points becomes Elite. These specialised troops are often called upon to fight in other battles and their availability is therefore limited. To represent this, Troops, Fast Attack and Heavy Support units with 3,000+ Experience Points count as Elites for choosing the army, deployment and so on in subsequent battles.

Designer's Note: *You will notice that, beyond a unit becoming elite, there is no cost incurred for becoming more experienced. This is because, so long as all the players in a campaign are playing the same number of games, they all have an equal chance of gaining Experience. In campaigns where a larger number of players are 'dropping in' to play games as and when they are able you might like to impose a cost of 10% of the unit's points value per battle honour, to even things out between those players that have played lots of games, and those that haven't. For example, a Tau Fire Warrior team costing 120 points, and having two battle honours would cost 144 points. Experience shows that charging a points cost for battle honours sometimes discourages players from making use of the battle honours system, as they must frequently alter their army lists, but we recommend this method if it's best for your campaign and your players.*

EXPERIENCE IN DIFFERENT MISSIONS

RESCUE MISSION

If the unit is in possession of the objective at the end of the game, it gains +200 Experience Points.

MEAT GRINDER MISSION

Every surviving unit on the winning side that counts as a scoring unit gains +150 Experience Points. Bear in mind that a unit brought back onto the table under the Sustained Attack scenario special rule counts as a different unit for the purposes of a campaign – the original will be counted as wiped out. Losing a battle in which your own side used the Meat Grinder tactic is a gruelling experience for the survivors, and so if the attacker loses, none of his units gain any Experience Points at all, though they can still lose them.

BUNKER ASSAULT MISSION

Every scoring unit occupying an uncontested bunker at the end of the battle gains +100 Experience Points.

SABOTAGE MISSION

If the unit destroys the objective it gains +100 Experience Points.

STRONGPOINT ASSAULT MISSION

Every scoring unit occupying an uncontested bunker at the end of the battle gains +100 Experience Points.

BREAKOUT MISSION

Every unit that leaves the table via a short table edge gains +100 Experience Points.

CHANGING A UNIT

A unit gains Experience by working together as a team and growing more familiar with its weapons. If new recruits are brought in, the unit's Experience will deteriorate as the overall level of expertise is brought down. This is represented by losing Experience Points when the unit is reduced to half strength or wiped out.

However, if a unit is issued new equipment or otherwise has its role altered, it may have to spend some time regaining its Experience, though it is also possible for a unit to be changed and the fighters to take to their new role without any loss of Experience. For every change made to a unit (each new member, different leader and so on), make a standard Leadership test. If the test is passed, the change has no effect on the unit, if the test is failed the unit loses a number of Experience Points as indicated on the chart.

For vehicles, use the Leadership characteristics listed on the chart.

VEHICLE LEADERSHIP	
Chaos Space Marines	9
Dark Eldar	8
Eldar	8
Imperial Guard	7
Lost and the Damned	6
Orks	7
Sisters of Battle	8
Space Marines	8
Tau	7

RETRAINING

Having failed the Leadership test for making a change, and determining the amount of Experience a unit will lose, it might prove time to send the unit back to boot camp for some retraining. You may choose to immediately retire the unit from the campaign for a number of battles, rather than reducing its Experience. For every battle the unit misses, it avoids losing 100 Experience Points for making a change. For example, an Imperial Guard Infantry squad has just had its Sergeant upgraded to a Veteran Sergeant, and been issued with frag grenades. Unfortunately, the player failed the Leadership test for the change of equipment (the farmboys didn't know whether to throw the grenade or the pin!). The unit would lose 100 Experience Points, but the player decides it will miss its next battle (while they receive retraining on their newfangled weapons or the respect of their new leader), and thus stay on the same Experience.

EXPERIENCE AND CODEXES

Some Warhammer 40,000 Codexes have details of how Experience relates to certain armies. For example, Necrons, being automatons devoid of any individual identity, do not learn from their experiences and do not gain battle honours. Other books may contain details of how units can gain bonus Experience Points, such as Codex: Daemonhunters, which awards any Daemonhunters unit +400 Experience Points should it slay a Greater Daemon.

Furthermore, Battlezone Codexes, such as Codex: Battlezone Cityfight, may contain extra battle honours that can be earned by units fighting a campaign in the specific environment detailed in that book. In most cases, units will be able to make use of both the battle honours detailed here, and those detailed in the book in question. Either way, see the relevant book for further details of yet more ways in which your units can advance and become veterans in your campaigns.

BATTLE HONOURS

Once a unit has accumulated 1,000 Experience Points, it rolls on the appropriate Battle Honours table. Each battle honour is represented by a re-roll, which may be used once per battle. This might be a re-roll of a failed To Wound dice, which could be used in either the Shooting phase, or in the Assault phase, or it could be a re-roll of failed Cover Saves. In every case, the re-roll applies to the entire unit, and all dice of the type specified must be re-rolled, even successful ones, and the result of the re-roll accepted. Also note that, if the unit already has a re-roll of the specified type, perhaps thanks to twin-linked weapons or a special ability, they must abide by the universal rule of 'no re-rolling re-rolls'.

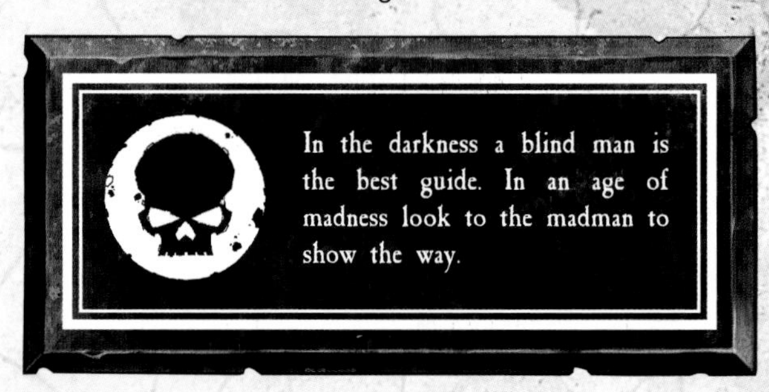

In the darkness a blind man is the best guide. In an age of madness look to the madman to show the way.

EXPERIENCE LOST FOR CHANGES

CHANGE MADE	EXPERIENCE LOST IF LD TEST FAILED
Change in numbers	-100 Experience for each squad member added or taken away.
Weapons/equipment change	-100 Experience for each weapon, piece of equipment changed.
Transport change	-100 Experience for a transport vehicle added or taken away.
Change of leader	-D3x100 Experience for changing a squad leader (adding or taking away an Exarch, Veteran Sergeant, Shas'ui, etc).

A unit may accumulate multiples of a given battle honour. For example, after gaining its first battle honour it may roll Street Fighters, allowing it to re-roll a Difficult Terrain test. Upon gaining its second battle honour, it rolls the same result. This means that the unit may re-roll two Difficult Terrain tests per game, but remember – you can't re-roll a re-roll, so each re-roll will have to be applied to a different Difficult Terrain test.

Designer's Note: *The idea of expressing a unit's ability through re-rolls is a simple one. Rather than applying special skills and abilities, which may change a unit's role or which might be inappropriate or just a pain to remember in the heat of battle, re-rolls provide a very simple way of keeping track of battle honours. Re-rolls do not make a unit 'better' or able to do new things; what they do is make the unit more reliable at what it already does. At the end of the day, that is what you, as the general of your army, are looking for most in your troops.*

If you wish to play in a campaign, it is a good idea to fill out a unit roster card for each squad and vehicle in your army. This card then becomes a record of the unit over your following battles. As units fight they will lose or gain Experience and any new skills or abilities they gain or penalties they suffer from are noted on the card. If you make any changes to the composition of the unit you alter the card to show this, and make up new roster cards if you add any more units to your army. Use the space on the back for noting Experience, battle honours and the unit's history.

The top line is for basic information which you can use when you're building up your force from your collection of army cards.

UNIT NAME:	UNIT TYPE:	POINTS COST:	EXPERIENCE POINTS:

Use the middle section to record the profiles of the unit's warriors and vehicles. Dreadnoughts can use either section – put their extra stats under 'Special'.

No.	TROOP TYPE	WS	BS	S	T	W	I	A	Ld	Save	Special

No.	VEHICLE TYPE	BS	Armour: Front	Side	Rear	Special

Put the unit's weapons' profiles here for easy reference during play.

WEAPONS	Range	Strength	AP	Shots	Special Rules

Classified

BATTLE HONOURS: INFANTRY, BIKES AND CAVALRY

D6	SKILL
1	**Street Fighters.** The unit may re-roll a Difficult or Dangerous Terrain test. (Jetbikes re-roll this result).
2	**Grizzled Veterans.** The unit may re-roll failed To Wound rolls from a single player turn of close combat or shooting.
3	**Seasoned Campaigner.** The unit may re-roll a failed Morale check (Fearless units re-roll this result).
4	**Tank Killers.** The unit may re-roll a failed Armour Penetration roll.
5	**Natural Survivors.** If the unit is the loser in an assault, it may re-roll its test to break off.
6	**Rapid Deployment.** If held in reserve, the unit may re-roll its Reserves roll.

All non-vehicle units roll on this chart for battle honours.

CAMPAIGN MODELLING

As well as finding ways to represent battle honours skills on your troops and vehicles, you might want to consider adding extra equipment, war paint, tokens and kill markings to old and new squads as they take part in the campaign.

Here are some examples of characters and squads that have earned their spurs on the battlefield.

Street Fighters *– Guardsman Kintaro, of the Cadian 3rd, has stripped his heavy bolter down to the bare essentials to allow for swifter movement through hindering terrain.*

Grizzled Veterans *– Khârvath, self-proclaimed prophet of the Chaos gods, records the name of every foe he has slain in a tome chained to his power armour.*

Seasoned Campaigner *– The suit of armour of the Exarch Ulthanuir has many distinctive trophies crafted into it, silent testimony to hundreds of campaigns, fought over a thousand lifetimes.*

Tank Killers *– Brother Masakari of the Helion Legion is an accomplished demolition expert, and always keeps a melta bomb close to hand for unexpected encounters.*

Natural Survivors *– Corporal Andor, of the Vernian XIth, is a veteran of many vicious assaults, and has the severed heads of his foes as the trophies to prove it.*

Rapid Deployment *– Like many in the White Scars Space Marine Chapter, Brother Torias specialises in lightning raids and has extensively customised his bike for greater speed.*

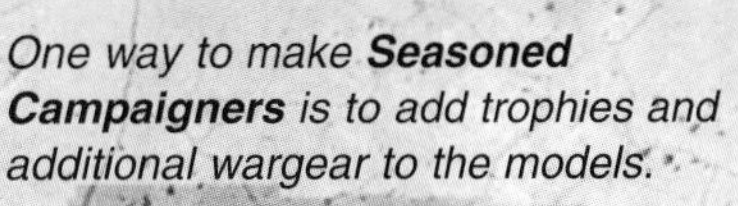

One way to make **Seasoned Campaigners** is to add trophies and additional wargear to the models.

The Carnifex has the remnants of an Eldar jetbike modelled onto it.

An Ork with an 'eavy shoota has a grisly Cadian head trophy.

A converted Disc of Tzeentch has been added to this Chaos Lord.

The helmets on this Ork Nob's bosspole have been painted to represent the different Space Marine Chapters he has faced.

A shoulder pad from the White Scars Space Marines has been added to this Nob.

This Tyranid Hunter has a piece of carapace added as an armoured shoulder pad and carries a knife made from a claw of a Gaunt attached to the knife haft.

This Ork Warlord has literally grown in stature during the course of a campaign. He starting out based on an Ogryn body, then a Warboss model and was eventually replaced by a converted Ghazghkull Thraka, with a pair of bionic eyes.

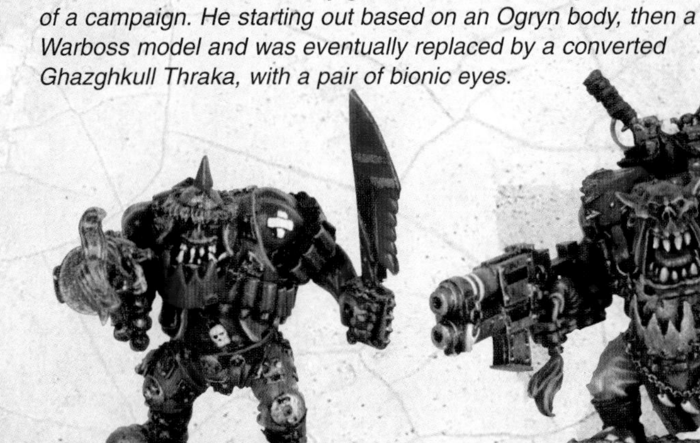

VEHICLE BATTLE HONOURS

D6	SKILL
1	**Terrifying.** The owning player may request that an enemy unit Tank Shocked by the vehicle re-roll its Morale check (Walkers re-roll this result).
2	**Hardened Crew.** The owning player may request that the result of a glancing hit scored against the vehicle is re-rolled.
3	**Reinforced armour.** The owning player may request that the result of a penetrating hit scored against the vehicle is re-rolled.
4	**Skilled Gunnery.** The vehicle may re-roll a failed To Hit roll, or may re-roll the Scatter dice.
5	**Skilled Pilot.** The vehicle may re-roll a Dangerous Terrain test (Skimmers re-roll this result).
6	**Tank Killers.** The vehicle may re-roll a failed Armour Penetration roll.

All vehicle units roll on this chart for battle honours.

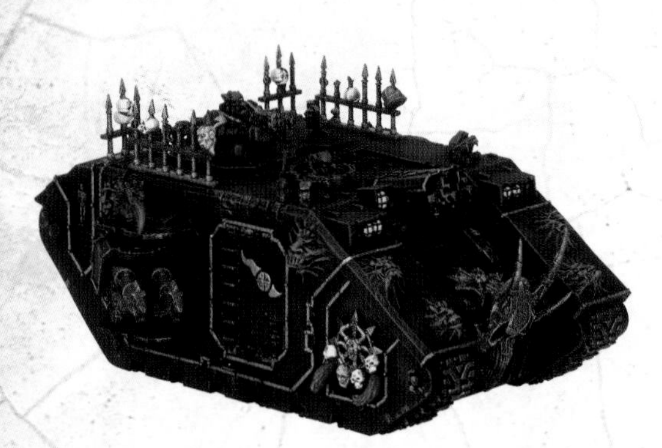

Terrifying *– The Chaos Land Raider Shrieking Death has assimilated the souls of those it has ground beneath its tracks, and emits a hellish roar as it smashes through the enemy lines.*

Hardened Crew *– The numerous purity seals, battle scars and campaign badges that festoon Brother Dorn's armoured carapace speak loudly of his illustrious history and war skill.*

Reinforced Armour *– This Leman Russ, from the Karax Defence force, has had the armour on its tracks reinforced, reducing its vulnerability to incoming fire.*

Skilled Gunnery *– Falcon grav tank pilots of the Saim-Hann craftworld are fiercely competitive in their battle record, painting a symbol on the gun turret of their vehicle for each enemy they destroy.*

Skilled Pilot *– The Bloodreaper, a heavily modified Defiler dedicated to Khorne, has 'evolved' an extra set of legs to better assist it in traversing potentially harmful terrain.*

Tank Killers *– The Sentinels of the Catachan Jungle Fighters are heavily camouflaged, all the better to buy those few extra seconds when finding a weak point in a foe's armour.*

Trophies and purity seals can represent ***Hardened Crew****.*

The base of this Sentinel features the body of a Black Templar Space Marine, a foe from a long-running campaign.

This Dark Angels Space Marines Dreadnought has extra armour plates and purity seals.

A Tyranid head has been added to this Battlewagon to taunt their alien opponents.

This Ork Battlewagon is liberally covered in trophies and kill markings.

BATTLE OF PHOENIX ISLAND

Armageddon Steel Legion units, supported by Thunderhawks of the Black Dragons Chapter of the Adeptus Astartes, landed at the relatively small Victorinus Airfield on Phoenix Island, responding to the Ork landings in the north that would cut off Imperial supply lines and cripple the war effort. Arriving just as the indigenous defence regiments were brought to their knees by the Ork assault, the Steel Legion and their Black Dragons allies found they were too late in many locations. Heliopolis Bridge had been completely destroyed, cutting the island off from reinforcements. The Orks had sent saboteur teams to destroy supply lines in Nadala Gorge ore mine and Ibis Reef Harbour. At Jabiru Quay, several gigatankers had been sunk in their berths by Ork Fighta-Bommerz, and the already polluted atmosphere of Phoenix Island was rapidly becoming totally unbreathable when the Imperium's armies struck.

The Imperium's forces were given the task of reclaiming those areas of Phoenix Island that had already fallen to the Orks. The Greenskins had made destruction their priority, burning acres and acres of land around the mineral storage facilities and Nadala Gorge. As the atmosphere became so caustic that it burnt unprotected skin, more and more of the Imperial defence forces stationed there went underground or fled the island completely, and only the Black Dragons were left to close in on the enemy. The Ork saboteurs were soon surrounded, and vicious close-quarter fighting erupted. Many of the Orks fled into the burning seas rather than face the wrath of the Dragon Claws, elites of the Black Dragons whose slashing bony crests and devastating charges had earned them a fearsome reputation amongst the ranks of their enemies.

It was at Valkyrie Bay refinery where the fate of the island was sealed. As hundreds of Orks set about the destruction of the facility, the Black Dragons attacked. Small arms fire riddled holes in cylinders full of poisonous chemicals, and the combatants were soon ankle-deep in corrosive slime and steaming acids. The Ork saboteurs could not escape the tide of volatile substances, and many died as their legs gave way and they collapsed into the lethal streams. The power armour of the Black Dragons protected them from harm, and they slaughtered their prey with a minimum of casualties. Sadly, the refinery is now useless to the Imperium, and this will undoubtedly break the back of major supply routes from the burning husk of Phoenix Island.

The task of consolidating what territory has been reclaimed now falls to the men and women of the Steel Legions, who have accepted the challenge of purging their homeworld of the Ork menace with grim resolve and stoic determination. Each has vowed to fight to the last in the name of the God-Emperor of Mankind.

Excerpt from Volume V, Chaper XII, The Chronicles of Armageddon

This section presents an example of a complete campaign. The Battle of Phoenix Island was a conflict that took place during the first phase of the Third Armageddon War, when the forces of the Ork Warlord Ghazghkull Mag Uruk Thraka returned fifty-seven years to the day after their first invasion had all but crippled the hive world. Phoenix Island was the scene of bitter fighting as a number of Ork roks dropped from orbit onto the island with the aim of capturing or destroying its vital refineries. Although initial defender casualties were heavy, the tenacity of the local Imperial Guard units, supported by the Black Dragons Chapter of the Adeptus Astartes, eventually put paid to the Orks' plans.

The campaign as presented here is effectively a ladder campaign, but the ladder is superimposed over a map of Phoenix Island, meaning that each 'node' in the campaign forms a pivotal battle in terms of both progress through the campaign and land controlled by each player.

Taking the background for the battle, we decided that each location on the map would correspond to a certain mission. Furthermore, as there are several potential routes between nodes, some easier to use than others, we decided that a dice roll was appropriate to cross certain areas.

Designer's Note: *You will notice that the campaign starts in the middle of the action, with the Orks already having captured a number of nodes on the campaign map. The reason for this is that experience shows that requiring an invading army to fight from a 'beachhead', with no territory held at the beginning of a campaign, can result in a few false starts should the invader have a run of bad luck at the beginning. It can also feel like a bit of an uphill struggle for the attacker, so we have started the Orks off on an equal footing to the Imperium's defenders.*

PLAYING THE CAMPAIGN

To play the Battle of Phoenix Island you will need two players, preferably one playing Imperial Guard or Space Marines and the other Orks, although there is no reason the background should not be adapted to cover any other armies you have available. For this example we've chosen to use the Armageddon Steel Legions and Orks.

The starting territories of each player are noted in the description of each node. At the beginning of each campaign turn, each player uses their army's Strategy Rating to decide who goes first to attack an occupied node, or move into and claim an unoccupied one. The player that won the Strategy roll may move into and occupy a single adjacent unclaimed node, or declare that he is attacking the other player if the node is occupied by the enemy. In either case, each player can only move or attack once each turn. If the result of a battle is a draw, each side withdraws and the node becomes unoccupied.

Each node contains a description of the area, what missions should be fought there, and any special notes that apply to terrain.

Routes between nodes may sometimes have a difficulty number attached. If this is the case, the player must roll equal to or higher than the number given in order to cross the area. If the roll is unsuccessful the route may not be crossed this turn, and the battle is not fought. Routes may not be occupied.

The campaign is deemed over when one player has captured all of the nodes.

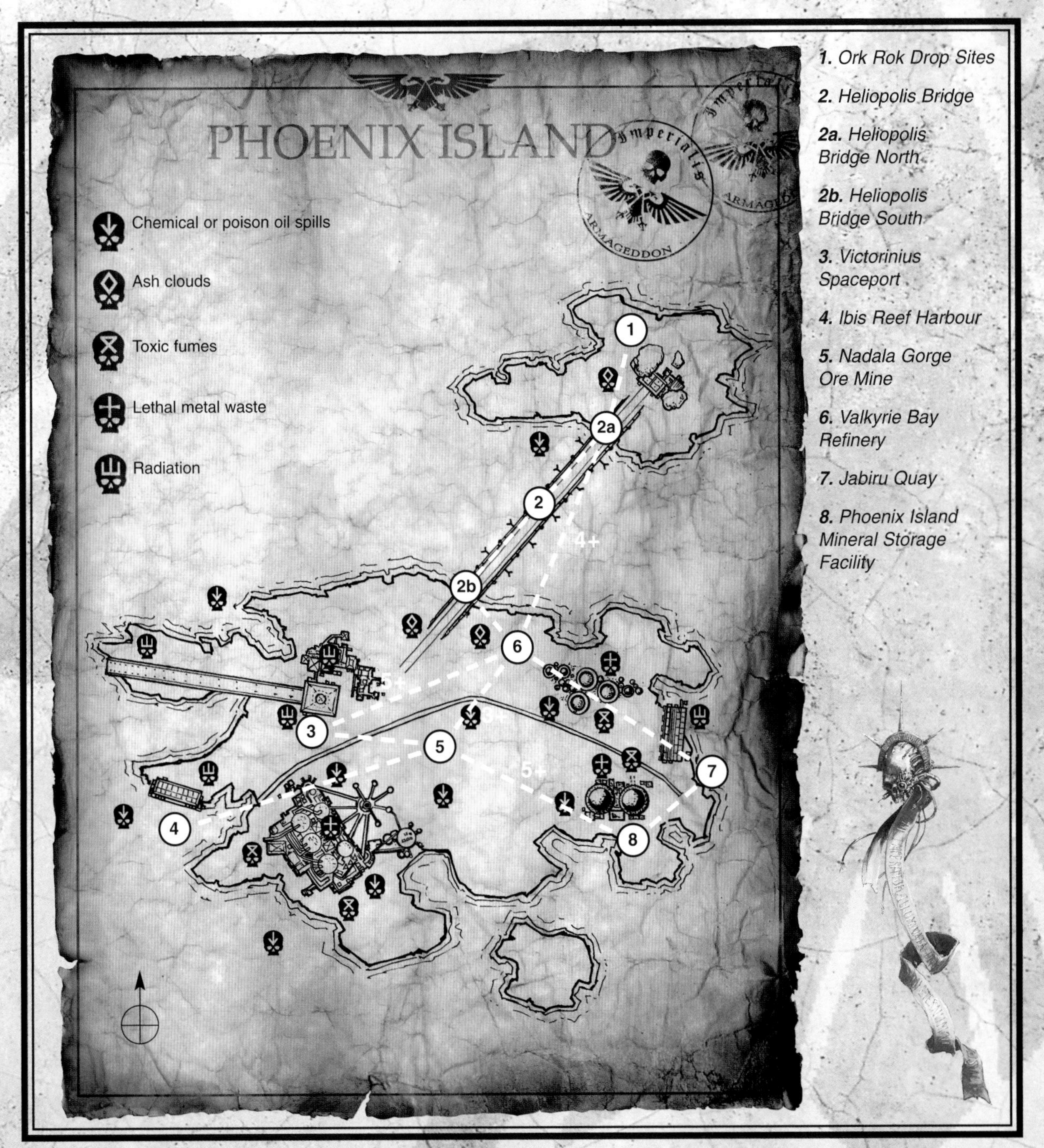

1. ORK ROK DROP SITES

Dozens of Ork roks have made landings throughout Armageddon, providing Ghazghkull's forces with gigantic ready-made citadels. Not only are these monstrous asteroid fortresses crammed with guns and missiles, but they also contain giant teleporter arrays the Ork Meks use to bring down Gargants, troops and heavy artillery to the planet's surface in vast numbers. The Phoenix Island rok has landed on the landward site of Heliopolis Bridge, cutting off the island from reinforcements that cannot be airlifted into Victorinius Airfield.

The Ork Rok Drop Sites begin the game in Ork hands.

Roll a D6 for missions played at this node:

D6	Mission played
1-2	Strongpoint Attack
3-6	Bunker Assault

Terrain in this area should be heavily fortified, with kunning Orky traps scattered about.

2. HELIOPOLIS BRIDGE

The entire length of the vast landbridge that links Phoenix Island with the Fire Wastes is defended by armoured bastions, guns and defence emplacements strong enough to hold off all but the most overwhelming enemies. It is defended on both sides by heavily fortified bunkers and vehicle traps. The Fire Wastes side has seen heavy fighting when the Ork rok landed and smashed these defences in their assault on the island. The roadway of the bridge is buckled and twisted, littered with burnt-out wreckage of Ork buggies and wartrukks.

Heliopolis Bridge begins the game held by the Orks.

Roll a D6 for missions played at this node:

D6	Mission played
1-4	Patrol
5-6	Take and Hold

Terrain in this area should be largely open, with scant cover afforded by wreckage and debris.

2A HELIOPOLIS BRIDGE NORTH

The north side of Heliopolis Bridge begins the game held by the Orks.

Roll a D6 for missions played at this node:

D6	Mission played
1-4	Blitz
5-6	Sabotage

2B HELIOPOLIS BRIDGE SOUTH

The south side of Heliopolis Bridge begins the game uncontested.

Roll a D6 for missions played at this node:

D6	Mission played
1-4	Seek and Destroy
5-6	Blitz

Terrain in this area should be set up according to the guidance given in the 'Organising a Battle' section.

3. VICTORINIUS SPACEPORT

Squadrons of Thunderbolts and Furies are based at Victorinius to provide air cover for the island as well as mounting strikes against Ork convoys and seaborne craft. Hardened underground hangars shelter the base's aircraft and the runways are constructed from modular adamantium segments that allow any damage to be repaired extremely rapidly. The base is defended from aerial attack by batteries of Hydras and from ground attack by a multitude of bunkers, defensive lines and regiments of the Imperial Guard. The Black Dragons Chapter of the Adeptus Astartes are currently preparing for a massed Thunderhawk landing at Victorinius to prevent the Nadala Gorge ore mine from falling into Ork hands.

Victorinius Spaceport begins the game in Imperial hands.

Roll a D6 for missions played at this node:

D6	Mission played
1-4	Patrol
5-6	Secure and Control

Terrain in this area should be set up with as many wrecked or damaged fortifications as you can muster.

4. IBIS REEF HARBOUR

The Imperial craft that escort the ore-laden gigatanker convoys across the Boiling Sea are berthed at Ibis Reef on the west coast of Phoenix Island. This military base is heaviliy fortified and is surrounded on the landward side by deep lines of trenches, bunkers and artillery. It also benefits from the protection of Imperial aircraft stationed at Victorinius Airfield. The seaward flank is constantly patrolled and is seeded with hundreds of minefields that require extremely precise information to navigate.

Ibis Reef Harbour begins the game in Imperial hands.

Roll a D6 for missions played at this node:

D6	Mission played
1-4	Patrol
5	Cleanse
6	Seek and Destroy

Terrain in this area should be feature as many fortifications, trenches and vehicle traps as possible.

5. NADALA GORGE ORE MINE

This drift mine provides many of the raw materials required to continue the war effort on Armageddon. The vast mine has cut deep into the planet and has created a highly toxic environment, continually blanketed in impenetrable clouds of ash and smoke. Ancient machineries and millennia old technologies continue to harvest the minerals beneath the island's surface and should many more of these mines fall into Ork hands, the war on Armageddon is lost.

Nadala Gorge Ore Mine begins the game in Ork hands.

Night Fight missions are fought at this node.

Terrain in the Nadala Gorge Ore Mine area should be set up to represent a hellish landscape of pollution, with chemical drifts as tall as a man, acid pools, corroded machinery and all manner of other such nasty terrain.

A Heretic may see the truth and seek redemption. He may be forgiven his past and will be absolved in death. A Traitor can never be forgiven. A Traitor will never find peace in this world or the next. There is nothing as wretched or as hated in all the world as a Traitor.

Cardinal Khrysdam - Instructum Absolutio

6. VALKYRIE BAY REFINERY

The vast ore refining facility produces invaluable chemicals and raw materials for the forges and machine shops of Armageddon. Its enormous filtration tanks and processing bays cover hundreds of square miles with twisting pipes, chemical spills and towering chimneys that spew corrosive fumes into the air, rendering the land uninhabitable for hundreds of miles in all directions. These refineries are vital to the continued resistance of Armageddon and without them the production of arms and ordnance will cease completely.

Valkyrie Bay Refinery begins the game uncontested.

Roll a D6 for missions played at this node:

D6	Mission played
1-2	Strongpoint Attack
3-5	Sabotage
6	Bunker Assault

The Valkyrie Bay Refinery area should be the most densely set up of the battlefields, with towering chimneys and massive storage tanks commonplace. If playing a Sabotage mission, try to find or build the most impressively dangerous and polluted looking storage tank possible to use as the objective.

7. JABIRU QUAY

Gigatankers laden with refined mineral ore from Valkyrie Bay transport their invaluable cargoes to the weapon shops of Armageddon from the easten docks of Phoenix Island. Hundreds of freight containers, lifting machines and mag-loader rails cover the ground here. The facility has suffered heavy damage from Ork Fighta-Bommerz, and the air defences are stretched to the limit in keeping the port open. Several tankers have been sunk in their berths, disastrously spilling billions of tonnes of weapons grade ore into the sea and fierce battles have been fought on the quayside between Ork saboteurs and Imperial defenders.

Jabiru Quay begins the game in Imperial hands.

Roll a D6 for missions played at this node:

D6	Mission played
1-3	Patrol
4-5	Cleanse
6	Sabotage

Terrain in this area should be set up to represent the industrial sprawl of Jabiru Quay, with plenty of cover for models to sneak around in.

8. PHOENIX ISLAND MINERAL STORAGE FACILITY

Precious minerals produced by the ore refineries that await shipping across the Boiling Sea are stored here. Huge warehouses packed with giant drums of chemicals pollute the landscape and exude toxic fumes. The defences of this region are largely automated due to the highly volatile chemicals stored here and regiments stationed at this facility are regularly rotated due to the hazardous nature of the posting.

Phoenix Island Mineral Storage Facility begins the game in Imperial hands.

Roll a D6 for missions played at this node:

D6	Mission played
1-2	Seek and Destroy
3-4	Take and Hold
5-6	Cleanse

The terrain for this area should be relatively built up, with lots of cover afforded by as many fuel drums as you can muster.

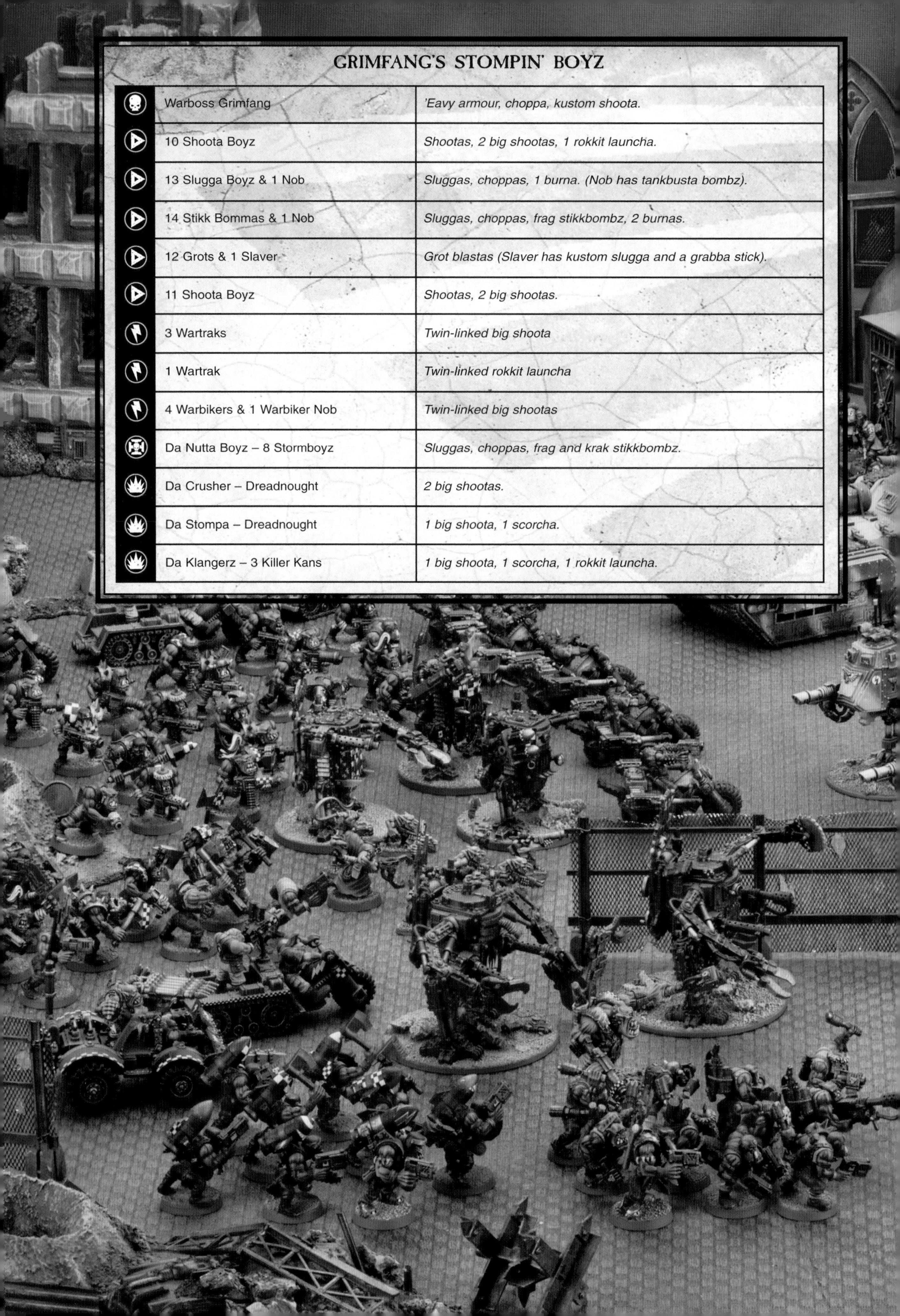

GRIMFANG'S STOMPIN' BOYZ

Unit	Wargear
Warboss Grimfang	*'Eavy armour, choppa, kustom shoota.*
10 Shoota Boyz	*Shootas, 2 big shootas, 1 rokkit launcha.*
13 Slugga Boyz & 1 Nob	*Sluggas, choppas, 1 burna. (Nob has tankbusta bombz).*
14 Stikk Bommas & 1 Nob	*Sluggas, choppas, frag stikkbombz, 2 burnas.*
12 Grots & 1 Slaver	*Grot blastas (Slaver has kustom slugga and a grabba stick).*
11 Shoota Boyz	*Shootas, 2 big shootas.*
3 Wartraks	*Twin-linked big shoota*
1 Wartrak	*Twin-linked rokkit launcha*
4 Warbikers & 1 Warbiker Nob	*Twin-linked big shootas*
Da Nutta Boyz – 8 Stormboyz	*Sluggas, choppas, frag and krak stikkbombz.*
Da Crusher – Dreadnought	*2 big shootas.*
Da Stompa – Dreadnought	*1 big shoota, 1 scorcha.*
Da Klangerz – 3 Killer Kans	*1 big shoota, 1 scorcha, 1 rokkit launcha.*

3RD BATTLEGROUP, 2ND ARMAGEDDON REGIMENT – 'THE FIREBIRDS'

Captain Kamarov's Command Squad	*Frag and krak grenades, heavy bolter, plasma gun, trademark item (sword), Xenos Hunters (Orks). Mounted in a Chimera.*
Lieutenant Lemesk's Command Section	*Frag grenades, missile launcher, plasma gun, Xenos Hunters (Orks). Mounted in a Chimera with a searchlight.*
Squad Primus	*Frag grenades, heavy bolter, grenade launcher, Xenos Hunters (Orks). Mounted in a Chimera.*
Squad Secundus	*Frag grenades, heavy bolter, grenade launcher, Xenos Hunters (Orks). Mounted in a Chimera.*
The Forlorn (*6 man Remnant Squad*)	*Plasma gun, Xenos Hunters (Orks). Mounted in a Chimera.*
Squad Tertius (*Armoured Fist Squad*)	*Missile launcher, plasma gun, Xenos Hunters (Orks). Mounted in a Chimera with extra armour.*
Cerberus (*Hellhound*)	*Inferno cannon*
Squad Recon (*Sentinel Squadron*)	*Lascannon, Xenos Hunters (Orks).*
The Deadeyes (*Ratling Snipers*)	*Sniper rifles*
Old Reliable (*Leman Russ*)	*Heavy bolter sponsons, hull-mounted lascannon.*

PHOENIX ISLAND - MULTI-PURPOSE TERRAIN

While you can create dedicated sets of gaming scenery for each battlezone in your campaign, it is possible to create boards that are just as enjoyable to game over with only a few large, focal pieces (such as a ruined factory complex) or a series of smaller, more general pieces. The boards on these pages were put together from only six focal pieces of terrain used in slightly different combinations with the following multi-purpose terrain pieces.

Five rubble heaps (hills) made from insulation foam and spare miniature components.

Tank traps from the Warhammer 40,000 Obstacles and Barricades set.

Four chain-link fences made from aluminium bodywork mesh and balsa wood.

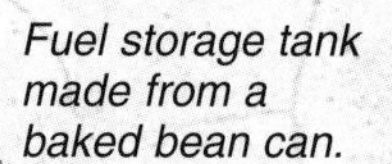

Fuel storage tank made from a baked bean can.

Two craters made from insulation foam.

VALKYRIE BAY REFINERY

The Valkyrie Bay Refinery consists of acres of filtration tanks, processing bays and countless miles of pipeline. Should the refinery fall to the Orks, the vital supplies of chemicals and raw materials will be severed – scores of factories across Armageddon will no longer be able to support the war effort.

Two sizable ruined buildings and a set of storage tanks form the focus of this board – the refinery complex itself. The remaining terrain has been used to suggest the idea of a perimeter about the refinery. It's worth noting how the terrain has been set up diagonally across the board, creating a sense of depth.

NADALA GORGE ORE MINE

Nadala Gorge is of vital importance to the continuing struggle against the Ork invasion. Countless assaults and counter-attacks have left the mine a battle-scarred and ruined site, with innummerable mortal remains lying scattered amongst the craters and acid pools.

As with the Valkyrie Bay Refinery board, the focal point of this table is formed by a pair of ruined buildings. The presence of the mining tower completely alters the theme of the terrain set, proving that very different layouts can be achieved with only a little variety in terrain.

VICTORINIUS SPACEPORT

This spaceport board is a little more ambitious than the others, using several new pieces of terrain, including a foam-board runway. Despite this, all of the multi-purpose terrain pieces make a reappearance to add depth and character to the board.

With underground hangars harbouring Thunderhawks and Furies, Victorinius Spaceport is the lynchpin for the defence of Phoenix Island. It is from here that the Black Dragons Space Marine Chapter launch their counter-attacks against the Orks.

THE GAMING HOBBY

The Warhammer 40,000 hobby is enormous. Underneath the surface of the rules and miniatures is a massive range of ideas and activities for you to take a look at. Over the next few pages we'll try to open your eyes to a few of these extra hobby activities and ideas, and hopefully show you the door into the vastness that is Warhammer 40,000. Whatever you do with the game, however, we hope you'll enjoy it for a very long time to come.

EVENTS

GAMING SHOWS

Gaming shows are all about showing the hobby. Organised both by Games Workshop and other groups of hobbyists, including some clubs or independent retailers, these events are always a popular addition to many people's Warhammer 40,000 experience. Most commonly shows are all about seeing some cool games, chatting to new people, and hopefully picking up the odd new model or tip that can make a difference to your own hobby.

TOURNAMENTS

One of the parts of the Warhammer 40,000 hobby are the tournaments which take place in most countries at some time in the annual calendar. Some of the most prestigious tournaments are organised by Games Workshop, under the banner of the Grand Tournament. There are, however, countless other competitions run not only by our own staff but by other enthusiasts and fans of the game. In short, tournaments are about testing your mettle against others to see who is the cleverest tabletop general; they also encourage you to show off your painted army and allow you to meet other fanatical commanders through the act of gaming. Tournaments are not for the faint hearted, but they are open to all with the tenacity and desire to conquer – and they all reward you with a social drink in the company of other players after the duelling is done.

CAMPAIGNS

Competition is not for everyone. With this in mind, it's also possible to take part in a variety of events that are all about creating a cool story through the gaming antics of a group of players. Many of these are organised as weekend or one-day events by clubs, our staff, or independent stockists. Yet, it doesn't stop there: campaigns sometimes grow into enormous affairs, and sometimes even boil over to engulf the entire globe, such as with the Eye of Terror Campaign that took place in 2003. Whatever your interest, you are going to be able to find people to band together with to create your own campaigns and exciting adventures on the battlefields of the 41st millennium. We reckon that you'll find something to broaden even the hoariest veteran's experience of the game we all enjoy – Warhammer 40,000.

GAMES DAYS

Each year across the globe Games Workshop hosts a series of Games Day events to showcase the whole of the hobby, including not only Warhammer 40,000 but our other games, miniatures and cool stuff too. Each event is unique, reflecting the style and scope of the hobby in the country that hosts it, providing a variety of scenarios to try, terrain and models to marvel at, and new ideas to explore. One of the many highlights of each Games Day is the prestigious Golden Demon painting competition. Knowing that pictures say far more than we ever could with words, have a look at these snapshots of UK Games Day 2003 and soak up the sheer size and impact of the experience.

GAMING CLUBS

Gaming is a sociable hobby and you will not be surprised to hear that there are many clubs that cater for gamers of all ages and tastes. If you live in a large city, you'll find there is a local games club where Games Workshop games are played. You don't need to be part of a club to enjoy gaming, but there are plenty of advantages, and it is nice to meet people who share your own passion for gaming.

One of the great things about clubs is there's always someone willing to show you how to play a particular game or improve your painting or modelling skills. In particular, clubs always seem to harbour at least one expert scenery maker who will only be too happy to rope you into whatever huge and ambitious project he happens to be working on. Many clubs also participate in bigger public events, putting on demonstration games or displays and helping to explain about the games and models.

Clubs come in all shapes and sizes. Actually, three or more hobbyists who meet regularly to enjoy a game count as a club. If there isn't a club near you why not consider starting your own? All you need is a group of like-minded friends and a place to meet. From humble beginnings many a large gaming club has grown.

TO FIND OUT MORE...

WARHAMMER 40,000 ON THE WEB

Regularly updated as and when new boxed sets and miniatures are released, the Games Workshop website is an ideal place to go to buy your models.

You can find lots of information about painting models, details of wargaming clubs and gaming events in your area and the location of Games Workshop stores and independent stockists. A large part of the Games Workshop website is dedicated to the wargaming community. This is a major forum that links together thousands of people across the world who are totally devoted to wargaming. Here you will find an abundance of advice written by fellow wargamers on all aspects of the hobby and also links to some of the thousands of websites on the Internet written by gamers.

Another great aspect of the site is that it enables players who live near each other to meet up and play a game. So even if you don't have a games store nearby you should be able to find a club near you or join up with someone wanting a battle.

For more details on Games Workshop releases, wargaming and hobby information, and links to our wargaming community check out:

www.games-workshop.com

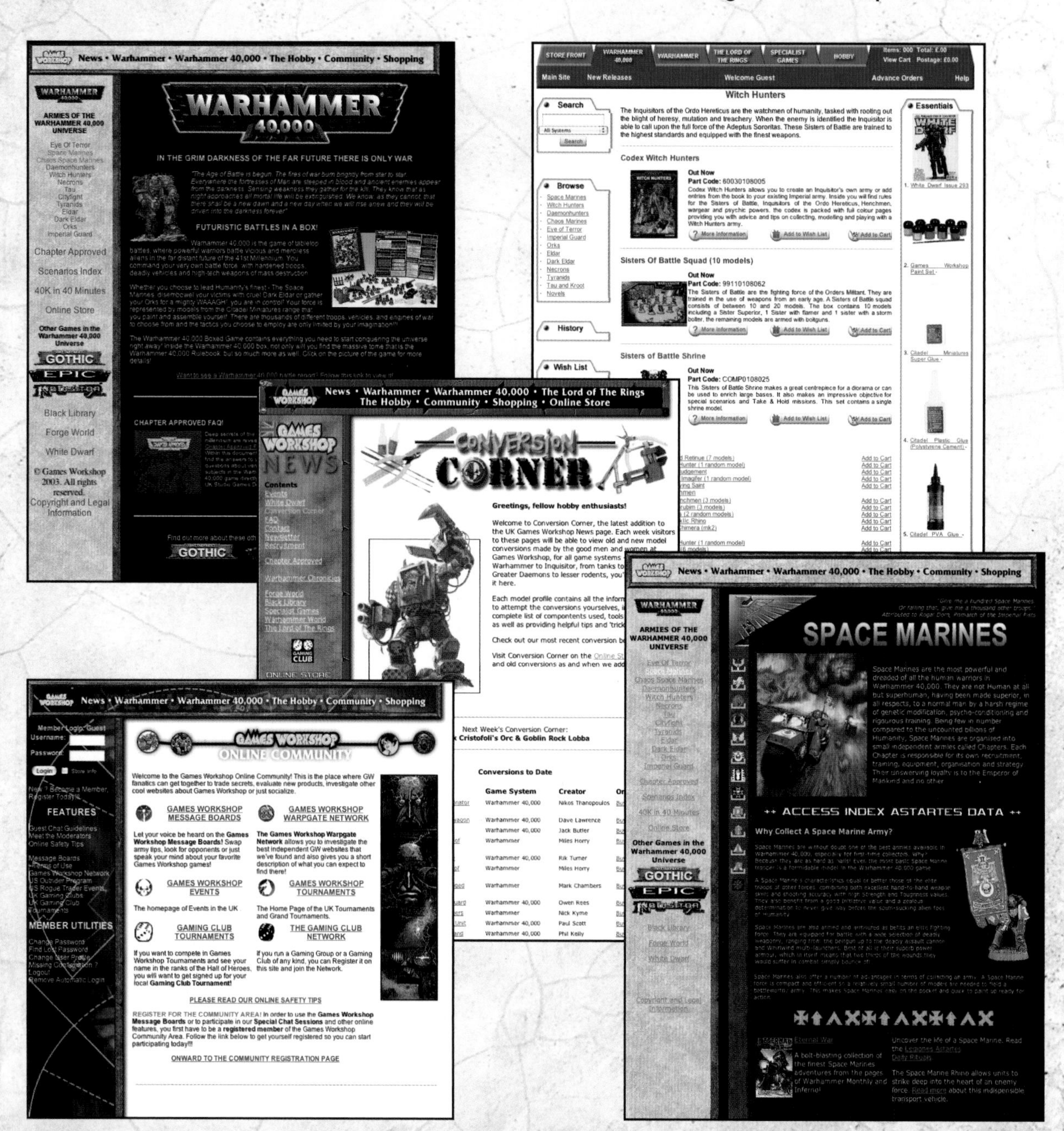

WHITE DWARF

Games Workshop's monthly hobby magazine, White Dwarf, is a great place to look if you want more information about the Warhammer 40,000 battle game or the wargaming hobby in general.

White Dwarf has loads of articles based on different aspects of Warhammer 40,000 so you can get the most out of your games, including:

- News on forthcoming releases.
- A look at the background of the 41st millennium.
- New missions to fight.
- Campaigns and battle reports.
- Advice on painting and converting your models.
- Terrain building.
- Gamer's armies.

White Dwarf is also the place to look if you want to find out where your nearest Games Workshop store or local stockist is.

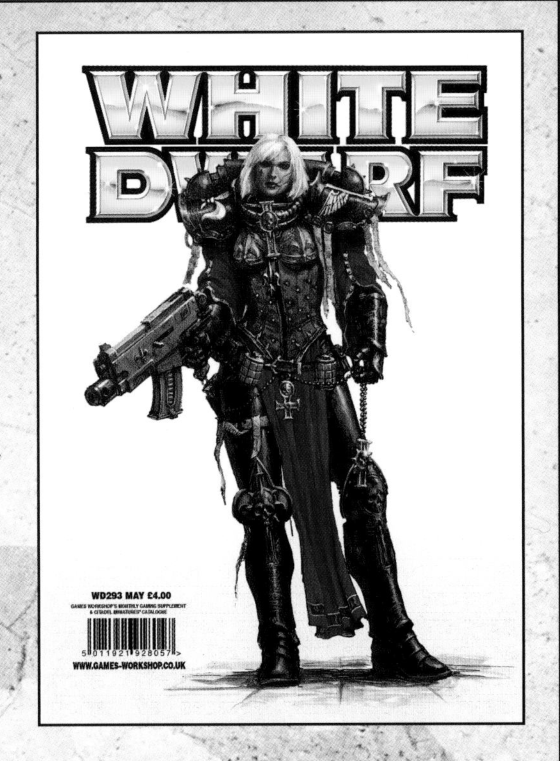

WHITE
DWARF
WD293 MAY £4.00
WWW.GAMES-WORKSHOP.CO.UK

GAMES WORKSHOP STORES

One of the best places to learn more about the game is at your local Games Workshop store. Not only can you find Warhammer 40,000 miniatures and vehicles there but also our stores are staffed by experienced gamers who can offer advice if you have any questions or wish to take part in an introductory game.

Our stores are also excellent places to meet other gamers. As most will have played other Games Workshop games, they're a good starting point if you're new to gaming.

INDEPENDENT RETAILERS

You can also find Warhammer 40,000 miniatures and books in a larger network of independent toy, hobby and game retailers across the world.

Many of these stores offer modelling advice in addition to stocking the Warhammer 40,000 range. They also stock a wide selection of Games Workshop paints and modelling equipment.

SHOWCASE – 'EAVY METAL TEAM

Grand Master Stern
Darren Latham

Death Guard Champion
Pete Foley

Imperial Guard Captain
Neil Langdown

Howling Banshee
Keith Robertson

Inquisitor
Kirsten Williams

Space Marine Sniper
Pete Foley

Ork Grot
Neil Green

Commissar Yarrick
Keith Robertson

Nurgle Daemon Prince
Seb Perbet

Ork Nob
Neil Green

Imperial Sage
Neil Green

Drazhar, Master of Blades
Keith Robertson

SHOWCASE - GOLDEN DEMON WINNERS

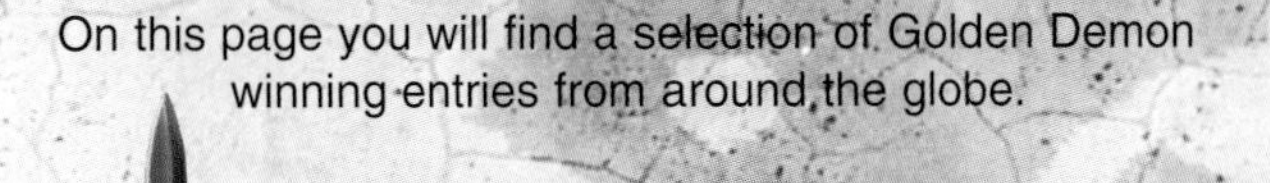

On this page you will find a selection of Golden Demon winning entries from around the globe.

Plague Marine Captain
Cyril Abati

Ulthwé Farseer Thalandee
Adam Rantz

Kroot
Michael Anderson

Sanguinius
Martin Sahlin

Eldar Farseer,
Bryan Shaw

Wulfen
Matt Gubser

Imperial Guardsman,
Joe Hill

Inquisitor,
Michael Anderson

Angels Renascent Space Marines Champion,
Jennifer Haley

EXISTING UNIT TYPES

TROOP TYPE	NEW UNIT TYPE
SPACE MARINES	
All Space Marines on foot	Infantry
All Space Marines with jump packs	Jump Infantry
All Space Marines with Bikes, Attack Bikes	Bikes
Dreadnoughts, Land Speeders, Predators, Rhinos, Whirlwinds, Land Raiders, Razorbacks, Vindicators	Vehicle
IMPERIAL GUARD	
All men on foot including Ogryns and Ratlings	Infantry
Rough Riders	Cavalry
Sentinels, Chimeras, Basilisks, Leman Russ & Demolisher	Vehicles
INQUISITION	
All troops on foot including Retinues & Daemonhosts	Infantry
Seraphim	Jump Infantry
Penitent Engines, Immolators, Exorcists, Rhinos Grey Knight Dreadnoughts, Land Raiders	Vehicle
ELDAR	
Avatar	Monstrous Creature
Farseers, Warlocks, Bonesingers, Guardians, Striking Scorpions, Howling Banshees, Wraithguard, Dark Reapers, Fire Dragons, Dire Avengers	Infantry
Farseers/Warlocks/Bonesingers on jet bikes, Guardian Jetbikes, Shining Spears	Eldar Jetbikes
Falcons, Fire Prism, Wave Serpent, Vyper, War Walker	Vehicle
Warp Spiders, Swooping Hawks	Jump Infantry
Wraithlords	Monstrous Creature
Grav Platform Battery	Artillery
TAU	
All models in Crisis suits, Stealth suits, Independent Drones	Jump Infantry (Jet Pack)
Ethereals, Fire Warriors, Pathfinders, Broadside teams, Kroot (even if Hounds or Ox included)	Infantry
Devilfish, Hammerhead	Vehicle
TYRANIDS	
Hive Tyrant	Monstrous Creature
Carnifex	Monstrous Creature
Rippers	Infantry – use Swarms special rule
Gargoyles	Jump Infantry
Tyrant Guard, Tyranid Warriors, Lictors, Termagants, Genestealers, Raveners, Zoanthropes, Biovores	Infantry
Hormagaunts	Beasts
Winged Hive Tyrant	Monstrous Creature (move as Jump Infantry)
Winged Tyranid Warriors or Gaunts	Jump Infantry
Leaping Tyranid Warriors or Gaunts	Beasts

TROOP TYPE NAME	NEW UNIT TYPE
CHAOS	
Lord with Daemonic Stature, Great Unclean One, Keeper of Secrets	Monstrous Creature
Lord with Daemonic Stature & Daemonic Flight, Bloodthirster, Lord of Change	Jump Infantry Monstrous creature
Model with Daemonic Flight but not Daemonic Stature	Jump Infantry
Chaos Space Marine Bikers	Bikes
Chaos Space Marines on foot, Chaos Terminators, Mutants, Obliterators, Daemons, Big Mutants, Traitors and Possessed (without Daemonic Flight)	Infantry
Predator, Land Raider, Rhino, Defiler, Dreadnought	Vehicle
Nurglings	Infantry – use Swarms special rule
Mounted Daemonettes, Flesh Hounds any model with a Daemonic Steed	Beasts/Cavalry
ORKS	
All Orks on foot	Infantry
Dethkoptas	Jetbikes
All Orks on Bikes	Bikes
Stormboyz	Jump Infantry
Dreadnoughts, Killer Kans, Buggies, Battlewagons, Gunwagons	Vehicles
Big Gunz	Artillery
Boarboyz	Cavalry
NECRONS	
Destroyer Lords, Destroyers, Heavy Destroyers, Wraiths	Jetbikes
Lords, Immortals, Warriors, Pariahs, Flayed Ones	Infantry
Scarabs	Infantry (move as Jetbikes, use Swarm special rule)
Monoliths	Vehicles
C'tan	Monstrous Creature
DARK ELDAR	
Archon, Dracon, Archite, Drachite, Haemonculi on foot	Infantry
Archon, Dracon, Archite, Drachite, Haemonculi on jetbikes	Jetbikes
Archon, Dracon, Archite, Drachite, Haemonculi on hellion skyboard	Jump Infantry
Grotesques, Mandrakes, Wyches, Warriors, Incubi	Infantry
Hellions, Scourges	Jump Infantry
Reavers	Jetbikes
Raider, Ravager	Vehicle
Talos	Monstrous creature
Warp Beasts	Beasts

Note that models are Independent Characters only if designated as such in their Codex entry.

BLAST MARKERS & FLAME TEMPLATE

To use these templates simply photocopy them, stick them to a piece of scrap card (old cereal packets are ideal) and cut them out.

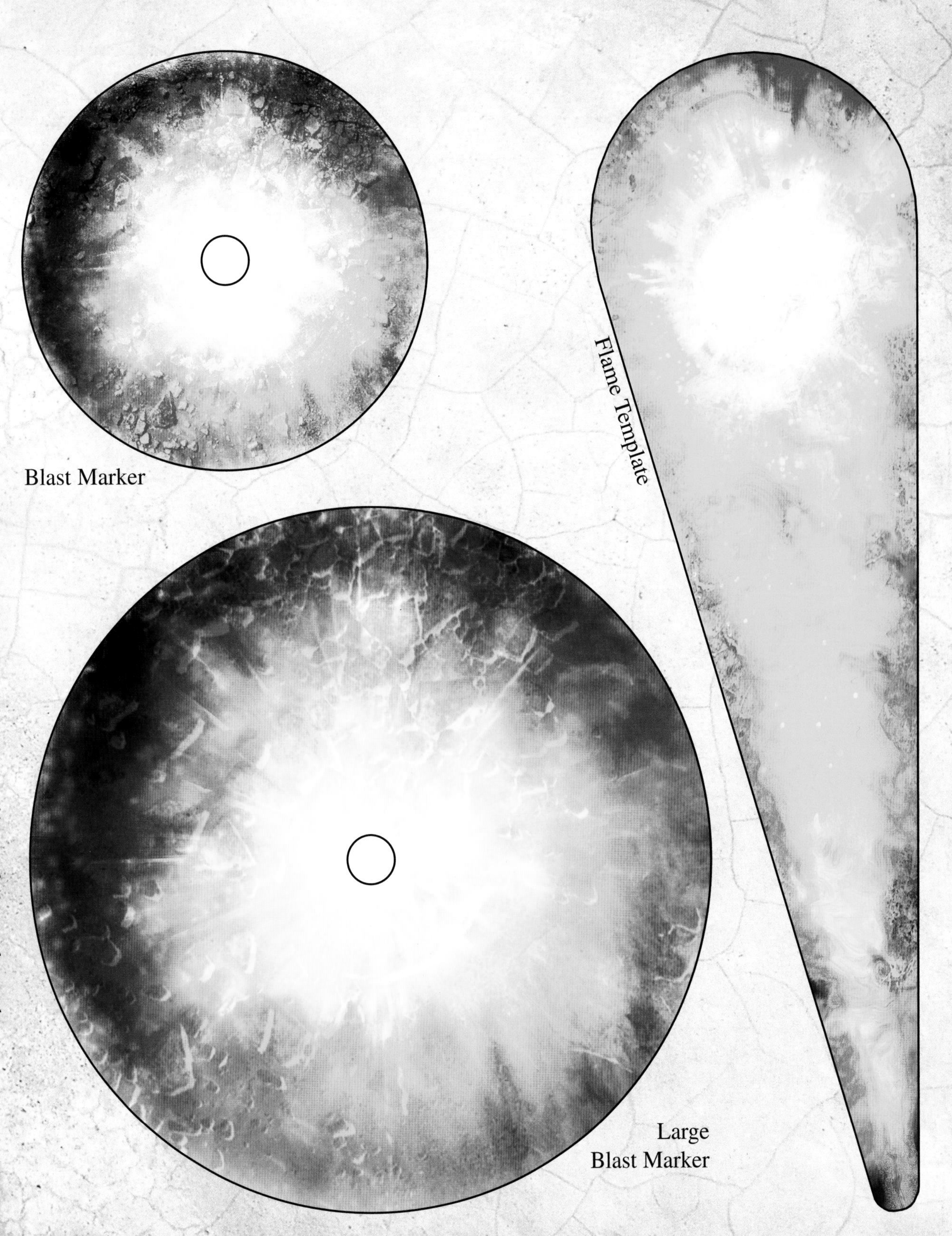

QUICK REFERENCE SHEET

THE MOVEMENT PHASE

SEQUENCE OF PLAY

1. Choose a unit to move.
2. Move any or all of the models in the unit up to their maximum move distance.
3. Repeat the above until movement is complete.

EMBARKING AND DISEMBARKING

Passengers may disembark before the vehicle moves. Both disembarked passengers and vehicle can then make a full normal move.

Passengers may disembark after the vehicle moves (no more than 12"). Neither disembarked passengers nor the vehicle may make further moves.

All of a unit must be embarked or disembarked.

THE SHOOTING PHASE

SEQUENCE OF PLAY

1. Choose a unit to shoot with.
2. Resolve the shooting process (see below) for the chosen unit.
3. Repeat the above until shooting is complete.

SHOOTING PROCESS

1. Choose a target.
2. Check line of sight and range.
3. Roll to hit.
4. Roll to wound.
5. Make Saving Throws.
6. Remove casualties.

Firer's BS	1	2	3	4	5+
Score to hit	6+	5+	4+	3+	2+

THE ASSAULT PHASE

RESOLVE CHARGES

1. Pick a unit.
2. Declare charge with it.
3. Move the charging unit.
4. Repeat the above until all charging units have moved.

RESOLVE COMBATS

1. Pick a combat.
2. Fight Close Combat.
3. Determine Assault Results.
4. Loser Checks Morale.
5. Breaking-off and Consolidation.
6. Pile in.
7. Repeat until all combats have been resolved.

ATTACK MODIFIERS

+1 Charge Bonus

+1 Two Weapons

SWEEPING ADVANCE

The falling back unit and the winning unit compare their Initiative characteristic plus the roll of a D6.

A) If the falling back unit's total is **higher,** they break off from the combat successfully. Make a Fall Back move for the losing unit. The winners can now consolidate 3".

B) If the winner's total is **equal or greater** they catch the fleeing enemy with a sweeping advance. The falling back unit is scattered and destroyed. The winners can now consolidate D6".

DIFFICULT TERRAIN – EFFECTS ON MOVEMENT

Unit Type	Slowed by difficult terrain?	Dangerous Terrain test required?
Infantry	Yes	No *
Bikes	No	Yes
Jetbikes	No	No if passing over. Yes if passing through
Monstrous creatures	Yes	No *
Jump Infantry	No	Yes if move ends in the terrain
Artillery	Yes	No for crew *. Yes for gun models.
Beasts & Cavalry	Yes	No *
Vehicles – Walkers	Yes	No *
Vehicles – Skimmers	No	No, always pass over it.
Vehicles – Other	No	Yes

** unless terrain is categorised as dangerous*

NON-VEHICLE WEAPON TYPE SUMMARY

Weapon Type	Moving and Firing	Firing and Charging
Pistol	Can move and fire once, or remain stationary and fire twice.	May fire once in the Shooting phase and then charge the same enemy unit in the Assault phase. Counts as an additional weapon in close combat.
Rapid Fire	Fire twice at up to 12", or remain stationary and fire once up to maximum weapon range.	Unit may not move in the Assault phase if the weapon was fired in the Shooting phase (unless allowed to by a special rule).
Assault	Can move and fire normally.	May fire in the Shooting phase and then charge the same enemy unit in the assault phase.
Heavy	Cannot move and fire.	Unit may not move in the Assault phase if the weapon was fired in the Shooting phase (unless allowed to by a special rule).

VEHICLES MOVING & SHOOTING SUMMARY

Type	Stationary	Up to 6"	Up to 12"	More than 12"
Any vehicle that is neither Fast nor a Walker	All main and defensive weapons OR 1 ordnance weapon OR 1 ordnance barrage weapon	1 main weapon and all defensive weapons OR 1 ordnance weapon	No weapons	Not applicable
Fast Vehicle	All main and defensive weapons	All main and defensive weapons	1 main weapon and all defensive weapons	No weapons
Walker	All main and defensive weapons OR 1 ordnance weapon OR 1 ordnance barrage weapon	2 main or defensive weapons OR 1 ordnance weapon	Not applicable	Not applicable

FIRING TEMPLATE WEAPONS

1. Place the Template.
2. Determine how many models are hit.
3. Roll to wound, make armour saves and remove casualties or roll armour penetration and resolve glancing/ penetrating hits against vehicles.

WHO IS HIT?

Models entirely covered by a blast marker or template, or partially covered by a template, are automatically hit.

Models partially covered by a blast marker are hit on a D6 score of 4+.

FIRING ORDNANCE OR BARRAGE WEAPONS

1. Place Blast Marker so that the blast marker's hole is centered on an enemy model.
2. Check range and line of sight.
3. Roll Scatter.
4. Determine how many models are hit.
5. Roll to wound, make armour saves and remove casualties or roll armour penetration and resolve glancing/ penetrating hits against vehicles.

FIRING BLAST WEAPONS

1. Roll to hit. If a hit occurs place the blast marker so that the blast marker's hole is centered on an enemy model, within range and line of sight.
2. Determine how many models are hit.
3. Roll to wound, make armour saves and remove casualties or roll armour penetration and resolve glancing/ penetrating hits against vehicles.

SCATTER DISTANCE

Roll 1D6 normally, 2D6 if firing ordnance from a moving vehicle, 2D6 if firing a barrage indirectly. Take the highest score.

ARMOUR PENETRATION

If the total of the **weapon strength + D6** is **equal** to vehicle armour value this is a **glancing hit** (unless the weapon firing is **AP1**, in which case it is a penetrating hit).

If the total of **weapon strength + D6** is **greater** than the vehicle armour then this is a **penetrating hit** (unless the weapon firing is **AP-**, in which case it is a glancing hit).

VEHICLE DAMAGE RESULTS

GLANCING HIT

D6	Result
1-2	Crew shaken
3	Crew stunned
4	Armament destroyed
5	Immobilised
6	Vehicle destroyed!

PENETRATING HIT

D6	Result
1	Crew stunned
2	Armament destroyed & Crew stunned
3	Immobilised & Crew stunned
4	Vehicle destroyed!
5	Vehicle destroyed!
6	Vehicle explodes!

ORDNANCE PENETRATING HIT

D6	Result
1	Crew stunned
2	Armament destroyed & Crew stunned
3	Immobilised & Crew stunned
4	Vehicle destroyed!
5	Vehicle explodes!
6	Vehicle annihilated!

MORALE CHECKS

A unit takes a Morale check:

A) If it takes 25% or more casualties from shooting in the turn – test at the end of the Shooting phase.

B) If it is defeated in close combat in the Assault phase – test once combat results are established.

C) If an enemy unit performs a Tank Shock attack on them – test once the vehicle has moved.

Leadership modifiers
-1 If the unit is below 50% of its starting strength.
-1 If the losing side is outnumbered by its opponents.*
-2 If the losing side is outnumbered 2:1 or more.*
-3 If the losing side is outnumbered 3:1 or more.*
-4 If the losing side is outnumbered 4:1 or more.*

** These modifiers only apply to units defeated in close combat. Use only the highest of these modifiers.*

COVER SUMMARY

Cover Type	Cover Save	Terrain Height range
Bushes, High Grass Crops, Fences, Railings	6+	Size 1/2
Crates, barrels, pipes, logs, jungles, partial cover from hill crests, woods.	5+	Size 1/2/3
Wrecks, vehicles, wreckage, rubble, rocks, emplacements, trenches, ruins, gun pits, craters, walls, buildings	4+	Size 2/3
Bunkers, fortified buildings.	3+	Size 2 / 3

ASSAULT – TO HIT CHART

Opponent's Weapon Skill (columns); Attacker's Weapon Skill (rows)

Attacker's Weapon Skill	1	2	3	4	5	6	7	8	9	10
1	4+	4+	5+	5+	5+	5+	5+	5+	5+	5+
2	3+	4+	4+	4+	5+	5+	5+	5+	5+	5+
3	3+	3+	4+	4+	4+	4+	5+	5+	5+	5+
4	3+	3+	3+	4+	4+	4+	4+	4+	5+	5+
5	3+	3+	3+	3+	4+	4+	4+	4+	4+	4+
6	3+	3+	3+	3+	3+	4+	4+	4+	4+	4+
7	3+	3+	3+	3+	3+	3+	4+	4+	4+	4+
8	3+	3+	3+	3+	3+	3+	3+	4+	4+	4+
9	3+	3+	3+	3+	3+	3+	3+	3+	4+	4+
10	3+	3+	3+	3+	3+	3+	3+	3+	3+	4+

DAMAGE CHART

Toughness (columns); Strength (rows)

Strength	1	2	3	4	5	6	7	8	9	10
1	4+	5+	6+	6+	N	N	N	N	N	N
2	3+	4+	5+	6+	6+	N	N	N	N	N
3	2+	3+	4+	5+	6+	6+	N	N	N	N
4	2+	2+	3+	4+	5+	6+	6+	N	N	N
5	2+	2+	2+	3+	4+	5+	6+	6+	N	N
6	2+	2+	2+	2+	3+	4+	5+	6+	6+	N
7	2+	2+	2+	2+	2+	3+	4+	5+	6+	6+
8	2+	2+	2+	2+	2+	2+	3+	4+	5+	6+
9	2+	2+	2+	2+	2+	2+	2+	3+	4+	5+
10	2+	2+	2+	2+	2+	2+	2+	2+	3+	4+

INDEX

HEROES OF THE IMPERIUM

GAMES DESIGN AND DEVELOPMENT
Rick Priestley and Andy Chambers
with Alessio Cavatore, Pete Haines,
Anthony Reynolds, Jervis Johnson, Adam Troke.

BACKGROUND
Gav Thorpe with Andy Chambers,
Phil Kelly, Alan Merrett,
Graham McNeill, Rick Priestley.

HOBBY SECTION
Dave Cross with Steve Cumiskey,
Tim Eagling, Andy Hoare, Phil Kelly,
Matthew Ward, Adrian Wood.

ILLUSTRATION
John Blanche, Alex Boyd, Paul Dainton,
David Gallagher, Jes Goodwin, Neil Hodgson,
Paul Jeacock, Nuala Kennedy, Karl Kopinski,
Stefan Kopinski, Adrian Smith.

COVER
Karl Kopinski and Stefan Kopinski

CITADEL MINIATURES DESIGNERS
Tim Adcock, Dave Andrews, Mark Bedford,
Juan Diaz, Martin Footitt, Jes Goodwin,
Mark Harrison, Alex Hedström,
Gary Morley, Aly Morrison, Brian Nelson,
Alan Perry, Michael Perry, Steve Saleh.

MINIATURES PAINTERS
Kevin Asprey, Neil Green, Neil Langdown,
Darren Latham, Matt Parkes, Keith Robertson,
Kirsten Williams, Pete Foley, Chris Blair,
George Dellapina, Kevan Downey, Guy Haley,
Gareth Harvey, Christopher Higson,
Richard Morgan, Roy Morris,
Gary Shaw, Mark Tait, Ted Williams.

TERRAIN MAKERS
Dave Andrews, Jason Buyaki,
Ray Dranfield, Mark Jones, Chad Mierzwa.

PROJECT MANAGEMENT
Gordon Davidson, Steve Pritchard,
Owen Branham, Ted Williams.

ART DIRECTION
John Blanche.

GRAPHIC DESIGN
John Blanche, Stefan Kopinski,
Alan Merrett, Markus Trenkner, Alun Davies.

PRODUCTION
Michelle Barson, Simon Burton,
Rowland Cox, Sean Cutler, Graham Davey,
Chris Eggar, Marc Elliott, Jason Foley,
Talima Fox, Matt Hutson, John Michelbach,
Glenn More, Muir Murdoch, Dave Musson,
Dylan Owen, Mark Owen, Owen Rees,
Lee Sanderson, Paul Sawyer, Adam Shaw,
Nicole Shewchuk, Simon Smith,
Andrew Stewart, Ian Strickland,
Sean Turtle, Nathan Winter.

THANKS TO
Christian Augst, Jes Bickham, Alan Borthwick,
CJ Cummings, Mike Derovchic, Paul Gebhart,
Andy Harris, Mark Havener, Marshall Jansen,
Tuomus Lähdeoja, Mike Major, Mike Marshall,
Jimmy Murphy, Tim Pearce, Matt Plonski,
Geoff Porritt, Ed Rusk, Will Thomas,
Darryl Trainer, and everyone at
Games Workshop and all of the
Warhammer 40,000 hobbyists across
the world without whom none
of this would have
been possible.

The Emperor will not
judge you by your
medals and diplomas
but by your scars.